HUMOROUS POEMS.

HUMOROUS POEMS.

SELECTED AND EDITED

BY

WILLIAM MICHAEL ROSSETTI.

> All wit does but divert men from the road
> In which things vulgarly are understood ;
> And force mistake and ignorance to own
> A better sense than commonly is known.
> BUTLER.
>
> Vivre est une chanson dont mourir est le refrain.
> VICTOR HUGO.

AMS PRESS
NEW YORK

Reprinted from the edition of 1879, London
First AMS EDITION published 1970
Manufactured in the United States of America

International Standard Book Number 0-404-05426-9

Library of Congress Card Catalog Number: 77-139260

AMS PRESS, INC.
NEW YORK, N.Y. 10003

DEDICATED

TO

ONE OF MY DEAREST AND OLDEST FRIENDS,

FORD MADOX BROWN,

A MAN EXCELLENTLY QUALIFIED,

BY THE TURN OF HIS OWN GENIUS,

TO SAY WHAT IS POETICAL,

OR HUMOROUS,

OR BOTH.

CONTENTS.

	PAGE
PREFACE	xvii

ENGLISH WRITERS.

GEOFFREY CHAUCER—
    The Chanoun's Yeman's Tale . . . 1
    The Nunne Priest's Tale 12

ADAM OF COBSAM—
    The Wright's Chaste Wife 26

ANDREW BORDE—
    An Irishman and a Lombard . . . 41

SIR THOMAS WYATT—
    The Recured Lover exulteth in his Freedom, and
        voweth to remain free until death . . 42
    Of his Love, that pricked her Finger with a Needle 43
    How to use the Court, and Himself therein . . 44

THOMAS TUSSER—
    Good Husband and Unthrift 46

HUGH RHODES—
    Cautions 48

EDMUND SPENSER—
    Prosopopoia 49

SIR JOHN HARINGTON—
    Of a Precise Tailor 77

CONTENTS

	PAGE
SIR JOHN DAVIES—	
A Riddle upon a Coffin	78
In Gerontem	78
JOHN DONNE—	
Song	79
Woman's Constancy	80
The Indifferent	80
The Will	81
BEN JONSON—	
On Giles and Joan	82
To Captain Hungry	82
A Fit of Rhyme against Rhyme	83
Epistle to my Lady Covell	84
BISHOP (JOSEPH) HALL—	
A Trencher Chaplain	85
JOHN FLETCHER—	
Laughing Song	86
BISHOP (RICHARD) CORBET—	
Dr. Corbet's Journey into France	87
Farewell to the Fairies	90
An Epitaph on Thomas Jonce	91
THOMAS CAREW—	
To A. D., unreasonably distrustful of her own beauty	92
To my Friend, G. N., from Wrest	93
The Hue and Cry	96
SAMUEL ROWLANDS—	
The Conjurer Cozened	97
ROBERT HERRICK—	
Upon a Wife that died mad with Jealousy	98
Upon Pagget	99
To the Detractor	99
The Invitation	99
FRANCIS QUARLES—	
Hey then up go we	100
EDMUND WALLER—	
An Epigram on a Painted Lady with Ill Teeth	101

	PAGE
THOMAS WASHBOURNE—	
Upon the People's Denying of Tithes in some places, and ejecting their Pastors	102
SAMUEL BUTLER—	
The Elephant in the Moon	103
Upon Plagiaries	114
Upon Modern Critics	118
A Palinode to the Honourable Edward Howard, Esq.	121
Description of Holland	123
Regal Adulation	123
Fear	124
A Jubilee	124
Scribblers	124
SIR JOHN SUCKLING—	
Sir J. S.	125
Love and Debt alike troublesome	125
Upon the Black Spots worn by my Lady D. E.	126
The Metamorphosis	126
JOHN CLEVELAND—	
The Long Parliament	126
The Puritan	128
R. WATKYNS—	
Black Patches, Vanitas Vanitatum	130
SIR JOHN DENHAM—	
On my Lord Croft's a..d my Journey into Poland	130
ABRAHAM COWLEY—	
The Chronicle, a Ballad	132
RICHARD LOVELACE—	
To a Lady that desired me I would bear my part with her in a song	134
The Duel	136
The Snail	137
THOMAS STANLEY—	
Note on Anacreon	138
ANDREW MARVELL—	
Mourning	140
The Character of Holland	141

CONTENTS.

	PAGE
HENRY VAUGHAN—	
To his Retired Friend, an Invitation to Brecknock	144
ALEXANDER BROME—	
The Prisoners	146
JOHN DRYDEN—	
On the Young Statesmen	148
KATHARINE PHILIPS—	
To Antenor, on a Paper of mine which J. J. threatens to publish, to prejudice him	149
EARL OF DORSET (Charles Sackville)—	
Song	50
WILLIAM WALSH—	
The Despairing Lover	151
MATTHEW PRIOR—	
To a Child of Quality	152
Merry Andrew	153
SAMUEL WESLEY (Senr.)—	
A Pindaric on the Grunting of a Hog	154
SIR JOHN VANBRUGH—	
Fable, related by a Beau to Æsop	156
JONATHAN SWIFT—	
Dean Swift's Curate	157
A True and Faithful Inventory	157
On the Little House by the Churchyard of Castlenock	158
Baucis and Philemon	159
A Description of the Morning	163
Stella's Birthday, 1718	163
Mary the Cook-Maid's Letter to Dr. Sheridan	164
Dr. Swift to Mr. Pope	165
To Dr. Delany, on the Libels written against him	166
Whitshed's Motto on his Coach	169
Death and Daphne	170
LORD LANSDOWNE (George Granville)—	
Lines	172
JOSEPH ADDISON—	
The Play-house	173

CONTENTS.

	PAGE
JOHN PHILIPS—	
The Splendid Shilling	175
GEORGE JEFFREYS—	
A Riddle of Dean Swift's, Versified	178
THOMAS SHERIDAN—	
Dr. Delany's Villa	180
JOSEPH MITCHELL—	
The Charms of Indolence	181
JOHN GAY—	
The Lion, the Fox, and the Geese	185
The Lion and the Cub	186
The Ratcatcher and Cats	186
The Old Woman and her Cats	188
The Butterfly and the Snail	189
The Fox at the point of Death	190
The Mastiff	191
The Turkey and the Ant	192
The Two Monkeys	192
The Man and the Flea	194
Verses to be placed under the Picture of Sir Richard Blackmore	195
A New Song of New Similes	195
LISLE—	
Eurydice	197
SAMUEL WESLEY (Junr.)—	
On the setting-up Mr. Butler's Monument in Westminster Abbey	198
Advice to one who was about to write, to avoid the Immoralities of the Ancient and Modern Poets	198
MATTHEW GREEN—	
An Epigram on the Rev. Mr. Laurence Eachard's and Bishop Gilbert Burnet's Histories	201
The Sparrow and Diamond	202
ROBERT DODSLEY—	
The Footman	203
SOAME JENYNS—	
Song	206

CONTENTS.

	PAGE
HENRY FIELDING—	
Plain Truth	206
An Epistle to Sir Robert Walpole	208
LORD LYTTELTON (George Lyttelton)—	
To Miss Lucy Fortescue, on her pleading want of time	209
JOHN BANCKS—	
To Boreas	210
WILLIAM WHITEHEAD—	
Variety	212
THOMAS GRAY—	
On the Death of a Favourite Cat	220
BISHOP (WILLIAM) BARNARD—	
Verses	221
THOMAS WARTON (Junior)—	
The Progress of Discontent	222
OLIVER GOLDSMITH—	
Description of an Author's Bedchamber	225
JOHN CUNNINGHAM—	
The Fox and the Cat	226
CHARLES CHURCHILL—	
The Journey	226
JOHN WOLCOT—	
To a Fish of the Brooke	230
The Pilgrims and the Peas	231
The Sailor-Boy at Prayers	232
Bozzy and Piozzi	233
A Poetical, Supplicating, Modest, and Affecting Epistle to those literary Colossuses the Reviewers	248
A Lyric Ode	251
To Myself	252
Farewell Odes (1786), I.	253
II.	255
CHARLES MORRIS—	
The Contrast	257
HANNAH MORE—	
The Bas Bleu	259

CONTENTS.

	PAGE
CHARLES DIBDIN—	
Jack at the Opera	269
One	270
RICHARD BRINSLEY SHERIDAN—	
Ode to Scandal	271
THOMAS CHATTERTON—	
February, an Elegy	275
GEORGE CRABBE—	
The Dumb Orators	277
The Widow	288
WILLIAM BLAKE—	
The Little Vagabond	298
Orator Prig	299
GEORGE COLMAN (Junr.)—	
The Newcastle Apothecary	299
ROBERT BLOOMFIELD—	
The Horkey	302
RICHARD ALFRED MILLIKIN—	
The Fair Maid of Passage	307
SIMON QUIN—	
The Town of Passage	308
MATTHEW GREGORY LEWIS—	
Grim, King of the Ghosts	309
ROBERT SOUTHEY—	
To a Goose	313
The Poet relates how he ole a lock of Delia's Hair	314
Epistle to Allan Cunningham	315
The Pious Painter	324
St. Romuald	327
CHARLES LAMB—	
A Farewell to Tobacco	329
JAMES SMITH—	
The Baby's Debut (Wordsworth)	332
The Theatre (Crabbe)	334

	PAGE
HORACE SMITH—	
Loyal Effusion (Fitzgerald)	337
A Tale of Drury Lane (Scott)	338
Drury's Dirge (Laura Matilda)	343
Architectural Atoms (Dr. B.)	344
The Jester Condemned to Death	349
PATRICK O'KELLY—	
The Doneraile Litany	350
ORLANDO THOMAS DOBBIN—	
My Manx Minx	352
A Dithyramb on Cats	354

POEMS BY UNKNOWN WRITERS.

Women	357
A Good Medicine for Sore Eyne	358
Trust in Women	358
Gossip Mine	360
Jolly Good Ale and Old	362
As it befell one Saturday	365
Mark More, Fool	367
The Poor Man and the King	371
Songs of Shepherds	377
Robin Goodfellow	379
The Song of the Beggar	381
A New-Year's Gift for Shrews	383
Lines on a Printing Office	384
The May-Pole	384
There was an Old Man came over the Lea	385
The New Litany	386
The Clean Contrary Way	388
The Anarchy	390
Joan's Ale was New	392
The Reformation	393
The Sale of Rebellion's Household Stuff	396
The Devil's Progress on Earth	398
The Desponding Whig	400

	PAGE
The Cameronian Cat	401
Titus Oates in the Pillory	402
Cosmelia	402
Phillida Flouts me	403
One Denial	405
An Echo Song	405
Chloe and Cœlia	406
Get up and Bar the Door	406
Nature and Fortune	407
At Church	408
Kissing	409
There was an Old Woman	409
The Merry Man	410
The Court of Aldermen at Fishmongers' Hall	412

AMERICAN WRITERS.

JOHN QUINCY ADAMS—
The Plague in the Forest	414

FITZ-GREENE HALLECK—
Red Jacket	417
Alnwick Castle	419

JOHN GARDNER CALKINS BRAINARD—
Sonnet to the Sea Serpent	422

GEORGE P. MORRIS—
The Retort	423

JOHN GREENLEAF WHITTIER—
The Demon of the Study	423

OLIVER WENDELL HOLMES—
The Treadmill Song	426
The Music-Grinders	427
To an Insect	429
The Spectre Pig	430

PARK BENJAMIN—
Indolence	433

MATTHEW C. FIELD—
To my Shadow	434

	PAGE
JOHN GODFREY SAXE—	
The Ghost-Player	434
I'm Growing Old	436
A Reflective Retrospect	437
Early Rising	439
Little Jerry the Miller	440
JAMES RUSSELL LOWELL—	
Festina Lente	441
The Courtin'	443
Birdofredom Sawin, I.	446
II.	448
III.	452
The Pious Editor's Creed	458
Sunthin' in the Pastoral Line	460
Mr. Hosea Biglow to the Editor of the Atlantic Monthly	467
WALT WHITMAN—	
A Boston Ballad	471
CHARLES G. LELAND—	
Manes	473
JOHN HAY—	
Jim Bludso	474
The Mystery of Gilgal	475
EDMUND CLARENCE STEDMAN—	
Pan in Wall Street	476
F. BRET HARTE—	
The Society upon the Stanislaus	478
Penelope	479
To the Pliocene Skull	480
ROBERT H. NEWELL—	
The American Traveller	481

PREFACE.

A VOLUME of Humorous Poems speaks for itself distinctly enough to save its editor the task of saying anything at great length. Most readers have a predilection for humorous writing. Many seek it as their natural and special *pabulum:* many others delight in it as an occasional variation and relief from more general or graver reading. If therefore the present Selection has been put together with any reasonable amount of discernment, I have little apprehension that my labour may have been spent in vain. This is of course far from being the first attempt of its kind; but I fancy it may be one of the most extensive in its range, and in the number, diversity, calibre, and in several instances in the length, of the pieces that it comprises. Ninety-six authors are here represented; and the number of compositions (including such as are anonymous) is two hundred and twenty-six.

I shall not essay to furnish anything like a true definition of the peculiar faculty or quality named Humour. Most people possess a tolerable internal perception of what it is, combined with a considerable indifference to having their perception distinctly formulated to themselves, whether by others or by an effort of their own reason. Perhaps the most essential thing to be remarked on the subject is that Humour is a matter mainly of character, while Wit is more an emanation of the mind.[1] We could not have a witty man who was not in some sense a clever man : but we might easily have—and in life we often come across—humorous men who are not exactly clever, but possess this endowment of humour as a part of their idiosyncrasy. It is a portion of their character, and a habit of their lives : they see things humorously, and can, with more or less nicety and vivacity, impart their perceptions, whether with or without the adjunct of wit. A rough or even a dull exterior is by no means incompatible with a humorous turn : and this latter argues very generally a certain robust kindliness of nature, of which the term "fellow-feeling" is perhaps the clearest expression. The humorous man is—in so far at least as he is humorous—never far removed from his kind : the strong lines of men's characters, their foibles, their oddities, the vicissitudes and contradictions of their lives, all find out in him one of like fibre with themselves, "a man and a brother." Not that every humourist is an amiable person—far from it but the faculty of humour belongs essentially to man as a gregarious animal—it is developed by society of the civilized kind (or at any rate some removes from barbarism), and in society it finds its subject-matter and continual incentive. A hermit or a Robinson Crusoe could not be, or could not long remain, a

---

[1] I dare say this is anything but an original observation. It is not consciously repeated here from any other writer ; but, if it has been said before, and is worth reclaiming, I can only leave it to be re-assigned by accurate memories to its proper source.

humourist: though some residuum of the faculty might indeed be exercised upon a parrot, monkey, or other congenial beast that the recluse might have been lucky enough to catch. The deficiency of humour in women (contrasting so markedly with their resources in wit) has often been noted. This volume may serve to confirm the observation. Out of ninety-six authors who figure here, only two (Katharine Philips and Hannah More) are women; and certainly the quality traceable in the specimens from them is not humour, properly so called—rather the quickness of eye and neatness of phrase which belong to wit.

Humour is, in an intense degree, at once individual and expansive. It depends upon a specialty of character; it affects all persons with whom it comes in contact; and it produces in the humourist's own mind a recast of all his experiences—they become to him very different from what they are *per se*, or what they would seem were he not a humourist. If he is furthermore a humourist with a gift of expression or of writing, he naturally produces something that has a flavour of its own—something fairly proper to himself, and (in the higher classes of humouristic writing) genuinely original. While humour is thus, as I have termed it, "expansive," wit is intensive or incisive. Humour modifies its subject-matter—and cannot help doing so, because the humourist is compelled to see everything through the spectacles of his own strong individuality: Wit irradiates or illustrates its subject-matter, but leaves it substantially unmodified.

I make no pretence, however, to confining this volume to such poems as are, strictly speaking, humorous, without admixture of those that are witty. Many are humorous, some witty: some are both witty and humorous: some may be sprightly, others quaint, without either humour or wit in any very large or definite proportion. Yet I trust and think that the volume will be found humorous in the main, and readable throughout, and well corresponding to its title of *Humorous Poems*.

For several generations past, the British nation has been celebrated among continental critics for its humour. Now, Englishmen can contemplate in their brethren across the Atlantic—in the Americans of the United States, a vigorously re-mixed race, arising out of the British and other mixed races of the old world—an offshoot of their own humour, perceptibly allied to that, yet very visibly varied from it too. We may fancy ourselves, in this regard, watching some such process as that so often spoken of by Darwin —the " Variation of Species under Domestication "; watching the wider and wider variation, until at last the divergence shall be so great as to constitute seemingly a new species—which we, however (more fortunate than the Darwinian man of science when he has to deal with animals living in a state of nature) shall know of a surety, having followed all the successive steps of modification, to be nothing more than a much transformed variety. Perhaps, on the whole, American humour at the present day is in somewhat closer alliance with wit than is English humour : there is more of the caprice of mind in it, and possibly less personal caprice. The English humourist is essentially an eccentric—a " queer fellow," or (as we so often say, touching herein the very core of humour) " quite a character." This tendency of the *insulaire britannique* has been continually recognized and enforced by foreign critics ; and so consentaneously that we may be assured it is true, even if we Britons, being ourselves the subject out of which the remark arises, perceive little of it of our own accord. The American humourist is not so much an eccentric, pursuing a devious path because his nature is to deviate : he is rather a fantastic person than an eccentric, and plays pranks because he finds in himself an endless facility for playing them. The Englishman's humour (I speak of c urse of the typical or crucial instances) is a dogged *quality*, innate, and more clearly manifest to others than to himself : the American's humour is a *faculty*, exercised masterfully and with a sense of enjoyment.

As regards the notices of authors which I have prefixed to the several specimens, it will be observed that, the more eminent a writer is, the less I say about him. This seems to me the only appropriate course in such an undertaking. Anything which I could here put forward about men of the rank and celebrity of Chaucer, Spenser, Butler, Dryden, or Swift, would be nugatory, if not even impertinent : but some brief remarks about less-known writers, such as Donne, Vaughan, or Whittier, highly deserving as they are of attention, or others who constitute the honourable rank and file of our array, appear to be both relevant and convenient. The arrangement of the works, as will readily be perceived, is chronological throughout, according to the dates of the writers' births wherever known.

There remain to be said a few words as to the precise scope of the present collection. It does not profess to be in any sense exhaustive ; yet none the less it has been compiled out of a great number of volumes; whether of single authors or of miscellaneous gatherings, and I have been heedful in choosing what seem to me the best and most appropriate pieces, to the exclusion of numberless others which come up nearly, but not quite, to an equal standard. There have besides been some definite limitations which require to be taken into account : otherwise the selection might seem in various respects arbitrary, and the exclusions wanton or even invidious. The reader should therefore understand that I have on system omitted —1, all copyright poems, and consequently (in general terms) anything published by a living British author,[1] or within the last forty-two years; 2, all poems by authors whose works form separate volumes in the series of *Moxon's Popular Poets*. Where the material for selection is so abundant, it has seemed to me unreasonable, and in other respects inexpedient, to reproduce writings of this class: but the limitation makes some rather startling gaps in our ranks—especially as regards Pope, Burns, and Hood; the latter a host in himself, and perhaps the very first author whom a reader expects to find in a Humorous compilation. I have further omitted—3, Songs or Ballads, which again may not improbably be included in our series in some other guise; and here I have had to decide for myself the question—in many cases a very nice one—whether a composition should be regarded as a lyric, and as such admissible, or rather as a song, and as such to be left aside. I have mostly considered that a composition actually set to music, or one that is obviously framed for being so set, or one with a burden, is a song; provided in each case the composition is of very moderate length. Or a short piece of a generally song-like character, and with much unity and little progression of subject-matter, has in like manner been regarded as more song than lyric. Again, my omissions apply to—4, all poems of really considerable length; 5, any and every mere extract (which I eschew on principle) from any poem whatsoever; 6, pieces that are so enormously well-known as to be—whatever their intrinsic merits—almost tiresome and pestering to encounter anew. Thus I have excluded Goldsmith's *Elegy on the Death of a Mad Dog*, Lowell's poem about "John P. Robinson," and Bret Harte's *Heathen*

---

[1] The only living (non-American) writer here represented is the Rev. Dr. Dobbin—see p. 352. I have gladly availed myself of his permission to include the two bright and quaint sallies which appear under his name: but these are not copyright in the ordinary sense,—*i.e.*, though previously printed, they had never been published.

Chinee. And, lastly—without, I hope, lapsing into utter and unmanly squeamishness—I have carefully avoided poems which are gross or indecent in general drift, or even in particular expressions; for the present volume is not put together for the use of any section—or rather so as to be ill-adapted to any other section—of the reading public, but for all readers, without exception, who may be minded to acquaint themselves with the riches of our humorous poetry, or to refresh their recollection of it. To any one who knows our elder writers—or I might broadly say all our writers save those of a very modern date—I need hardly observe that this precaution, especially where humorous poetry is concerned, entails very many exclusions, and often of the author's raciest and most characteristic work; for the British humourist has been a personage the reverse of mealy-mouthed. To take only the first instance in our volume, that of Chaucer: out of the several excellent examples of his sportive vein, I have, through this single consideration, been obliged to abandon all except the two that are here given; and of these the first, *the Chanoun's Yeman's Tale*, is hardly of his prime quality, and the second, *the Nunne Priest's Tale*, though most admirable in other respects, is less strictly and continuously humorous than various others. True, I might in many cases have managed to include poems mainly unexceptionable, if only I would have consented to miss out a verse or a phrase here and there; but this process I regard as wholly forbidden, by literary honesty and ordinary self-respect, to any serious editor.

I have also made very sparing use of poems in provincial and other *patois*—though I have freely admitted such as are in the Yankee dialect, and some in the Scottish; and I have mostly held aloof from the prepense narrative jocularity, the funny anecdotes in verse, of writers like the younger Colman and Dr. Wolcot. This is a sort of writing which seems to me, in general, more jocose than humorous, and deserving of only a very subordinate place in a collection like the present.

The reader will, I trust, agree with me that, while much has been omitted which might, on other grounds, rightly claim to be included, what figures here is good and choice, and sufficient to leave no qualm of regret behind it. Whatever the limitations and exclusions, enough and to spare is still before us. The Humourists are the "rulers of the feast"; and they have spread the table for us with a continual banquet.

W. M. ROSSETTI.

HUMOROUS POEMS.

ENGLISH WRITERS.

GEOFFREY CHAUCER.

[Circa 1340 to 1400.]

THE CHANOUN'S YEMAN'S TALE.

In London was a priest, an annueler,[1]
That therein dwelled hadde[2] many a year,
Which was so pleasant and so serviceable
Unto the wife whereas he was at table
That she would suffer him nothing for to pay
For board ne clothing, went he never so gay,
And spending-silver had he right enow.
Thereof no force : I wol proceed as now,
And telle forth my tale of the chanoun
That brought this prieste to confusion.

---

[1] *I. e.*, a priest employed solely in singing annuals, or anniversary masses, for the dead.

[2] For the purpose of a popular compilation like the present, it appears to me best (however unscholarly) to modernize the spelling of Chaucer in all cases where this can be done without obviously tampering with the pronunciation. As regards the use of the *e* mute at the end of words or elsewhere—a point of such prime importance to the rhythm—the reader should understand that, where this letter would not occur at all in modern spelling (as in the present word, "hadde"), I simply leave the letter, if it counts as a syllable, without marking it with any sign of accentuation ; but, in other cases, where the *e* would occur in modern spelling also (as in the words "dwellèd" and "falsè"), but would not be pronounced, I mark it with an accent, provided the rhythm of Chaucer demands its pronunciation. This is a very simple rule, and I hope an easy one to apply in practice. The same course is followed as regards the spelling of the ensuing poem by Adam of Cobsam.

This false chanoun came upon a day
Unto the prieste's chamber where he lay,
Beseeching him to lene him a certain
Of gold, and he would quit it him again.
"Lene me a mark," quod he, "but dayes three,
And at my day I will it quitè thee.
And, if so be that thou finde me false,
Another day hong me up by the halse."

This priest him took a mark, and that as swithe;
And this chanoun him thankèd ofte sithe,
And took his leave, and wente forth his way;
And attè thriddè day brought his money,
And to the priest he took his gold again—
Whereof this priest was wonder glad and fain.

"Certes," quod he, "nothing annoyeth me
To lene a man a noble, or two or three,
Or what thing were in my possession,
Whan he so true is of condition
That in no wise he breake wol his day:
To such a man I can never say nay."

"What!" quod this chanoun, "should I be untrue?
Nay, that were thing yfallen of the new!
Truth is a thing that I wol ever keep
Unto that day in which that I shall creep
Into my grave, and elles God forbede!
Believeth that as sicker as your creed.
God thank I, and in good time be it said,
That there was never man yet evil-apaid
For gold ne silver that he to me lent,
Ne never falsehood in my heart I meant.
And, sir," quod he, "now of my privity,
Sin' ye so goodlich have be unto me,
And kythèd to me so great gentilesse,
Somewhat to quitè with your kindeness,
I will you show, and, if you lust to lere,
I will you teache plainly, the mannere
How I can worken in philosophy.
Taketh good heed, ye shul seen well at ye
That I wol doon a maistry ere I go."

"Yea?" quod the priest, "yea, sir, and wul ye so?
Mary! thereof I pray you heartily."

"At your commandement, sir, truely,"
Quod the chanoun, "and elles God forbede!"

Lo how this thief couthè his service beed![1]
Full sooth it is that such proffered service

---

[1] Offer.

Stinketh, as witnessen these olde wise.
And that full soon I wol it verify
In this chanoun, root of all treachery,
That evermore delight hath and gladness
(Such fiendly thoughtes in his heart impress)
How Christe's people he may to mischief bring.
God keep us from his false dissimiling!
What wiste this priest with whom that he dealt?
Ne of his harm coming he nothing felt.
O silly priest, O silly innocent,
With covetise anon thou shalt be blent![1]
O gracëless! full blind is thy conceit:
Nothing art thou warè of the deceit
Which that this fox yshapen hath to thee!
His wily wrenches I wis thou mayst not flee.
Wherefore—to go to the conclusion
That rèferreth to thy confusion,
Unhappy man—anon I will me hie
To tellen thine unwit and thy folly,
And eke the falseness of that other wretch,
Als farforth as my cunning wollè stretch.

This chanoun was my lord, ye woulde ween?[2]
Sir ost, in faith, and by the heaven queen,
It was another chanoun, and not he,
That can an hundred-fold more subtlety.
He hath betrayèd folkes many time:
Of his falsenèss it dulleth me to rhyme.
Ever whan I speake of his falsehede,
For shame of him my cheekes wexen reed.
Algatès[3] they beginne for to glow;
For reedness have I none, right well I know,
In my visagè, for fumès diverse
Of metals, which ye han heard me rehearse,
Consumèd and wasted han my reednèss.—
Now take heed of this chanoun's cursedness.

"Sir," quod he to the priest, "let your man goen
For quicksilver, that we it had anon;
And let him bringe ounces two or three;
And, whan he cometh, as fast shul ye see
A wonder thing which ye saw never ere this."

"Sir," quod the priest, "it shall be done, I wis."

He bad his servant fetche him his things;
And he all ready was at his biddings,
And went him forth, and com anon again
With this quicksilver, shortly for to sayn,

---
[1] Blinded.
[2] This and some other allusions in the tale of the Canon's Yeoman refer back to what he had stated in his "prologue," given by Chaucer as introductory to his "tale." [3] Now, already.

And took these ounces three to the chanoun.
And he it laide fair and well adoun,
And bad the servant coales for to bring,
That he anon might go to his working.
The coales right anon weren yfett;
And this chanoun took out a croselet [1]
Of his bosòm, and showed it to the priest.

"This instrument," quod he, "which that thou seest,
Take in thine hond; and put thyself therein
Of this quicksilver an ounce; and here begin,
In the name of Christ, to wax a philosòpher.
There been full few which that I woulde proffer
To showe hem thus much of my science:
For ye shul seen here by experience
That this quicksilver I wul mortify
Right in your sight anon, withouten lie,
And make it as good silver and as fine
As there is any in your purse or mine,
Or ellèswhere; and make it malleable:—
And elles holdeth me false, and unable
Amonges folk forever to appear.
I have a powder here, that cost me dear,
Shall make all good; for it is cause of all
My cunning which that I you showe shall.
Voideth your man, and let him be thereout;
And shet the doore whiles we ben about
Our privity, that no man us aspie
Whilès we werken in this philosophy.

All, as he bad, fulfillèd was in deed.
This ilkè servant anon right out-yede;
And his maistèr shittè the door anon,
And to here labour speedily they gone.

This priest, at this cursèd chanoun's bidding,
Upon the fire anon sette this thing,
And blew the fire, and busied him full fast.
And this chanoun into the croslet cast
A powder—noot I whereof that it was
Ymade, outher of chalk outher of glass,
Or somewhat elles was nought worth a fly,
To blinde with this priest; and bad him hie,
These coales for to couchen all above
The croislet; for, "in tokening I thee love,"
Quod this chanoun, "thine owne handes two
Shall wirchè all thing which that shall be do."

"Graunt-mercy," quod the priest; and was full glad,
And couchèd coales as the chanoun bad.

---

[1] Crucible.

And, while he busy was, this fiendly wretch,
This false chanoun (the foule fiend him fetch!)
Out of his bosom took a bechen coal,
In which full subtilly was made an hole;
And therein put was of silver limayl[1]
An ounce, and stoppèd was withoute fail
The hole with wex, to keep the limayl in.
And understondeth that this falsè gin
Was not made there, but it was made before:
And other thinges I shall telle more
Hereafterward which that he with him brought,
Ere he com there, to bèguile him he thought,
And so he dedè, ere they went atwin:
Till he had turnèd him, couth he nought blyn.[2]
It dulleth me whan that I of him speak:
On his falsehedè fain would I me wreak,
If I wist how; but he is here and there,—
He is so variant he byt[3] nowhere.

But taketh heed now, sirs, for Goddes love.
He took his coal of which I spake above,
And in his hond he bare it privily:
And, whiles the prieste couchèd busily
The coales, as I tolde you ere this,
This chanoun saide: "Friend, ye doon amiss:
This is not couchèd as it oughte be;
But soon I shall amenden it," quod he.
"Now let me mellè therewith but awhile,
For of you have I pity, by Saint Gile!
Ye been right hot, I see well how ye sweat:
Have here a cloth, and wipe away the wet."

And, whilès that this priest him wipèd has,
This chanoun took his coal (I shrew his face!)
And laid it aboven on the midward
Of the croslet, and blew well afterward,
Till that the coales gonnè faste brenn.

"Now give us drinke," quod the chanoun then:
"Als swithe all shall be well, I undertake.
Sitte we down, and let us merry make."

And, whan that the chanounès bechen coal
Was brent, all the limayl out of the hole
Into the croslet anon fell adoun;
And so it muste needes by reasoun,
Since it so even abovè couchèd was.
But thereof wist the priest nothing, alas!
He deemèd all the coals ilikè good,
For of the sleight he nothing understood.

---

[1] Filings.   [2] Cease.   [3] Abides.

And, whan this alcamister saw his timè,
"Rise up, sir priest," quod he, "and stondè by me:
And, for I wot well ingot have ye none,
Goth, walketh forth, and bringe a chalk-stone;
For I wol make it of the samè shape
That is an ingold, if I may have hap.
And bring with you a bowle or a pan
Full of watèr; and ye shall well see than
How that our business shall hap and preve.
And yit, for you shoul have no misbelieve
Ne wrong conceit of me in your absence,
I ne wol nought ben out of your presence,
But go with you, and come with you again."

The chamber-doore, shortly for to sayn
They openèd and shet, and went here way;
And forth with hem they carrièd the key,
And comen again withouten any delay.
What should I tarry all the longe day?
He took the chalk, and shop[1] it in the wise
Of an ingòt, as I shall you devise :
I say, he took out of his owne sleeve
A teyne[2] of silver (evil mot he cheeve!)[3]
Which that was but an ounce of wight.
And taketh heed now of his cursèd sleight:
He shop his ingot in length and in brede
Of this teynè, withouten any dread,
So slyly that the priest it nought aspied;
And in his sleeve again he gan it hide;
And fro the fire he took up his matteer,
And into the ingot put it with merry cheer;
And into the water-vessel he it cast
Whan that him list; and bad this priest as fast—
"Look what there is: put in thine hond, and grope:
Thou finde there shalt silver, as I hope."
What, devil of helle, should it elles be?
Shaving of silver silver is, pardie!

He put in his hond, and took up a teyne
Of silver fine; and glad in every vein
Was this priest when he saw it was so.

"Goddes blessing, and his moder's also,
And alle halwes', have ye, sir chanoun!"
Saide this priest (and I, here malison):
"But, and ye vouchesauf to teache me
This noble craft and this subtility,
I will be your in all that ever I may."

---

[1] Shaped. [2] A thin piece. [3] End.

Quod this chanoun : " Yet wol I make assay
The second time, that ye mow taken heed
And ben expert of this ; and in your need
Another day assay in mine absence
This discipline and this crafty science.
Let take another ouncè," quod he tho,
" Of quicksilver, withouten wordes mo,
And do therewith as ye have done ere this
With that othèr which that now silver is."

The priest him busyeth in all that he can
To doon as this chanoun, this cursèd man,
Commanded him ; and faste blew the fire
For to come to the effect of his desire.
And this chanoun right in the meanewhile
All ready was this priest eft to beguile ;
And, for a countenance, in his hond bare
An hollow sticke (take keep and be ware)
In the end of which an ouncè and no more
Of silver limayl put was, as before
Was in his coal, and stoppèd with wex well
For to keep in his limayl every del.
But, while the priest was in his business,
This chanoun with his sticke gan him dress
To him anon, and his powder cast in,
As he did ere (the devil out of his skin
Him turn, I pray to God, for his falsehead,
For he was ever false in word and deed !)
And with this stick abovè the croslet,
That was ordainèd with that falsè get,[1]
He stirred the coales, till relente gan
The wex again the fire—as every man,
But it a fool be, woot well it moot need ;
And all that in the holè was out-yede,
And into the croslet hastily it fell.
Now, good sirès, what wol ye bet than well ?
Whan that this priest thus was beguiled again—
Supposing not but truthe, sooth to sayn,—
He was so glad that I can nought express
In no mannèr his mirth and his gladness :
And to the chanoun he proffèred eftsoon
Body and good.

"Yea," quod the chanoun, " soon,
Though poor I be, crafty thou shalt me find :
I warne thee, yet is there more behind.
Is there any copper here within ?" quod he.

" Yea, sir," quod this priest, " I trowe there be."

---

[1] Contrivance, device.

"Elles go buye some, and that as swithè.
Now, good sirè, go forth thy way and hie thee."

He went his way, and with this copper came :
And this chanoun it in his hondès name,[1]
And of that copper weighed out but an ounce.
All too simplè is my tongue to pronounce,
As minister of my wit, the doubleness
Of this chanoun, root of all cursedness.
He seemed friendly to hem that knew him nought,
But he *was* fiendly, both in work and thought.
It wearieth me to tell of his falseness :
And nathèless yit wol I it express,
To that intent men may be ware thereby,
And for none other causè truely.
He put this ounce of copper in the croslet ;
And on the fire als swithe he hath it set,
And cast in powder, and made the priest to blow :
And, in his worching for to stoope low,
As he did ere (and all nas but a jape),
Right as him list the priest he made his ape.
And afterward in the ingot he it cast ;
And in the panne put it, atte last,
Of water, and in he put his owne hond.
And in his sleevè, as ye bèfornhond
Hearde me tell, he had a silver teyne.
He slyly took it out, this cursèd heyne
(Unwittinge this priest of his false craft),
And in the panne's bottom he hath it laft,
And in the water rumbleth to and fro ;
And wonder privily took up also
The copper teynè (nought knowing this priest),
And hid it, and him hente by the breast,
And to him spake, and thus said in his game :
"Stoopeth adown ! by God, ye ben to blame !
Helpeth me now, as I dede you whilere :
Put in your hond, and looke what is there."

This priest took up this silver teyne anon.
And thannè said the chanoun : " Let us gone
With these three teynès which that we han wrought,
To some goldsmith, and wite if it be aught.
For by my faith I noldè, for mine hood,
But if they werè silver fine and good ;
And that as swithè provèd shall it be."

Unto the goldsmith with these teynès three
They went, and put these teynès in assay
To fire and hammer : might no man say nay
But that they werè as hem oughte be.

---

[1] Took.

This sotted priest, who was gladder than he?
Was never brid gladder again the day;
Ne nightingale in the seasoun of May
Was never none that list better to sing;
Ne lady lustier in caroling,
Or for to speak of love and womanhede;
Ne knight in armes doon an hardy deed
To stond in gracè of his lady dear,—
Than hadde this priest this craft for to lere.
And to the chanoun thus he spake and said:
"For the love of God, that for us alle deyd,
And as I may deserve it unto yow,
What shall this rèceipt costè? Telleth now."

"By our Lady," quod the chanoun, "it is dear,
I warn you well; for, save I and a frere,
In Engelond there can no man it make."

"No force," quod he; "now, sir, for Goddes sake,
What shall I paye? Telleth me, I pray."

"I wis," quoth he, "it is full dear, I say.
Sir, at a word, if that ye lust it have,
Ye shul pay fourty pound, so God me save:
And, nere the friendship that ye dede ere this
To me, ye shoulde paye more, I wis."

This priest the sum of fourty pound anon
Of nobles fett, and took hem everychone
To this chanoun, for this ilkè receipt.
All his working nas but fraud and deceit.

"Sir priest," he said, "I keepè have no los [1]
Of my craft, for I would it kept were close;
And, as ye loveth me, keep it secrè.
For, and men knewe all my subtlety,
By God, men woulden have so great envỳ
To me, because of my philosophy,
I should be dead—there were none other way."

"God it forbedè!" quoth the priest: "What say?
Yet had I liever spenden all the good
Which that I have (and elles wax I wood)
Than that ye shoulde fall in such mischief."

"For your good will, sir, have ye right good preef,"
Quoth the chanoun, "and farewell, graunt-mercy."

He went his way; and never the priest him sey
After this day. And, whan that this priest should
Maken assay, at such time as he would,
Of this receipt—farewell, it would not be.

---

[1] Praise.

Lo ! thus bejapèd and beguilt was he !
Thus maketh he his introduction
To bringe folk to here destruction.

Considereth, sirs, how that in each astate
Betwixe men and gold there is debate,
So ferforth that unnethè there is none.
This multiplying[1] blent so many one
That in good faith I trowe that it be
The causè grettest of swich scarcity.
Philosophers speaken so mistily
In this craft that men connot come thereby,
For any wit that men han now-on-days.
They may well chitteren, as doon these jays,
And in here termes sette lust and pain,
But to here purpose shul they never attain.
A man may lightly learn, if he have aught,
To multiply, and bring his good to naught.
Lo, such a lucre is in this lusty game !
A manne's mirth it wol turn into grame,
And empty also great and heavy purses,
And makè folk for to purchasè curses
Of hem that han here good thereto ylent.
Oh fie for shamè !   They that have been brent,
Alas ! can they not flee the firè's heat ?
Ye that it usen, I rede ye it lete,
Lest ye lesen all ; for bet than never is late,—
Never to thrivè were too long a date.
Though ye proll[2] all, ye shul it never find.
Ye been as bold as is Bayard the blind,[3]
That blundereth forth, and peril casteth none :
He is as bold to ren again a stone
As for to go besidès in the way :—
So farè ye that multiply, I say.
If that your eyen can nought see aright,
Look that your minde lacke nought his sight :
For, though ye look never so broad, and stare,
Ye shul nought win a mite on that chaffare,
But wasten all, that *they* may rape and ren.
Withdraw the fire, lest it too faste brenn :
Meddleth no morè with that art, I mean,—
For, gif ye doon, your thrift is gone full clean.
And right as swithe I wol you telle here
What philosòphers sayn in this mattere.

Lo thus saith Arnold of the Newe Toun,[4]
As his *Rosary* maketh mention,—

---

[1] Multiplying of precious metals, alchemy
[2] Prowl, search for.
[3] A popular old proverb—" Bayard " being understood as the name of a horse.
[4] Arnold de Villeneuve, author of the *Rosarius Philosophorum.*

He saith right thus, withouten any lie :
"There may no man Mercury mortify,
But it be with his brother knowleching.
Lo how that he which that first said this thing
Of philosòphers fader was, Hermès :
He saith how that the dragoun doubteless
He dieth nought but if that he be slain
With his brothèr :—and that is for to sayn,
By the dragoun, Mercury, and none other,
He understood, and brimstone be his brother,
That out of Sol and Luna were ydraw.
And therefore, said he, 'Take heed to my saw :—
Let no man busy him this art to seech
But if that he the intention and speech
Of philosòphers understondè can ;
And, if he do, he is a lewed man :
For this sciènce and this cunning,' quod he,
'Is of the Secrè of Secrets,[1] pardie.'"

Also there was a dìsciple of Platò
That on a time saide his master to,
As his book *Senior*[2] will bear witness,
And this was his demand in soothfastness :
"Tell me the name of thilkè privy stone."
And Plato answered unto him anon,
"Takè the stone that titanos men name."
"Which is that?" quod he. "Magnasia is the same,
Saide Platò. "Yea, sir, and is it thus?
This is *ignotum per ignotius*.
What is magnasia, good sir, I you pray?"
"It is a water that is made, I say,
Of elementes foure," quod Platò.
"Tell me the rotè,[3] good sir," quod he tho,
"Of that watèr, if it be your will."
"Nay, nay," quod Plato, "certain that I nill.
The philosòphers sworn were everychone
That they ne should discover it unto none,
Ne in no book it write in no mannere ;
For unto Christ it is so lief and dear
That he will not that it discovered be
But where it liketh to his deity
Man to inspire, and eke for to defend[4]
Whom that him liketh :—lo, this is the end."

Than thus conclude I : sin' that God of heaven
Ne wol not that the philosòphers neven[5]

---

[1] An allusion to a treatise, *Secreta Secretorum*, which was supposed to embody Aristotle's instructions to Alexander.
[2] The book is named *Senioris Zadith fil. Hamuelis Tabula Chymica.* The story in this work (quoted by Chaucer) is related of Solomon—not Plato.
[3] Root, source.   [4] Prohibit.   [5] Name, notify

How that a man shall come unto this stone,
I rede as for the beste, let it gone.
For whoso maketh God his adversary,
As for to work anything in contrary
Unto his will, cert's never shall he thrive,
Though that he multiply term of all his live.

And there a point, for ended is my tale.
God send every true man boot of his bale !

THE NUNNE PRIEST'S TALE.

A POORE widow, somedeal stope[1] in age,
Was whilom dwelling in a poor cottage,
Beside a grovè standing in a dale.
This widow of which I telle you my tale,
Sin' thilkè day that she was last a wife,
In patience leddè a full simple life,
For little was her cattle and her rent ;
For husbandry[2] of such as God her sent,
She fond herself, and eke her daughters two.
Three largè sowes had she, and no mo,
Three kine, and eke a sheep that hightè Mall.
Full sooty was her bower, and eke her hall,
In which she eat full many a sclender meal.
Of poinant sauce her needed never a deal:
None dainteth morsel passed thorough her throat ;
Her diet was accordant to her coat.
Repletïon ne made her never sick :
Attempre diet was all her physìc,
And exercise, and hearte's suffisance.
The goute let her nothing for to dance,
Ne poplexìè shentè not her heed.
No wine ne drank she, nother white ne reed :
Her board was servèd most with white and black,
Milk and brown bread, in which she fond no lack,
Saynd[3] bacon, and sometime an ey or twey;
For she was, as it were, a manner deye.[4]

A yard she had, enclosèd all about
With stickes, and a drye ditch without,
In which she had a cock hight Chanticleer :
In all the lond, of crowing was none his peer.
His voice was merrier than the merry orgòn
On masse-days that in the churche gone :
Well sickerer was his crowing in his lodge
Than is a clock or an abbey-orologe.
By nature knew he each ascension

---

[1] Stepped, advanced. [2] Husbanding, economizing.
[3] Singed, fried. [4] Hen-wife, dairy-maid.

Of equinoxial in thilkè town;
For whan degrees fifteene were ascended
Than crewe he, it might not ben amended.
His comb was redder than the fine coràl,
And battled as it were a castle-wall.
His bill was black, and like the jeet it shone;
Like azure were his legges and his toen;
His nailes whiter than the lily-flour;
And like the burnished gold was his colour.

This gentil cock had in his governance
Seven hennes, for to do all his pleasaunce,
Which were his susters and his paramours,
And wonder like to him as of colours;
Of which the fairest-huèd on her throat
Was clepèd fair damysel Pertilote.
Curteis she was, discreet, and debonnaire,
And companable, and bare herself full fair,
Sin' thilkè day that she was seven night old,—
That she hath truely the heart in hold
Of Chanticleer locken in every lith :[1]
He loved her so that well him was therewith.
But such a joy was it to hear him sing,
Whan that the brighte sunne gan to spring,
In sweet accord, "My lief is faren on lond."

Fro thilkè time, as I have understond,
Beastes and briddès coulde speake and sing.
And so befell that in a dawëning,
As Chanticleer among his wivès all
Sat on his perche that was in his hall,
And next him sat this faire Pertilote,
This Chanticleer gan groanen in his throat,
As man that in his dream is drecchèd sore.

And, whan that Pertilote thus heard him roar,
She was aghast, and saide: "Hearte dear,
What aileth you to groan in this mannere?
Ye ben a very sleeper! Fie for shame!"

And he answèred and saide thus : "Madame,
I pray you that ye take it nought agrief :
By God, me mett[2] I was in such mischief
Right now that yit mine heart is sore afright.
Now God," quod he, "my sweven[3] rede aright,
And keep my body out of foul prisoun!
Me mett how that I roamèd up and doun
Within our yard, whereas I saw a beast
Was like an hound, and would have made arrest
Upon my body, and would have had me deed.
His colour was betwix yellow and reed;

---

[1] Limb.   [2] I dreamed.   [3] Dream.

And tippèd was his tail and both his ears
With black, unlike the remnant of his heres.
His snout was small, with glowing eyen twey,—
Yet of his look for fear almost I dey:
This causèd me my groaning doubteless."

"Away!" quod she, "fie on you, heartless!
Alas!" quod she, "for by that God above
Now have ye lost my heart and all my love!
I can nought love a coward, by my faith!
For certes, whatso any woman saith,
We all desiren, if it mightè be,
To have husbondès hardy, rich, and free,
And secrè, and no niggard ne no fool,
Ne him that is aghast of every tool,
Ne none avaunter,[1] by that God above!
How durst ye say, for shame, unto your love,
That anything might makè you afeard?
Have ye no manne's heart, and han a beard?
Alas! and can ye been aghast of swevenès?
Nought, God wot, but vanity in sweven is.
Swevens engendred ben of repleccions,
And often of fume and of complexions,
Whan humours ben too abundant in a wight.
Certes this dream which ye han mett to-night
Cometh of the greate superfluity
Of youre reedè cholera, pardie,
Which causeth folk to dreamen in here dreams
Of arwes, and of fire with reedè beams,
Of reedè beastes that they will him bite,
Of contek,[2] and of whelpes greet and lite :[3]
Right as the humour of malencoly
Causeth in sleep full many a man to cry,
For fear of beares or of bulles blake,
Or elles blakè devils wol hem take.
Of other humours couth I tell also
That worken many a man in sleep full woe:
But I wol pass as lightly as I can.
Lo! Catoun, which that was so wise a man,
Said he not thus 'Ne do no force of dreams'—?
Now, sir," quod she, "whan we flee fro these beams,
For Goddes love as take some laxatif.
Up peril of my soul and of my life,
I counsel you the best, I wol not lie,
That both of choler and of malencoly
Ye purgè you; and for ye shul nought tarry,
Though in this town is nonè apotecary,
I shall myself two herbes teachen yow
That shall be for your hele and for your prow:[4]

---

[1] Braggart.   [2] Contention.   [3] Great and little.   [4] Benefit.

And in our yard tho herbes shall I find,
The which han of here property, by kind,
To purgen you beneath and eke above.
Forget not this, for Goddes owne love!
Ye ben full choleric of complexïon:
Warè the sun, in his ascensïon,
Ne find you not replete in humours hot:
And if it do, I dare well lay a groat
That ye shul have a fever tertian,
Or an agùe that may be youre bane.
A day or two ye shul have dìgestives
Of wormes, or ye take your laxatives
Of lauriol, century, and fumitere,
Or else of elderberry that groweth there,
Of catapus,[1] or of gaytre[2] berrïes,
Of erb ivy that groweth in our yard, that merry is:
Pick hem up right as they grow, and eat hem in.
Be merry, husband, for your fader kin:
Dreadeth none dreames. I can say no more."

"Madam," quod he, "graunt-mercy of your lore.
But nathëless, as touching Daun Catoun,
That hath of wisdom such a great renoun,
Though that he bad no dreames for to drede,
By God! men may in olde bookes read
Of many a man, more of auctority
Than ever Catoun was—so mot I the[3]—
That all the rèverse sayn of his sentence;
And han well founden by experience
That dreames ben significations
As well of joy as of tribulations
That folk enduren in this life present.
There needeth make of this none argument:
The very prevè showeth it in deed.
One of the grettest auctors that men read[4]
Saith thus: That whilom tway felawès went
On pilgrimage in a full good intent;
And happèd so they came unto a toun
Whereas there was such congregatïon
Of people, and eke so strait of herbergage,[5]
That they fond nought as much as one cottage
In which that they might both ylodgèd be.
Wherefore they musten of necessity,
As for that night, depart here compaigny:
And each of hem goth to his hostelry,
And took his lodging as it woulde fall.
That one of hem was lodgèd in a stall,
Fer in a yard, with oxen of the plough:
That other man was lodgèd well enow,

---
[1] A species of spurge.   [2] Dogwood.   [3] Thrive.   [4] Cicero.   [5] Lodging.

As was his àdventure or his fortune
That us govèrneth alle in comune.
And so befell that, long ere it were day,
This one mett in his bed, thereas he lay,
How that his felaw gan upon him call,
And said: 'Alas! for in an oxè-stall
This night I shall be murd'red there I lie.
Now help me, deare brother, or I die!
In alle hastè come to me!' he said.
This man out of his sleep for fear abrayd :[1]
But, whan that he was waked out of his sleep,
He turnèd him, and took of this no keep:
Him thought his dream nas but a vanity.
Thus twiès in his sleepe dreamèd he.
And at the thriddè time yet his felaw
Com, as him thought, and said: 'I am now slaw:
Behold my bloody woundes, deep and wide.
Arise up early in the morwè-tide;
And at the west gate of the toun,' quod he,
'A cart of dunge therè shalt thou see,
In which my body is hid privily.
Do thilkè cart arresten boldely.
My gold causèd my murdre, sooth to sayn :'—
And told him every point how he was slain,
With a full pitous facè, pale of hue.
And truste well, his dream he fond full true :—
For on the morwè, as soon as it was day,
To his felawè's inn he took the way;
And, whan that he came to this oxè-stall,
After his felaw he began to call.
The hosteller answerèd him anon,
And saide: 'Sir, your felaw is agone:
Als soon as day, he went out of the toun.'
This man gan fall in a suspeccïon,
Remembering on his dreames that he mett :
And forth he goth, no longer would he let,
Unto the west gate of the toun, and fond
A dung-cart went, as it were to dung lond,
That was arrayèd in the samè wise
As ye han heard the deedè man devise.
And with an hardy heart he gan to cry
Vengeance and justice of this felony.
'My felaw murd'red is this samè night,
And in this carte he lith here upright.
I cry out on the minsters,' quod he,
'That shoulde keep and rulè this citie!
Haro! alas! here lith my felaw slain!'—
What should I more unto this talè sayn?

---

[1] Started up awake.

The people upstert, and cast the cart to ground,
And in the middès of the dung they found
The deade man that murd'red was all new.
O blissful God, Thou art full just and true!
Lo how Thou bèwrayest murder all-day!
Murder will out—certes it is no nay.
Murder is so vlatsome[1] and abominable
To God, that is so just and reasonable,[2]
That he ne would not suffre it hilèd[3] be.
Though it abide a year, or two or three,
Murder will out—this is my cònclusioun.
And right anon the ministers of that toun
Han hent the carter; and so sore him pined,
And eke the hosteller so sore engined,[4]
That they beknew[5] here wickedness anon,
And were anhongèd by the necke-bone.—
Here may men see that dreames ben to dread:
And certes in the samè book I read,
Right in the next chapitre after this
(I gabbe nought, so have I joy or bliss),
Two men that would have passèd over sea
For certain causes into fer countrie,
If that the wind ne hadde been contràry,
That made hem in a city for to tarry,
That stood full merry upon an haven-side.
But on a day, again the eventide,
The wind gan change, and blew right as hem lest.
Jolyf and glad they wenten unto rest,
And casten hem full early for to sail.
But to that one man fell a great mervail.
That one of them, in his sleeping as he lay,
Him mett a wonder dream again the day.
Him thought a man stood by his bedde's side,
And him commanded that he should abide,
And said him thus: 'If thou tomorwè wend,
Thou shalt be dreynt:[6] my tale is at an end.'
He woke, and told his felaw what he mett,
And praydè him his viagè to let:
As for that day he prayed him for to abide.
His felaw, that lay by his bedde's side,
Gan for to laugh, and scornèd him full fast.
'No dream,' quod he, 'may so mine hearte ghast
That I will lettè for to do my things.
I sette not a straw by thy dreamings,
For swevens ben but vanities and japes.
Men dream all day of owles and of apes,
And eke of many a mazè[7] therewithall:

---

[1] Loathsome. [2] Equitable. [3] Hidden. [4] Racked, tortured.
[5] Confessed. [6] Drenched, drowned. [7] Wild fancy.

B

Men dream of thinges that nevèr be shall.
But, sith I see that thou wilt here abide,
And thus forslouthè[1] wilfully thy tide,
God wot it rueth me—and have good day.'
And thus he took his leave, and went his way.
But, ere he hadde half his course ysailed—
Noot I nought why, ne what mischance it ailed—
But casually the shippe's bottom rent ;
And ship and man under the water went
In sight of other shippes there-beside
That with him sailèd at the samè tide.—
And therefore, faire Pertilote so dear,
By such ensamples olde maistou lear
That no man shoulde be too rechëless
Of dreames : for I say thee doubteless
That many a dream full sore is for to dread.
Lo ! in the Life of Saint Kenelm I read
(That was Kenulphus' son, the noble King
Of Merkenrick[2]) how Kenelm mett a thing.
A little or he was murd'red, upon a day,
His murdre in his avisïon he sey.
His norice him expounèd every del
His sweven, and bad him for to keep him well
For traison : but he nas but seven year old,
And therefore little talè hath he told[3]
Of any dream, so holy was his hert.
By God, I hadde liever than my shirt
That ye had rad his legend, as have I.—
Dame Pertilote, I say you truely,
Macrobius, that writ the avision
In Afric of the worthy Scipion,
Affirmeth dreames, and saith that they been
Warning of thinges that men after seen.
And furthermore I pray you looketh well
In the Old Testament, of Danïel,
If he huld dreames any vanity.
Read eke of Joseph, and there shall ye see
Whether dreams ben sometime (I say nought all)
Warning of thinges that shul after fall.
Look of Egỳpt the King, Daun Pharäo,
His baker and his botteler also,
Whether they felte none effect in dreams.
Whoso wol seek actes of sundry rames[4]
May read of dreames many a wonder thing.
Lo Crœsus which that was of Lydes King,
Mett he not that he sat upon a tree,

---

[1] Neglect, miss.
[2] Mercia. Kenelm, succeeding to the throne in childhood, was murdered by order of his aunt, Quenedreda.
[3] Little account did he take.   [4] Realms.

Which signifièd he should hangèd be?
Lo her Andromachia, Ector's wife,
That day that Ector shoulde lese his life,
She dreamèd on the samè night beforn
How that the life of Ector should be lorn
If thilkè day he wentè to battail.
She warnèd him, but it might nought avail:
He wente forth to fighte nathëless,
And he was slain anon of Achilles.
But thilkè tale is all too long to tell:—
And eke it is nigh day—I may not dwell.
Shortly I say, as for conclusïon,
That I shall have, of this avisïon,
Adversity: and I say furthermore
That I ne tell of laxatifs no store,
For they ben venemous, I wot it well:
I hem defy—I love hem never a del.—
Now let us speak of mirth, and let all this.
Madamè Pertilote, so have I bliss,
Of o thing God hath me sent largè grace:
For, whan I see the beauty of your face,
Ye been so scarlet-hue about your eyen
It maketh all my dreade for to dien;
For, all so sicker as *in principio,
Mulier est hominis confusio:*
Madam, the sentence of this Latin is,
Woman is manne's joy and manne's bliss.
For, whan I feel anight your softe side
(Albeit that I may not on you ride,
For that your perch is made so narrow, alas!)
I am so full of joy and of solàs
That I defye both sweven and dream."

And with that word he fley doun fro the beam
(For it was day), and eke his hennes all;
And with a chuck he gan hem for to call,
For he had found a corn lay in the yerd.
Reäl he was, he was no more afeard.
He featherèd Pertilotè twenty time,
And trad as ofte, ere that it was prime.
He looketh as it were a grim lioun;
And on his toen he roameth up and doun,—
Him deignèd not to set his foot to ground.
He chucketh whan he hath a corn yfound,
And to him rennen than his wivès all.

Thus, reäl as a prince is in his hall,
Leave I this Chanticleer in his pasture:
And after wol I tell his àventure.

Whan that the month in which the world began,

That hightè March, whan God makèd first man,
Was còmplete, and ypassèd were also,
Sin' March began, tway months and dayes two,
Befell that Chanticleer in all his pride,
His seven wivès walking by his side,
Cast up his eyen to the brightè sun,
That in the sign of Taurus had yrun
Twenty degrees and one, and somewhat more:
He knew by kind, and by none other lore,
That it was prime, and crew with blissful steven.[1]

"The sun," he said, "is clomben up on heaven
Twenty degrees and one, and more, I wis.
Madamè Pertilote, my worlde's bliss,
Hearkeneth these blissful briddès how they sing,
And seeth these freshe flourès how they spring:
Full is mine heart of revel and solàce."

But suddenly him fell a sorrowful case,
For ever the latter end of joy is woe.
God wot that worldly joy is soon ago:
And, if a rhethor[2] couthè fair indite,
He in a chronique saufly might it write
As for a sovereign notability.

Now every wise man let him hearkne me.
This story is all so true, I undertake,
As is the book of Lancelot the Lake,
That woman huld in full gret reverence.
Now wol I turn again to my sentence.

A cole-fox,[3] full sly of iniquity,
That in the grove had wonnèd yeares three,
By high imagination forncast,
The samè nightè thurgh the hedgè brast
Into the yard there Chanticleer the fair
Was wont, and eke his wivès, to repair:
And in a bed of wortes[4] still he lay
Till it was passèd undern of the day,
Waiting his time on Chanticleer to fall;
As gladly doon these homicidès all
That in awaite lien to murder men.
O falsè murd'rer lurking in thy den!
O newe Scariot, newe Genilon!
Falsè dissimulor, O Greek Sinòn
That broughtest Troy all utterly to sorrow!
O Chanticleer, accursèd be the morrow

---

[1] Voice.   [2] Rhetorician.
[3] The word "cole," used as a compound with other words, is a term of opprobrium.
[4] Cabbages.

That thou into the yard flew fro the beams!
Thou werè full well warnèd by thy dreams
That thilkè day was perilous to thee!
But what that God forewot must needes be,
After the opinïon of certain clerkes.
Witness on him that any parfit clerk is
That in school is gret altercation
In this matteer, and gret disputeson,
And hath been of an hundred-thousand men.
But yet I cannot bult it to the bren,[1]
As can the holy doctor Aùgustin,
Or Boece, or the bishop Bradwardin,
Whether that Goddes worthy foreweeting
Straineth me needly for to do a thing
("Needly" clepe I simple necessity);
Or elles if free choice be granted me
To do that same thing or to do it nought,
Though God forewot it ere that it was wrought,
Or, of his witting, straineth never a deal
But by necessity conditionel.
I wol not have to do of such matteer.
My tale is of a cock, as ye shall hear,
That took his counsel of his wife with sorrow
To walken in the yard upon the morrow
That he had mett the dreame that I told.
Women's counseilès been full ofte cold:
Womane's counseil brought us first to woe,
And made Adàm fro paradise to go,
Thereas he was full merry and well at ease.
But, for I not to whom it might displease
If I counsell of woman wouldè blame,
Pass over, for I said it in my game.
Read auctours where they treat of such matteer,
And what they sayn of women ye may hear.
These been the cocke's wordes, and not mine:
I can none harme of womàn divine.

Fair in the sond,[2] to bathe her merrily,
Li'th Pertilote, and all her susters by,
Again the sun: and Chanticleer so free
Sang merrier than the meermaid in the sea—
For Physiologus[3] saith sickerly
How that they singen well and merrily.
And so befell that, as he cast his eye
Among the wortes on a butterfly,
He was ware of this fox that lay full low.
Nothing ne list him thannè for to crow;

---

[1] Bolt (sift) it to the bran.   [2] Sand.
[3] A popular metrical Latin treatise on the nature of animals.

But cried anon "Cok cok," and up he stert,
As man that was affrayèd in his hert.
For naturally a beast desireth flee
Fro his contràry, if he may it see,
Though he never ere had seyn it with his eye.

This Chanticleer, whan he gan it aspie,
He would han fled ; but that the fox anon
Said : "Gentil sir, alas ! why wol ye go'n ?
Be ye afraid of me that am your friend ?
Certes I werè worse than any fiend
If I to you would harm or villany.
I am nought come your counsel to espie.
But truely the cause of my comìng
Was only for to hearken how ye sing :
For truely ye have als merry a steven
As any angel hath that is in heaven ;
Therewith ye han of music more feelìng
Than had Boece, or any that can sing.
My lord your fader (God his soule bless !)
And youre moder, of her gentiless,
Han in mine housè been, to my gret ease :
And certes, sir, full fain would I you please.
But for men speak of singing, I wol say—
So mot I brookè[1] well mine eyen twey,
Save ye I hearde never man so sing
As dede your fader in the morwening.
Certes it was of heart all that he song.
And, for to make his voice the morè strong,
He would so painen him that with both his eyen
He muste wink—so loud he woulde cryen ;
And stonden on his tiptoen therewithal,
And stretche forth his necke long and small.
And eke he was of such discretion
That there was no man in no region
That him in song or wisdom mighte pass.
I have well rad in Daun Burnel[2] the ass,
Among his verses, how there was a cock
That, for a prieste's son gave him a knock
Upon his leg while he was young and nice,
He made him for to lese his benefice.
But certain there is no comparison
Betwix the wisdom and discretion
Of youre fader and of his subtlety.
Now singeth, sir, for Sainte Charity !
Let see can ye your fader counterfeit."

This Chanticleer his winges gan to beat,

---

[1] Use.
[2] The satirical poem, *Burnellus*, written by Nigellus Wireker.

As man that couth his treason nought espie,
So was he ravished with his flattery.
Alas! ye lordlings, many a false flattour
Is in your house, and many a losengour,[1]
That pleasen you well morè, by my faith,
Than he that soothfastness unto you saith.
Readeth Ecclesiast of flattery :
Beware, ye lordes, of here treachery.

This Chanticleer stood high upon his toes,
Stretching his neck ; and held his eyen close,
And gan to crowe loude for the nonce :
And Daun Russèl the fox stert up at once,
And by the garget hentè Chanticleer,
And on his back toward the wood him bare—
For yit was there no man that had him sued.
O destiny, that mayst not ben eschewed !
Alas that Chanticleer fley fro the beams !
Alas his wife ne roughtè nought of dreams !
And on a Friday fell all this mischance.
O Venus, that art goddess of pleasance,
Sin' that thy servant was this Chanticleer,
And in thy service did all his powère,
More for delight than th' world to multiply,
Why wouldst thou suffer him on thy day to die?
O Gaufred,[2] deare maister soveraign,
That, whan the worthy King Richàrd was slain
With shot, complainedest his death so sore,
Why n'had I nought thy sentence and thy lore
The Friday for to chiden as dede ye—
For on a Friday soothly slain was he?
Than would I showe how that I couth plain
For Chanticleere's dread and for his pain.

Certes such cry ne lamentation
Was never of ladies made whan Ilion
Was won, and Pyrrhus with his streitè[3] swerd,
Whan he had hent King Priam by the berd,
And slaw him (as saith us Eneïdos),
As maden all the hennes in the close
Whan they had seyn of Chanticleer the sight.
But sovereignly dame Pertilotè shright
Full louder than did Hasdrubaldè's wife,
Whan that her housèbond had lost his life,
And that the Romans had ybrent Cartage :

---

[1] Sycophant.
[2] Geoffrey de Vinsauf, author of a treatise named *Nova Poetria*. In this work he gives, as a specimen of the plaintive style, some lines on the death of Richard I., referring to the *dies Veneris*, or Friday, on which that event occurred.
[3] Stretched, drawn.

She was so full of torment and of rage
That wilfully unto the fire she stert,
And brenned herselven with a stedfast hert.
O woful hennes! right-so criede ye
As, whan that Nero brentè the citee
Of Rome, crieden the senatoures' wives,
For that here housbonds losten all here lives :
Withouten gult, this Nero had hem slayn.

Now wol I turn to my matteer again.
The silly widow and her daughters two
Hearden these hennes cry and maken woe ;
And out at doores starten they anon,
And seyen the fox toward the wood is gone,
And bare upon his back the cock away.
They crieden : " Out, haro, and wellaway !
Ha ha ! The fox !"—And after him they ran,
And eke with staves many another man.
Ran Coll our dog, and Talbot, and Garlond,
And Malkin with a distaff in her hond :
Ran cow and calf, and eke the very hogs ;—
So were they feared for barking of the dogs,
And shouting of the men and women eke,
They ronnè that they thought here hearte breke.
They yellëden as fiendes doon in hell :
The duckes crieden as men would hem quell.[1]
The geese for feare flow'n over the trees :
Out of the hivè came the swarm of bees.
So hidous was the noise—ah benedicite !—
Certes he Jacke Straw, and his meynè,
Ne maden shoutes never half so shrill
Whan that they woulden any Fleming kill
As thilkè day was made upon the fox.
Of brass they broughten hornes, and of box,
Of horn and bone, in which they blew and pouped,[2]
And therewithal they shriekèd and they whooped :
It seemèd as that heaven shoulde fall.

Now, goode men, I pray you hearkeneth all :
Lo how fortunè turneth suddenly
The hope and pride eke of her enemy.
This cock that lay upon this fox's back,
In all his dread unto the fox he spak,
And saide : " Sir, if that I were as ye,
Yet should I sayn, as wise God helpe me—
' Turneth again, ye proude churles all !
A very pestilence upon you fall !
Now am I come unto this woode's side,

---

[1] Kill. [2] Sounded.

Maugre your head the cock shall here abide :
I wol him eat in faith, and that anon.' "

The fox answèred : " In faith, it shall be done ! "

And, while he spake that word, all suddenly,
This cock brake from his mouth deliverly,
And high upon a tree he fley anon.

And, whan the fox sey that he was ygone,
" Alas ! " quod he, " O Chanticleer, alas !
I have to you," quod he, " ydone trespàss,
Inàsmuch as I makèd you afeard,
Whan I you hent, and brought out of the yerd.
But, sir, I dede it in no wicked intent :
Come doun, and I shall tell you what I meant.
I shall say sooth to you, God help me so ! "

" Nay than," quod he, " I shrew us bothe two,
And first I shrew myself, both blood and bones,
If thou beguile me any oftèr than once.
Thou shalt no more thorough thy flattery
Do me to sing and winke with mine eye :
For he that winketh whan he shoulde see,
All wilfully, God let him never the "

" Nay," quod the fox, " but God give him mischance
That is so undiscreet of governance
That jangleth whan he shoulde hold his peace ! "

Lo such it is for to be rechëless
And negligent, and trust on flattery.
But ye that holde this tale a follìe—
As of a fox, or of a cock or hen,—
Tak'th the morality thereof, good men :
For Saint Poul saith that all that written is,
To our doctrìne it is ywrit, I wis.
Taketh the fruit, and let the chaff be still.

Now goode God, if that it be thy will
(As saith my lord), so make us all good men,—
And bring us alle to his bliss, Amen !

ADAM OF COBSAM.

[Nothing seems to be known about this writer, except that his poem must bear date somewhere towards 1462. It was discovered by that indefatigable student of our early literature Mr. F. J. Furnivall, in a MS. in the Library of the Archbishop of Canterbury; and was by him published in 1865 for the Early English Text Society].

THE WRIGHT'S CHASTE WIFE.

ALMIGHTY God, Maker of all,
Save you, my sovereigns, in tower and hall,
    And send you good grace!
If ye will a stoundè blyn,
Of a story I will begin,
    And tell you all the case,
Many farleyes [1] that I have heard;
Ye would have wonder how it fared:
    Listen, and ye shall hear:
Of a wright I will you tell
That sometime in this land gan dwell,
    And lived by his mystere.

Whether that he were in or out,
Of earthly man had he no doubt
    To work house, harrow, nor plough,
Or other works, whatso they were:
Thus wrought he hem far and near,
    And did them well enow.
This wright would wed no wife,
But in youth to lead his life
In mirth and other melody:
Overall where he gan wend,
Alle they said: "Welcome, friend;
    Sit down, and do gladly."
Till on a time he was willing
(As time cometh of all thing,
    So saith the prophecy)
A wife for to wed and have
That might his goodes keep and save,
    And for to leave all folly.

There dwelled a widow in that countrie
That had a daughter fair and free:
    Of her, word sprang wide—
For she was both stable and true,
Meek of manners, and fair of hue:
    So said men in that tide.

The wright said: "So God me save,
Such a wifè would I have
To lie nightly by my side."

---

[1] Rarities.

He thought to speake with that may,
And rose early on a day,
 And thider gan he to ride.

The wright was welcome to the wife,
And her salùed all so blyve,
 And so he did her daughter free.

For the errand that he for came
Tho he spake, that good yemane.
 Than to him said she,
The widow said : "By heaven king,
I may give with her no thing,
 And that forthinketh me;[1]
Save a garland I will thee give ;
Ye shall never see, while ye live,
 None such in this countrie.
Have here this garland of roses rich :
In all this lond is none it lich,
 For it will ever be new.
Weet thou well, withouten fable,
All the while thy wife is stable
 The chaplet wol hold hue ;
And, if thy wife use putry,[2]
Or toll[3] any man to lie her by,
 Than will it change hue :
And by the garland thou may see
Fickle or false if that she be,
 Or else if she be true."

Of this chaplet him was full fain,
And of his wife, was not to layn.[4]
 He wedded her full soon ;
And lad her home with solempnity,
And hild her bridal dayes three.—
 Whan they home come,
This wright in his heart cast,
If that he walked east or west,
 As he was wont to doon :
" My wife, that is so bright of blee,
Men wol desire her fro me,
 And that hastly and soon."

But soon he him bethought
That a chamber should be wrought
 Both of lime and stone.
With walles strong as any steel,
And doors subtly made and wele,
 He outframed it soon.
The chamber he let make fast
With plaster of Paris that will last ;—

---

[1] Is a subject of regret to me.   [2] Unchastity.
[3] Take.   [4] Conceal.

   Such ouse know I never none;
There is king ne emperour,
And he were locken in that tower,
   That could get out of that wonne.
Now hath he done as he thought,
And in the mids of the floor wrought
   A wonder strange guile—
A trapdoore round-about,
That no man might come in nor out.
   It was made with a wile
That whoso touched it anything
Into the pit he should fling
   Within a little while.
For his wife he made that place,
That no man should beseek her of grace,
   Nor her to beguile.

By that time the lord of the town
Had ordained timber ready bown,[1]
   An hall to make of tree.
After the wright the lord let send
For that he should with him lend [2]
   Moneths two or three.
The lord said: "Wolt thou have thy wife?
I will send after her blyve,
   That she may come to thee."
The wright his garland had take with him,
That was bright and nothing dim;
   It was fair on to see.
The lord axed him as he sat:
"Fellow, where hadst thou this hat,
   That is so fair and new?"
The wright answered all so blyve,
And said: "Sir, I had it with my wife,
   And that dare me never rue.
Sir, by my garland I may see
Fickle or false if that she be,
   Or if that she be true:
And if my wife love a paramour,
Than will my garland vade colour,
   And change will it the hue."
The lord thought: "By Goddes might,
That will I weet this same night,
   Whether this tale be true."
To the wright's house anon he went.
He found the wife therein present,
   That was so bright and sheen.
Soon he hailèd her truly,
And so did she the lord courtisly:

---

[1] Prepared.   [2] Stay.

She said: "Welcome ye be."
Thus said the wife of the house:
"Sir, how fareth my sweet spouse,
    That heweth upon your tree?"

"Certes, damè," he said, "wele;
And I am come, so have I hele,
    To weet the will of thee:
My love is upon thee cast,
That methinketh my heart wol brest,
    It wol none otherwise be.
Good dame, grant me thy grace,
To play with thee in some privy place
    For gold and eke for fee."

"Good sir, let be your fare,
And of such words speak no mair,
    For his love that died on rood.[1]
Had we once begun that glee,
My husband by his garland might see:
    For sorrow he would wax wood."[2]

"Certes, damè," he said, "nay:
Love me, I pray you, in that ye may:
    For God's love, change thy mood!
Forty mark shall be your meed
Of silver and of gold so rede,
    And that shall do thee good."

"Sir, that deede shall be done:
Take me that money here anon."

    "I swear by the holy rood,
I thought, when I came hidder,
For to bring it all togider,
    As I mot break my hele!"[3]

There she tooke forty mark
Of silver and gold stiff and stark;
    She took it fair and well.
She said: "Into the chamber will we,
There no man shall us see:
    No lenger will we spare."

Up the staier they gan hie:
The steps were made so quaintly [4]
    That farther might he not fare.
The lord stumbled as he went in haste;
He fell down into that chast [5]
    Forty foot and somedele mair.

---

[1] I have ventured to substitute, for the rhyme's sake, "rood," in lieu of "tree," which I find in my text: so also, a little further on, "mair," in lieu of "more,"—and, on p. 34, "done," in lieu of "do."
[2] Frantic.
[3] Or otherwise may I forfeit my salvation
[4] Curiously, ingeniously.
[5] Chest, receptacle.

The lord began to cry:
The wife said to him in high,
 "Sir, what do ye there?"

"Dame, I cannot say how
That I am come hidder now
 To this house that is so new:
I am so deep in this sure floor
That I ne can come out at no door:
 Good dame, on me thou rue!"

"Nay," she said, "so mut I the,
Till mine husband come and see,
 I shrew him that it thought."
The lord arose and looked about
If he might anywhere get out;
 But it holp him right nought.
The walles were so thick within
That he nowhere might out win,
 But help to him were brought:
And ever the lord made evil cheer,
And said: "Dame, thou shalt buy this dear!"
 She said that she ne rought.[1]

She said: "I recke ne'er;
While I am here and thou art there,
 I shrew her that thee doth dread."
The lord was soon out of her thought:
The wife went into her loft;
 She sat, and did her deed.

Then it fell on that other day
Of meat and drink he gan her pray;
 Thereof he had great need.
He said: "Dame, for Saint Charity,
With some meat thou comfort me!"

 She said: "Nay, so God me speed!
For I swear by sweet St. John,
Meat ne drink ne gett'st thou none
 But thou wilt sweat or swink;
For I have both hemp and line,
And a beating-stock full fine,
 And a swingle[2] good and great.
If thou wilt work, tell me soon."

"Dame, bring it forth, it shall be done;
 Full gladly would I eat."

She took the stock in her hond,
And into the pit she it sclang[3]

---

[1] Recked not, cared not.
[2] A wooden instrument used for the clearing of hemp and flax from the stalks &c.   [3] Slung, threw.

With a greate heat:
She brought the line and hemp on her back:
"Sir lord," she said, "have thou that,
And learne for to sweat."

There she tooke him a bond [1]
For to occupy his hond,
And)ade him fast on to beat.
He laid it down on the stone,
And laid on strockes well good wone,
And spared not on to lain.
Whan that he had wrought a thrave,
Meat and drink he gan to crave,
And would have had it fain.
"That I had somewhat for to eat
Now after my great sweat,
Methinketh it were right:
For I have laboured night and day
Thee for to please; dame, I say,
And thereto put my might."

The wife said, "So mut I have hele,
And if thy worke be wrought wele,
Thou shalt have to dine."

Meat and drink she him bare,
With a thrafe of flex mair
Of full long bounden line.
So fair the wife the lord gan pray
That he should be working aye,
And nought that he should blyn:
The lord was fain to work tho:—
But his men knew not of his woe,
Nor of their lord's pine.

The steward to the wright gan say:
"Saw thou aught of my lord to-day,
Whether that he is wend?"

The wright answered and said: "Nay;
I saw him not sith yesterday:
I trow that he be shent."[3]

The steward stood the wright by,
And of his garland had ferly
What that it bemeant.
The steward said: "So God me save,
Of thy garland wonder I have,
And who it hath thee sent.'

"Sir," he said, "be the same hat
I can know if my wife be bad

---
[1] Bundle, bavin, bush of thorns.   [2] Number.   [3] Destroyed, dead.

To me by any other man:
If my flowers other fade or fall,
Then doth my wife me wrong withal,
　　As many a woman can."

The steward thought: "By Goddes might,
That shall I preve this same night,
　　Whether thou bliss or ban."
And into his chamber he gan gone,
And took treasure full good wone,
　　And forth he sped him than.
But he ne stint at no stone
Till he unto the wright's house come
　　That ilkè samè night.
He met the wife about the gate:
About the neck he gan her take,
　　And said: "My deare wight,
All the good that is mine
I will thee give to be thine,
　　To lie by thee all night."

She said: "Sir, let be thy fare:
My husband wol weet withouten mair
　　And I him did that unright.
I would not he might it weet
For all the good that I might gete,
　　So Jesus mut me speed:
For, and any man lay me by,
My husband would it weet truly,—
　　It is withouten any drede."

The steward said: "For him that is[1] wrought:
Thereof, dame, dread thee nought
　　With me to do that deed:
Have here of me twenty mark
Of gold and silver stiff and stark;
　　This treasure shall be thy meed."

"Sir, and I grant that to you,
Let no man weet but we two now."

　　He said: "Nay, withouten dread."
The steward thought: "Sickerly,
Women beth both quaint and sly."
　　The money he gan her bede:
He thought well to have be sped,
And of his errand he was onredd[2]
　　Or he were fro hem ygone.

---

[1] The text gives "ys" [is]. With this word, the meaning of the sentence appears to be: "The transaction will turn to *his* advantage too (considering the pay that you will receive):" or perhaps, "He is safely provided for." But I suspect we ought to read "us": in that case, the clause would be a simple adjuration—"For the sake of Him [God] who made us!"
[2] Cheerless, anxious?

Up the staires she him led,
Till he saw the wrighte's bed :
   Of treasure rought he none.
He went and stumbled at a stone :
Into the cellar he fill soon,
   Down to the bare floor.

The lord said : "What devil art thou?
And thou haddest fall on me now,
   Thou hadst hurt me full sore !"

The steward stert and stared about,
If he might ower get out
   At holè, less or mair.

The lord said : "Welcome, and sit betime ;
For thou shalt help to dight[1] this line,
   For all thy fierce fare."[2]

The steward lookèd on the knight :—
He said : "Sir, for Goddes might,
   My lord, what do you here ?"

He said : "Fellow, withouten oath,
For o errand we come both :
   The sooth wol I not lete."[3]

Tho came the wife them unto,
And said : "Sirs, what do you two?
   Will ye not learn to sweat ?"

Than said the lord her unto :
"Damè, your line is ydo :
   Now would I fain eat :
And I have made it all ilike,—
Full clear, and nothing thick :
   Methinketh it great pain."

The steward said : "Withouten doubt,
And ever I may win out,
   I will break her brain !"

"Fellow, let be, and say not so ;
For thou shalt work or ever thou go,—
   Thy words thou turn again.
Fain thou shalt be so to do,
And thy good-will put thereto :
   As a man buxom and bayn,[4]
Thou shalt rubbe, reel, and spin,
And thou wolt any meat win,—
   That I give to God a gift !"

---

[1] Dress, prepare.   [2] Goings-on, project.
[3] I will not disguise the truth.   [4] Alert.

The steward said : " Then have I wonder !
Rather would I die for hunger
   Without hosel or shrift !"

The lord said : " So have I hele,
Thou wilt work, if thou hunger well,
   What work that thee be brought."
The lord sat, and did his work :
The steward drew into the derk ;
   Great sorrow was in his thought.
The lord said : " Dame, here is your line :
Have it in God's blessing and mine ;
   I hold it well ywrought."

Meat and drink she gave him in.
" The steward," she said, " wol he not spin ?
   Will he do right nought ?"

The lord said : " By sweet Sen John,
Of this meat shall he have none
   That ye have me hidder brought !"

The lord eat and dranke fast :
The steward hungered at the last,
   For he gave him nought.
The steward sat all in a study
His lord had forgot courtesy.
Tho said the steward : " Give me some."

The lord said : " Sorrow have the morsel or sop
That shall come into thy throat !
   Not so much as a crumb !
But thou wilt help to dight this line,
Much hunger it shall be thine,
   Though thou make much moan !"

Up he rose, and went thereto :—
" Better is me thus to do,
   While it must needs be done."

The steward he gan fast to knock :
The wife threw him a swingling-stock,
   His meat therewith to win.
She brought a swingle at the last :
" Good sirs," she said, " swingle on fast ;
   For nothing that ye blyn."
She gave him a stock to sit upon,
And said : " Sirs, this work must needs be done,
   All that that is herein."
The steward took up a stick to say :—
" See, see,[1]—swingle better if ye may :
   It will be the better to spin."

---

[1] Printed in my original " Sey, seye." I am not clear as to the sense of

Were the lord never so great,
Yet was he fain to work for his meat,
   Though he were never so sad:
But the steward, that was so stout,
Was fain to swingle the scales out;
   Thereof he was not glad.

The lord's meynè [1] that were at home
Wist not where he was become:
   They were full sore adrad.

The proctor of the parish-church right
Came and lookèd on the wright;
   He looked as he were mad.
Fast the proctor gan him frayn: [2]
"Where hadst thou this garland gayn?
   It is ever like-new."

The wright gan say: "Fellòw,—
With my wife, if thou wilt know:
   That dare me not rue:
For, all the while my wife true is,
My garland wol hold hue, I wis,
   And never fall nor fade;
And, if my wife take a paramour,
Than wol my garland vade the floure,—
   That dare I lay mine head."

The proctor thought: "In good fay,
That shall I weet this same day,
   Whether it may so be."

To the wrighte's house he went:
He greet the wife with fair intent:
   She said: "Sir, welcome be ye."

"Ah dame! my love is on you fast,
Sith the time I saw you last!
   I pray you it may so be
That ye would grant me of your grace
To play with you in some privy place,
   Or else to death mut me!"

Fast the proctor gan to pray;
And ever to him she said: "Nay,
   That wol I not do.

---

these three lines. The steward, it seems, "took up a stick to say:" but why or what "to say" I can't make out, nor (for certain) whether he "took up a stick" for some flax-dressing purpose, or perhaps in exasperation at the preachments of the wright's wife. Then the two following lines seem to be spoken by that lady: who, with bantering and ruthless calmness, persists in ignoring every aspect of the transaction save the simple matter of business—efficient workmanlike flax-dressing.

  [1] Household, dependents.   [2] Ask.

Hadst thou done that deed with me,
My spouse by his garland might see;
   That should turn me to woe."

The proctor said: "By heaven King,
If he say to thee anything,
   He shall have sorrow unsought:
Twenty mark I wol thee give;
It wol thee helpe well to live:
   The money here have I brought."

Now hath she the treasure ta'en;
And up the staire be they gane—
   (What helpeth it to lie?)
The wife went to the stair beside;
The proctor went a little too wide:
   He fell down by and by.
When he into the cellar fell,
He went[1] to have sunk into hell;
   He was in heart full sorry.
The steward lookèd on the knight,
And said: "Proctor, for Goddes might,
   Come and sit us by."

The proctor began to stare,
For he was he wist never where:
   But well he knew the knight,
And the steward that swingled the line.
He said: "Sirs, for Goddes pine,
   What do ye here this night?"

The steward said: "God give thee care!
Thou camest to look how we fare.
   Now help this line were dight!"

He stood still in a great thought;
What to answer he wist nought.
   "By Mary full of might,"
The proctor said, "What do ye in this inn,
For to beat this wife's line?
   For Jesus' love full of might,"
The proctor said right as he thought,
"For me it shall be evil-wrought,
   And I may see aright!
For I learnèd never in lond
For to have a swingle in hond,
   By day nor be night."

The steward said: "As good as thou
We hold us that be here now,
   And let preve it be sight:

---

[1] Weened.

Yet must us work for oure meat;
Or elles shall we none get
    Meat nor drink to our hond."

The lord said: "Why flyte[1] ye two?
I trow ye will work or ye go,
    If it be as I understond."

About he goës twice or thrice:
They eat and drink in such wise
    That they give him right nought.

The proctor said: "Think ye no shame?
Give me some meat (ye be to blame!)
    Of that the wife ye brought."

The steward said: "Evil speed the sop,
If any morsel come in thy throat,
    But thou with us hadst wrought!"

The proctor stood in a study
Whether he might work hem by:
    And so, to turn his thought,
To the lord he drewe near,
And to him said with mild cheer,
    "That Mary mot thee speed!"

The proctor began to knock:
The goodwife raught[2] him a rock,
    For thereto had she need.
She said: "When I was maid at home,
Other work could I do none,
    My life therewith to lead."
She gave him in hand a rocke-hynd,
And badè hem[3] fast for to wind,
    Or else to let-be his deed.

"Yes, dame," he said, "so have I hele,
I shall it work both fair and well,
    As ye have taughte me."
He wavèd up a strick[4] of line;
And he span well and fine
    Before the swingle-tree.

The lord said: "Thou spinnest too great;
Therefore thou shalt have no meat—
    That thou shalt well see."

Thus they sat and wrought fast
Till the weeke-days were past:
    Then the wright home came he.

---

[1] Wrangle.   [2] Reached.   [3] Hem = them; but I think it should be "him."
[4] A strike; as much as is heckled at one handful.

And, as he came by his house side,
He heard noise that was not ryde,[1]
   Of persons two or three :—
One of hem knockèd line ;
Another swingled good and fine
   Before the swingle-tree ;
The third did reel and spin,
Meat and drink therewith to win—
   Great need thereof had he.
Thus the wright stood hearkening :
His wife was ware of his coming,
   And against him went she.
"Dame," he said, "what is this din?
I hear great noise here within :
   Tell me, so God thee speed."

"Sir," said she, "workmen three
Be come to helpe you and me :
   Thereof we have great need."

"Fain would I weet what they were !"
But when he saw his lord there,
   His heart began to drede.
To see his lord in that place,
He thought it was a strange case,—
   And said, so God him speed !
"What do ye here, my lord and knight?
Tell me now, for Goddes might,
   How came this unto."

The knight said : "What is best rede?
Mercy I ask for my misdeed !
   My heart is wonder woe !"

"So is minè, verament ;
To see you among this flex and hemp,
   Full sore it rueth me ;
To see you in such heaviness,
Full sore mine heart it doth oppress,
   By God in trinity !"

The wright bade his wife let hem out.—
"Nay then, sorrow come on my snout
   If they pass hence to-day,
Till that my lady come and see
How they would have done with me !
   But now late me say."

Anon she sent after the lady bright
For to fett home her lord and knight :

---

[1] Slight.

Thereto she said nought.
She told her what they had meant,
And of their purpose and their intent
   That they would have wrought.
Glad was that lady of that tiding,
When she wist her lord was living :
   Thereof she was full fain.

Whan she came unto the stair aboun,
She looked unto the cellar down,
   And said (this is not to layn) :
"Good sirs, what do ye here?"

"Dame, we buy our meat full dear,
   With great travail and pain.
I pray you help that we were out ;
And I will swear withouten doubt
   Never to come here again."

The lady spake the wife until,
And said : "Dame, if it be your will,
   What do these meyne here?"

The carpenter's wife her answered sickerly :
"All they would have lain me by,
   Everich in their manneer :
Gold and silver they me brought,
And forsook it and would it nought,
   The rich gifts so clear.
Willing they were to do me shame :
I took their gifts withouten blame,
   And there they be all three."

The lady answered her anon :
"I have things to do at home
   Mo than two or three.
I wist my lord never do right nought
Of no thing that should be wrought
   Such as falleth to me."

The lady laughed and made good game
Whan they came out, all in same,
   From the swingle-tree.

The knight said : "Fellows in fere,
I am glad that we be here,
   By Goddes dear pity.
Dame, and ye had been with us,
Ye would have wrought, by sweet Jesus,
   As well as did we."
And, when they came up aboun,
They turned about and lookèd down.
   The lord said : "So God save me,

>   Yet had I never such a fytt
>   As I have had in that low pit—
>   So Mary so mut me speed!"

The knight and this lady bright,
How they would home that night,—
    For nothing they would abide.
And so they went home:
This said Adam of Cobsam.
    By the way as they rode
Through a wood in their playing,
For to hear the fowles sing
    They hovèd still, and bode.
The steward sware by Goddes ore,[1]
And so did the proctor much more,
    That never in their life
Would they no more come in that wonne,[2]
Whan they were ones thence come,
    This forty year and five.
Of the treasure that they brought
The lady would give them right nought,
    But gave it to the wright's wife.

Thus the wright's garland was fair of hue,
And his wife both good and true:
    Thereof was he full blithe.
I take witness at great and small,
Thus true been good women all
    That now been on live:
So come thryst on their heads,
Whan they mumble on their beds
    Their paternoster rive.[3]
Here is written a geste of the wright
That had a garland well ydight—
    The colour will never fade.
Now God that is heaven King
Grant us all his dear blessing
    Our heartes for to glad!
And all tho that do her husbands right,
Pray we to Jesu full of might
    That fair mot hem befall,
And that they may come to heaven bliss,
For thy dear moder's love thereof not to miss,
    All good wivës all!

Now all tho that this treatise have hard,
Jesu grant hem for her reward
    As true lovers to be
As was the wright unto his wife,

---
[1] Grace.   [2] Dwelling.   [3] Rife, abundantly.

And she to him during her life:
 Amen, for charity.

Here endeth the wright's process true,
With his garland fair of hue
 That never did fade the colour.
It was made by the avise
Of his wive's moder, witty and wise,
 Of flowers most of honour,—
Of roses white that will not fade;
Which flower all Englond doth glad
 With true-loves meddled [1] in sight;
Unto the which flower, I wis,
The love of God and of the commenys [2]
 Subdued been of right.

ANDREW BORDE.

[Born towards 1485, died in 1549. Became a Carthusian Monk at an early age, but was released from his vows, and practised physic. Borde was a great traveller, for his time; a man of wit, sense, and learning, author of various books of a substantial kind: others which show him in the light of a "Merry Andrew" (and it has been said that that term took its origin from him) have been attributed to him with little apparent reason—such as the *Tales of the Mad Men of Gotham*. Accusations of incontinence were brought against him both in early and in late life: finally he was confined in the Fleet Prison, probably on a charge of this kind, and soon afterwards died,—some say that he poisoned himself.—Our extracts are taken from *The First Book of the Introduction of Knowledge*, wherein Borde puts into the mouths of the natives of various countries some characteristic particulars regarding themselves.]

AN IRISHMAN AND A LOMBARD.

I AM an Irishman, in Ireland I was born;
I love to wear a saffron shirt, although it be to-torn.
My anger and my hastiness doth hurt me full sore;
I cannot leave it, it creaseth more and more;
And, although I be poor, I have an angry heart.
I can keep a hobby, a garden, and a cart;
I can make good mantles, and good Irish fryce; [3]
I can make aqua vitæ, and good square dice.
Pediculus otherwhile do bite me by the back,
Wherefore divers times I make their bones crack.
I do love to eat my meat, sitting upon the ground,
And do lie in oaten straw, sleeping full sound.
I care not for riches, but for meat and drink;
And divers times I wake when other men do wink.

---

[1] *I.e.*, mingled with true-loves. The question remains whether "true-loves" are to be understood as figures like true-lovers'-knots (which I should rather suppose), or as the herb true-love, a sort of quatrefoil otherwise termed Herb Paris.

[2] Commons. The reader will recognize in this whole passage the Yorkist sympathies of its writer. [3] Frieze.

I do use no pot to seeth my meat in,
Wherefore I do boil it in a beaste's skin;
Then, after my meat, the broth I do drink up;
I care not for my master, neither cruse nor cup.
I am not newfangled, nor never will be;
I do live in poverty, in mine own countree.

I AM a Lombart, and subtle craft I have,
To deceive a gentleman, a yeman, or a knave;
I work by policy, subtlety, and craught,[1]
The which, otherwhile, doth bring me to nought.
I am the next neighbour to the Italian;
We do bring many things out of all fashion;
We care for no man, and no man careth for us;
Our proud hearts maketh us to fare the worse.
In our country we eat adders, snails, and frogs,
And above all thing we be sure of cur dogs;
For men's shins they will lie in wait;
It is a good sport to see them so to bait.

SIR THOMAS WYATT.

[Born in 1503, at Allington Castle, Kent, the seat of his father, who stood deservedly high in favour with Henry VII.; died in October 1542, at Sherborne, Dorsetshire. Wyatt was a man of many gifts: handsome in person, having a form wherein "force and beauty met," as Lord Surrey said; skilled in languages, music, and other accomplishments; a soldier and negociator; and in poetry surpassing all his predecessors since the time of Chaucer—manly both in his force and in his tenderness, and every now and then thrilling the reader with his deep, true, and direct touches of passionate appeal. Being an influential man in the court of Henry VIII., he used his opportunities for the advancement of others, rather than himself. He married very early; but there is some ground for thinking that he was not insensible at a later date to the charms of Anne Boleyn. He afterwards spent some considerable time in diplomatic services in Spain, and as ambassador in Paris. Returning to England in 1540, he was accused of treasonable complicity with Cardinal Pole, and was imprisoned in the Tower; but had the good fortune of triumphantly vindicating himself, even in the eyes of that decapitating monarch Henry VIII., whose good opinion he continued to enjoy. He was travelling on the service of the state to Falmouth, when his exertions brought on a fever of which he died. Wyatt had a leaning to the Protestant side in religion: his son, also named Sir Thomas Wyatt, conspired against Queen Mary, and was executed in 1554.]

THE RECURED LOVER
EXULTETH IN HIS FREEDOM, AND VOWETH TO REMAIN FREE UNTIL DEATH.

I AM as I am, and so will I be;
But how that I am none knoweth truly.
Be it evil, be it well, be I bond, be I free,
I am as I am, and so will I be.

I lead my life indifferently;
I mean no thing but honesty;
And, though folks judge full diversely,
I am as I am, and so will I die.

---

[1] Craft.

I do not rejoice, nor yet complain ;
Both mirth and sadness I do refrain,
And use the means since folks will feign ;
Yet I am as I am, be it pleasure or pain.

Divers do judge as they do trow,
Some of pleasure and some of woe,
Yet, for all that, nothing they know,
But I am as I am, wheresoever I go.

But, since judgers do thus decay,
Let every man his judgment say ;
I will it take in sport and play,
For I am as I am, whosoever say nay.

Who judgeth well, well God him send ;
Who judgeth evil, God them amend ;
To judge the best therefore intend,
For I am as I am, and so will I end.

Yet some there be that take delight
To judge folks' thought for envy and spite,
But, whether they judge me wrong or right,
I am as I am, and so do I write.

Praying you all that this do read
To trust it as you do your creed ;
And not to think I change my weed,
For I am as I am, however I speed.

But how that is I leave to you ;
Judge as ye list, false or true.
Ye know no more than afore ye knew ;
Yet I am as I am, whatever ensue.

And from this mind I will not flee ;
But, to you all that misjudge me,
I do protest, as ye may see,
That I am as I am, and so will be.

OF HIS LOVE, THAT PRICKED HER FINGER WITH A NEEDLE.

SHE sat and sewed that hath done me the wrong
   Whereof I plain, and have done many a day :
And, whilst she heard my plaint, in piteous song
   She wished my heart the sampler, as it lay.
The blind master whom I have served so long,
   Grudging to hear that he did hear her say,
Made her own weapon do her finger bleed,
To feel if pricking were so good indeed.

What man hath heard such cruelty before?
  That, when my plaint remembered her my woe
That causèd it, she, cruel more and more,
  Wishèd each stitch, as she did sit and sew,
Had pricked my heart for to increase my sore.
  And, as I think, she thought it had been so:
For, as she thought " this is his heart indeed,"
She prickèd hard, and made herself to bleed.

HOW TO USE THE COURT, AND HIMSELF THEREIN.
WRITTEN TO SIR FRANCIS BRYAN.

A SPENDING hand that alway poureth out
Had need to have a bringer-in as fast;
And on the stone that still doth turn about
There grow'th no moss: these proverbs yet do last;
Reason hath set them in so sure a place
That length of years their force can never waste.
When I remember this, and eke the case
Wherein thou stand'st, I thought forthwith to write,
Bryan, to thee, who knows how great a grace
In writing is, to counsel man the right.
To thee therefore that trots still up and down,
And never rests, but, running day and night
From realm to realm, from city, street, and town,—
Why dost thou wear thy body to the bones?
And mightst at home sleep in thy bed of down,
And drink good ale so nappy for the nones,
Feed thyself fat, and heap up pound by pound.
Lik'st thou not this? "No." Why? "For swine so groins
In sty, and chaw dung moulded on the ground,
And drivel on pearls, with head still in the manger:
So of the harp the ass doth hear the sound:
So sacks of dirt be filled up in the cloister,
That serve for less than do these fatted swine.
Though I seem lean and dry, withouten moisture,
Yet will I serve my prince, my lord and thine;
And let them live to feed the paunch that list;
So I may live to feed both me and mine."
By God! well said. But what and if thou wist
How to bring in, as fast as thou dost spend?
"That would I learn." And it shall not be missed
To tell thee how. Now hark what I intend:
Thou know'st well first, whoso can seek to please
Shall purchase friends, where truth shall but offend.
Flee therefore truth,—it is both wealth and ease;
For, though that truth of every man hath praise,
Full near that wind go'th truth in great misease.

Use virtue, as it goeth now-a-days,
In word alone, to make thy language sweet:
And of thy deed yet do not as thou says.
Else be thou sure thou shalt be far unmeet
To get thy bread, each thing is now so scant:
Seek still thy profit upon thy bare feet.
Lend in no wise, for fear that thou do want,
Unless it be as to a calf a cheese,—
But if thou can be sure to win a cant [1]
Of half at least. It is not good to leese.
Learn at the lad that, in a long white coat,
From under the stall, withouten lands or fees,
Hath leaped into the shop; who knows by rote
This rule that I have told thee here before.
Some time also rich age begins to dote;
See thou when there thy gain may be the more.
Stay him by the arm whereso he walk or go;
Be near alway; and, if he cough too sore,
What he hath spit tread out; and please him so.
A diligent knave that picks his master's purse
May please him so that he, withouten mo,
Executor is: and what is he the worse?
But, if so chance thou get nought of the man,
The widow may for all thy pain disburse.
A rivelled skin, a stinking breath; what than?
A toothless mouth shall do thy lips no harm.
The gold is good: and though she curse or ban,
Yet where thee list thou mayst lie good and warm;
Let the old mule bite upon the bridle,
Whilst there do lie a sweeter in thy arm.
In this also see that thou be not idle :—
Thy niece, thy cousin, sister, or thy daughter,
If she be fair, if handsome be her middle,
If thy better hath her love besought her,
Advance his cause, and he shall help thy need:
It is but love, turn thou it to a laughter.
But ware, I say, so gold thee help and speed,
That in this case thou be not so unwise
As Pandar was in such a likè deed;
For he, the fool of conscience, was so nice
That he no gain would have for all his pain.
Be next thyself, for friendship bears no price.
Laughest thou at me? Why? Do I speak in vain?
"No, not at thee, but at thy thrifty jest.
Wouldst thou I should, for any loss or gain,
Change that for gold that I have ta'en for best,—
Next godly things, to have an honest name?
Should I leave that? Then take me for a beast!"

---

[1] A portion, or eantle.

Nay then, farewell ; and, if thou care for shame,
Content thee then with honest poverty ;
With a free tongue what thee dislikes to blame,
And, for thy truth, sometime adversity.
And therewithal this gift I shall thee give ;—
In this world now little prosperity,
And coin to keep, as water in a sieve.

THOMAS TUSSER.

[Born towards 1515, died towards 1582. Being a chorister in the collegiate chapel of Wallingford Castle, he was impressed into the service of the royal chapel ; afterwards became a retainer of Lord Paget ; and then a farmer at Kadwade (or Cattiwade) in Suffolk, and in 1557 published his noted work, *A Hundred Points of good Husbandry* (from which our specimen is taken). The "Hundred" became ultimately "Five-hundred." It is disheartening to learn that this lawgiver of the olden farmers was himself, according to Fuller, the reverse of successful in farming. "He traded at large in oxen, sheep, dairies, grain of all kinds, to no profit : whether he bought or sold, he lost, and, when a renter, impoverished himself, and never enriched his landlord."]

GOOD HUSBAND AND UNTHRIFT.

Comparing good husband with unthrift his brother
The better discerneth the t'one from the t'other,

Ill husbandry braggeth
  To go with the best :
Good husbandry baggeth
  Up gold in his chest.

Ill husbandry trudgeth
  With unthrifts about :
Good husbandry snudgeth,
  For fear of a doubt.

Ill husbandry spendeth
  Abroad, like a mome :
Good husbandry tendeth
  His charges at home.

Ill husbandry selleth
  His corn on the ground :
Good husbandry smelleth
  No gain that way found.

Ill husbandry loseth,
  For lack of good fence ;
Good husbandry closeth,
  And gaineth the pence.

Ill husbandry trusteth
  To him and to her ;

Good husbandry lusteth
   Himself for to stir.

Ill husbandry eateth
   Himself out of door :
Good husbandry meateth
   His friend and the poor.

Ill husbandry dayeth,
   Or letteth it lie :
Good husbandry payeth,
   The cheaper to buy.

Ill husbandry lurketh,
   And stealeth a sleep :
Good husbandry worketh
   His household to keep.

Ill husbandry liveth
   By that and by this :
Good husbandry giveth
   To every man his.

Ill husbandry taketh,
   And spendeth up all:
Good husbandry maketh
   Good shift with a small.

Ill husbandry prayeth
   His wife to make shift :
Good husbandry sayeth
   "Take this of my gift."

Ill husbandry drowseth
   At fortune so awk :
Good husbandry rouseth
   Himself as a hawk.

Ill husbandry lieth
   In prison for debt :
Good husbandry spieth
   Where profit to get.

Ill husbandry ways hath
   To fraud what he can ;
Good husbandry praise hath
   Of every man.

Ill husbandry never
   Hath wealth to keep touch :
Good husbandry ever
   Hath penny in pouch.

Good husband his boon
  Or request hath afar :
Ill husband as soon
  Hath a toad with an R.[1]

HUGH RHODES.

[Was a gentleman of the King's Chapel towards 1550. Wrote a *Book of Nurture* (whence our extract), and a *Song of the Child-Bishop*.]

CAUTIONS.

He that spendeth much,
  And getteth nought ;
He that oweth much,
  And hath nought ;
He that looketh in his purse
  And findeth nought,—
He may be sorry,
  And say nought.

He that may and will not,
He then that would shall not.
He that would and cannot
May repent and sigh not.

He that sweareth
  Till no man trust him ;
He that lieth
  Till no man believe him ;
He that borroweth
  Till no man will lend him,—
Let him go where
  No man knoweth him.

He that hath a good master,
  And cannot keep him ;
He that hath a good servant,
  And not content with him ;
He that hath such conditions
  That no man loveth him,—
May well know other,
  But few men will know him.

---

[1] One of the editors of Tusser understands this expression to amount to much the same as "getting more kicks than halfpence." He quotes from Brockett the proverb, "Over-many masters, as the toad said when under the harrow."

EDMUND SPENSER.

[Born in London, 1553; died in Westminster, 16 January 1599. The *Prosopopoia* is an early poem, published in 1591, and then spoken of by the author as "long sithens composed in the raw conceit of my youth." It is evidently in large measure a satire: the Lord Treasurer Burleigh is regarded as the main object of attack.]

PROSOPOPOIA: OR, MOTHER HUBBARD'S TALE.

It was the month in which the righteous maid
That, for disdain of sinful world's upbraid,
Fled back to heaven whence she was first conceived,
Into her silver bower the Sun received;
And the hot Syrian dog on him awaiting,
After the chaféd lion's cruel baiting,
Corrupted had the air with his noisome breath,
And poured on the earth plague, pestilence, and death.
Amongst the rest, a wicked malady
Reigned amongst men, that many did to die,
Deprived of sense and ordinary reason,
That it to leeches seeméd strange and geason.
My fortune was, 'mongst many others moe,
To be partaker of their common woe,
And my weak body, set on fire with grief,
Was robbed of rest and natural relief.
In this ill plight there came to visit me
Some friends, who, sorry my sad case to see,
Began to comfort me in cheerful wise,
And means of gladsome solace to devise.
But, seeing kindly Sleep refuse to do
His office, and my feeble eyes forego,
They sought my troubled sense how to deceive
With talk, that might unquiet fancies reave;
And, sitting all on seats about me round,
With pleasant tales, fit for that idle stound,
They cast in course to waste the weary hours.
Some told of ladies and their paramours:
Some of brave knights and their renownéd squires;
Some of the fairies and their strange attires;
And some of giants hard to be believed;
That the delight thereof me much relieved.
Amongst the rest a good old woman was,
Hight Mother Hubbard, who did far surpass
The rest in honest mirth, that 'seemed her well.
She, when her turn was come her tale to tell,
Told of a strange adventure that betided
Betwixt the Fox and the Ape, by him misguided;
The which, for that my sense it greatly pleased,
All were my spirit heavy and dis-eased,
I'll write in terms as she the same did say,
So well as I her words remember may.

No Muse's aid me needs hereto to call;
Base is the style, and matter mean withal.
   "Whilom" (said she) "before the world was civil,
The Fox and the Ape, disliking of their evil
And hard estate, determinèd to seek
Their fortunes far abroad, like with his like;
For both were crafty and unhappy-witted;
Two fellows might nowhere be better fitted.
   "The Fox, that first this cause of grief did find,
'Gan first thus plain his case with words unkind.
'Neighbour Ape, and my gossip eke beside,
(Both two sure bands in friendship to be tied)
To whom may I more trustily complain
The evil plight that doth me sore constrain,
And hope thereof to find due remedy?
Hear then my pain and inward agony.
Thus many years I now have spent and worn
In mean regard and basest fortune's scorn,
Doing my country service as I might,—
No less, I dare say, than the proudest wight;
And still I hopèd to be up advanced
For my good parts, but still it hath mischanced.
Now therefore that no longer hope I see,
But froward fortune still to follow me,
And losels lifted high where I did look,
I mean to turn the next leaf of the book;
Yet, ere that any way I do betake,
I mean my gossip privy first to make.'
   "'Ah! my dear gossip,' (answered then the Ape)
'Deeply do your sad words my wits awhape,
Both for because your grief doth great appear,
And eke because myself am touchèd near;
For I likewise have wasted much good time,
Still waiting to preferment up to climb,
Whilst others always have before me stepped,
And from my beard the fat away have swept,
That now unto despair I 'gin to grow,
And mean for better wind about to throw;
Therefore, to me, my trusty friend, aread
Thy counsel: two is better than one head.'
   "'Certes' (said he) 'I mean me to disguise
In some strange habit, after uncouth wise,
Or like a pilgrim or a limiter,
Or like a gipsy or a juggeler,
And so to wander to the worlde's end,
To seek my fortune where I may it mend,—
For worse than that I have I cannot meet.
Wide is the world, I wot, and every street
Is full of fortunes and adventures strange,
Continually subject unto change.

Say, my fair brother, now, if this device
Do like you, or may you to look entice.'
"'Surely' (said the Ape) 'it likes me wondrous well;
And, would ye not poor fellowship expel,
Myself would offer you to accompany
In this adventure's chanceful jeopardy,—
For to wex old at home in idleness
Is disadventrous, and quite fortuneless:
Abroad, where change is, good may gotten be.'
"The Fox was glad, and quickly did agree.
So both resolved the morrow next ensuing,
So soon as day appeared to people's viewing,
On their intended journey to proceed;
And overnight whatso thereto did need
Each did prepare in readiness to be.
The morrow next, so soon as one might see
Light out of heaven's windows forth to look,
Both their habiliments unto them took,
And put themselves a' God's name on their way;—
Whenas the Ape, beginning well to weigh
This hard adventure, thus began to advise.
"'Now rede, Sir Reynold, as ye be right wise,
What course ye ween is best for us to take,
That for ourselves we may a living make.
Whether shall we profess some trade or skill,
Or shall we vary our device at will,
Even as new occasion appears?
Or shall we tie ourselves for certain years
To any service, or to any place?
For it behoves, ere that into the race
We enter, to resolve first hereupon.'
"'Now, surely, brother,' (said the Fox anon)
'Ye have this matter motioned in season;
For everything that is begun with reason
Will come by ready means unto his end,
But things miscounselled must needs miswend.
Thus therefore I advise upon the case;
That not to any certain trade or place,
Nor any man, we should ourselves apply;
For why should he that is at liberty
Make himself bond? Sith then we are free-born,
Let us all servile base subjection scorn;
And, as we be sons of the world so wide,
Let us our father's heritage divide,
And challenge to ourselves our portions due
Of all the patrimony, which a few
Now hold in hugger-mugger in their hand,
And all the rest do rob of good and land.
For now a few have all, and all have nought,
Yet all be brethren ylike dearly bought.
There is no right in this partition,

Ne was it so by institution
Ordainèd first, ne by the law of Nature,
But that she gave like blessing to each creature,
As well of worldly livelode as of life,
That there might be no difference nor strife,
Nor aught called mine or thine. Thrice happy then
Was the condition of mortal men.
That was the Golden Age of Saturn old,
But this might better be the World of Gold;
For without gold now nothing will be got.
Therefore (if please you) this shall be our plot;—
We will not be of any occupation.
Let such vile vassals, born to base vocation,
Drudge in the world, and for their living droyl,
Which have no wit to live withouten toil;
But we will walk about the world at pleasure,
Like two free-men, and make our ease our treasure.
Free-men some 'beggars' call; but they be free,
And they which call them so more beggars be:
For they do swink and sweat to feed the other,
Who live like lords of that which they do gather,
And yet do never thank them for the same,
But as their due by Nature do it claim.
Such will we fashion both ourselves to be,
Lords of the world, and so will wander free
Whereso us listeth, uncontrolled of any.
Hard is our hap if we (amongst so many)
Light not on some that may our state amend;
Sildom but some good cometh ere the end.'
 "Well seemed the Ape to like this ordinance;
Yet, well considering of the circumstance,
As pausing in great doubt awhile he stayed,
And afterwards with grave advisement said;—
'I cannot, my lief brother, like but well
The purpose of the complot which ye tell;
For well I wot (compared to all the rest
Of each degree) that beggars' life is best,
And they that think themselves the best of all
Oft-times to begging are content to fall.
But this I wot withal, that we shall run
Into great danger, like to be undone,
Wildly to wander thus in the world's eye,
Withouten passport or good warranty;
For fear lest we like rogues should be reputed,
And for ear-markèd beasts abroad be bruited.
Therefore I rede that we our counsels call
How to prevent this mischief ere it fall,
And how we may with most security
Beg amongst those that beggars do defy.'
 "'Right well, dear gossip, ye advisèd have,
(Said then the Fox), 'but I this doubt will save;

For, ere we farther pass, I will devise
A passport for us both in fittest wise,
And by the names of soldiers thus protect,
That now is thought a civil begging sect.
Be you the soldier, for you likest are
For manly semblance and small skill in war;
I will but wait on you, and, as occasion
Falls out, myself fit for the same will fashion.'

"The passport ended, both they forward went,
The Ape clad soldier-like, fit for the intent,
In a blue jacket, with a cross of red,
And many slits, as if that he had shed
Much blood through many wounds therein received,
Which had the use of his right arm bereaved.
Upon his head an old Scotch cap he wore,
With a plume feather all to pieces tore;
His breeches were made after the new cut,
Al Portugese, loose like an empty gut,
And his hose broken high above the heeling,
And his shoes beaten out with travelling.
But neither sword nor dagger he did bear;
Seems that no foe's revengement he did fear:
Instead of them a handsome bat he held,
On which he leanèd, as one far in eld.
Shame light on him that through so false illusion
Doth turn the name of soldiers to abusion,
And that which is the noblest mystery
Brings to reproach and common infamy!

"Long they thus travellèd, yet never met
Adventure which might them a-working set;
Yet many ways they sought, and many tried,
Yet for their purposes none fit espied.
At last they chanced to meet upon the way
A simple husbandman in garments grey;
Yet, though his vesture were but mean and base,
A good yeomàn he was, of honest place,
And more for thrift did care than for gay clothing:
Gay without good is good heart's greatest loathing.
The Fox, him spying, bade the Ape him dight
To play his part, for lo he was in sight
That (if he erred not) should them entertain,
And yield them timely profit for their pain.
Eftsoons the Ape himself 'gan to uprear,
And on his shoulders high his bat to bear,
As if good service he were fit to do,
But little thrift for him he did it to;
And stoutly forward he his steps did strain,
That like a handsome swain it him became.[1]

---

[1] I feel greatly tempted to set the rhyming here correct by writing "That it became him like a handsome swain."

"Whenas they nigh approachèd, that good man,
Seeing them wander loosely, first began
To enquire, of custom, what and whence they were.
To whom the Ape ; 'I am a Soldïer,
That late in war have spent my dearest blood,
And in long service lost both limbs and good ;
And, now constrained that trade to over-give,
I driven am to seek some means to live ;
Which might it you in pity please to afford,
I would be ready both in deed and word
To do you faithful service all my days.
This iron world' (that same he weeping says)
'Brings down the stoutest hearts to lowest state ;
For misery doth bravest minds abate,
And make them seek for that they wont to scorn,
Of fortune and of hope at once forlorn.'

"The honest man, that heard him thus complain,
Was grieved, as he had felt part of his pain,
And, well disposed him some relief to show,
Asked if in husbandry he aught did know ;
To plough, to plant, to reap, to rake, to sow,
To hedge, to ditch, to thresh, to thatch, to mow,
Or to what labour else he was prepared—
For husband's life is laborous and hard.

"Whenas the Ape him heard so much to talk
Of labour, that did from his liking baulk,
He would have slipped the collar handsomely,
And to him said : ' Good Sir ! full glad am I
To take what pains may any living wight ;
But my late-maimèd limbs lack wonted might
To do their kindly services as needeth.
Scarce this right hand the mouth with diet feedeth,
So that it may no painful work endure,
Ne to strong labour can itself inure.
But, if that any other place you have,
Which asks small pains, but thriftiness to save,
Or care to overlook, or thrust to gather,
Ye may me trust as your own ghostly father.'

"With that the husbandman 'gan him avise
That it for him was fittest exercise
Cattle to keep, or grounds to oversee ;
And askèd him if he could willing be
To keep his sheep, or to attend his swine,
Or watch his mares, or take his charge of kine.

"'Gladly' (said he) 'whatever such-like pain
Ye put on me, I will the same sustain.
But gladliest I of your fleecy sheep
(Might it you please) would take on me to keep ;
For, ere that unto arms I me betook,
Unto my father's sheep I used to look,

That yet the skill thereof I have not lost.
Thereto right well this curdog, by my cost,'
(Meaning the Fox) 'will serve my sheep to gather,
And drive to follow after their bellwether.'
　"The husbandman was meanly well content
Trial to make of his endeavourment;
And, home him leading, lent to him the charge
Of all his flock, with liberty full large,
Giving account of the annual increase
Both of their lambs and of their woolly fleece.
　"Thus is this Ape become a shepherd swain,
And the false Fox his dog. God give them pain!
For, ere the year have half his course outrun,
And do return from whence he first begun,
They shall him make an ill account of thrift.
　"Now whenas Time, flying with winges swift,
Expirèd had the term that these two javels
Should render up a reckoning of their travails
Unto their master, which it of them sought,
Exceedingly they troubled were in thought,—
Ne wist what answer unto him to frame,
Ne how to escape great punishment or shame
For their false treason and vile thievery;
For not a lamb of all their flock's supply
Had they to show, but ever as they bred
They slew them, and upon their fleshes fed;
For that disguisèd dog loved blood to spill,
And drew the wicked shepherd to his will.
So 'twixt them both they not a lambkin left,
And, when lambs failed, the old sheep's lives they reft;
That how to acquit themselves unto their lord
They were in doubt, and flatly set aboard.
The Fox then counselled the Ape for to require
Respite till morrow to answer his desire;
For time's delay new hope of help still breeds.
The good man granted, doubting nought their deeds,
And bade next day that all should ready be.
But they more subtle meaning had than he;
For the next morrow's meed they closely meant,
For fear of afterclaps, for to prevent.
And that same evening, when all shrouded were
In careless sleep, they without care or fear
Cruelly fell upon their flock in fold,
And of them slew at pleasure what they wold;
Of which whenas they feasted had their fill,
For a full complement of all their ill,
They stole away, and took their hasty flight,
Carried in clouds of all-concealing night.
So was the husbandman left to his loss,
And they unto their fortune's change to toss.

After which sort they wanderèd long while,
Abusing many through their cloakèd guile,—
That at the last they 'gan to be descried
Of every one, and all their sleights espied,
So as their begging now them failèd quite,
For none would give, but all men would them wite.
Yet would they take no pains to get their living,
But seek some other way to gain by giving ;
Much like to begging, but much better named,
For many beg which are thereof ashamed.
  " And now the Fox had gotten him a gown,
And the Ape a cassock sidelong hanging down ;
For they their occupation meant to change,
And now in other state abroad to range ;
For, since their soldier's pass no better sped,
They forged another, as for clerks book-red :
Who passing forth, as their adventures fell,
Through many haps which needs not here to tell,
At length chanced with a formal priest to meet,
Whom they in civil manner first did greet,
And after asked an alms for God's dear love.
The man straightway his choler up did move,
And with reproachful terms 'gan them revile
For following that trade so base and vile,
And asked what licence or what pass they had.
  " ' Ah ! ' (said the Ape, as sighing wondrous sad)
' It's an hard case when men of good deserving
Must either driven be perforce to sterving,
Or askèd for their pass by every squib
That list at will them to revile or snib ;
And yet (God wot) small odds I often see
'Twixt them that ask and them that askèd be.
Nathless, because you shall not us misdeem,
But that we are as honest as we seem,
Ye shall our passport at your pleasure see,
And then ye will (I hope) well movèd be.'
  " Which when the priest beheld, he viewed it near,
As if therein some text he studying were ;
But little else (God wot) could thereof skill,
For read he could not evidence nor will,
Ne tell a written word, ne write a letter,
Ne make one tittle worse, ne make one better.
Of such deep learning little had he need,
Ne yet of Latin, ne of Greek, that breed
Doubts 'mongst divines, and difference of texts,
From whence arise diversity of sects,
And hateful heresies, of God abhorred.
But this good Sir did follow the plain word,
Ne meddled with their controversies vain ;
All his care was his service well to fain,

And to read homilies on holy-days;
When that was done, he might attend his plays:
An easy life, and fit high God to please.
He, having over-looked their pass at ease,
'Gan at the length them to rebuke again,
That no good trade of life did entertain,
But lost their time in wandering loose abroad,—
Seeing the world, in which they bootless bode,
Had ways enow for all therein to live,
Such grace did God unto his creatures give.
 "Said then the Fox, 'Who hath the world not tried
From the right way full eath may wander wide.
We are but novices new come abroad;
We have not yet the tract of any trod,
Nor on us taken any state of life,
But ready are of any to make prief.
Therefore might please you, which the world have proved,
Us to devise, which forth but lately moved,
Of some good course that we might undertake,
Ye shall for ever us your bondmen make.'
 "The priest 'gan wex half proud to be so prayed,
And thereby willing to afford them aid.
'It seems' (said he) 'right well that ye be clerks,
Both by your witty words and by your works.
Is not that name enough to make a living
To him that hath a whit of Nature's giving?
How many honest men see ye arise
Daily thereby, and grow to goodly prize—
To deans, to archdeacons, to commissaries,
To lords, to principals, to prebendaries!
All jolly prelates, worthy rule to bear,
Whoever them envy; yet spite bites near.
Why should ye doubt then but that ye likewise
Might unto some of those in time arise?
In the meantime to live in good estate,
Loving that love, and hating those that hate,
Being some honest curate or some vicar,
Content with little in condition sicker.'
 "'Ah! but' (said the Ape) 'the charge is wondrous great
To feed men's souls, and hath an heavy threat.'
 "'To feed men's souls' (quoth he) 'is not in man,
For they must feed themselves, do what we can;
We are but charged to lay the meat before;
Eat they that list, we need to do no more.
But God it is that feeds them with his grace,
The bread of life poured down from heavenly place
Therefore said he that with the budding rod
Did rule the Jews, 'All shall be taught of God.'
That same hath Jesus Christ now to him raught,
By whom the flock is rightly fed and taught;

He is the Shepherd, and the Priest is he;
We but his shepherd swains ordained to be.
Therefore herewith do not yourself dismay;
Ne is the pains so great but bear ye may;
For not so great as it was wont of yore
It's nowadays, ne half so strait and sore.
They whilom usèd duly every day
Their service and their holy things to say
At morn and even, besides their anthems sweet,
Their penny masses, and their complynes meet,
Their dirges, and their trentals, and their shrifts,
Their memories, their singings, and their gifts.
Now all these needless works are laid away;
Now once a week, upon the sabbath-day,
It is enough to do our small devotion,
And then to follow any merry motion.
Ne are we tied to fast but when we list,
Ne to wear garments base, of woollen twist,
But with the finest silks us to array,
That before God we may appear more gay,
Resembling Aaron's glory in his place.
For far unfit it is that persons base
Should with vile clothes approach God's majesty,
Whom no uncleanness may approachen nigh;—
Or that all men which *any* master serve
Good garments for their service should deserve;
But he that serves the Lord of Hosts most high,
And that in highest place to approach him nigh,
And all the people's prayers to present
Before his throne, as on ambàssage sent
Both to and fro, should not deserve to wear
A garment better than of wool or hair.
Beside, we may have lying by our sides
Our lovely lasses, or bright-shining brides:
We be not tied to wilful chastity,
But have the gospel of free liberty.'

"'By that he ended had his ghostly sermon,
The Fox was well induced to be a parson,
And of the priest eftsoons 'gan to enquire
How to a benefice he might aspire.

"''Marry, there' (said the priest) 'is art indeed;
Much good deep learning one thereout may rede:
For that the groundwork is and end of all,
How to obtain a beneficial.
First, therefore, when ye have in handsome wise
Yourselves attirèd, as you can devise,
Then to some noble man yourself apply,
Or other great one in the worlde's eye,
That hath a zealous disposition
To God, and so to his religion.

There must thou fashion eke a goodly zeal,
Such as no carpers may contrayr reveal,
For each thing feignèd ought more wary be.
There thou must walk in sober gravity,
And seem as saint-like as Saint Radegund;
Fast much, pray oft, look lowly on the ground,
And unto every one do court'sy meek.
These looks (nought saying) do a benefice seek;
And be thou sure one not to lack ere long.
But if thee list unto the Court to throng,
And there to hunt after the hopèd prey,
Then must thou thee dispose another way;
For there thou needs must learn to laugh, to lie,
To face, to forge, to scoff, to company,
To crouch, to please, to be a beetle-stock
Of thy great master's will, to scorn, to mock.
So mayst thou chance mock out a benefice,—
Unless thou canst one conjure by device,
Or cast a figure for a bishopric;
And, if one could, it were but a school-trick.
These be the ways by which without reward
Livings in courts be gotten, though full hard;
For nothing there is done without a fee.
The courtier needs must recompensèd be
With a benevolence, or have in gage
The *primitias* of your parsonage:
Scarce can a bishopric forpass them by,
But that it must be gelt in privity.
Do not thou, therefore, seek a living there,
But of more private persons seek elsewhere
Whereas thou mayst compound a better penny;
Ne let thy learning questioned be of any:
For some good gentleman that hath the right
Unto his church for to present a wight
Will cope with thee in reasonable wise,
That if the living yearly do arise
To forty pound, that then his youngest son
Shall twenty have, and twenty thou hast won.
Thou hast it won, for it is of frank gift,
And he will care for all the rest to shift,
Both that the bishop may admit of thee,
And that therein thou mayst maintainèd be.
This is the way for one that is unlearned
Living to get, and not to be discerned.
But they that are great clerks have nearer ways,
For learning-sake to living them to raise:
Yet many eke of them (God wot) are driven
To accept a benefice in pieces riven.
How sayst thou, friend, have I not well discoursed
Upon this common-place,—though plain, not worst?

Better a short tale than a bad long shriving;
Needs any more to learn to get a living?'
  "'Now sure, and by my hallidom,' (quoth he)
'Ye a great master are in your degree;
Great thanks I yield you for your discipline,
And do not doubt but duly to incline
My wits thereto, as ye shall shortly hear.'
  " The priest him wished good speed, and well to fare;
So parted they as either's way them led.
But the Ape and Fox ere long so well them sped,
Through the priest's wholesome counsel lately taught,
And through their own fair handling wisely wrought,
That they a benefice 'twixt them obtained;
And crafty Reynold was a priest ordained,
And the Ape his Parish-Clerk procured to be.
Then made they revel-rout and goodly glee.
But, ere long time had passèd, they so ill
Did order their affairs that the evil-will
Of all their parish'ners they had constrained;
Who to the Ordinary of them complained,
How foully they their offices abused,
And them of crimes and heresies accused,
That Pursuivants he often for them sent.
But they, neglecting his commandement,
So long persisted obstinate and bold,
Till at the length he publishèd to hold
A Visitation, and them cited thether;
Then was high time their wits about to gether.
What did they then but made a composition
With their next neighbour priest for light condition?
To whom their living they resignèd quite
For a few pence, and ran away by night.
  " So, passing through the country in disguise,
They fled far off, where none might them surprise;
And after that long strayèd here and there,
Through every field and forest far and near,—
Yet never found occasion for their turn,
But, almost starved, did much lament and mourn.
At last they chanced to meet upon the way
The Mule all decked in goodly rich array,
With bells and bosses that full loudly rung,
And costly trappings that to ground down hung.
Lowly they him saluted in meek wise;
But he through pride and fatness 'gan despise
Their meanness, scarce vouchsafed them to requite:
Whereat the Fox, deep growling in his sprite,
Said: 'Ah! Sir Mule, now blessed be the day
That I see you so goodly and so gay
In your attires, and eke your silken hide
Filled with round flesh, that every bone doth hide.

Seems that in fruitful pastures ye do live,
Or Fortune doth you secret favour give.'
  "'Foolish Fox' (said the Mule) 'thy wretched need
Praises the thing that doth thy sorrow breed ;
For well I ween thou canst not but envy
My wealth, compared to thine own misery,
That art so lean and meagre waxen late
That scarce thy legs uphold thy feeble gait.'
  "'Ay me !' (said then the Fox) 'whom evil hap
Unworthy in such wretchedness doth wrap,
And makes the scorn of other beasts to be !
But rede, fair Sir, of grace, from whence come ye ?
Or what of tidings you abroad do hear?
News may perhaps some good unweeting bear.'
  "'From royal court I lately came' (said he)
Where all the bravery that eye may see,
And all the happiness that heart desire,
Is to be found. He nothing can admire
That hath not seen that heaven's portraiture.
But tidings there is none, I you assure,
Save that which common is, and known to all,—
That courtiers, as the tide, do rise and fall.'
  "'But tell us' (said the Ape), 'we do you pray,
Who now in court doth bear the greatest sway.
That, if such fortune do to us befall,
We may seek favour of the best of all.'
  "'Marry' (said he) 'the highest now in grace
Be the wild beasts that swiftest are in chace ;
For in their speedy course and nimble flight
The Lion now doth take the most delight,
But chiefly joys on foot them to behold,
Enchased with chain and circulet of gold.
So wild a beast so tame ytaught to be,
And buxom to his bands, is joy to see ;
So well his golden circlet him beseemeth.
But his late chain his liege unmeet esteemeth,
For so brave beasts he loveth best to see
In the wild forest ranging fresh and free.
Therefore, if fortune thee in court to live,
In case thou ever there wilt hope to thrive,
To some of these thou must thyself apply ;
Else, as a thistle-down in the air doth fly,
So vainly shalt thou to and fro be tossed,
And lose thy labour and thy fruitless cost.
And yet full few that follow them, I see,
For virtue's bare regard advancèd be ;
But either for some gainful benefit,
Or that they may for their own turns be fit.
Nathless, perhaps, ye things may handle so
That ye may better thrive than thousands moe.'

"'But' (said the Ape) 'how shall we first come in,
That after we may favour seek to win?'
"'How else' (said he) 'but with a good bold face,
And with big words, and with a stately pace?
That men may think of you in general
That to be in you which is not at all;
For not by that which is the world now deemeth
(As it was wont), but by that same that seemeth.
Ne do I doubt but that ye well can fashion
Yourselves thereto according to occasion.
So fare ye well, good courtiers may ye be.'
So, proudly neighing, from them parted he.
  "Then 'gan this crafty couple to devise
How for the court themselves they might aguize;
For thither they themselves meant to address,
In hope to find their happier success.
So well they shifted that the Ape anon
Himself had clothèd like a gentleman,
And the sly Fox as like to be his groom,—
That to the court in speedy sort they come;
Where the fond Ape, himself uprearing high
Upon his tiptoes, stalketh stately by,
As if he were some great Magnifico,
And boldly doth amongst the boldest go;
And his man Reynold with fine counterfesànce
Supports his credit and his countenance.
Then 'gan the courtiers gaze on every side,
And stare on him with big looks basen wide,
Wondering what mister wight he was, and whence;
For he was clad in strange accoutrements,
Fashioned with quaint devices, never seen
In court before, yet there all fashions been.
Yet he them in newfangleness did pass.
But his behaviour altogether was
Alla turchesca, much the more admired,
And his looks lofty, as if he aspired
To dignity, and 'sdained the low degree;
That all which did such strangeness in him see
By secret means 'gan of his state enquire,
And privily his servant thereto hire;
Who, throughly armed against such coverture,
Reported unto all that he was sure
A noble gentleman of high regard,
Which through the world had with long travel fared,
And seen the manners of all beasts on ground,
Now here arrived, to see if like he found.
  "Thus did the Ape at first him credit gain;
Which afterwards he wisely did maintain
With gallant show, and daily more augment
Through his fine feats and courtly complement.

For he could play, and dance, and vaute, and spring,
And all that else pertains to revelling,
Only through kindly aptness of his joints.
Besides, he could do many other points,
The which in court him servèd to good stead;
For he 'mongst ladies could their fortunes read
Out of their hands, and merry leasings tell,
And juggle finely, that became him well.
But he so light was at legerdemain
That what he touched came not to light again.
Yet would he laugh it out, and proudly look,
And tell them that they greatly him mistook.
So would he scoff them out with mockery,
For he therein had great felicity,
And with sharp quips joyed others to deface,
Thinking that their disgracing did him grace.
So, whilst that other like vain wits he pleased,
And made to laugh, his heart was greatly eased.
 " But the right gentle mind would bite his lip,
To hear the javel so good men to nip;
For though the vulgar yield an open ear,
And common courtiers love to gibe and flear
At every thing which they hear spoken ill,
And the best speeches with ill-meaning spill,
Yet the brave courtier, in whose beauteous thought
Regard of honour harbours more than aught,
Doth loathe such base condition, to backbite
Any's good name for envy or despite.
He stands on terms of honourable mind,
Ne will be carried with the common wind
Of court's inconstant mutability,
Ne after every tattling fable fly;
But hears and sees the follies of the rest,
And thereof gathers for himself the best.
He will not creep, nor crouch with feignèd face,
But walks upright with comely stedfast pace,
And unto all doth yield due courtesy,—
But not with kissèd hand below the knee,
As that same apish crew is wont to do,
For he disdains himself to embase thereto.
He hates foul leasings and vile flattery,
Two filthy blots in noble gentery;
And loathful idleness he doth detest,
The canker-worm of every gentle breast;
The which to banish with fair exercise
Of knightly feats he daily doth devise;
Now menaging the mouths of stubborn steeds,
Now practising the proof of warlike deeds;
Now his bright arms assaying, now his spear,
Now the nigh-aimèd ring away to bear.

At other times he casts to sue the chace
Of swift wild beasts, or run on foot a race,
To enlarge his breath (large breath in arms most needful),
Or else by wrestling to wex strong and heedful ;
Or his stiff arms to stretch with yewen bow,
And manly legs, still passing to and fro;
Without a gownèd beast him fast beside,
A vain ensample of the Persian pride,
Who, after he had won the Assyrian foe,
Did ever after scorn on foot to go.
Thus when this courtly gentleman with toil
Himself hath wearièd, he doth recoil
Unto his rest, and there with sweet delight
Of music's skill revives his toilèd sprite;
Or else with loves and ladies' gentle sports,
The joy of youth, himself he recomforts.
Or, lastly, when the body list to pause,
His mind unto the Muses he withdraws;
Sweet Lady Muses! ladies of delight,
Delights of life, and ornaments of light,
With whom he close confers with wise discourse
Of Nature's works, of heaven's continual course,
Of foreign lands, of people different,
Of kingdoms' change, of diverse government,
Of dreadful battles of renownèd knights,
With which he kindleth his ambitious sprites
To like desire and praise of noble fame,
The only upshot whereto he doth aim.
For all his mind on honour fixèd is,
To which he levels all his purposes;
And in his prince's service spends his days,
Not so much for to gain, or for to raise
Himself to high degree, as for his grace,
And in his liking to win worthy place,
Through due deserts and comely carriage,
In whatso please employ his personage,
That may be matter meet to gain him praise.
For he is fit to use in all assays,
Whether for arms and warlike amenance,
Or else for wise and civil governance;
For he is practised well in policy,
And thereto doth his courting most apply;
To learn the enterdeal of princes strange,
To mark the intent of counsels, and the change
Of states, and eke of private men somewhile,
Supplanted by fine falsehood and fair guile ;
Of all the which he gathereth what is fit
To enrich the storehouse of his powerful wit,
Which through wise speeches and grave conference
He daily ekes, and brings to excellence.

"Such is the rightful courtier in his kind;
But unto such the Ape lent not his mind.
Such were for him no fit companions;
Such would discry his lewd conditions.
But the young lusty gallants he did chose
To follow, meet to whom he might disclose
His witless pleasance and ill-pleasing vein.
A thousand ways he them could entertain,
With all the thriftless games that may be found,
With mumming and with masking all around,
With dice, with cards, with balliards far unfit,
With shuttlecocks, mis-seeming manly wit,
With courtesans and costly riotize,
Whereof still somewhat to his share did rise.
Ne, them to pleasure, would he sometimes scorn
A pandar's coat (so basely was he born).
Thereto he could fine loving-verses frame,
And play the poet oft. But ah! for shame,
Let not sweet poets' praise, whose only pride
Is virtue to advance, and vice deride,
Be with the work of losels' wit defamed,
Ne let such verses poetry be named.
Yet he the name on him would rashly take,
Maugre the sacred Muses, and it make
A servant to the vile affection
Of such as he depended most upon,
And with the sugary sweet thereof allure
Chaste ladies' ears to fantasies impure.
To such delights the noble wits he led
Which him relieved, and their vain humours fed
With fruitless follies and unsound delights.
But, if perhaps into their noble sprites
Desire of honour or brave thought of arms
Did ever creep, then with his wicked charms
And strong conceits he would it drive away,
Ne suffer it to house there half a day.
And, whenso love of letters did inspire
Their gentle wits, and kindle wise desire,
That chiefly doth each noble mind adorn,
Then he would scoff at learning, and eke scorn
The sectaries thereof, as people base,
And simple men, which never came in place
Of world's affairs, but, in dark corners mewed,
Muttered of matters as their books them shewed,
Ne other knowledge ever did attain,
But with their gowns their gravity maintain.
From them he would his impudent lewd speech
Against God's holy ministers oft reach,
And mock divines and their profession:
What else then did he by progression

But mock high God himself, whom they profess?
But what cared he for God or godliness?
All his care was himself how to advance,
And to uphold his courtly countenance
By all the cunning means he could devise.
Were it by honest ways or otherwise,
He made small choice; yet sure his honesty
Got him small gains, but shameless flattery,
And filthy brocage, and unseemly shifts,
And borrow base, and some good ladies' gifts.
But the best help which chiefly him sustained
Was his man Reynold's purchase which he gained;
For he was schooled by kind in all the skill
Of close conveyance, and each practice ill
Of cosenage and cleanly knavery,
Which oft maintained his master's bravery.
Besides, he used another slippery sleight,
In taking on himself in common sight
False personages, fit for every stead,
With which he thousands cleanly cosened;
Now like a merchant, merchants to deceive,
With whom his credit he did often leave
In gage for his gay master's hopeless debt;
Now like a lawyer, when he land would let,
Or sell fee-simples in his master's name,
Which he had never, nor aught like the same.
Then would he be a broker, and draw in
Both wares and money, by exchange to win.
Then would he seem a farmer, that would sell
Bargains of woods which he did lately fell,
Or corn, or cattle, or such other ware,
Thereby to cosen men not well aware.
Of all the which there came a secret fee
To the Ape, that he his countenance might be.
Besides all this, he used oft to beguile
Poor suitors that in court did haunt somewhile;
For he would learn their business secretly,
And then inform his master hastily,
That he by means might cast them to prevent,
And beg the suit the which the other meant.
Or otherwise, false Reynold would abuse
The simple suitor, and wish him to choose
His master, being one of great regard
In court, to compass any suit not hard,
In case his pains were recompensed with reason.
So would he work the silly man by treason
To buy his master's frivolous good-will,
That had not power to do him good or ill.
    "So pitiful a thing is suitor's state!
Most miserable man! whom wicked Fate

Had brought to court to sue for had-I-wist,
That few have found, and many one hath missed!
Full little knowest thou, that hast not tried,
What hell it is in suing long to bide;
To lose good days that might be better spent,
To waste long nights in pensive discontent;
To speed to-day, to be put back to-morrow;
To feed on hope, to pine with fear and sorrow;
To have thy prince's grace, yet want her peers';
To have thy asking, yet wait many years;
To fret thy soul with crosses and with cares;
To eat thy heart through comfortless despairs;
To fawn, to crouch, to wait, to ride, to run,
To spend, to give, to want, to be undone.
Unhappy wight, born to disastrous end,
That doth his life in so long tendance spend!
Whoever leaves sweet home, where mean estate
In safe assurance, without strife or hate,
Finds all things needful for contentment meek,
And will to court for shadows vain to seek,
Or hope to gain, himself a daw will try;
That curse God send unto mine enemy!
For none but such as this bold Ape unblest
Can ever thrive in that unlucky quest,—
Or such as have a Reynold to his man,
That by his shifts his master furnish can.

"But yet this Fox could not so closely hide
His crafty feats but that they were descried
At length by such as sate in Justice' seat;
Who for the same him foully did intreat,
And, having worthily him punishèd,
Out of the court for ever banishèd.
And now the Ape, wanting his huckster-man,
That wont provide his necessaries, 'gan
To grow into great lack, ne could uphold
His countenance in those his garments old;
Ne new ones could he easily provide,
Though all men him uncasèd 'gan deride,
Like as a puppet placèd in a play,
Whose part, once past, all men bid take away;—
So that he driven was to great distress,
And shortly brought to hopeless wretchedness.
Then, closely as he might, he cast to leave
The court, not asking any pass or leave;
But ran away in his rent rags by night,—
Ne never stayed in place, ne spake to wight,
Till that the Fox his copesmate he had found;
To whom complaining his unhappy stound,
At last again with him in travel joined,
And with him fared, some better chance to find.

So in the world long time they wanderèd,
And mickle want and hardness sufferèd,
That them repented much so foolishly
To come so far to seek for misery,
And leave the sweetness of contented home,
Though eating hips, and drinking watery foam.
 "Thus as they them complainèd to and fro,
Whilst through the forest reckless they did go,
Lo where they spied how in a gloomy glade
The Lion sleeping lay in secret shade;
His crown and sceptre lying him beside,
And having doffed for heat his dreadful hide.
Which when they saw, the Ape was sore afraid,
And would have fled, with terror all dismayed;
But him the Fox with hardy words did stay,
And bad him put all cowardice away,
For now was time (if ever they would hope)
To aim their counsels to the fairest scope,
And them for ever highly to advance,
In case the good which their own happy chance
Them freely offered they would wisely take.
 "Scarce could the Ape yet speak, so did he quake;
Yet, as he could, he asked how good might grow
Where nought but dread and death do seem in show.
 "'Now' (said he) 'whiles the Lion sleepeth sound,
May we his crown and mace take from the ground,
And eke his skin, the terror of the wood,
Wherewith we may ourselves (if we think good)
Make kings of beasts, and lords of forests all
Subject unto that power imperial.'
 "'Ah! but' (said the Ape) 'who is so bold a wretch
That dare his hardy hand to those outstretch,
Whenas he knows his meed, if he be spied,
To be a thousand deaths, and shame beside?'
 "'Fond Ape' (said then the Fox) 'into whose breast
Never crept thought of honour nor brave geste,
Who will not venture life a king to be,
And rather rule and reign in sovereign see
Than dwell in dust inglorious and base,
Where none shall name the number of his place!
One joyous hour in blissful happiness
I choose before a life of wretchedness.
Be therefore counsellèd herein by me,
And shake off this vile-hearted cowardry.
If he awake, yet is not death the next,
For we may colour it with some pretext
Of this or that, that may excuse the crime.
Else we may fly; thou to a tree mayst climb,
And I creep underground; both from his reach:
Therefore be ruled to do as I do teach.'

"The Ape, that erst did nought but chill and quake,
Now 'gan some courage unto him to take,
And was content to attempt that enterprise,
Tickled with glory and rash covetise;
But first 'gan question whether should assay
Those royal ornaments to steal away.
"'Marry, that shall yourself,' (quoth he thereto)
'For ye be fine and nimble it to do;
Of all the beasts which in the forests be,
Is not a fitter for his turn than ye.
Therefore, mine own dear brother! take good heart,
And ever think a kingdom is your part.'
"Loth was the Ape (though praisèd) to adventure;
Yet faintly 'gan into his work to enter,
Afraid of every leaf that stirred him by,
And every stick that underneath did lie.
Upon his tiptoes nicely he up went,
For making noise, and still his ear he lent
To every sound that under heaven blew;
Now went, now stepped, now crept, now backward drew,
That it good sport had been him to have eyed.
Yet at the last (so well he him applied),
Through his fine handling and his cleanly play,
He all those royal signs had stoln away,
And with the Fox's help them borne aside
Into a secret corner unespied:
Whither whenas they came, they fell at words
Whether of them should be the lord of lords.
For the Ape was strifeful and ambitious,
And the Fox guileful, and most covetous,—
That neither pleasèd was to have the rein
Twixt them divided into even twain,
But either algates would be lord alone;
For love and lordship bide no paragon.
"'I am most worthy' (said the Ape), 'sith I
For it did put my life in jeopardy;
Thereto I am in person and in stature
Most like a man, the lord of every creature,
So that it seemeth I was made to reign,
And born to be a kingly sovereign.'
"'Nay,' (said the Fox) 'Sir Ape, you are astray;
For though to steal the diadem away
Were the work of your nimble hand, yet I
Did first devise the plot by policy,
So that it wholly springeth from my wit;
For which also I claim myself more fit
Than you to rule. For government of state
Will without wisdom soon be ruinate.
And, where ye claim yourself for outward shape
Most like a man, man is not like an Ape

In his chief parts, that is, in wit and spirit ;
But I, therein most like to him, do merit,
For my sly wiles and subtle craftiness,
The title of the kingdom to possess.
Nathless, my brother, since we passèd are
Unto this point, we will appease our jar ;
And I with reason meet will rest content
That ye shall have both crown and government,
Upon condition that ye rulèd be
In all affairs, and counsellèd by me,
And that ye let none other ever draw
Your mind from me, but keep this as a law,
And hereupon an oath unto me plight.'
  " The Ape was glad to end the strife so light,
And thereto swore ; for who would not oft swear,
And oft unswear, a diadem to bear?
Then freely up those royal spoils he took,
Yet at the Lion's skin he inly quook,
But it dissembled ; and upon his head
The crown, and on his back the skin, he did ;
And the false Fox, he helpèd to array.
Then when he was all dight, he took his way
Into the forest, that he might be seen
Of the wild beasts in his new glory sheen.
There the two first whom he encountered were
The Sheep and the Ass, who, stricken both with fear
At sight of him, 'gan fast away to fly.
But unto them the Fox aloud did cry,
And in the king's name bade them both to stay,
Upon the pain that thereof follow may.
Hardly nathless were they restrainèd so,
Till that the Fox forth toward them did go,
And there dissuaded them from needless fear,
For that the king did favour to them bear,
And therefore dreadless bade them come to court,—
For no wild beasts should do them any torte
There or abroad, ne would his majesty
Use them but well, with gracious clemency,
As whom he knew to him both fast and true.
So he persuaded them with homage due
Themselves to humble to the Ape prostrate,
Who, gently to them bowing in his gait,
Receivèd them with cheerful entertain.
  " Thence, forth proceeding with his princely train,
He shortly met the Tiger and the Boar,
Which with the simple Camel ragèd sore
In bitter words, seeking to take occasion
Upon his fleshy corps to make invasion.
But, soon as they this mock-king did espy,
Their troublous strife they stinted by and by,

Thinking indeed that it the Lion was.
He then, to prove whether his power would pass
As current, sent the Fox to them straightway,
Commanding them their cause of strife bewray;
And, if that wrong on either side there were,
That he should warn the wronger to appear
The morrow next at court it to defend,—
In the meantime upon the king to attend.

"The subtle Fox so well his message said
That the proud beasts him readily obeyed;
Whereby the Ape in wondrous stomach wox,
Strongly encouraged by the crafty Fox,
That king indeed himself he shortly thought.
And all the beasts him fearèd as they ought,
And followèd unto his palace high;
Where taking congee, each one by and by
Departed to his home in dreadful awe,
Full of the fearèd sight which late they saw.

"The Ape, thus seizèd of the regal throne,
Eftsoons, by counsel of the Fox alone,
'Gan to provide for all things in assurance,
That so his rule might longer have endurance.
First to his gate he 'pointed a strong guard,
That none might enter but with issue hard;
Then, for the safeguard of his personage,
He did appoint a warlike equipage
Of foreign beasts, not in the forest bred,
But part by land and part by water fed;
For tyranny is with strange aid supported.
Then unto him all monstrous beasts resorted,
Bred of two kinds, as griffons, minotaurs,
Crocodiles, dragons, beavers, and centaurs.
With those himself he strengthened mightily,
That fear he need no force of enemy.
Then 'gan he rule and tyrannize at will,
Like as the Fox did guide his graceless skill,
And all wild beasts made vassals of his pleasures,
And with their spoils enlarged his private treasures.
No care of justice, nor no rule of reason,
No temperance, nor no regard of season,
Did thenceforth ever enter in his mind;
But cruelty, the sign of currish kind,
And 'sdainful pride and wilful arrogance;
Such follows those whom Fortune doth advance.

" But the false Fox most kindly played his part,
For whatsoever mother-wit or art
Could work he put in proof. No practice sly,
No counterpoint of cunning policy,
No reach, no breach, that might him profit bring,
But he the same did to his purpose wring.

Nought suffered he the Ape to give or grant,
But through his hand alone must pass the fiant.
All offices, all leases, by him leapt,
And of them all whatso he liked he kept.
Justice he sold, injustice for to buy,
And for to purchase for his progeny.
Ill might it prosper that ill gotten was;
But, so he got it, little did he pass.
He fed his cubs with fat of all the soil,
And with the sweat of others' sweating toil;
He crammèd them with crumbs of benefices,
And filled their mouths with meeds of malefices;
He clothèd them with all colours, save white,
And loaded them with lordships and with might,
So much as they were able well to bear,
That with the weight their backs nigh broken were;
He chaffered chairs in which churchmen were set,
And breach of laws to privy farm did let.
No statute so establishèd might be,
Nor ordinance so needful, but that he
Would violate, though not with violence,
Yet under colour of the confidence
The which the Ape reposed in him alone,
And reckoned him the kingdom's corner-stone.
And ever, when he aught would bring to pass,
His long experience the platform was;
And, when he aught not pleasing would put by,
The cloak was care of thrift and husbandry,
For to increase the common treasure's store.
But his own treasure he increasèd more,
And lifted up his lofty towers thereby,
That they began to threat the neighbour sky:
The whiles the prince's palaces fell fast
To ruin (for what thing can ever last?)
And whilst the other peers, for poverty,
Were forced their ancient houses to let lie,
And their old castles to the ground to fall,
Which their forefathers, famous over all,
Had founded for the kingdom's ornament,
And for their memories' long moniment.
But he no count made of nobility,
Nor the wild beasts whom arms did glorify,
The realm's chief strength, and girlond of the crown;
All these, through feignèd crimes, he thrust adown,
Or made them dwell in darkness of disgrace,
For none but whom he list might come in place.
Of men of arms he had but small regard,
But kept them low, and straitened very hard;
For men of learning little he esteemed;
His wisdom he above their learning deemed.

As for the rascal commons, least he cared,
For not so common was his bounty shared;
'Let God,' (said he) 'if please, care for the many;
I for myself must care before else any.'
So did he good to none, to many ill,
So did he all the kingdom rob and pill;
Yet none durst speak, nor none durst of him plain,
So great he was in grace, and rich through gain.
Ne would he any let to have access
Unto the prince but by his own address;
For all that else did come were sure to fail.
Yet would he further none but for avail:
For on a time the Sheep, to whom of yore
The Fox had promisèd of friendship store,
What time the Ape the kingdom first did gain,
Came to the court, her case there to complain,
How that the Wolf, her mortal enemy,
Had sithence slain her lamb most cruelly,
And therefore craved to come unto the king,
To let him know the order of the thing.
'Soft, Goody Sheep,' (then said the Fox) 'not so:
Unto the king so rash ye may not go;
He is with greater matter busièd
Than a lamb, or the lamb's own mother's head;
Ne certes may I take it well in part
That ye my cousin Wolf so foully thwart,
And seek with slander his good name to blot;
For there was cause, else do it he would not.
Therefore surcease, good dame, and hence depart.'
So went the Sheep away with heavy heart;
So many moe, so every one, was used,
That to give largely to the Fox refused.
 "Now when high Jove, in whose almighty hand
The care of kings and power of empires stand,
(Sitting one day within his turret high
From whence he views with his black-lidded eye
Whatso the heaven in his wide vault contains,
And all that in the deepest earth remains)
The troubled kingdom of wild beasts beheld,—
Whom not their kindly sovereign did weld,
But an usurping Ape, with guile suborned,
Had all subversed,—he 'sdainfully it scorned
In his great heart, and hardly did refrain
But that with thunderbolts he had him slain,
And driven down to hell, his duest meed.
But, him avising, he that dreadful deed
Forbore, and rather chose with scornful shame
Him to avenge, and blot his brutish name
Unto the world, that never after any
Should of his race be void of infamy;

And his false counsellor, the cause of all,
To damn to death, or dole perpetual,
From whence he never should be quit nor stalled.
Forthwith he Mercury unto him called,
And bade him fly with never-resting speed
Unto the forest, where wild beasts do breed,
And there, enquiring privily, to learn
What did of late chance to the Lion stern,
That he ruled not the empire as he ought,
And whence were all those plaints unto him brought
Of wrongs and spoils by salvage beasts committed.
Which done, he bade the Lion be remitted
Into his seat, and those same treachours vile
Be punishèd for their presumptuous guile.
" The son of Maia, soon ás he received
That word, straight with his azure wings he cleaved
The liquid clouds and lucid firmament,
Ne stayed till that he came with steep descent
Unto the place where his prescript did show.
There, stooping like an arrow from a bow,
He soft arrivèd on the grassy plain,
And fairly pacèd forth with easy pain,
Till that unto the palace nigh he came.
Then 'gan he to himself new shape to frame;
And that fair face and that ambrosial hue
Which wonts to deck the gods' immortal crew,
And beautify the shiny firmament,
He doffed, unfit for that rude rabblement.
So, standing by the gates in strange disguise,
He 'gan enquire of some, in secret wise,
Both of the king and of his government,
And of the Fox, and his false blandishment.
And evermore he heard each one complain
Of foul abuses both in realm and reign;
Which yet to prove more true he meant to see,
And an eye-witness of each thing to be.
Tho on his head his dreadful hat he dight,
Which maketh him invisible to sight,
And mocketh the eyes of all the lookers-on,
Making them think it but a vision.
Through power of that he runs through enemies' swerds;
Through power of that he passeth through the herds
Of ravenous wild beasts, and doth beguile
Their greedy mouths of the expected spoil;
Through power of that his cunning thieveries
He wonts to work, that none the same espies;
And through the power of that he putteth on
What shape he list in apparition.
That on his head he wore, and in his hand
He took Caduceus, his snaky wand,

With which the damnèd ghosts he governeth,
And Furies rules, and Tartare tempereth.
With that he causeth sleep to seize the eyes,
And fear the hearts of all his enemies;
And, when him list, an universal night
Throughout the world he makes on every wight,
As when his sire with Alcumena lay.
Thus dight, into the court he took his way,
Both through the guard, which never him descried,
And through the watchmen, who him never spied.
Thence forth he passed into each secret part,
Whereas he saw (that sorely grieved his heart)
Each place abounding with foul injuries,
And filled with treasure racked with robberies;
Each place defiled with blood of guiltless beasts,
Which had been slain to serve the Ape's beheasts:
Gluttony, malice, pride, and covetize,
And lawlessness reigning with riotize;
Besides the infinite extortions
Done through the Fox's great oppressions,
That the complaints thereof could not be told.

"Which when he did with loathful eyes behold,
He would no more endure, but came his way,
And cast to seek the Lion where he may,
That he might work the avengement for his shame
On those two caitives which had bred him blame.
And, seeking all the forest busily,
At last he found where sleeping he did lie.
The wicked weed which there the Fox did lay
From underneath his head he took away;
And then him waking forcèd up to rise.
The lion, looking up, 'gan him avize,
As one late in a trance, what had of long
Become of him, for fantasy is strong.

"'Arise,' (said Mercury) 'thou sluggish beast,
That here liest senseless, like the corpse deceased,
The whilst thy kingdom from thy head is rent,
And thy throne royal with dishonour blent;
Arise, and do thyself redeem from shame,
And be avenged on those that breed thy blame!'

"Thereat enragèd, soon he 'gan up-start,
Grinding his teeth, and greating his great heart;
And, rousing up himself, for his rough hide
He 'gan to reach, but nowhere it espied.
Therewith he 'gan full terrible to roar,
And chafed at that indignity right sore.
But, when his crown and sceptre both he wanted,
Lord how he fumed, and swelled, and raged, and panted,
And threatened death and thousand deadly dolours
To them that had purloined his princely honours!

With that in haste, disrobèd as he was,
He towards his own palace forth did pass;
And all the way he roarèd as he went,
That all the forest with astonishment
Thereof did tremble, and the beasts therein
Fled fast away from that so dreadful din.
"At last he came unto his mansion,
Where all the gates he found fast locked anon,
And many warders round about them stood.
With that he roared aloud, as he were wood,
That all the palace quakèd at the stound,
As if it quite were riven from the ground,
And all within were dead and heartless left.
And the Ape himself, as one whose wits were reft,
Fled here and there, and every corner sought,
To hide himself from his own fearèd thought.
But the false Fox, when he the Lion heard,
Fled closely forth, straightway of death afeared;
And to the Lion came full lowly creeping,
With feignèd face, and watery eyn half weeping,
To excuse his former treason and abusion,
And turning all unto the Ape's confusion.
Nathless the royal beast forbore believing,
But bade him stay at ease till further prieving.
Then when he saw no entrance to him granted,
Roaring yet louder, that all hearts it daunted,
Upon those gates with force he fiercely flew;
And, rending them in pieces, felly slew
Those warders strange, and all that else he met.
But the Ape, still flying, he nowhere might get.
From room to room, from beam to beam, he fled,
All breathless, and for fear now almost dead.
Yet him at last the Lion spied, and caught,
And forth with shame unto his judgment brought.
"Then all the beasts he caused assembled be,
To hear their doom, aud sad ensample see.
The Fox, first author of that treachery,
He did uncase, and then away let fly;
But the Ape's long tail (which then he had) he quite
Cut off, and both ears parèd of their height;
Since which all apes but half their ears have left,
And of their tails are utterly bereft."

So Mother Hubbard her discourse did end,
Which pardon me if I amiss have penned;
For weak was my remembrance it to hold,
And bad her tongue that it so bluntly told.

SIR JOHN HARINGTON.

[Born in 1561, son of a natural daughter of Henry VIII.; died in 1612. Author of the celebrated translation of Ariosto's *Orlando Furioso*].

OF A PRECISE TAILOR.

A TAILOR, a man of an upright dealing,
True but for lying, honest but for stealing,
Did fall one day extremely sick by chance,
And on the sudden was in wondrous trance.
The Fiends of hell, mustering in fearful manner,
Of sundry-coloured silks displayed a banner,
Which he had stoln; and wished, as they did tell,
That one day he might find it all in hell.
The man, affrighted at this apparition,
Upon recovery grew a great precisian.
He bought a Bible of the new translation,
And in his life he showed great reformation.
He walkèd mannerly and talkèd meekly;
He heard three lectures and two sermons weekly;
He vowed to shun all companies unruly,
And in his speech he used no oath but "truly:"
And, zealously to keep the Sabbath's rest,
His meat for that day on the even was dressed.
And, lest the custom that he had to steal
Might cause him sometime to forget his zeal,
He gives his journeyman a special charge
That, if the stuff allowed fell out too large,
And that to filch his fingers were inclined,
He then should put the Banner in his mind.
This done, I scant the rest can tell for laughter.
A Captain of a ship came three days after,
And brought three yards of velvet and three quarters,
To make Venetians down below the garters.
He, that precisely knew what was enough,
Soon slipped away three quarters of the stuff.
His man, espying it, said in derision,
"Remember, Master, how you saw the vision!"
"Peace, knave," quoth he; "I did not see one rag
Of such-a-coloured silk in all the flag."

SIR JOHN DAVIES.

[Born in 1570; died in 1626, in which year he had been appointed Lord Chief Justice. Author of the noted work *Nosce Teipsum,* published in 1599, and accounted one of the prime specimens of the so-called " Metaphysical School" of poetry.]

A RIDDLE UPON A COFFIN.

THERE was a man bespake a thing,
Which when the owner home did bring,
He that made it did refuse it;
And he that brought it would not use it;
And he that hath it doth not know
Whether he hath it yea or no.

IN GERONTEM.

GERON his mouldy memory corrects
Old Holinshed, our famous Chronicler,
With moral rules; and policy collects
Out of all actions done these fourscore year;
Accounts the time of every old event,
Not from Christ's birth, nor from the Prince's reign,
But from some other famous accident,
Which in men's general notice doth remain,—
The siege of Boulogne and the Plaguy Sweat,
The going to St. Quintin's and New-haven,
The rising in the North, the Frost so great
That cart-wheels' prints on Thamis' face were graven,
The fall of money, and burning of Paul's steeple,
The blazing star, and Spaniard's overthrow.
By these events, notorious to the people,
He measures times, and things forepast doth show.
But, most of all, he chiefly reckons by
A private chance,—the death of his curst wife;
This is to him the dearest memory,
And the happiest accident of all his life.

JOHN DONNE.

[Born in London, 1573; died there, 31 March 1631. Donne was at first destined for the law: afterwards he travelled in Italy, Spain, and elsewhere; and then became Secretary to Lord Chancellor Egerton. He incurred great displeasure by contracting a clandestine marriage with the Chancellor's niece, daughter of Sir George More. Finally, after serious studies, he entered holy orders, and became Dean of St. Paul's. In all his vocations he excited great admiration, and as a clergyman he was highly revered. The poems of Donne are loaded with ingenious thought; often provokingly involved or paradoxical, and thwarting the true and natural course of poesy,—yet it is constantly thought, not mere whim or wire-drawing. A large and keen intellect, and a fervid poetic sense, are united in Donne; and combine to produce poetry much of which is truly fine, and can even become fascinating to a reader willing to "acclimatize" himself in this rarefied and vibrating atmosphere. Few English poetic writers give indication of a more masculine capacity. The man of the world, of adventure and gallantry, is quite as prominent in the verses as the student or divine; and it is often startling to reflect that the personage so thorough-going in th former character was the same who shone with genuine sanctity in the latter.]

SONG.

Go and catch a falling star,
  Get with child a mandrake root;
Tell me where all past years are,
  Or who cleft the Devil's foot;
Teach me to hear Mermaids singing,—
Or to keep off envy's stinging,
    And find
    What wind
Serves to advance an honest mind.

If thou beest born to strange sights,
  Things invisible to see,
Ride ten thousand days and nights,
  Till age snow white hairs on thee;
Thou, when thou return'st, wilt tell me
All strange wonders that befell thee,
    And swear
    Nowhere
Lives a woman true and fair.

If thou find'st one, let me know;
  Such a pilgrimage were sweet.
Yet do not; I would not go,
  Though at next door we might meet.
Though she were true when you met her,
And last till you write your letter,
    Yet she
    Will be
False, ere I come, to two or three.

WOMAN'S CONSTANCY.

Now thou hast loved me one whole day,
To-morrow, when thou leav'st, what wilt thou say?
Wilt thou then antedate some new-made vow?
    Or say that now
We are not just those persons which we were?
Or that oaths made in reverential fear
Of Love, and his wrath, any may forswear?
(For, as true deaths true marriages untie,
So lovers' contracts, images of those,
Bind but till sleep, death's image, them unloose);
    Or, your own end to justify,
For, having purposed change and falsehood, you
Can have no way but falsehood to be true?
Vain lunatic! against these scapes I could
    Dispute, and conquer, if I would;—
    Which I abstain to do,
For by to-morrow I may think so too.

THE INDIFFERENT.

I can love both fair and brown;
Her whom abundance melts, and her whom want betrays;
Her who loves loneness best, and her who masks and plays;
Her whom the country formed, and whom the town;
Her who believes, and her who tries;
Her who still weeps with spongy eyes,
And her who is dry cork, and never cries;
I can love her, and her, and you, and you,—
I can love any, so she be not true.

Will no other vice content you?
Will it not serve your turn to do as did your mothers?
Or have you all old vices spent, and now would find out others?
Or doth a fear that men are true torment you?
Oh we are not; be not you so!
Let me, and do you, twenty know!
Rob me, but bind me not, and let me go.
Must I, who came to travel thorough you,
Grow your fixed subject, because you are true?

Venus heard me sigh this song;
And by Love's sweetest part, Variety, she swore,
She heard not this till now; it should be so no more.
She went, examined, and returned ere long,
And said: "Alas! some two or three
Poor Heretics in love there be
Which think to stablish dangerous constancy.
But I have told them, Since you will be true,
You shall be true to them who are false to you."

THE WILL.

BEFORE I sigh my last gasp, let me breathe,
Great Jove, some legacies.   Here I bequeath
Mine eyes to Argus, if mine eyes can see ;
If they be blind, then, Love, I give them thee.
My tongue to Fame ; to Embassadors mine ears ;
    To women or the sea, my tears.
  Thou, Love, hast taught me heretofore
By making me serve her who had twenty more,
That I should give to none but such as had too much before.

My constancy I to the Planets give ;
My truth to them who at the Court do live ;
Mine ingenuity and openness,
To Jesuits, to Buffoons my pensiveness ;
My silence to any who abroad hath been ;
    My money to a Capuchin.
  Thou, Love, taught'st me, by appointing me
To love there where no love received can be,
Only to give to such as have an incapacity.

My faith I give to Roman Catholics ;
All my good works unto the Schismatics
Of Amsterdam ; my best civility
And courtship, to an University ;
My modesty I give to Soldiers bare ;
    My patience let gamesters share.
  Thou, Love, taught'st me, by making me
Love her that holds my love disparity,
Only to give to those that count my gifts indignity.

I give my reputation to those
Which were my friends ; mine industry to foes ;
To schoolmen I bequeath my doubtfulness ;
My sickness to Physicians, or excess ;
To Nature, all that I in rhyme have writ ;
    And to my company my wit.
  Thou, Love, by making me adore
Her who begot this love in me before,
Taught'st me to make as though I gave when I do but restore.

To him for whom the passing-bell next tolls,
I give my physic-books ; my written rolls
Of moral counsels I to Bedlam give ;
My brazen medals, unto them which live
In want of bread ; to them which pass among
    All foreigners, mine English tongue.
  Thou, Love, by making me love one
Who thinks her friendship a fit portion
For younger lovers, dost my gift thus disproportion.

Therefore I'll give no more, but I'll undo
The world by dying ; because love dies too.
Then all your beauties will be no more worth
Than gold in mines, where none doth draw it forth ;
And all your graces no more use shall have
    Than a sun-dial in a grave.
    Thou, Love, taught'st me, by making me
  Love her who doth neglect both me and thee,
To invent and practise this one way to annihilate all three.

BEN JONSON.
[Born in Westminster, 1574 ; died there, 6 August 1637].
ON GILES AND JOAN.

Who says that Giles and Joan at discord be ?
The observing neighbours no such mood can see.
Indeed, poor Giles repents he married ever ;
But *that* his Joan doth too. And Giles would never,
By his free will, be in Joan's company ;
No more would Joan he should. Giles riseth early,
And, having got him out of doors, is glad ;
The like is Joan :—but, turning home, is sad ;
And so is Joan. Ofttimes when Giles doth find
Harsh sights at home, Giles wisheth he were blind ;
All this doth Joan : or that his long-yearned life
Were quite out-spun ; the like wish hath his wife.
The children that he keeps Giles swears are none
Of his begetting ; and so swears his Joan.
In all affections she concurreth still.
If now, with man and wife, to will and nill
The selfsame things a note of concord be,
I know no couple better can agree.

TO CAPTAIN HUNGRY.

Do what you come for, captain, with your news,—
That's sit and eat ; do not my ears abuse.
I oft look on false coin to know't from true ;
Not that I love it more than I will you.
Tell the gross Dutch those grosser tales of yours ;
How great you were with their two emperors,
And yet are with their princes : fill them full
Of your Moravian horse, Venetian bull ;
Tell them what parts you've ta'en, whence run away,
What states you gulled, and which yet keeps you in pay ;
Give them your services, and embassies
In Ireland, Holland, Sweden, pompous lies !
In Hungary and Poland, Turkey too ;
What at Leghorn, Rome, Florence, you did do ;

And, in some year, all these together heaped,—
For which there must more sea and land be leaped
(If but to be believed you have the hap)
Than can a flea at twice skip i' the map.
Give your young statesmen (that first make you drunk,
And then lie with you, closer than a punk,
For news) your Villeroys, and Silleries,
Janins, your Nuncios, and your Tuileries,
Your Arch-dukes' agents, and your Beringhams,
That are your words of credit. Keep your names
Of Hannow, Shieter-huissen, Popenheim,
Hans-spiegle, Rotteinberg, and Boutersheim,
For your next meal; *this* you are sure of. Why
Will you part with them here, unthriftily?
Nay, now you puff, tusk, and draw up your chin,
Twirl the poor chain you run a-feasting in.
Come, be not angry; you are hungry,—eat;
Do what you come for, captain; there's your meat.

A FIT OF RHYME AGAINST RHYME.

RHYME, the rack of finest wits,
That expresseth but by fits
        True conceit,
Spoiling senses of their treasure,
Cozening judgment with a measure,
        But false weight;
Wresting words from their true calling;
Propping verse for fear of falling
        To the ground;
Jointing syllabes, drowning letters,
Fastening vowels, as with fetters
        They were bound!
Soon as lazy thou wert known,
All good poetry hence was flown,
        And art banished;
For a thousand years together,
All Parnassus' green did wither,
        And wit vanished.
Pegasus did fly away;
At the wells no Muse did stay,
        But bewailed
So to see the fountain dry,
And Apollo's music die,
        All light failed.
Starveling rhymes did fill the stage,—
Not a poet in an age,
        Worthy crowning;
Not a work deserving bays,
Nor a line deserving praise,
        Pallas frowning.

Greek was free from rhyme's infection;
Happy Greek, by this protection,
    Was not spoiled;
Whilst the Latin, queen of tongues,
Is not yet free from rhyme's wrongs,
    But rests foiled.
Scarce the Hill again doth flourish,
Scarce the world a wit doth nourish,
    To restore
Phœbus to his crown again,
And the Muses to their brain,
    As before.
Vulgar languages that want
Words and sweetness, and be scant
    Of true measure,
Tyrant rhyme hath so abused
That they long since have refused
    Other censure.
He that first invented thee,
May his joints tormented be,
    Cramped for ever;
Still may syllabes jar with time,
Still may reason war with rhyme,
    Resting never!

May his sense, when it would meet
The cold tumour in his feet,
    Grow unsounder;
And his title be long Fool,
That in rearing such a school
    Was the founder!

EPISTLE TO MY LADY COVELL.

You won not verses, madam, you won me,
When you would play so nobly and so free,
A book to a few lines! But it was fit
You won them too; your odds did merit it.
So have you gained a servant and a Muse:
The first of which I fear you will refuse;
And you *may* justly,—being a tardy, cold,
Unprofitable chattel, fat and old,
Laden with belly, and doth hardly approach
His friends, but to break chairs or crack a coach.
His weight is twenty stone within two pound;
And that's made up as doth the purse abound.
Marry, the Muse is one can tread the air,
And stroke the water, nimble, chaste, and fair,—
Sleep in a virgin's bosom without fear,
Run all the rounds in a soft lady's ear,

Widow or wife, without the jealousy
Of either suitor or a servant by.
Such, if her manners like you, I do send ;
And can for other graces her commend,—
To make you merry on the dressing-stool
A' mornings, and at afternoons to fool
Away ill company, and help in rhyme
Your Joan to pass her melancholy time.
By this, although you fancy not the man,
Accept his Muse ; and tell, I know you can,
How many verses, madam, are your due.
I can lose none in tendering these to you.
I gain in having leave to keep my day,—
And should grow rich, had I much more to pay.

BISHOP (JOSEPH) HALL.

[Born in 1574 died in 1656. He became Bishop of Exeter in 1627, and of Norwich in 1641 ; soon after which, the troubles of the time, in church and state, ousted him from his see, and he expired unrestored, but much esteemed for character and piety. His Satires are the first compositions of that kind, in a regular form, in the English language. So at least they are generally accounted ; though I hardly know why the claims of Wyatt in this respect should be ignored. Even as regards Hall himself, some of his Satires are of a very curt and casual sort, as our specimen shows].

A TRENCHER CHAPLAIN.

A GENTLE squire would gladly entertain
Into his house some trencher-chapelain ;
Some willing man that might instruct his sons,
And that would stand to good conditions.
First, that he lie upon the truckle-bed,
Whiles his young master lieth o'er his head.
Second, that he do, on no default,
Ever presume to sit above the salt.
Third, that he never change his trencher twice.
Fourth, that he use all common courtesies ;
Sit bare at meals, and one half rise and wait.
Last, that he never his young master beat,
But he must ask his mother to define
How many jerks she would his breech should line.
All these observed, he could contented be
To give five marks and winter livery.

JOHN FLETCHER.

[Born in Northamptonshire, 1576, son of a Bishop of London; died of the plague, 1625. The constant colleague of Francis Beaumont as a dramatist, and in daily life as well: it is said "that they lived together on the Bank-side, and not only pursued their studies in close companionship, but carried their community of habits so far that they had only one bench between them, and used the same clothes and cloaks in common." Fletcher is believed to have composed the larger portion of the plays, and the great majority of the interspersed songs. The following comes from a drama, *The Nice Valour*, which is ascribed to Fletcher singly].

LAUGHING SONG.

[For several voices.]

OH how my lungs do tickle! ha ha ha!
Oh how my lungs do tickle! ho ho ho ho!
   Set a sharp jest
   Against my breast,
Then how my lungs do tickle!
   As nightingales,
   And things in cambric rails,
Sing best against a prickle.
   Ha ha ha ha!
   Ho ho ho ho ho!
Laugh! Laugh! Laugh! Laugh!
Wide! Loud! And vary!
A smile is for a simpering novice,—
   One that ne'er tasted caviarë,
Nor knows the smack of dear anchovies.
   Ha ha ha ha ha!
   Ho ho ho ho ho!
A giggling waiting-wench for me,
That shows her teeth how white they be,—
A thing not fit for gravity,
For theirs are foul and hardly three.
   Ha ha ha!
   Ho ho ho!
"Democritus, thou ancient fleerer,
  How I miss thy laugh, and ha' since!"[1]
There thou named the famous[est] jeerer
  That e'er jeered in Rome or Athens.
   Ha ha ha!
   Ho ho ho!
"How brave lives he that keeps a fool,
  Although the rate be deeper!"
But he that is his own fool, sir,
  Does live a great deal cheaper.
"Sure I shall burst, burst, quite break,
  Thou art so witty."

---

[1] Changed by Seward to
    "How I miss thy laugh, and ha-sense.'
Neither reading is very convincing.

" 'Tis rare to break at court,
   For that belongs to the city."
Ha ha ! my spleen is almost worn
   To the last laughter.
" Oh keep a corner for a friend !
   A jest may come hereafter."

BISHOP (RICHARD) CORBET.

[Born in 1582, died in 1635. Bishop of Oxford and of Norwich. The humorous turn of his verses was the reflex of the like quality in himself. Indeed, his deportment appears to have often been eminently unepiscopal: he had, however, substantial merits of kindliness and sound sense to set off against this].

DR. CORBET'S JOURNEY INTO FRANCE.

I WENT from England into France,
Nor yet to learn to cringe nor dance,
   Nor yet to ride nor fence ;
Nor did I go like one of those
That do return with half a nose
   They carrièd from hence.

But I to Paris rode along,
Much like John Dory in the song,
   Upon a holy-tide ;
I on an ambling nag did jet
(I trust he is not paid for yet),
   And spurred him on each side.

And to St. Denis fast we came,
To see the sights of Notre Dame,
   (The man that shows them snuffles) ;
Where who is apt for to believe
May see our Lady's right-arm sleeve,
   And eke her old pantofles ;

Her breast, her milk, her very gown
That she did wear in Bethlehem town
   When in the inn she lay ;
Yet all the world knows that's a fable,
For so good clothes ne'er lay in stable
   Upon a lock of hay.

No carpenter could by his trade
Gain so much coin as to have made
   A gown of so rich stuff ;
Yet they, poor souls, think, for their credit,
That they believe old Joseph did it,
   'Cause he deserved enough.

There is one of the cross's nails,
Which whoso sees his bonnet vails,
   And, if he will, may kneel.
Some say 'twas false, 'twas never so ;
Yet, feeling it, thus much I know,
   It is as true as steel.

There is a lanthorn which the Jews,
When Judas led them forth, did use,—
   It weighs my weight downright ;
But, to believe it, you must think
The Jews did put a candle in't.
   And then 'twas very light.

There's one saint there hath lost his nose,
Another's head, but not his toes,
   His elbow and his thumb.
But, when that we had seen the rags,
We went to the inn, and took our nags,
   And so away did come.

We came to Paris, on the Seine ;
'Tis wondrous fair, 'tis nothing clean,
   'Tis Europe's greatest town ;
How strong it is I need not tell it,
For all the world may easily smell it,
   That walk it up and down.

There many strange things are to see ;—
The palace and great gallery,
   The Place Royal doth excel,
The New Bridge, and the statues there,—
At Notre Dame St. Q. Pater
   The steeple bears the bell ;

For learning the University,
And for old clothes the Frippery ;
   The house the queen did build ;
St. Innocence, whose earth devours
Dead corps in four-and-twenty hours,
   And there the king was killed.

The Bastille and St. Denis Street,
The Shafflenist like London Fleet,
   The Arsenal no toy ;
But, if you'll see the prettiest thing,
Go to the court and see the king—
   Oh 'tis a hopeful boy !

He is, of all his dukes and peers,
Reverenced for much wit at's years,
   Nor must you think it much ;

For he with little switch doth play,
And make fine dirty pies of clay,—
   Oh never king made such !

A bird that can but kill a fly,
Or prate, doth please his majesty,
   'Tis known to every one ;
The Duke of Guise gave him a parrot,
And he had twenty cannons for it,
   For his new galleon.

Oh that I e'er might have the hap
To get the bird which in the map
   Is called the Indian ruck !
I'd give it him, and hope to be
As rich as Guise or Liviné,
   Or else I had ill-luck.

Birds round about his chamber stand,
And he them feeds with his own hand,
   'Tis his humility ;
And, if they do want anything,
They need but whistle for their king,
   And he comes presently.

But now, then, for these parts he must
Be enstyled Lewis the Just,
   Great Henry's lawful heir ;
When, to his style to add more words,
They'd better call him King of Birds
   Than of the great Navarre.

He hath besides a pretty quirk,
Taught him by nature, how to work
   In iron with much ease.
Sometimes to the forge he goes,
There he knocks and there he blows,
   And makes both locks and keys ;

Which puts a doubt in every one
Whether he be Mars' or Vulcan's son,—
   Some few believe his mother ;
But, let them all say what they will,
I came resolved, and so think still,
   As much the one as th' other.

The people too dislike the youth,
Alleging reasons, for, in truth.
   Mothers should honoured be ;
Yet others say he loves her rather
As well as e'er she loved her father,
   And that's notoriously.

His queen, a pretty little wench,
Was born in Spain, speaks little French,
   She's ne'er like to be mother;
For her incestuous house could not
Have children which were not begot
   By uncle or by brother.

Nor why should Lewis, being so just,
Content himself to take his lust
   With his Lucina's mate,
And suffer his little pretty queen
From all her race that yet hath been
   So to degenerate?

'Twere charity for to be known
To love others' children as his own
   And why? It is no shame;
Unless that he would greater be
Than was his father Henery,
   Who, men thought, did the same.

FAREWELL TO THE FAIRIES.

"FAREWELL, rewards and fairies!"
   Good housewives now may say,
For now foul sluts in dairies
   Do fare as well as they.
And, though they sweep their hearths no less
   Than maids were wont to do,
Yet who of late, for cleanliness,
   Finds sixpence in her shoe?

Lament, lament, old Abbeys,
   The fairies lost command!
They did but change priests' babies,
   But some have changed your land;
And all your children stoln from thence
   Are now grown Puritans;
Who live as changelings ever since,
   For love of your domains.

At morning and at evening both,
   You merry were and glad,
So little care of sleep or sloth
   These pretty ladies had;
When Tom came home from labour,
   Or Cis to milking rose,
Then merrily went their tabor,
   And nimbly went their toes.

Witness those rings and roundelays
   Of theirs, which yet remain,

Were footed in Queen Mary's days
   On many a grassy plain;
But, since of late Elizabeth,
   And later James, came in,
They never danced on any heath
   As when the time hath been.

By which we note the fairies
   Were of the old profession,
Their songs were Ave-Maries,
   Their dances were procession:
But now, alas! they all are dead,
   Or gone beyond the seas;
Or further for religion fled,
   Or else they take their ease.

A tell-tale in their company
   They never could endure,
And whoso kept not secretly
   Their mirth was punished sure;
It was a just and Christian deed
   To pinch such black and blue:
Oh how the commonwealth doth need
   Such justices as you!

AN EPITAPH ON THOMAS JONCE.[1]

Here, for the nonce,
Came Thomas Jonce,
   In St. Giles' church to lie.
None Welsh before,
None Welshman more,
   Till Shon Clerk die.

I'll toll the bell,
I'll ring his knell;
He died well,
He's saved from hell;
And so farewell
   Tom Jonce.

---

[1] Thomas Jonce (Jones), a Welsh clergyman, who lived in St. Giles' parish, Oxford.

THOMAS CAREW.

[Born towards 1589, died in 1639. Carew was in great favour with Charles I. and his court; a man of pleasure, gallantry, fancy, and wit. When these allurements came to their close in a mortal illness, very different cares possessed him, and he died an "edifying" death].

TO A. D., UNREASONABLY DISTRUSTFUL OF HER OWN BEAUTY.

Fair Doris, break thy glass; it hath perplexed,
With a dark comment, beauty's clearest text;
It hath not told thy face's story true,
But brought false copies to thy jealous view.
No colour, feature, lovely hair, or grace,
That ever yet adorned a beauteous face,
But thou must read in thine, or justly doubt
Thy glass hath been suborned to leave it out;
But, if it offer to thy nice survey
A spot, a stain, a blemish, or decay,
It not belongs to thee—the treacherous light
Or faithless stone abuse thy credulous sight.
Perhaps the magic of thy face hath wrought
Upon the enchanted crystal, and so brought
Fantastic shadows to delude thine eyes
With airy repercussive sorceries;
Or else the enamoured image pines away
For love of the fair object, and so may
Wax pale and wan, and, though the substance grow
Lively and fresh, that may consume with woe.
Give then no faith to the false specular stone,
But let thy beauties by the effects be known.
Look, sweetest Doris, on my lovesick heart;
In that true mirror see how fair thou art.
There, by Love's never-erring pencil drawn,
Shalt thou behold thy face, like the early dawn,
Shoot through the shady covert of thy hair,
Enamelling and perfuming the calm air
With pearls and roses, till thy suns display
Their lids, and let out the imprisoned day;
Whilst Delphic priests, enlightened by their theme,
In amorous numbers court thy golden beam,
And from Love's altars clouds of sighs arise
In smoking incense to adore thine eyes.
If then love flow from beauty as the effect,
How canst thou the resistless cause suspect?
Who would not brand that fool that should contend
There was no fire where smoke and flames ascend?
Distrust is worse than scorn; not to believe
My harms is greater wrong than not to grieve;
What cure can for my festering sore be found,
Whilst thou believ'st thy beauty cannot wound?

Such humble thoughts more cruel tyrants prove
Than all the pride that e'er usurped in love;
For beauty's herald *here* denounceth war,—
There are false spies betray me to a snare.
If fire disguised in balls of snow were hurled,
It unsuspected might consume the world;
Where our prevention ends, danger begins.
So wolves in sheep's, lions in asses' skins,
Might far more mischief work, because less feared;
Those the whole flock, these might kill all the herd.
Appear then as thou art, break through this cloud,
Confess thy beauty, though thou thence grow proud;
Be fair though scornful; rather let me find
Thee cruel than thus mild, and more unkind;
Thy cruelty doth only me defy,
But these dull thoughts thee to thyself deny.
Whether thou mean to barter or bestow
Thyself, 'tis fit thou thine own value know.
I will not cheat thee of thyself, nor pay
Less for thee than thou art worth; thou shalt not say
That is but brittle glass which I have found
By strict enquiry a firm diamond.
I'll trade with no such Indian fool as sells
Gold, pearls, and precious stones, for beads and bells;
Nor will I take a present from your hand
Which you or prize not or not understand.
It not endears your bounty that I do
Esteem your gift, unless you do so too;
You undervalue me when you bestow
On me what you nor care for, nor yet know.
No, lovely Doris, change thy thoughts, and be
In love first with thyself, and then with me.
You are afflicted that you are not fair,
And I as much tormented that you are.
What I admire you scorn; what I love, hate;
Through different faiths, both share an equal fate.
Fast to the truth, which you renounce, I stick;
I die a martyr, you an heretic.

TO MY FRIEND G. N., FROM WREST.

I BREATHE, sweet Ghib, the temperate air of Wrest,
Where I, no more with raging storms oppressed,
Wear the cold nights out by the banks of Tweed,
On the bleak mountains where fierce tempests breed,
And everlasting winter dwells; where mild
Favonius and the vernal winds, exiled,
Did never spread their wings; but the wild north
Brings sterile fern, thistles, and brambles forth.

Here, steeped in balmy dew, the pregnant earth
Sends forth her teeming womb a flowery birth ;
And, cherished with the warm sun's quickening heat,
Her porous bosom doth rich odours sweat,
Whose perfumes through the ambient air diffuse
Such native aromatics as we use
No foreign gums, nor essence fetched from far,
No volatile spirits, nor compounds that are
Adulterate ; but, as nature's cheap expense,
With far more genuine sweets refresh the sense.
Such pure and uncompounded beauties bless
This mansion with an useful comeliness,
Devoid of art ; for here the architect
Did not with curious skill a pile erect
Of carvèd marble, touch, or porphyry,
But built a house for hospitality.
No sumptuous chimney-piece of shining stone
Invites the stranger's eye to gaze upon,
And coldly entertains his sight ; but clear
And cheerful flames cherish and warm him here.
No Doric nor Corinthian pillars grace
With imagery this structure's naked face.
The lord and lady of this place delight
Rather to be in act than seem in sight.
Instead of statues to adorn their wall,
They throng with living men their merry hall,
Where, at large tables filled with wholesome meats,
The servant, tenant, and kind neighbour, eats.
Some of that rank spun of a finer thread
Are, with the women, steward, and chaplain, fed
With daintier cates. Others of better note,
Whom wealth, parts, office, or the herald's coat,
Have severed from the common, freely sit
At the lord's table ; whose spread sides admit
A large access of friends, to fill those seats
Of his capacious circle, filled with meats
Of choicest relish, till his oaken back
Under the load of piled-up dishes crack.
 Nor think, because our pyramids and high
Exalted turrets threaten not the sky,
That therefore Wrest of narrowness complains,
Or strengthened walls ; for she more numerous trains
Of noble guests daily receives, and those
Can with far more convenïence dispose,
Than prouder piles, where the vain builder spent
More cost in outward gay embellishment
Than real use, which was the sole design
Of our contriver, who made things not fine,
But fit for service. Amalthea's horn
Of plenty is not in effigy worn

Without the gate; but she within the door
Empties her free and unexhausted store.
Nor, crowned with wheaten wreaths, doth Ceres stand
In stone, with a crook'd sickle in her hand;
Nor, on a marble tun, his face besmeared
With grapes, is curled, unscissored Bacchus reared:
We offer not in emblems to the eyes,
But to the taste, those useful deities.
We press the juicy god, and quaff his blood,
And grind the yellow goddess into food.
Yet we decline not all the work of art;
But, where more bounteous Nature bears a part,
And guides her handmaid if she but dispense
Fit matter, she with care and diligence
Employs her skill. For where the neighbour source
Pours forth her waters, she directs their course,
And entertains the flowing streams in deep
And spacious channels, where they slowly creep
In snaky windings as the shelving ground
Leads them in circles, till they twice surround
This island mansion; which, i' the centre placed,
Is with a double crystal heaven embraced,
In which our watery constellations float,
Our fishes, swans, our waterman and boat,
Envied by those above, who wish to slake
Their star-burnt limbs in our refreshing lake.
But they stick fast, nailed to the barren sphere;
Whilst our increase, in fertile waters here,
Disport and wander freely where they please,
Within the circuit of our narrow seas.
   With various trees we fringe the water's brink,
Whose thirsty roots the soaking moisture drink;
And whose extended boughs, in equal ranks,
Yield fruit and shade and beauty to the banks.
On this side young Vertumnus sits, and courts
His ruddy-cheeked Pomona; Zephyr sports
On the other with loved Flora, yielding there
Sweets for the smell, sweets for the palate here.
But, did you taste the high and mighty drink
Which from that fountain flows, you'd clearly think
The god of wine did his plump clusters bring,
And crush the Falerne grape into our spring;
Or else, disguised in watery robes, did swim
To Ceres' bed, and make her big of him,
Begetting to himself on her; for know
Our vintage here in March doth nothing owe
To theirs in autumn, but our fire boils here
As lusty liquor as the sun makes there.
   Thus I enjoy myself, and taste the fruit
Of this bless'd peace; whilst, toiled in the pursuit

Of bucks and stags, th' emblem of war, you strive
To keep the memory of our arms alive.

THE HUE AND CRY.

In Love's name you are charged hereby
To make a speedy hue and cry
After a face which, t'other day,
Stole my wandering heart away.
To direct you, these, in brief,
Are ready marks to know the thief.
  Her hair, a net of beams, would prove
Strong enough to captive Jove
In his eagle's shape ; her brow
Is a comely field of snow ;
Her eye so rich, so pure a grey,
Every beam creates a day ;
And if she but sleep (not when
The sun sets) 'tis night again.
In her cheeks are to be seen
Of flowers both the king and queen,
Thither by the Graces led,
And freshly laid in nuptial bed ;
On whom lips like nymphs do wait
Who deplore their virgin state ;
Oft they blush,—and blush for this,
That they one another kiss.
But observe : besides the rest,
You shall know this felon best
By her tongue ; for, if your ear
Once a heavenly music hear,
Such as neither gods nor men,
But from that voice, shall hear again—
That, that is she. Oh straight surprise,
And bring her unto Love's assize.
If you let her go, she may
Antedate the latter day,
Fate and philosophy control,
And leave the world without a soul.

SAMUEL ROWLANDS.

[A prolific humorous and satirical writer of the 17th century].

THE CONJURER COZENED.

A SHIFTING knave about the town
Did challenge wondrous skill:
To tell men's fortunes and good haps,
He had the stars at will.
What day was best to travel on,
Which fit to choose a wife;
If violent or natural
A man should end his life;
Success of any suit in law,
Which party's cause prevails;
When it is good to pick one's teeth,
And ill to pare his nails.
So cunningly he played the knave
That he deluded many
With shifting, base, and cozening tricks;
For skill he had not any.
    Amongst a crew of simple gulls,
That plied him to their cost,
A butcher comes and craves his help,
That had some cattle lost.
Ten groats he gave him for his fee;
And he to conjure goes,
With characters, and vocables,
And divers antic shows.
The butcher, in a beastly fear,
Expected spirits still,
And wished himself within his shop,
Some sheep or calf to kill.
At length out of an old blind hole,
Behind a painted cloth,
A devil comes with roaring voice,
Seeming exceeding wroth.
With squibs and crackers round-about
Wild-fire he did send;
Which swaggering Ball, the butcher's dog,
So highly did offend
That he upon the devil flies,
And shakes his horns so sore,
Even like an ox, most terrible
He made hobgoblin roar.
The cunning man cries, "For God's love, help!
Unto your mastiff call!"
"Fight dog, fight devil!" butcher said,
And claps his hands at Ball.
The dog most cruelly tore his flesh,

The devil went to wrack,
And lookèd like a tattered rogue,
With ne'er a rag on's back.
"Give me my money back again,
Thou slave," the butcher said,
"Or I will see your devil's heart,
Before he can be laid !
He gets not back again to hell,
Ere I my money have ;
And I will have some interest too,
Besides mine own I gave.
Deliver first mine own ten groats,
And then a crown to boot :
I smell your devil's knavery out,
He wants a cloven foot."

The conjurer, with all his heart,
The money back repays,
And gives five shillings of his own :
To whom the butcher says,—
"Farewell, most scurvy conjurer !
Think on my valiant deed,
Which has done more than English George
That made the dragon bleed.
He and his horse, the story tells,
Did but a serpent slay :
I and my dog the devil spoiled,—
We two have got the day."

ROBERT HERRICK.

[Born in 1591, son of a goldsmith in Cheapside, of good family connexions ; died towards 1674. Herrick entered the church, in what year is uncertain : the year 1629 is the first clear date relating to this matter, when Herrick, aged thirty-eight, was appointed to the living of Dean Prior, Devonshire. In 1648 he was ejected as a royalist ; but restored in 1660. He lived a bachelor ; much more (if we may judge from his verses) in the style of a jovial celibate than of a clerical ascetic. A certain section of his poems is religious or moral ; the great majority of them, however, testify to a keen enjoyment of the good things of this world, whether simple or refined. Many of his compositions are, in the fullest sense of the term, trifles ; others are at least exquisite trifles ; some are not trifles, and are exquisite. After more than a century of neglect, ensuing upon their first ample popularity, Herrick's writings have for years been kept freshened with a steady current of literary laudation—certainly not unjustified, so far as their finer qualities go, but tending a little to the indiscriminate].

UPON A WIFE THAT DIED MAD WITH JEALOUSY.

In this little vault she lies
Here, with all her jealousies ;
Quiet yet ; but, if ye make
Any noise, they both will wake,
And such spirits raise 'twill then
Trouble Death to lay again.

UPON PAGGET.

PAGGET, a schoolboy, got a sword, and then
He vowed destruction both to birch and men;
Who would not think this younker fierce to fight?
Yet, coming home but somewhat late last night,
"Untruss," his master bade him; and that word
Made him take up his shirt, lay down his sword.

TO THE DETRACTOR.

WHERE others love and praise my verses, still
Thy long black thumb-nail marks 'em out for ill;
A fellon take it, or some white-flaw come
For to unslate or to untile that thumb!
But cry thee mercy; exercise thy nails
To scratch or claw, so that thy tongue not rails.
Some numbers prurient are, and some of these
Are wanton with their itch; scratch, and 'twill please.

THE INVITATION.

To sup with thee thou didst me home invite,
And mad'st a promise that mine appetite
Should meet and tire on such lautitious meat
The like not Heliogàbalus did eat;
And richer wine wouldst give to me, thy guest,
Than Roman Sylla poured out at his feast.
I came, 'tis true; and looked for fowl of price,
The bustard, phœnix, bird of paradise;
And for no less than aromatic wine
Of maiden's-blush commixed with jessamine.
Clean was the hearth; the mantel larded jet,
Which, wanting Lar and smoke, hung weeping wet.
At last, i'the noon of winter, did appear
A ragg'd soused neat's-foot with sick vinegar;
And in a burnished flagonet stood by
Beer small as comfort, dead as charity.
At which amazed, and pondering on the food,—
How cold it was, and how it chilled my blood,—
I cursed the master, and I damned the souce,
And swore I'd got the ague of the house.
Well, when to eat thou dost me next desire,
I'll bring a fever, since thou keep'st no fire.

FRANCIS QUARLES.

[Born in 1592, died in 1644. Chiefly known as the author of the *Emblems*. Quarles held the post of cup-bearer to the Queen of Bohemia, daughter of James I.; afterwards of secretary to Archbishop Usher in Ireland, and of Chronologer to the City of London. He adhered to the royal party in the civil war: hence his property was sequestrated, and his mishaps are supposed to have accelerated his death].

HEY, THEN, UP GO WE.

Know this, my brethren, heaven is clear,
    And all the clouds are gone;
The righteous man shall flourish,
    Good days are coming on.
Then come, my brethren, and be glad,
    And eke rejoice with me;
Lawn sleeves and rochets shall go down,
    And hey, then, up go we!

We'll break the windows which the whore
    Of Babylon hath painted;
And, when the popish saints are down,
    Then Barrow shall be sainted;
There's neither cross nor crucifix
    Shall stand for men to see,
Rome's trash and trumpery shall go down,
    And hey, then, up go we!

Whate'er the Popish hands have built
    Our hammers shall undo;
We'll break their pipes and burn their copes,
    And pull down churches too;
We'll exercise within the groves,
    And teach beneath a tree;
We'll make a pulpit of a cask,
    And hey, then, up go we!

We'll put down Universities,
    Where learning is professed,
Because they practise and maintain
    The language of the Beast;
We'll drive the doctors out of doors,
    And all that learned be;
We'll cry all arts and learning down,
    And hey, then, up go we!

We'll down with deans and prebends, too,
    And I rejoice to tell ye
We then shall get our fill of pig,
    And capons for the belly.
We'll burn the Fathers' weighty tomes,
    And make the Schoolmen free;
We'll down with all that smells of wit,
    And hey, then, up go we!

If once the Antichristian crew
    Be crushed and overthrown,
We'll teach the nobles how to stoop,
    And keep the gentry down.
Good manners have an ill report,
    And turn to pride, we see ;
We'll therefore put good manners down,
    And hey, then, up go we !

The name of lords shall be abhorred,
    For every man's a brother;
No reason why in Church and State
    One man should rule another ;
But, when the change of government
    Shall set our fingers free,
We'll make these wanton sisters stoop,
    And hey, then, up go we !

What though the King and Parliament
    Do not accord together,
We have more cause to be content,—
    This is our sunshine weather:
For, if that reason should take place,
    And they should once agree,
Who would be in a Roundhead's case?
    For hey, then, up go we !

What should we do, then, in this case?
    Let's put it to a venture ;
If that we hold out seven years' space
    We'll sue out our indenture.
A time may come to make us rue,
    And time may set us free,—
Except the gallows claim his due,
    And hey, then, up go we !

EDMUND WALLER.

[Born on 3d March 1605, died on 21st October 1687. Was not only an admired poet and man of fashion, but also an active though not highly consistent politician ; negociating for the Parliament, plotting for Charles I., lauding Cromwell, and acclaiming Charles II. As a poet, Waller is now chiefly remembered by his delightful lyric, "Go, lovely rose," and as the poetic suitor of "Saccharissa"—*i. e.*, Lady Dorothy Sidney, whom he courted, but did not secure in marriage].

AN EPIGRAM ON A PAINTED LADY WITH ILL TEETH.

WERE men so dull they could not see
That Lyce painted,—should they flee,
Like simple birds, into a net
So grossly woven and ill set,—
Her own teeth would undo the **knot,**
And let all go that she had got.

Those teeth fair Lyce must not show
If she would bite ; her lovers, though
Like birds they stoop at seeming grapes,
Are disabused when first she gapes ;
The rotten bones discovered there
Show 'tis a painted sepulchre.

THOMAS WASHBOURNE.

[Born in 1606, died in 1687. He belonged to a good Worcestershire family, entered holy orders, and was on the royalist side, in the contest between the parliament and the king. His volume of verse is named *Divine Poems*].

UPON THE PEOPLE'S DENYING OF TITHES IN SOME PLACES, AND EJECTING THEIR PASTORS.

THE shepherd heretofore did keep
    And watch the sheep :
Whiles they, poor creatures, did rejoice
    To hear his voice ;
But now, they, that were used to stray,
    Do know the way
So perfectly that they can guide
The shepherd when he goes aside.

To pay the tenth fleece they refuse,
    As shepherd's dues.
They know a trick worth two of that ;
    They can grow fat,
And wear their fleece on their own back,
    But let him lack
Meat, drink, and cloth, and everything
Which should support and comfort bring.

What silly animals be these,
    Themselves to please
With fancies that they nothing need,
    But safely feed
Without the shepherd's careful eye !
    When lo ! they die
Ere they be ware, being made a prey
Unto the wolf by night and day.

Besides, they're subject to the rot,
    And God knows what
Diseases more, which they endure,
    And none can cure
But the shepherd's skilful hand ;
    In need they stand
Of his physic and his power
To heal and help them every hour.

    The danger set before their eyes, —
        Let them be wise,
    Not trusting to their own direction
        Nor protection,
    But to his rod, his staff, submit;
        His art, his wit,
    For every sore a salve hath found,
    And will preserve them safe and sound.

SAMUEL BUTLER.

[The author of *Hudibras* was born in 1612 at Strensham, Worcestershire, son of a farmer; died in London, 25 September 1680].

THE ELEPHANT IN THE MOON.[1]

    A LEARN'D society of late,
    The glory of a foreign state,
    Agreed, upon a summer's night,
    To search the Moon by her own light;
    To make an inventory of all
    Her real estate, and personal;
    And make an accurate survey
    Of all her lands, and how they lay,
    As true as that of Ireland, where
    The sly surveyors stole a shire:[2]
    To observe her country, how 'twas planted,
    With what she abounded most, or wanted;
    And make the proper'st observations
    For settleing of new plantations,
    If the society should incline
    To attempt so glorious a design.
      This was the purpose of their meeting,
    For which they chose a time as fitting;
    When at the full her radiant light
    And influence too were at their height.
    And now the lofty tube, the scale
    With which they heaven itself assail,
    Was mounted full against the Moon;
    And all stood ready to fall on,
    Impatient who should have the honour
    To plant an ensign first upon her.
    When one,[3] who for his deep belief
    Was virtuoso then in chief,

---

[1] This is a satire on the Royal Society, first founded in 1645, and incorporated by royal charter in 1662. The notes here given are (very greatly) condensed from those in Mr. Robert Bell's careful edition of Butler.

[2] Probably an allusion to Sir William Petty, who was employed to take a survey of Ireland in Cromwell's time, and was afterwards impeached for mismanagement in the distribution and allotments of land.

[3] Lord Brouncker, the first President of the Royal Society under the charter. He was a zealous member, and distinguished himself as a mathematician.

Approved the most profound and wise
To solve impossibilities,
Advancing gravely, to apply
To the optic glass his judging eye,
Cried "Strange!"—then reinforced his sight
Against the Moon with all his might,
And bent his penetrating brow,
As if he meant to gaze her through ;
When all the rest began to admire,
And, like a train, from him took fire,
Surprised with wonder, beforehand,
At what they did not understand,
Cried out, impatient to know what
The matter was they wondered at.

   Quoth he, "The inhabitants o' the Moon;—
Who, when the Sun shines hot at noon,[1]
Do live in cellars under ground
Of eight miles deep and eighty round,
In which at once they fortify
Against the sun and the enemy,
Which they count towns and cities there,—
Because their people's civiller
Than those rude peasants that are found
To live upon the upper ground,
Called Privolvans,[2] with whom they are
Perpetually in open war.
And now both armies, highly enraged,
Are in a bloody fight engaged,
And many fall on both sides slain,
As by the glass 'tis clear and plain.
Look quickly then, that every one
May see the fight before 'tis done."

   With that a great philosopher,
Admired and famous far and near,[3]
As one of singular invention,
But universal comprehension,
Applied one eye and half a nose
Unto the optic engine close.
For he had lately undertook
To prove, and publish in a book,
That men whose natural eyes are out
May, by more powerful art, be brought

---

[1] The notion of digging caverns to seek shelter in from the great heat of the sun is a satire upon one of Kepler's speculations.

[2] Kepler called the earth *volva*, because of its diurnal revolutions; the inhabitants of the moon who live on the side facing the earth he named *Subvolvani*, because they enjoy the sight of our world ; and the others, who live on the opposite side, he named *Privolvani*, because they are deprived of that privilege.

[3] There is some reason to think that Sir Christopher Wren is here glanced at, but some of the details apply to Sir Kenelm Digby instead.

To see with the empty holes as plain
As if their eyes were in again,
And, if they chanced to fail of those,
To make an optic of a nose;
As clearly it may, by those that wear
But spectacles, be made appear;
By which both senses being united
Does render them much better-sighted.
This great man, having fixed both sights
To view the formidable heights,
Observed his best, and then cried out,—
"The battle's desperately fought;
The gallant Subvolvani rally,
And from their trenches make a sally
Upon the stubborn enemy,
Who now begin to rout and fly.
These silly ranting Privolvans
Have every summer their campaigns,
And muster, like the warlike sons
Of Rawhead and of Bloodybones,
As numerous as Soland geese
I' the islands of the Orcades,
Courageously to make a stand,
And face their neighbours hand to hand,
Until the longed-for winter's come;
And then return in triumph home,
And spend the rest o' the year in lies,
And vapouring of their victories.
From the old Arcadians they're believed
To be, before the Moon, derived;
And, when her orb was new created,
To people her were thence translated.
For, as the Arcadians were reputed
Of all the Grecians the most stupid,
Whom nothing in the world could bring
To civil life, but fiddleing,
They still retain the antique course
And custom of their ancestors;
And always sing and fiddle to
Things of the greatest weight they do."
    While thus the learn'd man entertains
The assembly with the Privolvans,
Another of as great renown
And solid judgment in the Moon,
That understood her various soils,
And which produced best genet-moyles,[1]

---

[1] A species of sweet apple, generally called moyle. This may be an allusion to Evelyn, who speaks of the genet-moyle in his *Pomona,* a treatise on fruit-trees annexed to the *Sylva,* published in 1664 "by express order of the Royal Society."

And in the register of fame
Had entered his long-living name,—
After he had pored long and hard
In the engine, gave a start, and stared.
    Quoth he : " A stranger sight appears
Than e'er was seen in all the spheres,
A wonder more unparallelled
Than ever mortal tube beheld;
An elephant from one of those
Two mighty armies is broke loose,[1]
And with the horror of the fight
Appears amazed, and in a fright ;
Look quickly, lest the sight of us
Should cause the startled beast to imboss.[2]
It is a large one, far more great
Than e'er was bred in Afric yet ;
From which we boldly may infer
The moon is much the fruitfuller.
And, since the mighty Pyrrhus brought
Those living castles first, 'tis thought,
Against the Romans in the field,
It may an argument be held
(Arcadia being but a piece,
As his dominions were, of Greece)
To prove what this illustrious person
Has made so noble a discourse on;
And amply satisfied us all
Of th' Privolvans' original.
That elephants are in the Moon,
Though we had now discovered none,
Is easily made manifest ;
Since, from the greatest to the least,
All other stars and constellations
Have cattle of all sorts of nations,
And heaven, like a Tartars' horde,
With great and numerous droves is stored :
And, if the Moon produce by nature
A people of so vast a stature,
'Tis consequent she should bring forth
Far greater beasts too than the earth,
As by the best accounts appears
Of all our great'st discoverers ;
And that those monstrous creatures there
Are not such rarities as here."
    Meanwhile the rest had had a sight
Of all particulars o' the fight ;

---

[1] The story is related of Sir Paul Neal, one of the early promoters of the Royal Society, who is said to have announced the discovery of an elephant in the moon, which turned out upon investigation to be a mouse that had got into the telescope.   [2] Properly imbosk, to hide in bushes.

And every man, with equal care,
Perused of the elephant his share,
Proud of his interest in the glory
Of so miraculous a story;
When one who, for his excellence
In heightening words and shadowing sense,
And magnifying all he writ
With curious microscopic wit,
Was magnified himself no less
In home and foreign colleges,[1]
Began, transported with the twang
Of his own trillo, thus t' harangue:
"Most excellent and virtuous friends,
This great discovery makes amends
For all our unsuccessful pains,
And lost expense of time and brains.
For, by this sole phenomenon,
We have gotten ground upon the Moon;
And gained a pass, to hold dispute
With all the planets that stand out;
To carry this most virtuous war
Home to the door of every star,
And plant the artillery of our tubes
Against their proudest magnitudes;
To stretch our victories beyond
The extent of planetary ground;
And fix our engines and our ensigns
Upon the fixed stars' vast dimensions,—
Which Archimede, so long ago,
Durst not presume to wish to do,—
And prove if they are other suns,
As some have held opinions,
Or windows in the empyreum,
From whence those bright effluvias come—
Like flames of fire, as others guess,
That shine i' the mouths of furnaces.
Nor is this all we have achieved,
But more, henceforth to be believed,
And have no more our best designs,
Because they're ours, believed ill signs.
To out-throw, and stretch, and to enlarge,
Shall now no more be laid t' our charge;
Nor shall our ablest virtuosos
Prove arguments for coffeehouses;
Nor those devices that are laid
Too truly on us, nor those made
Hereafter, gain belief among
Our strictest judges, right or wrong;

---

[1] Dr. Hooke, whose microscopical speculations excited considerable notice and discussion, appears to be indicated here.

Nor shall our past misfortunes more
Be charged upon the ancient score;
No more our making old dogs young[1]
Make men suspect us still i' the wrong;
Nor new-invented chariots draw
The boys to course us, without law;
Nor putting pigs to a bitch to nurse,
To turn 'em into mongrel-curs,
Make them suspect our sculls are brittle,
And hold too much wit, or too little;
Nor shall our speculations whether
An elder-stick will save the leather
Of schoolboys' breeches from the rod[2]
Make all we do appear as odd.
This one discovery's enough
To take all former scandals off.
But, since the world's incredulous
Of all our scrutinies, and us,
And with a prejudice prevents
Our best and worst experiments,
As if th' were destined to miscarry,
In consort tried, or solitary,—
And since it is uncertain when
Such wonders will occur again,—
Let us as cautiously contrive
To draw an exact narrative
Of what we every one can swear
Our eyes themselves have seen appear,
That, when we publish the account,
We all may take our oaths upon't."

This said, they all with one consent
Agreed to draw up th' instrument,
And, for the general satisfaction,
To print it in the next "Transaction."

But, whilst the chiefs were drawing up
This strange memoir o' the telescope,
One, peeping in the tube by chance,
Beheld the elephant advance,
And from the west side of the Moon
To the east was in a moment gone.
This, being related, gave a stop
To what the rest were drawing up;
And every man, amazed anew
How it could possibly be true
That any beast should run a race

---

[1] This was one of the experiments actually made under the direction of the Society in 1666, by transfusion of blood from one dog into another.

[2] The allusion is to the custom of wearing a sprig of elder in the breeches-pocket, as an effectual preventive against what is called losing leather, or galling, in riding.

So monstrous in so short a space,
Resolved, howe'er, to make it good,—
At least, as possible as he could ;
And rather his own eyes condemn
Than question what he had seen with them.
   While all were thus resolved, a man
Of great renown there thus began :—
  " 'Tis strange, I grant ! But who can say
What cannot be, what can and may ?
Especially at so hugely vast
A distance as this wonder's placed ;
Where the least error of the sight
May show things false, but never right ;
Nor can we try them, so far off,
By any sublunary proof.
For who can say that nature there
Has the same laws she goes by here ?
Nor is it like she has infused,
In every species there produced,
The same efforts she doth confer
Upon the same productions here :
Since those with us, of several nations,
Have such prodigious variations,
And she affects so much to use
Variety in all she does.
Hence may be inferred that, though I grant
We've seen i' the Moon an elephant,
That elephant may differ so
From those upon the earth below,
Both in his bulk and force and speed,
As being of a different breed,
That, though our own are but slow-paced,
Theirs there may fly, or run as fast,—
And yet be elephants no less
Than those of Indian pedigrees."
   This said, another of great worth,
Famed for his learned works, put forth,
Looked wise, then said—" All this is true,
And learnedly observed by you ;
But there's another reason for't,
That falls but very little short
Of mathematic demonstration,
Upon an accurate calculation:
And that is—As the Earth and Moon
Do both move contrary upon
Their axes, the rapidity
Of both their motions cannot be
But so prodigiously fast
That vaster spaces may be passed
In less time than the beast has gone,

Though he had no motion of his own;
Which we can take no measure of,
As you have cleared by learned proof.
This granted, we may boldly thence
Lay claim to a nobler inference;
And make this great phenomenon,
Were there no other, serve alone
To clear the grand hypothesis
Of the motion of the Earth, from this."
   With this they all were satisfied,
As men are wont o' the biased side;
Applauded the profound dispute;
And grew more gay and resolute,
By having overcome all doubt,
Than if it never had fallen out;
And, to complete their narrative,
Agreed to insert this strange retrieve.
   But, while they were diverted all
With wording the memorial,
The footboys, for diversion too,
As having nothing else to do,
Seeing the telescope at leisure,
Turned virtuosos for their pleasure;
Began to gaze upon the Moon,
As those they waited on had done,
With monkeys' ingenuity
That love to practise what they see.
When one, whose turn it was to peep,
Saw something in the engine creep;
And, viewing well, discovered more
Than all the learn'd had done before.
Quoth he; "A little thing is slunk
Into the long star-gazing trunk;
And now is gotten down so nigh
I have him just against mine eye."
   This being overheard by one
Who was not so far overgrown
In any virtuous speculation
To judge with mere imagination,
Immediately he made a guess
At solving all appearances,—
A way far more significant
Than all their hints of the elephant;
And found, upon a second view,
His own hypothesis most true.
For he had scarce applied his eye
To the engine, but immediately
He found a mouse was gotten in
The hollow tube, and, shut between
The two glass windows in restraint,

Was swelled into an elephant;
And proved the virtuous occasion
Of all this learned dissertation:
And, as a mountain heretofore
Was great with child, they say, and bore
A silly mouse, this mouse, as strange,
Brought forth a mountain, in exchange.
 Meanwhile, the rest in consultation
Had penned the wonderful narration;
And set their hands, and seals, and wit,
To attest the truth of what they'd writ;
When this accurst phenomenon
Confounded all they'd said or done.
For 'twas no sooner hinted at
But th' all were in a tumult straight,
More furiously enraged by far
Than those that in the Moon made war,
To find so admirable a hint,
When they had all agreed to have seen't,
And were engaged to make it out,
Obstructed with a paltry doubt.
When one whose task was to determine
And solve the appearances of vermin,
Who'd made profound discoveries
In frogs and toads and rats and mice[1]
(Though not so curious, 'tis true,
As many a wise rat-catcher knew),
After he had with signs made way
For something great he had to say,
[2]At last quoth he: "This disquisition
Is, half of it, in my discission;
For, though the elephant, as beast,
Belongs of right to all the rest,
The mouse, being but a vermin, none
Has title to but I alone;
And therefore hope I may be heard,
In my own province, with regard.
It is no wonder we're cried down,
And made the talk of all the town,
That rants and swears, for all our great
Attempts, we have done nothing yet,
If every one have leave to doubt
When some great secret's half made out;
And, 'cause perhaps it is not true,
Obstruct and ruin all we do.
As no great act was ever done,
Nor ever can, with truth alone,

---

[1] It is probable that Digby was chiefly pointed at here.
[2] These four words appear in a second version of this poem, written by Butler. In the first version, as ordinarily printed, there is a gap.

If nothing else but truth we allow,
'Tis no great matter what we do.
For truth is too reserved and nice
To appear in mixed societies;
Delights in solitary abodes,
And never shows herself in crowds;
A sullen little thing, below
All matters of pretence and show
That deal in novelty and change,—
Not of things true, but rare and strange,
To treat the world with what is fit
And proper to its natural wit;
The world, that never sets esteem
On what things are, but what they seem,
And, if they be not strange and new,
They're ne'er the better for being true.
For what has mankind gained by knowing
His little truth, but his undoing,
Which wisely was by nature hidden,
And only for his good forbidden?
And therefore with great prudence does
The world still strive to keep it close;
For, if all secret truths were known,
Who would not be once more undone?
For truth has always danger in't,
And here, perhaps, may cross some hint
We have already agreed upon,
And vainly frustrate all we've done,
Only to make new work for Stubbes,[1]
And all the academic clubs.
How much then ought we have a care
That no man know above his share,
Nor dare to understand henceforth
More than his contribution's worth;[2]
That those who've purchased of the college
A share or half a share of knowledge,
And brought in none, but spent repute,
Should not be admitted to dispute,
Nor any man pretend to know
More than his dividend comes to;
For partners have been always known
To cheat their public interest prone;
And, if we do not look to ours,
'Tis sure to run the self-same course."
 This said, the whole assembly allowed
The doctrine to be right and good;
And, from the truth of what they'd heard,

---

[1] Henry Stubbe, a physician, one of the ablest opponents of the Royal Society.
[2] The contribution to the Society was one shilling weekly.

Resolved to give truth no regard,
But what was for their turn to vouch,
And either find or make it such:
That 'twas more noble to create
Things like truth, out of strong conceit,
Than, with vexatious pains and doubt,
To find or think to have found her out.
   This being resolved, they, one by one,
Reviewed the tube, the mouse, and moon;
But still, the narrower they pried,
The more they were unsatisfied,—
In no one thing they saw agreeing,
As if they'd several faiths of seeing.
Some swore, upon a second view,
That all they'd seen before was true,
And that they never would recant
One syllable of the elephant;
Avowed his snout could be no mouse's,
But a true elephant's proboscis.
Others began to doubt and waver,
Uncertain which o' the two to favour;
And knew not whether to espouse
The cause of the elephant or mouse.
Some held no way so orthodox
To try it as the ballot-box,
And, like the nation's patriots,
To find, or make, the truth by votes.
Others conceived it much more fit
To unmount the tube, and open it;
And, for their private satisfaction,
To re-examine the "Transaction,"
And after explicate the rest,
As they should find cause for the best.
   To this, as the only expedient,
The whole assembly gave consent;
But, ere the tube was half let down,
It cleared the first phenomenon;
For, at the end, prodigious swarms
Of flies and gnats, like men in arms,
Had all passed muster, by mischance,
Both for the Sub- and Pri-volvans.
This, being discovered, put them all
Into a fresh and fiercer brawl,
Ashamed that men so grave and wise
Should be caldesed[1] by gnats and flies,
And take the feeble insects' swarms
For mighty troops of men at arms;
As vain as those who, when the Moon

---

[1] Chaldeized, juggled.

Bright in a crystal river shone,
Threw casting-nets as subtly at her,
To catch and pull her out o' the water.
But, when they had unscrewed the glass
To find out where the impostor was,
And saw the mouse, that by mishap
Had made the telescope a trap,
Amazed, confounded, and afflicted,
To be so openly convicted,
Immediately they get them gone,—
With this discovery alone:
That those who greedily pursue
Things wonderful, instead of true,
That in their speculations choose
To make discoveries strange news,
And natural history a gazette
Of tales stupendous and far-fet,—
Hold no truth worthy to be known
That is not huge and overgrown,
And explicate appearances
Not as they are but as they please,—
In vain strive Nature to suborn,
And for their pains are paid with scorn.

UPON PLAGIARIES.

Why should the world be so averse
To plagiary privateers,
That all men's sense and fancy seize,
And make free prize of what they please?
As if, because they huff and swell,
Like pilferers full of what they steal,
Others might equal power assume
To pay 'em with as hard a doom;
To shut them up, like beasts in pounds,
For breaking into others' grounds;
Mark 'em with characters and brands,
Like other forgers of men's hands;
And in effigy hang and draw
The poor delinquents by club-law;
When no indictment justly lies,
But where the theft will bear a price.
   For, though wit never can be learned,
It may be assumed, and owned, and earned;
And, like our noblest fruits, improved
By being transplanted and removed.
And, as it bears no certain rate,
Nor pays one penny to the state,
With which it turns no more to account
Than virtue, faith, and merit's wont;

Is neither moveable nor rent,
Nor chattel, goods, nor tenement;
Nor was it ever passed by entail,
Nor settled upon the heirs-male,
Or, if it were, like ill-got land,
Did never fall to a second hand;—
So 'tis no more to be engrossed
Than sunshine, or the air enclosed,
Or to propriety confined
Than the uncontrolled and scattered wind.
   For why should that which Nature meant
To owe its being to its vent,
That has no value of its own,
But as it is divulged and known,
Is perishable and destroyed
As long as it lies unenjoyed,
Be scanted of that liberal use
Which all mankind is free to choose,
And idly hoarded where 'twas bred,
Instead of being dispersed and spread?
And, the more lavish and profuse,
'Tis of the nobler general use;
As riots, though supplied by stealth,
Are wholesome to the commonwealth,
And men spend freelier what they win
Than what they've freely coming in.
   The world's as full of curious wit
Which those that father never writ
As 'tis of bastards which the sot
And cuckold owns that ne'er begot,
Yet pass as well as if the one
And the other by-blow were their own.
For why should he that's impotent
To judge, and fancy, and invent,
For that impediment be stopped
To own and challenge and adopt
At least the exposed and fatherless
Poor orphans of the pen and press,
Whose parents are obscure, or dead,
Or in far countries born and bred?
   As none but kings have power to raise
A levy which the subject pays,
And, though they call that tax a loan,
Yet, when 'tis gathered, 'tis their own;
So he that's able to impose
A wit-excise on verse or prose,
And, still the abler authors are,
Can make them pay the greater share,
Is prince of poets of his time,
And they his vassals, that supply'm

Can judge more justly of what he takes
Than any of the best he makes,
And more impartially conceive
What's fit to choose and what to leave.
For men reflect more strictly upon
The sense of others than their own;
And wit that's made of wit and sleight
Is richer than the plain downright:
As salt that's made of salt's more fine
Than when it first came from the brine,
And spirit's of a nobler nature,
Drawn from the dull ingredient matter.
   Hence mighty Virgil's said, of old,
From dung to have extracted gold,—
As many a lout and silly clown,
By his instructions, since has done,—
And grew more lofty by that means
Than by his livery-oats and beans,
When from his carts and country-farms
He rose a mighty man at arms;
To whom th' heroics ever since
Have sworn allegiance as their prince,
And faithfully have in all times
Observed his customs in their rhymes.
   'Twas counted learning once and wit
To void but what some author writ,
And what men understand by rote
By as implicit sense to quote.
Then many a magisterial clerk
Was taught, like singing birds, i' the dark,
And understood as much of things
As the ablest blackbird what it sings,
And yet was honoured and renowned
For grave and solid and profound.
Then why should those who pick and choose
The best of all the best compose,
And join it, by mosaic art,
In graceful order, part to part,
To make the whole in beauty suit,
Not merit as complete repute
As those who, with less art and pains,
Can do it with their native brains,
And make the home-spun business fit
As freely with their mother-wit?
Since what by Nature was denied
By art and industry's supplied,—
Both which are more our own, and brave,
Than all the alms that Nature gave.
For what we acquire by pains and art
Is only due to our own desert;

While all the endowments she confers
Are not so much our own as hers,
That, like good fortune, unawares
Fall not to our virtue, but our shares,
And all we can pretend to merit
We do not purchase, but inherit.
 Thus all the great'st inventions, when
They first were found out, were so mean
That the authors of them are unknown,
As little things they scorned to own;
Until by men of nobler thought
Th' were to their full perfection brought.
This proves that wit does but rough-hew,
Leaves art to polish and review,
And that a wit at second hand
Has greatest interest and command;
For to improve, dispose, and judge,
Is nobler than to invent and drudge.
 Invention's humorous and nice,
And never at command applies;
Disdains to obey the proudest wit,
Unless it chance to be in the fit,—
Like prophecy, that can presage
Successes of the latest age,
Yet is not able to tell when
It next shall prophesy again;
Makes all her suitors course and wait
Like a proud minister of state,
And, when she's serious in some freak,
Extravagant and vain and weak,
Attend her silly lazy pleasure,
Until she chance to be at leisure;
When 'tis more easy to steal wit.
To clip, and forge, and counterfeit,
Is both the business and delight,
Like hunting-sports, of those that write;
For thievery is but one sort,
The learned say, of hunting-sport.
 Hence 'tis that some who set up first
As raw and wretched and unversed,
And opened with a stock as poor
As a healthy beggar with one sore;
That never writ in prose or verse,
But picked or cut it, like a purse,
And at the best could but commit
The petty-larceny of wit;
To whom to write was to purloin,
And printing but to stamp false coin;
Yet, after long and sturdy endeavours
Of being painful wit-receivers,

With gathering rags and scraps of wit
(As paper's made, on which 'tis writ),
Have gone forth authors, and acquired
The right—or wrong—to be admired;
And, armed with confidence, incurred
The fool's good luck, to be preferred.
   For, as a banker can dispose
Of greater sums he only owes
Than he who honestly is known
To deal in nothing but his own,
So whosoe'er can take up most
May greatest fame and credit boast.

UPON MODERN CRITICS.
A PINDARIC ODE.

'Tis well that equal Heaven has placed
  Those joys above that to reward
  The just and virtuous are prepared,
Beyond their reach until their pains are past;
Else men would rather venture to possess
    By force, than earn, their happiness;
    And only take the devil's advice,
As Adam did, how soonest to be wise,
   Though at the expense of Paradise.
For, as some say to fight is but a base
  Mechanic handiwork, and far below
    A generous spirit to undergo,
    So 'tis to take the pains to know,—
Which some, with only confidence and face,
    More easily and ably do;
For daring nonsense seldom fails to hit,
Like scattered shot, and pass with some for wit.
Who would not rather make himself a judge,
     And boldly usurp the chair,
    Than with dull industry and care
    Endure to study, think, and drudge,
For that which he much sooner may advance
With obstinate and pertinacious ignorance?

    For all men challenge, though in spite
    Of Nature and their stars, a right
      To censure, judge, and know;
    Though *she* can only order who
     Shall be, and who shall ne'er be, wise.
      Then why should those whom she denies
    Her favour and good graces to
Not strive to take opinion by surprise,
And ravish what it were in vain to woo?
    For he that desperately assumes

  The censure of all wits and arts,
  Though without judgment, skill, and parts,
   Only to startle and amuse,
And mask his ignorance, as Indians use
    With gaudy-coloured plumes
  Their homely nether parts to adorn,
   Can never fail to captive some,
That will submit to his oraculous doom,
  And reverence what they ought to scorn;
  Admire his sturdy confidence
   For solid judgment and deep sense;—
And credit purchased without pains or wit,
Like stolen pleasures, ought to be most sweet.

  Two self-admirers, that combine
  Against the world, may pass a fine[1]
  Upon all judgment, sense, and wit,
   And settle it, as they think fit,
   On one another, like the choice
Of Persian princes by one horse's voice.[2]
  For those fine pageants, which some raise,
   Of false and disproportioned praise,
  To enable whom they please to appear
  And pass for what they never were,
   In private only being but named,
   Their modesty must be ashamed,[3]
    And not endure to hear;
  And yet may be divulged and famed,
   And owned in public everywhere.
  So vain some authors are to boast
Their want of ingenuity, and club
   Their affidavit wits, to dub
  Each other but a Knight o' the Post,
  As false as suborned perjurers,
That vouch away all right they have to their own ears.

  But, when all other courses fail,
   There is one easy artifice
  That seldom has been known to miss,—
  To cry all mankind down, and rail:
  For he whom all men do contemn
May be allowed to rail again at them,
   And in his own defence
  To outface reason, wit, and sense,

---

[1] A mode of changing or alienating real property. The phrase is most usually adopted when a person has a limited interest in an estate, and, wishing to divest himself of a reversionary interest in it, settles the whole on himself absolutely. And this is the sense in which Butler here uses it.

[2] The well-known story of the election of Darius.

[3] Alluding to the custom of ushering books of poetry to the public with commendatory verses.

And all that makes against himself condemn;
  To snarl at all things right or wrong,
Like a mad dog that has a worm in his tongue;
Reduce all knowledge back of good and evil
  To its first original, the devil;
And, like a fierce inquisitor of wit,
To spare no flesh that ever spoke or writ;
  Though, to perform his task, as dull
As if he had a toadstone in his skull,
  And could produce a greater stock
Of maggots than a pastoral poet's flock.

  The feeblest vermin can destroy,
  As sure as stoutest beasts of prey;
  And only with their eyes and breath
  Infect and poison men to death.
  But that more impotent buffoon
That makes it both his business and his sport
  To rail at all is but a drone,
That spends his sting on what he cannot hurt;
Enjoys a kind of lechery in spite,
Like o'ergrown sinners that in whipping take delight;
  Invades the reputation of all those
    That have, or have it not, to lose:
And, if he chance to make a difference,
  'Tis always in the wrongest sense:
  As rooking gamesters never lay
  Upon those hands that use fair play,
    But venture all their bets
Upon the slurs and cunning tricks of ablest cheats.

  Nor does he vex himself much less
    Than all the world beside,
  Falls sick of other men's excess,
    Is humbled only at their pride,
  And wretched at their happiness;
  Revenges on himself the wrong
  Which his vain malice and loose tongue
  To those that feel it not have done;
And whips and spurs himself, because he is outgone;
  Makes idle characters and tales,
    As counterfeit, unlike, and false,
As witches' pictures are, of wax and clay,
To those whom they would in effigy slay.
And as the devil, that has no shape of his own,
  Affects to put the ugliest on,
And leaves a stink behind him when he's gone:
So he that's worse than nothing strives to appear
    I' the likeness of a wolf or bear,
    To fright the weak; but, when men dare
Encounter with him, stinks, and vanishes to air.

A PALINODE TO THE HONOURABLE EDWARD HOWARD, ESQ.

UPON HIS INCOMPARABLE POEM OF "THE BRITISH PRINCES."

It is your pardon, sir, for which my Muse
Thrice humbly thus, in form of paper, sues;
For, having felt the dead weight of your wit,
She comes to ask forgiveness, and submit;
Is sorry for her faults, and, while I write,
Mourns in the black, does penance in the white:
But such is her belief in your just candour,
She hopes you will not so misunderstand her
To wrest her harmless meaning to the sense
Of silly emulation or offence.
No: your sufficient wit does still declare
Itself too amply; they are mad that dare
So vain and senseless a presumption own
To yoke your vast parts in comparison.
And yet you might have thought upon a way
To instruct us how you'd have us to obey;
And not command our praises, and then blame
All that's too great or little for your fame;[1]
For who could choose but err, without some trick
To take your elevation to a nick?
As he that was desired, upon occasion,
To make the Mayor of London an oration,
Desired his lordship's favour that he might
Take measure of his mouth, to fit it right;
So, had you sent a scantling of your wit,
You might have blamed us if it did not fit;
But 'tis not just to impose, and then cry down
All that's unequal to your huge renown;
For he that writes below your vast desert
Betrays his own, and not your, want of art.
Praise, like a robe of state, should not sit close
To the person 'tis made for, but, wide and loose,
Derives its comeliness from being unfit;
And such have been our praises of your wit,
Which is so extraordinary no height
Of fancy, but your own, can do it right;
Witness those glorious poems you have writ
With equal judgment, learning, art, and wit,
And those stupendious discoveries
You've lately made of wonders in the skies.
For who, but from yourself, did ever hear
The "sphere of atoms" was the "atmosphere?"[2]

---

[1] Mr. Howard was very angry with his critics, and particularly with those who ridiculed him under the disguise of burlesque panegyric.

[2] A space transparent entertains the eye;
The sphere of atoms called.
British Princes.

Who ever shut those stragglers in a room,
Or put a circle about *vacuum*,
That should confine those undetermined crowds,
And yet extend no further than the clouds?
Who ever could have thought, but you alone,
A "sign" and an "ascendant" were all one?
Or how 'tis possible the Moon should shroud
Her face, to peep at Mars, behind a cloud;
Since clouds below are so far distant placed
They cannot hinder her from being barefaced?
Who ever did a language so enrich
To scorn all little particles of speech?
For, though they make the sense clear, yet they're found
To be a scurvy hindrance to the sound;
Therefore you wisely scorn your style to humble,
Or for the sense's sake to waive the rumble.
Had Homer known this art, he had ne'er been fain
To use so many particles in vain,
That to no purpose serve but as he haps
To want a syllable to fill up gaps.
You justly coin new verbs, to pay for those
Which in construction you o'ersee and lose;
And by this art do Priscïan no wrong
When you break's head, for 'tis as broad as long.
These are your own discoveries, which none
But such a Muse as yours could hit upon,
That can, in spite of laws of art or rules,
Make things more intricate than all the schools:
For what have laws of art to do with you,
More than the laws with honest men and true?
He that's a prince in poetry should strive
To cry 'em down, by his prerogative,
And not submit to that which has no force
But o'er delinquents and inferiors.
Your poems will endure to be tried
I' the fire like gold, and come forth purified;
Can only to eternity pretend,
For they were never writ to any end.
All other books bear an uncertain rate;
But those *you* write are always sold by weight,—
Each word and syllable brought to the scale,
And valued to a scruple in the sale.
For, when the paper's charged with your rich wit,
'Tis for all purposes and uses fit;
Has an abstersive virtue to make clean
Whatever nature made in man obscene;
Boys find, by experiment, no paper kite,
Without your verse, can make a noble flight;
It keeps our spice and aromatics sweet;
In Paris they perfume their rooms with it:

For burning but one leaf of yours, they say,
Drives all their stinks and nastiness away.
Cooks keep their pies from burning with your wit,
Their pigs and geese from scorching on the spit;
And vintners find their wines are ne'er the worse,
When arsenic's only wrapped up in the verse.
These are the great performances that raise
Your mighty parts above all reach of praise,
And give us only leave to admire your worth;
For no man but yourself can set it forth,—
Whose wondrous power's so generally known,
Fame is the echo, and her voice your own.

DESCRIPTION OF HOLLAND.[1]

A COUNTRY that draws fifty foot of water,
In which men live as in the hold of Nature;
And, when the sea does in upon them break,
And drown a province, does but spring a leak;
That always ply the pump, and never think
They can be safe, but at the rate they stink;[2]
That live as if they had been run aground,
And, when they die, are cast away and drowned;
That dwell in ships, like swarms of rats, and prey
Upon the goods all other nations' fleets convey;
And, when their merchants are blown up and cracked,
Whole towns are cast away in storms and wrecked;
That feed, like cannibals, on other fishes,
And serve their cousin-germans up in dishes.
A land that rides at anchor, and is moored;
In which they do not live, but go aboard.

REGAL ADULATION.

IN foreign universities,
When a king's born, or weds, or dies,
Straight other studies are laid by,
And all apply to poetry.
Some write in Hebrew, some in Greek;
And some, more wise, in Arabic,
To avoid the critic, and the expense
Of difficulter wit and sense,
And seem more learnedish than those

---

[1] Compare these verses with the *Character of Holland*, by Marvell, p. 141. Butler's lines had not been published during Marvell's lifetime.
[2] Should this word be "sink"? If so, the sense appears to be that the Hollanders do not so much as think of being absolutely safe, but only think (reckon) at what rate they are sinking: if that rate is slow, they have to be contented. If "stink" is correct, I do not seize the sense.

That at a greater charge compose.
The doctors lead, the students follow;
Some call him Mars, and some Apollo,
Some Jupiter, and give him the odds,
On even terms, of all the gods.
Then Cæsar he's nicknamed,—as duly as
He that in Rome was christened Julius,
And was addressed to by a crow
As pertinently long ago,—
And with more heroes' names is styled
Than saints' are clubbed to an Austrian child.
And, as wit goes by colleges,
As well as standing and degrees,
He still writes better than the rest
That's of the house that's counted best.

FEAR.

There needs no other charm nor conjurer,
To raise infernal spirits up, but fear;
That makes men pull their horns in, like a snail,
That's both a prisoner to itself, and jail;
Draws more fantastic shapes than in the grains
Of knotted wood, in some men's crazy brains;
When all the cocks they think they see, and bulls,
Are only in the inside of their skulls.

A JUBILEE.

A jubilee is but a spiritual fair
To expose to sale all sorts of impious ware;
In which his Holiness buys nothing in
To stock his magazines, but deadly sin,
And deals in extraordinary crimes,
That are not vendible at other times;
For, dealing both for Judas and th' High-Priest,
He makes a plentifuller trade of Christ.

SCRIBBLERS.

As he that makes his mark is understood
To write his name, and 'tis in law as good:
So he that cannot write one word of sense
Believes he has as legal a pretence
To scribble what he does not understand
As idiots have a title to their land.

SIR JOHN SUCKLING.

[Born in 1613, son of the Controller of the Household to Charles I. ; died in 1641. An elegant courtier, and man of gallantry and wit. He saw some service under Gustavus Adolphus, and raised a troop of horse in the cause of Charles I., but with no successful result].

SIR J. S.

Out upon it, I have loved
    Three whole days together ;
And am like to love three more,
    If it prove fair weather.

Time shall moult away his wings,
    Ere he shall discover
In the whole wide world again
    Such a constant Lover.

But the spite on't is, no praise
    Is due at all to me :
Love with me had made no stays,
    Had it any been but she.

Had it any been but she,
    And that very face,
There had been at least ere this
    A dozen dozen in her place.

LOVE AND DEBT ALIKE TROUBLESOME.

This one request I make to him that sits the clouds above,—
That I were freely out of debt, as I am out of love.
Then for to dance, to drink and sing, I should be very willing ;
I should not owe one lass a kiss, nor ne'er a knave a shilling.
'Tis only being in love and debt that breaks us of our rest ;
And he that is quite out of both of all the world is blest :
He sees the Golden Age wherein all things were free and common ;
He eats, he drinks, he takes his rest, he fears no man nor woman.
Though Crœsus compassèd great wealth, yet he still cravèd more ;
He was as needy a beggar still as goes from door to door.
Though Ovid was a merry man, love ever kept him sad ;
He was as far from happiness as one that is stark mad.
Our merchant he in goods is rich, and full of gold and treasure ;
But, when he thinks upon his debts, that thought destroys his
    pleasure.
Our courtier thinks that he's preferred, whom every man envies ;
When love so rumbles in his pate, no sleep comes in his eyes.
Our Gallant's case is worst of all, he lies so just betwixt them ;
For he's in love, and he's in debt, and knows not which most vex
    him.
But he that can eat beef, and feed on bread which is so brown,
May satisfy his appetite, and owe no man a crown :

And he that is content with lasses clothèd in plain woollen
May cool his heat in every place ; he need not to be sullen,
Nor sigh for love of lady fair ; for this each wise man knows,—
As good stuff under flannel lies as under silken clothes.

UPON THE BLACK SPOTS WORN BY MY LADY D.

I KNOW your heart cannot so guilty be
That you should wear those spots for vanity ;
Or, as your beauty's trophies, put on one
For every murder which your eyes have done.
No, they're your mourning-weeds for hearts forlorn,
Which, though you must not love, you could not scorn ;
To whom since cruel honour does deny
Those joys could only cure their misery,
Yet you this noble way to grace 'em found,
Whilst thus your grief their martyrdom has crowned :—
Of which take heed you prove not prodigal ;
For, if to every common funeral,
By your eyes martyred, such grace were allowed,
Your face would wear not patches, but a cloud.

THE METAMORPHOSIS.

THE little boy to show his might and power,
Turned Io to a cow, Narcissus to a flower ;
Transformed Apollo to a homely swain,
And Jove himself into a golden rain.
These shapes were tolerable ; but, by the mass,
He has metamorphosed me into an ass !

JOHN CLEVELAND.

[Born at Loughborough in 1613, son of a clergyman ; died in London in 1658. Cleveland is said to have been the first champion in verse of the cause of Charles I., when the parliamentary struggle began. He was imprisoned for awhile, but had been set at large some time before his death. A satire named *The Rebel Scots* is his principal performance].

THE LONG PARLIAMENT.

MOST gracious and omnipotent
And everlasting Parliament,
  Whose power and majesty
Are greater than all kings' by odds,—
And to account you less than gods
  Must needs be blasphemy,—

Moses and Aaron ne'er did do
More wonder than is wrought by you
  For England's Israel ;

But, though the Red Sea we have passed,
If you to Canaan bring's at last,
   Is't not a miracle?

In six years' space you have done more
Than all the parliaments before;
   You have quite done the work.
The King, the Cavalier, and Pope,
You have o'erthrown, and next we hope
   You will confound the Turk.

By you we have deliverance
From the design of Spain and France,
   Ormond, Montrose, the Danes;
You, aided by our brethren Scots,
Defeated have malignant plots,
   And brought your sword to Cain's.

What wholesome laws you have ordained
Whereby our property's maintained
   'Gainst those would us undo!
So that our fortunes and our lives—
Nay, what is dearer, our own wives—
   Are wholly kept by you.

Oh what a flourishing Church and State
Have we enjoyed e'er since you sate!
   What a glorious King (God save him!)
Have you not made his Majesty,—
Had he the grace but to comply,
   And do as you would have him!

Your *Directory* how to pray
By the Spirit shows the perfect way;
   In zeal you have abolished
The Dagon of the *Common Prayer*,
And next we see you will take care
   That churches be demolished.

A multitude, in every trade,
Of painful preachers you have made,
   Learned by revelation;
Cambridge and Oxford made poor preachers,
Each shop affordeth better teachers,—
   Oh blessed reformation!

Your godly wisdom hath found out
The true religion, without doubt;
   For sure among so many
(We have five hundred at the least)
Is not the gospel much increased?
   All must be pure, if any.

Could you have done more piously
Than sell church-lands the King to buy,
   And stop the city's plaints?
Paying the Scots' church-militant,
That the new gospel helped to plant;
   God knows they are poor saints!

Because the Apostles' Creed is lame,
The Assembly doth a better frame,
   Which saves us all with ease;
Provided still we have the grace
To believe the House in the first place,
   Our works be what they please.

'Tis strange your power and holiness
Can't the Irish devils dispossess,
   His end is very stout:
But, though you do so often pray,
And every month keep fasting-day,
   You cannot cast them out.

THE PURITAN.

With face and fashion to be known
For one of sure election;
With eyes all white, and many a groan;
With neck aside to draw in tone;
With harp in's nose, or he is none:
   See a new teacher of the town,
   Oh the town, oh the town's new teacher!

With pate cut shorter than the brow;
With little ruff starched, you know how;
With cloak like Paul, no cape I trow;
With surplice none, but lately now;
With hands to thump, no knees to bow:
   See a new teacher, &c.

With cozening cough, and hollow cheek,
To get new gatherings every week;
With paltry change of *and* to *eke;*
With some small Hebrew, and no Greek,
To find out words, when stuff's to seek:
   See a new teacher, &c.

With shop-board breeding and intrusion;
With some outlandish institution;
With Ursine's catechism to muse on;
With system's method for confusion;
With grounds strong laid of mere illusion:
   See a new teacher, &c.

With rites indifferent all damnèd,
And made unlawful if commanded,
Good works of Popery down banded,
And moral laws from him estrangèd,
Except the Sabbath still unchangèd :
    See a new teacher, &c.

With speech unthought, quick revelation ;
With boldness in predestination ;
With threats of absolute damnation,—
Yet *Yea*-and-*Nay* hath some salvation
For his own tribe, not every nation :
    See a new teacher, &c.

With after-license cost a crown,
When Bishop new had put him down ;
With tricks called repetition,
And doctrine, newly brought to town,
Of teaching men to hang and drown :
    See a new teacher, &c.

With flesh-provision to keep Lent ;
With shelves of sweetmeats often spent,
Which new maid bought, old lady sent,—
Though, to be saved, a poor presènt,
Yet legacies assure to event :
    See a new teacher, &c.

With troops expecting him at the door,
That would hear sermons, and no more,—
With noting-tools, and sighs great store,
With Bibles great, to turn them o'er,
While he wrests places by the score :
    See a new teacher, &c.

With running text, the named forsaken ;
With *for* and *but*, both by sense shaken,
Cheap doctrines forced, wild uses taken,
Both sometimes one by mark mistaken ;
With anything to any shapen :
    See a new teacher, &c.

With new-wrought caps, against the canon,
For taking cold, though sure he ha' none ;
A sermon's end where he began one
A new hour long, when's glass had ran one ;
New use, new points, new notes to stand on :
    See a new teacher, &c.

R. WATKYNS.

[Author of *Flamma sine Fumo*, published in 1662].

BLACK PATCHES—VANITAS VANITATUM.

Ladies turn conjurers, and can impart
The hidden mystery of the black art;
Black artificial patches do betray
They more affect the works of night than day.
The creature strives the Creator to disgrace,
By patching that which is a perfect face.
A little stain upon the purest dye
Is both offensive to the heart and eye:
Defile not then with spots that face of snow,
Where the wise God His workmanship doth show.
The light of nature and the light of grace
Is the complexion for a lady's face.

SIR JOHN DENHAM.

[Born in Dublin, of an English family, in 1615; died in 1668. The author of the descriptive poem of *Cooper's Hill* was in his own day admired also as a playwright, in virtue of his tragedy, *The Sophy*. He was noted moreover as a gambler, and he rendered some important services in conducting correspondence for Charles I. The monarch for whom his journey to Poland was made (see the ensuing poem) was Charles II., towards 1650. "According to some accounts, Denham first discovered the merits of Milton's *Paradise Lost*; and went about with the book new from the press in his hands, showing it to everybody, and exclaiming, 'This beats us all, and the ancients too!'"]

ON MY LORD CROFT'S AND MY JOURNEY INTO POLAND,

FROM WHENCE WE BROUGHT £10,000 FOR HIS MAJESTY, BY THE DECIMATION OF HIS SCOTTISH SUBJECTS THERE.

Toll, toll,
Gentle bell, for the soul
Of the pure ones in Pole
Which are damned in our scroll!

Who having felt a touch
Of Cockram's greedy clutch—
(Which though it was not much,
Yet their stubbornness was such

That, when we did arrive,
'Gainst the stream we did strive)—
They would neither lead nor drive;

Nor lend
An ear to a friend,
Nor an answer would send
To our letter so well penned;

Nor assist our affairs
With their moneys nor their wares,

As their answer now declares,—
But only with their prayers.

Thus they did persist,
Did and said what they list,
Till the Diet was dismissed;
But then our breech they kissed.

For, when
It was moved there and then
They should pay one in ten,
The Diet said Amen.

And, because they are loth
To discover the troth,
They must give word and oath,
Though they will forfeit both.

Thus the constitution
Condemns them every one,
From the father to the son.

But John
(Our friend) Mollesson
Thought us to have outgone
With a quaint invention.

Like the prophets of yore,
He complained long before
Of the mischiefs in store,
Aye, and thrice as much more;

And, with that wicked lie,
A letter they came by
From our King's majesty.

But fate
Brought the letter too late;
'Twas of too old a date
To relieve their damned state.

The letter's to be seen,
With seal of wax so green,
At Dantzig, where't has been
Turned into good Latin.

But he that gave the hint
This letter for to print
Must also pay his stint.

That trick,
Had it come in the nick,
Had touched us to the quick;
But the messenger fell sick.

Had it later been wrote,
And sooner been brought,
They had got what they sought;
But now it serves for nought.

On Sandys they ran aground;
And our return was crowned
With full ten-thousand pound.

ABRAHAM COWLEY.

[Born in London, 1618, the son of a grocer; died at Chertsey, 28 July 1667. He was extraordinarily precocious, publishing at the age of fifteen a volume of *Poetical Blossoms*. During the Parliamentary War he was mostly abroad, and was laboriously employed in conducting a correspondence in cipher between the King and Queen. Afterwards he became a doctor of medicine, paying some considerable attention to botany. At the age of forty-two he retired to a life of rural and lettered seclusion at Chertsey: this also, it would seem, palled upon him, and death put a period to it after a brief interval of years. Cowley is one of the poets of remote and brilliant turns of thought, and elaborated literary distinction. One does not love his poetry; but one can admire it often—if only one would read it].

THE CHRONICLE, A BALLAD.

MARGARITA first possessed,
If I remember well, my breast,
Margarita first of all;
But, when a while the wanton maid
With my restless heart had played,
Martha took the flying ball.

Martha soon did it resign
To the beauteous Catharine:
Beauteous Catharine gave place
(Though loth and angry she to part
With the possession of my heart)
To Eliza's conquering face.

Eliza till this hour might reign,
Had she not evil counsels ta'en:
Fundamental laws she broke,
And still new favourites she chose,
Till up in arms my passions rose,
And cast away her yoke.

Mary then, and gentle Anne,
Both to reign at once began;
Alternately they swayed;
And sometimes Mary was the fair,
And sometimes Anne the crown did wear,
And sometimes both I obeyed.

Another Mary then arose,
And did rigorous laws impose;

A mighty tyrant she!
Long, alas! should I have been
Under that iron-sceptred queen,
Had not Rebecca set me free.

When fair Rebecca set me free,
'Twas then a golden time with me:
But soon those pleasures fled;
For the gracious princess died
In her youth and beauty's pride,
And Judith reigned in her stead.

One month, three days, and half an hour,
Judith held the sovereign power.
Wondrous beautiful her face;
But so weak and small her wit
That she to govern was unfit,
And so Susanna took her place.

But, when Isabella came,
Armed with a resistless flame,
And the artillery of her eye,
Whilst she proudly marched about,
Greater conquests to find out,
She beat out Susan by the bye.

But in her place I then obeyed
Black-eyed Bess, her viceroy made, —
To whom ensued a vacancy.
Thousand worst passions then possessed
The interregnum of my breast.
Bless me from such an anarchy!

Gentle Henrietta then,
And a third Mary, next began:
Then Joan, and Jane, and Audria;
And then a pretty Thomasine,
And then another Catharine.
And then a long *et cætera*.

But should I now to you relate
The strength and riches of their state,
The powder, patches, and the pins,
The ribands, jewels, and the rings,
The lace, the paint, and warlike things,
That make up all their magazines;

If I should tell the politic arts
To take and keep men's hearts,
The letters, embassies, and spies,
The frowns, the smiles, and flatteries,
The quarrels, tears, and perjuries,
Numberless, nameless mysteries;—

And all the little lime-twigs laid
By Machiavel the waiting-maid ;
I more voluminous should grow
(Chiefly if I like them should tell
All change of weathers that befell)
Than Holinshed or Stow.

But I will briefer with them be,
Since few of them were long with *me*.
An higher and a nobler strain
My present Empress does claim,—
Heleonora, first o' the name,
Whom God grant long to reign !

RICHARD LOVELACE.

[Born in 1618, son of Sir William Lovelace, of Woolwich : died in London, 1658. He was twice imprisoned in the royal cause—firstly, in the Gatehouse, Westminster, in 1642, for delivering to the House of Commons the Kentish petition "for restoring the king to his rights" &c., and again in 1648, when he remained in confinement until the execution of Charles I. was past. His miscellaneous poems appeared under the title of *Lucasta:* he wrote also a tragedy and a comedy, never printed. Lovelace died in poverty and obscurity, though probably not in such abject want as some writers have represented. He was, in his early youth, "accounted," says Wood, "the most amiable and beautiful person that ever eye beheld ; a person also of innate modesty, virtue, and courtly deportment"].

TO A LADY THAT DESIRED ME I WOULD BEAR MY PART WITH HER IN A SONG.

MADAM A. L.

THIS is the prettiest motion ![1]
Madam, the alarums of a drum
That calls your lord, set to your cries,
To mine are sacred symphonies.

What though 'tis said I have a voice ;
I know 'tis but that hollow noise
Which (as it through my pipe doth speed)
Bitterns do carol through a reed ;
In the same key with monkeys' jigs,
Or dirges of proscribèd pigs,
Or the soft serenades above
In calm of night, when cats make love.

Was ever such a consort seen ?
Fourscore-and-fourteen with fourteen !
Yet sooner they'll agree, one pair,
Than we in our spring-winter air.
They may embrace, sigh, kiss, the rest :

---

[1] "Motion" and "drum" make up a very extraordinary rhyme. True, Lovelace was loose in his rhymes, and in his execution generally : yet I almost think a word must be missed here—perhaps "come !" (in the sense of "go to !")

   Our breath knows nought but east and west.
Thus have I heard to children's cries
The fair nurse still such lullabies
That well, all said (for what there lay),
The pleasure did the sorrow pay.

   Sure there's another way to save
Your fancy, madam; that's to have
('Tis but a petitioning kind fate)
The organs sent to Billingsgate,
Where they, to that soft murmuring choir,
Shall teach you all you can admire!
Or do but hear how love-bang Kate
In pantry dark, for freage of mate,
With edge of steel the square wood shapes,
And *Dido*[1] to it chaunts or scrapes.
The merry Phaeton o' the car,
You'll vow, mades a melodious jar;
Sweeter and sweeter whistleth he
To unanointed axletree;
Such swift notes he and 's wheels do run,
For me, I yield him Phœbus' son.

   Say, fair commandress, can it be
You should ordain a mutiny?
For, where I howl, all accents fall,
As kings' harangues, to one and all.

   Ulysses' art is now withstood:
You ravish both with sweet and good.
Saint Siren, sing, for I dare hear;
But, when I ope, oh stop your ear!

   Far less be't emulation
To pass me or in trill or tone,—
Like the thin throat of Philomel,
And the smart lute, who should excel;
As if her soft chords should begin,
And strive for sweetness with the pin.[2]

   Yet can I music too; but such
As is beyond all voice or touch.
My mind can in fair order chime,
Whilst my true heart still beats the time.
My soul's so full of harmony
That it with all parts can agree.
If you wind up to the highest fret,[3]
It shall descend an eight from it;
And, when you shall vouchsafe to fall,

---

[1] The ballad of *Queen Dido*. "Love-bang" seems to mean "fond of noise, obstreperous." "Freage" is a word unknown to me.
[2] A musical peg.
[3] A piece of wire attached to the finger-board of a guitar.

Sixteen above you it shall call,
And yet, so dis-assenting one,
They both shall meet in unison.

Come then, bright cherubim, begin!
My loudest music is within.
Take all notes with your skilful eyes;
Hark if mine do not sympathize!
Sound all my thoughts, and see expressed
The tablature of my large breast.
Then you'll admit that I too can
Music above dead sounds of man;
Such as alone doth bless the spheres,
Not to be reached with human ears.

THE DUEL.

LOVE drunk, the other day, knocked at my breast;
   But I, alas! was not within.
My man, my ear, told me he came to attest
   That without cause he'd boxèd him,
And batterèd the windows of mine eyes,
And took my heart for one of's nunneries.

I wondered at the outrage, safe returned,
   And stormèd at the base affront;
And by a friend of mine, bold faith, that burned,
   I called him to a strict accompt.
He said that, by the law, the challenged might
Take the advantage both of arms and fight.

Two darts of equal length and points he sent,
   And nobly gave the choice to me;
Which I not weighed, young and indifferent,
   Now full of nought but victory.
So we both met in one of his mother's groves;—
The time, at the first murmuring of her doves.

I stripped myself naked all o'er, as he:
   For so I was best armed, when bare.
His first pass did my liver raze: yet I
   Made home a falsify[1] too near:
For, when my arm to its true distance came,
I nothing touched but a fantastic flame.

This, this is Love we daily quarrel so,—
   An idle Don-Quichoterie:
We whip ourselves with our own twisted woe,
   And wound the air for a fly.
The only way to undo this enemy
Is to laugh at the boy, and he will cry.

---

[1] "To falsify a thrust," says Phillips (*World of Words*), "is to make a feigned pass." Lovelace here employs the word as a substantive.

THE SNAIL.

Wise emblem of our politic world,
Sage Snail, within thine own self curled,
Instruct me softly to make haste,
Whilst these my feet go slowly fast.

Compendious Snail ! thou seem'st to me
Large Euclid's strict epitome ;
And in each diagram dost fling
Thee from the point unto the ring.
A figure now triangular,
And oval now, and now a square,
And then a serpentine, dost crawl ;
Now a straight line, now crook'd, now all.

Preventing rival of the day,
Thou art up and openest thy ray ;
And, ere the morn cradles the moon,
Thou art broke into a beauteous noon.
Then, when the Sun sups in the deep,
Thy silver horns ere Cynthia's peep ;
And thou, from thine own liquid bed,
New Phœbus, heav'st thy pleasant head.

Who shall a name for thee create,
Deep riddle of mysterious state ?
Bold Nature, that gives common birth
To all products of seas and earth,
Of thee, as earthquakes, is afraid,
Nor will thy dire delivery aid.

Thou, thine own daughter, then, and sire,
That son and mother art entire,
That big still with thy self dost go,
And liv'st an aged embryo ;
That, like the cubs of India,
Thou from thyself awhile dost play ;
But, frighted with a dog or gun,
In thine own belly thou dost run,
And as thy house was thine own womb,
So thine own womb concludes thy tomb

But now I must (anàlysed king)
Thy economic virtues sing ;
Thou great staid husband still within,
Thou thee (that's thine) dost discipline ;
And, when thou art to progress bent,
Thou mov'st thy self and tenement.
As warlike Scythians travelled, you
Remove your men and city too.

Then, after a sad dearth and rain,
Thou scatterest thy silver train ;
And, when the trees grow nak'd and old,
Thou cloathest them with cloth of gold,
Which from thy bowels thou dost spin,
And draw from the rich mines within.

Now hast thou changed thee saint, and made
Thyself a fane that's cupulaed ;
And in thy wreathèd cloister thou
Walkest thine own grey-friar too ;
Strict and locked up, thou art hood all o'er,
And ne'er eliminat'st thy door.
On salads thou dost feed severe,
And 'stead of beads thou dropp'st a tear.
And, when to rest each calls the bell,
Thou sleep'st within thy marble cell,
Where, in dark contemplation placed,
The sweets of Nature thou dost taste ;
Who now, with Time, thy days resolve,
And in a jelly thee dissolve,—
Like a shot star, which doth repair
Upward, and rarify the air.

THOMAS STANLEY.

[Son of a knight in Hertfordshire : born in 1620, died in 1678. Author of a laborious *History of Philosophy*, and of various poetical compositions, including translations from the classic and some modern languages].

NOTE ON ANACREON.

LET's not rhyme the hours away ;
Friends ! we must no longer play :
Brisk Lyæus—see !—invites
To more ravishing delights.
Let's give o'er this fool Apollo,
Nor his fiddle longer follow :
Fie upon his forked hill,
With his fiddlestick and quill !
And the Muses, though they're gamesome,
They are neither young nor handsome ;
And their freaks, in sober sadness,
Are a mere poetic madness :
Pegasus is but a horse ;
He that follows him is worse.
See, the rain soaks to the skin,—
Make it rain as well within.
Wine, my boy ! we'll sing and laugh,
All night revel, rant, and quaff ;

Till the morn, stealing behind us,
At the table sleepless find us.
When our bones, alas ! shall have
A cold lodging in the grave,
When swift Death shall overtake us,
We shall sleep and none can wake us.
Drink we then the juice o' the vine,
Make our breasts Lyæus' shrine.
Bacchus, our debauch beholding,—
By thy image I am moulding,
Whilst my brains I do replenish
With this draught of unmixed Rhenish ;
By thy full-branched ivy-twine ;
By this sparkling glass of wine ;
By thy thyrsus so renowned ;
By the healths with which thou'rt crowned ;
By the feasts which thou dost prize ;
By thy numerous victories ;
By the howls by Mænads made ;
By this haut-gout carbonade ;
By thy colours red and white ;
By the tavern, thy delight ;
By the sound thy orgies spread ;
By the shine of noses red ;
By thy table free for all.;
By the jovial carnival ;
By thy language cabalistic ;
By thy cymbal, drum, and his stick ;
By the tunes thy quart-pots strike up ;
By thy sighs, the broken hiccup ;
By thy mystic set of ranters ;
By thy never-tamèd panthers ;
By this sweet, this fresh and free air ;
By thy goat, as chaste as we are ;
By thy fulsome Cretan lass ;
By the old man on the ass ;
By thy cousins in mixed shapes ;
By the flower of fairest grapes ;
By thy bisks famed far and wide ;
By thy store of neats'-tongues dried ;
By thy incense, Indian smoke ;
By the joys thou dost provoke ;
By this salt Westphalia gammon ;
By these sausages that inflame one ;
By thy tall majestic flagons ;
By mass, tope, and thy flapdragons ;
By this olive's unctuous savour ;
By this orange, the wine's flavour ;
By this cheese o'errun with mites ;
By thy dearest favourites ;—

To thy frolic order call us,
  Knights of the deep bowl install us;
And, to show thyself divine,
  Never let it want for wine.

ANDREW MARVELL.

[Born at Hull, 1620; died on 16th August 1678, with some vague suspicion of poison. He became assistant to Milton as Cromwell's Latin secretary, and was afterwards (1660) elected to Parliament, where he continued till the close of his life—a zealous delegate of his constituents, and opponent of arbitrary measures. Marvell appears, in biographic and political record, as a thoroughly manly person; and the same is the prevailing character of his poetic work. We observe vigorous strenuous lines, a bluff and sometimes boisterous humour, keen fencing-play of wit, a strong temper, as ready to overstate a prejudice as to pile a panegyric; often too a sharp thrill of tenderness, and a full sense and full power of expressing beauty].

MOURNING.

You that decipher out the fate
  Of human offsprings from the skies,
What mean these infants which of late
  Spring from the stars of Chlora's eyes?

Her eyes, confused and doubled o'er
  With tears suspended ere they flow,
Seem bending upwards, to restore
  To heaven, whence it came, their woe:—

When, moulding of the watery spheres,
  Slow drops untie themselves away;
As if she, with those precious tears,
  Would strew the ground where Strephon lay.

Yet some affirm, pretending art,
  Her eyes have so her bosom drowned,
Only to soften, near her heart,
  A place to fix another wound.

And, while vain pomp does her restrain
  Within her solitary bower,
She courts herself in amorous rain;
  Herself both Danae and the shower.

Nay, others, bolder, hence esteem
  Joy now so much her master grown
That whatsoever does but seem
  Like grief is from her windows thrown;—

Nor that she pays, while she survives,
  To her dead love this tribute due;
But casts abroad these donatives
  At the installing of a new.

How wide they dream ! the Indian slaves
  Who sink for pearl through seas profound
Would find her tears yet deeper waves,
  And not of one the bottom sound.

I yet my silent judgment keep,
  Disputing not what they believe :
But sure, as oft as women weep,
  It is to be supposed they grieve.

THE CHARACTER OF HOLLAND.

Holland, that scarce deserves the name of land,
As but the offscouring of the British sand,
And so much earth as was contributed
By English pilots when they heaved the lead,
Or what by the ocean's slow alluvion fell,
Of shipwrecked cockle and the mussel-shell,—
This indigested vomit of the sea
Fell to the Dutch by just propriety.
  Glad then, as miners who have found the ore,
They, with mad labour, fished the land to shore,
And dived as desperately for each piece
Of earth as if't had been of ambergreece ;
Collecting anxiously small loads of clay,
Less than what building swallows bear away,
Or than those pills which sordid beetles roll,
Transfusing into them their dunghill soul.
  How did they rivet, with gigantic piles,
Thorough the centre their new-catchèd miles,
And to the stake a struggling country bound,
Where barking waves still bait the forcèd ground ;
Building their watery Babel far more high,
To reach the sea, than those to scale the sky !
  Yet still his claim the injured ocean laid,
And oft at leap-frog o'er their steeples played ;
As if on purpose it on land had come
To show them what's their *mare liberum*.
A daily deluge over them does boil ;
The earth and water play at level-coyl.
The fish oft-times the burgher dispossessed,
And sat, not as a meat, but as a guest ;
And oft the tritons and the sea-nymphs saw
Whole shoals of Dutch served up for cabillau ;
Or, as they over the new level ranged,
For pickled herring, pickled heeren changed.
Nature, it seemed, ashamed of her mistake,
Would throw their land away at duck and drake :
Therefore necessity, that first made kings,
Something like government among them brings.
For, as with pygmies, who best kills the crane,

Among the hungry he that treasures grain,
Among the blind the one-eyed blinkard reigns,
So rules among the drownèd he that drains.
Not who first see the rising sun commands,
But who could first discern the rising lands.
Who best could know to pump an earth so leak,
Him they their lord and country's father speak.
To make a bank was a great plot of state;
Invent a shovel, and be a magistrate.
Hence some small dyke-grave, unperceived, invades
The power, and grows, as 'twere, a king of spades;
But, for less envy, some joined states endures,
Who look like a commission of the sewers:
For these half-anders, half wet and half dry,
Nor bear strict service nor pure liberty.
 'Tis probable religion, after this,
Came next in order; which they could not miss.
How could the Dutch but be converted when
The apostles were so many fishermen?
Besides, the waters of themselves did rise,
And, as their land, so them did re-baptize;
Though Herring[1] for their God few voices missed,
And Poor-John to have been the evangelist.
Faith, that could never twins conceive before,
Never so fertile, spawned upon this shore
More pregnant than their Margaret, that lay down,
For Hans-in-Kelder, of a whole Hans-town.
 Sure, when religion did itself embark,
And from the east would westward steer its ark,
It struck, and, splitting on this unknown ground,
Each one thence pillaged the first piece he found:
Hence Amsterdam, Turk-Christian-Pagan-Jew,
Staple of sects and mint of schism grew;
That bank of conscience, where not one so strange
Opinion but finds credit and exchange.
In vain for Catholics ourselves we bear;
The Universal Church is only there.
Nor can civility there want for tillage,
Where wisely for their court they chose a village.
How fit a title clothes their governors,—
Themselves the *hogs*, as all their subjects *boars!*
Let it suffice, to give their country fame,
That it had one Civilis called by name,
Some fifteen hundred and more years ago;
But surely never any that *was* so.
 See but their mairmaids, with their tails of fish,
Reeking at church over the chafing dish.

---

[1] See the pun, on p. 141, between "herring" and "heeren." Here again there is the same sort of pun upon "Heer" or "Herr" in its signification of "Lord" (God).

A vestal turf, enshrined in earthenware,
Fumes through the loopholes of a wooden square.
Each to the temple with these altars tend,
But still does place it at her western end ;
While the fat steam of female sacrifice
Fills the priest's nostrils, and puts out his eyes.
  Or what a spectacle the skipper gross,
A water-Hercules, butter-coloss,
Tunned up with all their several towns of beer ;
When, staggering upon some land, sniek and sneer,
They try, like statuaries, if they can
Cut out each other's Athos to a man ;
And carve in their large bodies, where they please,
The arms of the united provinces.
But, when such amity at home is showed,
What then are their confederacies abroad ?
Let this one courtesy witness all the rest ;
When their whole navy they together pressed,
Not Christian captives to redeem from bands,
Or intercept the western golden sands ;
No, but all ancient rights and leagues must fail,
Rather than to the English strike their sail ;
To whom their weather-beaten province owes
Itself, when, as some greater vessel tows
A cock-boat tossed with the same wind and fate,
We buoyed so often up their sinking state.
Was this *jus belli et pacis?* Could this be
Cause why their burgomaster of the sea,
Rammed with gunpowder, flaming with brand-wine,
Should raging hold his linstock to the mine ?
While, with feigned treaties, they invade by stealth
Our sore new-circumcisèd commonwealth.
Yet of his vain attempt no more he sees
Than of case-butter shot and bullet-cheese ;
And the torn navy staggered with him home,
While the sea laughed itself into a foam.
'Tis true, since that (as fortune kindly sports)
A wholesome danger drove us to our ports ;
While half their banished keels the tempest tossed,
Half bound at home in prison to the frost,
That ours, meantime, at leisure might careen,
In a calm winter, under skies serene,—
As the obsequious air and waters rest
'Till the dear halcyon hatch out all its nest.
The Commonwealth doth by its losses grow,
And, like its own seas, only ebbs to flow.
Besides, that very agitation laves,
And purges out the corruptible waves.
  And now again our armèd bucentore
Doth yearly their sea nuptials restore ;

And now the hydra of seven provinces
Is strangled by our infant Hercules.
Their tortoise wants its vainly stretchèd neck;
Their navy, all our conquest, or our wreck:
Or what is left their Carthage overcome
Would render fain unto our better Rome,—
Unless our senate, lest their youth disuse
The war, (but who would?) peace, if begged, refuse.
For now of nothing may our state despair,
Darling of heaven, and of men the care;
Provided that they be, what they have been,
Watchful abroad, and honest still within;
For, while our Neptune doth a trident shake
Steeled with those piercing heads, Dean, Monck, and Blake,
And while Jove governs in the highest sphere,
Vainly in hell let Pluto domineer!

HENRY VAUGHAN.

[Born at Newton, near Usk, Monmouthshire, 1622, of an ancient line; died, 23 April 1695. From the locality of his birth and usual residence, he termed himself the Silurist: he practised as a physician in Brecon. Like the great majority of the poetical writers of the time, he was on the side of royalism. Vaughan has continued to enjoy a certain reputation among literary students, chiefly as a satellite of George Herbert, and sometimes almost his rival. The quality and degree of his poetic excellence are, however, in fact, very uncommon. He is in various respects diverse from Herbert, and in some even superior to him: he has a larger range, and, in point of thought and of perception, a certain subtlety mingled with intensity which brings him into specially close relation to the modern tone in poetry. It may be hoped that the writings of this fine thinker and deep poet will be better known henceforth, in consequence of the zealous care with which he has been lately edited by the Rev. Mr. Grosart in his important series, *The Fuller Worthies Library*. Of course a volume of Humorous Poetry is not the place where the deservings of Vaughan can be shown forth in any sufficient measure].

TO HIS RETIRED FRIEND, AN INVITATION TO BRECKNOCK.

SINCE last we met, thou and thy horse, my dear,
Have not so much as drunk or littered here.
I wonder, though thyself be thus deceased,
Thou hast the spite to coffin up thy beast;
Or is the palfrey sick, and his rough hide
With the penànce of one spur mortified?
Or taught by thee—like Pythagoras's ox—
Is than his master grown more orthodox?
Whatever 'tis, a sober cause't must be
That thus long bars us of thy company.
The town believes thee lost; and, didst thou see
But half her sufferings, now distressed for thee,
Thou'ldst swear—like Rome—her foul polluted walls
Were sacked by Brennus and the salvage Gauls.
Abominable face of things! Here's noise
Of bangèd mortars, blue aprons, and boys,

Pigs, dogs, and drums, with the hoarse hellish notes
Of politicly-deaf usurers' throats,
With new fine Worships, and the old cast team
Of Justices vexed with the cough and phlegm.
Midst these the Cross looks sad, and in the Shire-
Hall furs of an old Saxon Fox appear,
With brotherly ruffs and beards, and a strange sight
Of high monumental hats, ta'en at the fight
Of Eighty eight; while every Burgess foots
The mortal pavement in eternal boots.
 Hadst thou been bachelor, I had soon divined
Thy close retirements and monastic mind;
Perhaps some nymph had been to visit, or
The beauteous churl was to be waited for,
And, like the Greek, ere you the sport would miss,
You stayed, and stroked the distaff for a kiss.
But in this age, when thy cool settled blood
Is tied to one flesh, and thou almost grown good,
I know not how to reach the strange device,
Except—Domitian-like—thou murderest flies.
Or is't thy piety? for who can tell
But thou mayst prove devout, and love a cell,
And—like a badger—with attentive looks
In the dark hole sit rooting up of books.
Quick hermit! what a peaceful change hadst thou,
Without the noise of hair-cloth, whip, or vow!
But is there no redemption? must there be
No other penance but of liberty?
Why! two months hence, if thou continue thus,
Thy memory will scarce remain with us.
The drawers have forgot thee, and exclaim
They have not seen thee here since Charles his reign;
Or, if they mention thee, like some old man
That at each word inserts—" Sir, as I can
Remember "—so the Cipherers puzzle me
With a dark cloudy character of thee;
That—certs—I fear thou wilt be lost, and we
Must ask the fathers, ere't be long, for thee.
 Come! leave this sullen state, and let not wine
And precious wit lie dead for want of thine.
Shall the dull market landlord, with his rout
Of sneaking tenants, dirtily swill out
This harmless liquor? shall they knock and beat
For sack, only to talk of rye and wheat?
Oh let not such preposterous tippling be
In our metropolis; may I ne'er see
Such tavern-sacrilege, nor lend a line
To weep the rapes and tragedy of wine!
Here lives that chemic, quick fire which betrays
Fresh spirits to the blood, and warms our lays.

K

  I have reserved 'gainst thy approach a cup
That, were thy Muse stark dead, shall raise her up,
And teach her yet more charming words and skill
Than ever Cœlia, Chloris, Astrophil,
Or any of the threadbare names, inspired
Poor rhyming lovers, with a mistress fired.
Come then! and, while the slow icicle hangs
At the stiff thatch, and Winter's frosty pangs
Benumb the year, blithe—as of old—let us,
'Midst noise and war, of peace and mirth discuss.
This portion thou wert born for: why should we
Vex at the time's ridiculous misery?
An age that thus hath fooled itself, and will
—Spite of thy teeth and mine—persist so still!
Let's sit then at this fire; and, while we steal
A revel in the town, let others seal,
Purchase, or cheat, and who can, let them pay,
Till those black deeds bring on the darksome day.
Innocent spenders we! a better use
Shall wear out our short lease, and leave the obtuse
Rout to their husks. They and their bags at best
Have cares in earnest; we, care for a jest.

ALEXANDER BROME.

[Born in 1623, died in 1666. Was an untiring producer of verse in ridicule of the Puritans and the parliamentary party: it has even been said that he "was the author of the greater part of the songs and epigrams published against the Rump." He was also concerned in translations of Horace and Lucretius, and other literary work. His profession was that of attorney].

THE PRISONERS.

Come, a brimmer, my bullies! drink whole ones or nothing,
 Now healths have been voted down.
'Tis sack that can heat us; we care not for clothing,—
 A gallon's as warm as a gown.
  'Cause the Parliament sees
  Nor the former nor these
Could engage us to drink their health,
  They may vote that we shall
  Drink no healths at all,
Not to King nor to Commonwealth,
So that now we must venture to drink 'em by stealth.

But we've found out a way, that's beyond all their thinking,
 To keep up good-fellowship still
We'll drink their destruction that would destroy drinking,—
 Let 'em vote *that* a health if they will!

    Those men that did fight,
    And did pray day and night,
For the Parliament and its attendant,
    Did make all that bustle
    The King out to justle,
And bring in the Independent,
But now we all clearly see what was the end on't.[1]

Now their idol's thrown down with their sooterkin also,
 About which they did make such a pother ;
And, though their contrivance did make one thing to fall so,
 We have drank ourselves into another ;
    And now, my lads, we
    May still Cavaliers be,
In spite of the Còmmittee's frown ;
    We will drink and we'll sing,
    And each health to our King
Shall be loyally drunk in the ' *Crown*,"
Which shall be the standard in every town.

Their politic would-be's do but show themselves asses,
 That other men's calling invade ;
We only converse with pots and with glasses,—
 Let the rulers alone with their trade.
    The Lion of the Tower
    Their estates does devour,
Without showing law for't or reason ;
    Into prison we get
    For the crime called debt,
Where our bodies and brains we do season,
And that is ne'er taken for murder or treason.

Where our ditties still be, " Give's more drink, give's more drink,
    boys !
 Let those that are frugal take care !"
Our gaolers and we will live by our chink, boys,
 While our creditors live by the air.
    Here we live at our ease,
    And get craft and grease,
'Till we've merrily spent all our store ;
    Then, as drink brought us in,
    'Twill redeem us agen ;
We got in because we were poor,
And swear ourselves out on the very same score.

---

   [1] A reference to the project of making Cromwell king.

JOHN DRYDEN.

[Born in Aldwinkle All Saints, Northamptonshire, towards 1631; died in London, 1 May 1700].

ON THE YOUNG STATESMEN.

WRITTEN IN 1680.

CLARENDON had law and sense;
    Clifford was fierce and brave;
Bennet's grave look was a pretence;
And Danby's matchless impudence
    Helped to support the knave.

But Sunderland, Godolphin, Lory.
These will appear such chits in story
    'Twill turn all politics to jests,—
To be repeated like John Dory,
    When fiddlers sing at feasts.

Protect us, mighty Providence!
    What would these madmen have?
First, they would bribe us without pence.
Deceive us without common sense,
    And without power enslave.

Shall freeborn men, in humble awe,
    Submit to servile shame,—
Who from consent and custom draw
The same right to be ruled by law
    Which kings pretend to reign?

The duke shall wield his conquering sword,
    The chancellor make a speech,
The king shall pass his honest word,
The pawned revenue sums afford,
    And then, come kiss my breech.

So have I seen a king on chess
    (His rooks and knights withdrawn,
His queen and bishops in distress)
Shifting about grow less and less,
    With here and there a pawn.

KATHARINE PHILIPS.

[Born towards 1632, died of small-pox in 1664. Her maiden name was Fowler, and she married James Philips Esq., of the Priory of Cardigan. Herself and all her immediate society assumed philandering fancy-names: she was "Orinda," or, as several of her highly distinguished contemporaries lavishly called her, "the matchless Orinda." Some of her poems got about during her brief lifetime, but without her sanction. Orinda, though not exactly "matchless," must have been a very gifted woman—of elevated mind and character, warm attachments, and no inconsiderable poetic endowment: she was full mistress of the faculty of nervous and direct expression in verse].

TO ANTENOR,[1]
ON A PAPER OF MINE WHICH J. J. THREATENS TO PUBLISH TO PREJUDICE HIM.

Must then my crimes become thy scandal too?
Why, sure the devil hath not much to do!
The weakness of the other charge is clear,
When such a trifle must bring up the rear.
But this is mad design, for who before
Lost his repute upon another's score?
My love and life, I must confess, are thine,—
But not my errors, they are only mine.
And, if my faults must be for thine allowed,
It will be hard to dissipate the cloud:
For Eve's rebellion did not Adam blast,
Until himself forbidden fruit did taste.
'Tis possible this magazine of hell
(Whose name would turn a verse into a spell,
Whose mischief is congenial to his life)
May yet enjoy an honourable wife.
Nor let his ill be reckoned as *her* blame,
Nor yet *my* follies blast Antenor's name.
But, if those lines a punishment could call
Lasting and great as this dark-lantern's gall,
Alone I'd court the torments with content,
To testify that thou art innocent.
So, if my ink through malice proved a stain,
My blood should justly wash it off again.
But, since that mint of slander could invent
To make so dull a rhyme his instrument,
Let verse revenge the quarrel. But he's worse
Than wishes, and below a poet's curse;
And more than this wit knows not how to give,—
Let him be still himself, and let him live.

---

[1] The authoress's husband.

EARL OF DORSET (CHARLES SACKVILLE).

[Born in 1637, died in 1706. Witty and dissipated in his youth, he became, as age advanced, a political personage of some importance, and, concurring in the revolution under William III., was created Lord Chamberlain of the Household. He was at all times a generous supporter of men of genius].

SONG.[1]

To all you ladies now at land
  We men at sea indite ;
But first would have you understand
  How hard it is to write ;
The Muses now, and Neptune too,
We must implore, to write to you,
    With a fa, la, la, la, la.[2]

For though the Muses should prove kind,
  And fill our empty brain,
Yet, if rough Neptune rouse the wind
  To wave the azure main,
Our paper, pen and ink, and we,
Roll up and down our ships at sea.

Then, if we write not by each post,
  Think not we are unkind ;
Nor yet conclude our ships are lost,
  By Dutchmen or by wind ;
Our tears we'll send a speedier way,—
The tide shall bring them twice a-day.

The king, with wonder and surprise,
  Will swear the seas grow bold,
Because the tides will higher rise
  Than e'er they used of old :
But let him know, it is our tears
Bring floods of grief to Whitehall stairs.

Should foggy Opdam chance to know
  Our sad and dismal story,
The Dutch would scorn so weak a foe,
  And quit their fort at Goree :
For what resistance can they find
From men who've left their hearts behind ?

Let wind and weather do its worst,
  Be you to us but kind ;
Let Dutchmen vapour, Spaniards curse,
  No sorrow we shall find :

---

[1] Written at sea in the Dutch War, 1665 : composed (or at any rate completed) the night before the great engagement in which the Dutch Admiral, Opdam, and all his crew, were blown up.
[2] Burden repeated to each stanza.

'Tis then no matter how things go,
Or who's our friend, or who's our foe.

To pass our tedious hours away,
　We throw a merry main,
Or else at serious ombre play:
　But why should we in vain
Each other's ruin thus pursue?
We were undone when we left you.

But now our fears tempestuous grow,
　And cast our hopes away;
Whilst you, regardless of our woe,
　Sit careless at a play:
Perhaps, permit some happier man
To kiss your hand, or flirt your fan.

When any mournful tune you hear,
　That dies in every note,
As if it sighed with each man's care
　For being so remote,
Think then how often love we've made
To you, when all those tunes were played.

In justice you cannot refuse
　To think of our distress,
When we for hopes of honour lose
　Our certain happiness;
All those designs are but to prove
Ourselves more worthy of your love.

And now we've told you all our loves,
　And likewise all our fears,
In hopes this declaration moves
　Some pity from your tears;
Let's hear of no inconstancy,—
We have too much of that at sea.
　　With a fa, la, la, la, la.

WILLIAM WALSH.

[Born in 1663, died towards 1709. He was a friend of Dryden, who termed him "the best critic of our nation:" he also encouraged Pope in his early career].

THE DESPAIRING LOVER.

DISTRACTED with care
For Phyllis the fair;
Since nothing could move her,
Poor Damon, her lover,
Resolves in despair
No longer to languish,

Nor bear so much anguish;
But, mad with his love,
To a precipice goes,
Where a leap from above
Would soon finish his woes.

When in rage he came there,
Beholding how steep
The sides did appear,
And the bottom how deep;
His torments projecting,
And sadly reflecting
That a lover forsaken
A new love may get,
But a neck, when once broken,
Can never be set;

And that he could die
Whenever he would,
But that he could live
But as long as he could:—
How grievous soever
The torment might grow,
He scorned to endeavour
To finish it so.
But bold, unconcerned
At thoughts of the pain,
He calmly returned
To his cottage again.

MATTHEW PRIOR.

[Born in 1664, died in 1721. His father was a joiner in London: but Matthew, under the patronage of the Earl of Dorset, was even in boyhood brought into a higher social sphere, and he soon became a public personage of consequence, deep in the diplomatic machinations of the time, as well as a successful poet of the lighter kind. Beginning as a Whig, he turned into a Tory in 1701; acted as ambassador in France in 1713; was afterwards impeached for his share in negociating the treaty of Utrecht; and remained a long while in custody, but was finally released untried. After this failure of his political career, a college-fellowship, literature, and the active practical friendship of Lord Oxford, formed his chief resources. Prior was a loose liver; and, spite of his high station, was not disinclined to shift off at times his outward social decorum. "I have been assured," says Spence, "that Prior—after having spent the evening with Oxford, Bolingbroke, Pope, and Swift—would go and smoke a pipe, and drink a bottle of ale, with a common soldier and his wife, in Long Acre, before he went to bed"].

TO A CHILD OF QUALITY
FIVE YEARS OLD, 1704, THE AUTHOR THEN FORTY.

Lords, knights, and squires, the numerous band
That wear the fair Miss Mary's fetters,
Were summoned by her high command
To show their passions by their letters.

My pen amongst the rest I took,
Lest those bright eyes that cannot read
Should dart their kindling fires, and look
The power they have to be obeyed.

Nor quality nor reputation
Forbid me yet my flame to tell;
Dear five-years-old befriends my passion,
And I may write till she can spell.

For, while she makes her silkworms' beds
With all the tender things I swear,—
Whilst all the house my passion reads
In papers round her baby's hair,—

She may receive and own my flame;
For, though the strictest prudes should know it,
She'll pass for a most virtuous dame,
And I for an unhappy poet.

Then, too, alas! when she shall tear
The lines some younger rival sends,
She'll give me leave to write, I fear,
And we shall still continue friends:

For, as our different ages move,
'Tis so ordained (would fate but mend it!)
That I shall be past making love
When she begins to comprehend it.

MERRY ANDREW.

Sly Merry Andrew, the last Southwark fair,
(At Bartholomew he did not much appear,
So peevish was the edict of the Mayor)—
At Southwark, therefore, as his tricks he showed,
To please our masters and his friends the crowd,
A huge neat's tongue he in his right hand held,
His left was with a good black-pudding filled.
With a grave look, in this odd equipage,
The clownish mimic traverses the stage.
"Why, how now, Andrew!" cries his brother droll,
"To-day's conceit methinks is something dull.
Come on, Sir, to our worthy friends explain
What does your emblematic Worship mean?"
Quoth Andrew, "Honest English let us speak;
Your emble—(what d'ye call it?) is Heathen Greek.
To tongue or pudding thou hast no pretence;
Learning thy talent is, but mine is sense.
That busy fool I was which thou art now;
Desirous to correct, not knowing how,—

With very good design, but little wit,
Blaming or praising things as I thought fit :
I for this conduct had what I deserved,
And, dealing honestly, was almost starved.
But, thanks to my indulgent stars, I eat,
Since I have found the secret to be great."
"O dearest Andrew," says the humble droll,
"Henceforth may I obey, and thou control;
Provided thou impart thy useful skill."—
"Bow then," says Andrew, "and for once I will.—
Be of your patron's mind, whate'er he says ;
Sleep very much ; think little, and talk less :
Mind neither good nor bad, nor right nor wrong,
But eat your pudding, slave, and hold your tongue."
 A reverend prelate stopped his coach-and-six
To laugh a little at our Andrew's tricks :
But, when he heard him give this golden rule,
"Drive on" (he cried) "this fellow is no fool."

SAMUEL WESLEY (SENR.)

[The Rev. Samuel Wesley (or Westley) was born towards 1666, and died in 1735. He came of a dissenting family, but entered the Established Church in his youth, and was appointed to the living of Epworth, Lincolnshire. He published *Maggots, or Poems on several Subjects*, 1685 ; *The Life of Christ*, a heroic poem, 1693 ; a Latin Commentary on Job ; and other works in verse and prose. He had a family of nineteen children, including Samuel Wesley, Jun. (see p. 198), and the celebrated John Wesley].

A PINDARIC ON THE GRUNTING OF A HOG.

FREEBORN Pindaric never does refuse
Either a lofty or a humble muse :—
Now in proud Sophoclean buskins sings
 Of heroes and of kings,
 Mighty numbers, mighty things ;
  Now out of sight she flies,
  Rowing with gaudy wings
  Across the stormy skies ;
   Then down again
   Herself she flings,
 Without uneasiness or pain,
  To lice and dogs,
  To cows and hogs,
And follows their melodious grunting o'er the plain.

  Harmonious hog, draw near !
  No bloody butcher's here,—
  Thou need'st not fear.
Harmonious hog, draw near, and from thy beauteous snout
 (Whilst we attend with ear,
 Like thine, pricked up devout,

To taste thy sugary voice, which here and there,
With wanton curls, vibrates around the circling air),
  Harmonious hog ! warble some anthem out !
As sweet as those which quavering Monks, in days of yore,
      With us did roar,
      When they (alas
That the hard-hearted abbot such a coil should keep,
  And cheat 'em of their first, their sweetest sleep !)
  When they were ferreted up to midnight mass :
  Why should not other pigs on organs play,
      As well as they ?

    Dear hog ! thou king of meat !
    So near thy lord, mankind,
  The nicest taste can scarce a difference find !
  No more may I thy glorious gammons eat—
      No more
Partake of the free farmer's Christmas store,
Black puddings which with fat would make your mouth run o'er,—
If I (though I should ne'er so long the sentence stay,
And in my large ears' scale the thing ne'er so discreetly weigh),
  If I can find a difference in the notes
      Belched from the applauded throats
Of rotten play-house songsters all-divine,—
If any difference I can find between their notes and thine.
  A noise they keep, with tune and out of tune,
      And round and flat,
      High, low, and this and that,
That Algebra or thou or I might understand as soon.

Like the confounding lute's innumerable strings
      One of them sings.
  Thy easier music's ten times more divine :
More like the one-stringed, deep, majestic trump-marine.
Prythee strike up, and cheer this drooping heart of mine !—
    Not the sweet harp that's claimed by Jews,
Nor that which to the far more ancient Welsh belongs,
  Nor that which the wild Irish use,
Frighting even their own wolves with loud hubbubbaboos,
    Nor Indian dance, with Indian songs,
      Nor yet
    (Which how should I so long forget ?)
      The crown of all the rest,
      The very cream o' the jest,
  Amphion's noble lyre—the tongs ;
Nor, though poetic Jordan bite his thumbs
At the bold world, my Lord Mayor's flutes and kettledrums ;
    Not all this instrumental dare
With thy soft, ravishing, vocal music ever to compare !

SIR JOHN VANBRUGH.

[Born in 1666, died in 1726. Dramatist and architect].

FABLE, RELATED BY A BEAU TO ÆSOP.

A Band, a Bob-wig, and a Feather,
Attacked a lady's heart together.
The Band, in a most learned plea
Made up of deep philosophy,
Told her, if she would please to wed
A reverend beard, and take instead
    Of vigorous youth,
      Old solemn truth,
With books and morals, into bed,
    How happy she would be.

The Bob he talked of management,
What wondrous blessings Heaven sent
On care, and pains, and industry:
And truly he must be so free
To own he thought your airy beaux,
With powdered wigs and dancing-shoes,
Were good for nothing (mend his soul!)
But prate, and talk, and play the fool.

He said 'twas wealth gave joy and mirth,
And that to be the dearest wife
Of one who laboured all his life
To make a mine of gold his own,
And not spend sixpence when he'd done,
Was heaven upon earth.

When these two blades had done, d'ye see,
The Feather (as it might be me)
Steps out, sir, from behind the screen,
With such an air and such a mien—
"Look you, old gentleman,"—in short,
He quickly spoiled the statesman's sport.

  It proved such sunshine weather
That, you must know, at the first beck
The lady leaped about his neck,
    And off they went together!

JONATHAN SWIFT.
[Born in Dublin, 30 November 1667; died there, 19 October 1745].

DEAN SWIFT'S CURATE.

I MARCHED three miles through scorching sand,
With zeal in heart, and notes in hand;
I rode four more to great St. Mary,
Using four legs when two were weary.
To three fair virgins I did tie men
In the close bands of pleasing Hymen;
I dipped two babes in holy water,
And purified their mothers after.
Within an hour and eke an half,
I preachèd three congregations deaf,
Which, thundering out with lungs long-winded,
I chopped so fast that few there minded.
My emblem, the laborious sun,
Saw all these mighty labours done
Before one race of his was run.
All this performed by Robert Hewit;
What mortal else could e'er go through it?

A TRUE AND FAITHFUL INVENTORY
OF THE GOODS BELONGING TO DR. SWIFT, VICAR OF LARACOR, UPON LENDING HIS HOUSE TO THE BISHOP OF MEATH TILL HIS PALACE WAS REBUILT.

AN oaken broken elbow-chair;
A caudle-cup without an ear;
A battered shattered ash bedstead;
A box of deal, without a lid;
A pair of tongs, but out of joint;
A back-sword poker, without point;
A pot that's cracked across, around
With an old knotted garter bound;
An iron lock, without a key;
A wig, with hanging quite grown grey;
A curtain, worn to half a stripe;
A pair of bellows, without pipe;
A dish, which might good meat afford once;
An Ovid, and an old Concordance;
A bottle-bottom, wooden platter,—
One is for meal, and one for water.
There likewise is a copper skillet,
Which runs as fast out as you fill it;
A candlestick, snuff-dish, and save-all:
And thus his household goods you have all.
These to your lordship, as a friend,
Till you have built, I freely lend:
They'll serve your lordship for a shift;
Why not, as well as Doctor Swift?

ON THE
LITTLE HOUSE BY THE CHURCHYARD OF CASTLENOCK.

Whoever pleaseth to enquire
Why yonder steeple wants a spire,
The grey old fellow, poet Joe,
The philosophic cause will show.
Once on a time, a western blast
At least twelve inches overcast,
Reckoning roof, weathercock, and all;
Which came with a prodigious fall,
And, tumbling topsy-turvy round,
Lit with its bottom on the ground,
For by the laws of gravitation
It fell into its proper station.
  This is the little strutting pile
You see just by the churchyard stile.
The walls in tumbling gave a knock,
And thus the steeple gave a shock:
From whence the neighbouring farmer calls
The steeple, Knock; the Vicar, Walls.
  The vicar once a week creeps in,
Sits with his knees up to his chin;
Here cons his notes, and takes a whet,
Till the small ragged flock is met.
  A traveller who by did pass
Observed the roof behind the grass,
On tiptoe stood, and reared his snout,
And saw the parson creeping out;
Was much surprised to see a crow
Venture to build his nest so low.
A schoolboy ran unto't, and thought
The crib was down, the blackbird caught.
A third, who lost his way by night,
Was forced for safety to alight,
And, stepping o'er the fabric-roof,
His horse had like to spoil his hoof
  Warburton took it in his noddle
This building was designed a model
Or of a pigeon-house, or oven,
To bake one loaf, and keep one dove in.
Then Mrs. Johnson[1] gave her verdict,
And every one was pleased that heard it:
"All that you make this stir about
Is but a still which wants a spout."
The Rev. Dr. Raymond guessed
More probably than all the rest;
He said, but that it wanted room,

---

[1] Stella.

It might have been a pygmy's tomb.
The doctor's family came by,
And little miss began to cry,
"Give me that house in my own hand!"
Then madam bade the chariot stand,
Called to the clerk, in manner mild;
"Pray reach that thing here to the child,—
That thing, I mean, among the kale;
And here's to buy a pot of ale."
The clerk said to her, in a heat;
"What, sell my master's country-seat,
Where he comes every week from town?
He would not sell it for a crown."
"Poh, fellow, keep not such a pother,
In half an hour thou'lt make another."
Says Nancy; "I can make for miss
A finer house ten times than this;
The Dean will give me willow-sticks,
And Joe my apronful of bricks."

BAUCIS AND PHILEMON.
IMITATED FROM THE EIGHTH BOOK OF OVID.

IN ancient times, as story tells,
The saints would often leave their cells,
And stroll about, but hide their quality,
To try good people's hospitality.
    It happened on a winter-night,
As authors of the legend write,
Two brother hermits, saints by trade,
Taking their tour in masquerade,
Disguised in tattered habits, went
To a small village down in Kent;
Where, in the strollers' canting strain,
They begged from door to door in vain,
Tried every tone might pity win;
But not a soul would let them in.
    Our wandering saints in woful state,
Treated at this ungodly rate,
Having through all the village passed,
To a small cottage came at last;
Where dwelt a good old honest ye'man,
Called in the neighbourhood Philemon;
Who kindly did these saints invite
In his poor hut to pass the night.
And then the hospitable sire
Bid goody Baucis mend the fire;
While he from out the chimney took
A flitch of bacon off the hook,

And freely from the fattest side
Cut out large slices to be fried;
Then stepped aside to fetch 'em drink,
Filled a large jug up to the brink,
And saw it fairly twice go round;
Yet (what is wonderful!) they found
'Twas still replenished to the top,
As if they had not touched a drop.
The good old couple were amazed,
And often on each other gazed;
For both were frightened to the heart,
And just began to cry "What art?"
Then softly turned aside to view
Whether the lights were burning blue.
The gentle pilgrims, soon aware on't,
Told them their calling and their errant.
"Good folks, you need not be afraid,
We are but saints," the hermits said.
"No hurt shall come to you or yours:
But, for that pack of churlish boors,
Not fit to live on Christian ground,
They and their houses shall be drowned;
Whilst you shall see your cottage rise,
And grow a church before your eyes."
    They scarce had spoke when fair and soft
The roof began to mount aloft;
Aloft rose every beam and rafter;
The heavy wall climbed slowly after.
The chimney widened, and grew higher,
Became a steeple with a spire.
The kettle to the top was hoist,
And there stood fastened to a joist,
But with the upside down, to show
Its inclination for below.
In vain; for a superior force
Applied at bottom stops its course:
Doomed ever in suspense to dwell,
'Tis now no kettle but a bell.
    A wooden jack, which had almost
Lost by disuse the art to roast,
A sudden alteration feels,
Increased by new intestine wheels;
And, what exalts the wonder more,
The number made the motion slower.
The flier, though't had leaden feet,
Turned round so quick you scarce could see't;
But, slackened by some secret power,
Now hardly moves an inch an hour.
The jack and chimney, near allied,
Had never left each other's side:

The chimney to a steeple grown,
The jack would not be left alone,
But, up against the steeple reared,
Became a clock, and still adhered ;
And still its love to household-cares,
By a shrill voice at noon, declares,
Warning the cook-maid not to burn
That roast-meat which it cannot turn.
  The groaning chair began to crawl,
Like a huge snail, along the wall ;
There stuck aloft in public view,
And, with small change, a pulpit grew.
The porringers, that in a row
Hung high, and made a glittering show,
To a less noble substance changed,
Were now but leathern buckets ranged.
The ballads pasted on the wall,
Of Joan of France, and English Moll,
Fair Rosamond, and Robin Hood,
The little children in the wood,
Now seemed to look abundance better,
Improved in picture, size, and letter ;
And, high in order placed, describe
The heraldry of every tribe.[1]
  A bedstead of the antique mode,
Compact of timber many a load,
Such as our ancestors did use,
Was metamorphosed into pews ;
Which still their ancient nature keep,
By lodging folks disposed to sleep.
  The cottage, by such feats as these,
Grown to a church by just degrees,
The hermits then desired their host
To ask for what he fancied most.
Philemon, having paused a while,
Returned them thanks in homely style ;
Then said ; "My house is grown so fine,
Methinks I still would call it mine ;
I'm old, and fain would live at ease ;
Make me the parson, if you please."
  He spoke ; and presently he feels
His grazier's coat fall down his heels :
He sees, yet hardly can believe,
About each arm a pudding-sleeve ;
His waistcoat to a cassock grew,
And both assumed a sable hue ;
But, being old, continued just

---

[1] Of the twelve tribes of Israel, which in country-churches were sometimes distinguished by the ensigns appropriated to them by Jacob on his deathbed.

As threadbare, and as full of dust.
His talk was now of tithes and dues:
He smoked his pipe, and read the news;
Knew how to preach old sermons next,
Vamped-in the preface and the text;
At christ'nings well could act his part,
And had the service all by heart;
Wished women might have children fast,
And thought whose sow had farrowed last;
Against dissenters would repine,
And stood up firm for right divine;
Found his head filled with many a system:
But classic authors—he ne'er missed 'em.

 Thus having furbished up a parson,
Dame Baucis next they played their farce on.
Instead of home-spun coifs, were seen
Good pinners edged with colberteen;
Her petticoat, transformed apace,
Became black satin flounced with lace.
Plain *Goody* would no longer down;
'Twas *Madam*, in her grogram gown.
Philemon was in great surprise,
And hardly could believe his eyes,
Amazed to see her look so prim;
And she admired as much at him.

 Thus happy in their change of life
Were several years this man and wife;
When on a day, which proved their last,
Discoursing o'er old stories past,
They went by chance, amidst their talk,
To the church-yard to take a walk;
When Baucis hastily cried out,
"My dear, I see your forehead sprout!"
"Sprout!" quoth the man; "what's this you tell us?
I hope you don't believe me jealous.
But yet, methinks, I feel it true;
And really yours is budding too——
Nay,—now I cannot stir my foot;
It feels as if 'twere taking root."

 Description would but tire my Muse;
In short, they both were turned to yews.

 Old Goodman Dobson of the green
Remembers he the trees has seen.
He'll talk of them from noon till night,
And goes with folks to show the sight.
On Sundays, after evening-prayer,
He gathers all the parish there;
Points out the place of either yew;
"Here Baucis, there Philemon grew:
Till once a parson of our town,

> To mend his barn, cut Baucis down;
> At which 'tis hard to be believed
> How much the other tree was grieved,—
> Grew scrubby, died a-top, was stunted;
> So the next parson stubbed and burnt it."

A DESCRIPTION OF THE MORNING.

Now hardly here and there an hackney-coach
Appearing showed the ruddy morn's approach.
Now Betty from her master's bed had flown,
And softly stole to discompose her own:
The slipshod prentice from his master's door
Had pared the dirt, and sprinkled round the floor.
Now Moll had whirled her mop with dextrous airs,
Prepared to scrub the entry and the stairs.
The youth[1] with broomy stumps began to trace
The kennel's edge, where wheels had worn the place.
The small-coal man was heard with cadence deep,
Till drowned in shriller notes of chimney-sweep:
Duns at his Lordship's gate began to meet;
And brick-dust Moll had screamed through half the street.
The turnkey now his flock returning sees,
Duly let out a-nights to steal for fees:
The watchful bailiffs take their silent stands;
And schoolboys lag with satchels in their hands.

STELLA'S BIRTHDAY, 1718.

Stella this day is thirty-four
(We shan't dispute a year or more).
However, Stella, be not troubled;
Although thy size and years are doubled
Since first I saw thee at sixteen,
The brightest virgin on the green,
So little is thy form declined;
Made up so largely in thy mind.
  Oh would it please the gods to split
Thy beauty, size, and years, and wit!
No age could furnish out a pair
Of nymphs so graceful, wise, and fair,
With half the lustre of your eyes,
With half your wit, your years, and size.
And then, before it grew too late,
How should I beg of gentle fate
(That either nymph might have her swain)
To split my worship too in twain!

---

[1] To find old nails.

MARY THE COOK-MAID'S LETTER TO DR. SHERIDAN

WELL, if ever I saw such another man since my mother bound my head!
You a gentleman! marry come up, I wonder where you were bred!
I am sure such words do not become a man of your cloth;
I would not give such language to a dog, faith and troth.
Yes, you called my master a knave: fie, Mr. Sheridan! 'tis a shame
For a parson, who should know better things, to come out with such a name.
Knave in your teeth, Mr. Sheridan! 'tis both a shame and a sin;
And the Dean my master is an honester man than you and all your kin.
He has more goodness in his little finger than you have in your whole body:
My master is a personable man, and not a spindle-shanked hoddy-doddy.
And now, whereby I find you would fain make an excuse,
Because my master one day, in anger, called you goose;
Which and I am sure I have been his servant four years since October,
And he never called me worse than *sweetheart*, drunk or sober.
Not that I know his Reverence was ever concerned, to my knowledge,
Though you and your come-rogues keep him out so late in your wicked college.
You say you will eat grass on his grave: A Christian eat grass!
Whereby you now confess yourself to be a goose or an ass.
But that's as much as to say that my master should die before ye;
Well, well, that's as God pleases; and I don't believe that's a true story.
And so say I told you so, and you may go tell my master; what care I?
And I don't care who knows it; 'tis all one to Mary.
Every body knows that I love to tell truth, and shame the devil.
I am but a poor servant; but I think gentle-folks should be civil.
Besides, you found fault with our victuals one day that you was here;
I remember it was on a Tuesday, of all days in the year.
And Saunders the man says you are always jesting and mocking:
"Mary," said he one day, as I was mending my master's stocking,
"My master is so fond of that minister that keeps the school:
I thought my master a wise man, but that man makes him a fool."
"Saunders," said I, "I would rather than a quart of ale
He would come into our kitchen, and I would pin a dishclout to his tail."
And now I must go, and get Saunders to direct this letter;
For I write but a sad scrawl; but my sister Marget she writes better.

Well, but I must run and make the bed, before my master comes
    from prayers;
And see now, it strikes ten, and I hear him coming up stairs.
Whereof I could say more to your verses, if I could write written
    hand :
And so I remain, in a civil way, your servant to command,
                                           MARY.

DR. SWIFT TO MR. POPE, WHILE HE WAS WRITING THE DUNCIAD.

POPE has the talent well to speak,
  But not to reach the ear;
His loudest voice is low and weak,
  The Dean too deaf to hear.

Awhile they on each other look,
  Then different studies choose.
The Dean sits plodding on a book;
  Pope walks, and courts the muse.

Now backs of letters, though designed
  For those who more will need 'em,
Are filled with hints, and interlined,—
  Himself can hardly read 'em.

Each atom, by some other struck,
  All turns and motions tries:
Till, in a lump together stuck,
  Behold a poem rise !

Yet to the Dean his share allot;
  He claims it by a canon;
"That without which a thing is not
  Is causa sine quâ non."

Thus, Pope, in vain you boast your wit;
  For, had our deaf divine
Been for your conversation fit,
  You had not writ a line.

Of prelate thus for preaching famed
  The sexton reasoned well;
And justly half the merit claimed,
  Because he rang the bell.

TO DR. DELANY, ON THE LIBELS WRITTEN AGAINST HIM.

As some raw youth in country bred,
To arms by thirst of honour led,
When at a skirmish first he hears
The bullets whistling round his ears,
Will duck his head aside, will start,
And feel a trembling at his heart;
Till scaping oft without a wound
Lessens the terror of the sound;
Fly bullets now as thick as hops,
He runs into a cannon's chops:
An author thus who pants for fame
Begins the world with fear and shame.
When first in print, you see him dread
Each pop-gun levelled at his head:
The lead yon critic's quill contains
Is destined to beat out his brains.
As if he heard loud thunders roll,
Cries Lord have mercy on his soul!
Concluding that another shot
Will strike him dead upon the spot.
But, when with squibbing, flashing, popping,
He cannot see one creature dropping;
That, missing fire or missing aim,
His life is safe (I mean his fame);
The danger past, takes heart of grace,
And looks a critic in 'the face.

Though splendour gives the fairest mark
To poisoned arrows from the dark,
Yet, in yourself when smooth and round,[1]
They glance aside without a wound.

'Tis said the gods tried all their art
How Pain they might from Pleasure part;
But little could their strength avail,—
Both still are fastened by the tail.
Thus Fame and Censure with a tether
By fate are always linked together.

Why will you aim to be preferred
In wit before the common herd,
And yet grow mortified and vexed
To pay the penalty annexed?

'Tis eminence makes envy rise,
As fairest fruits attract the flies.
Should stupid libels grieve your mind,
You soon a remedy may find;

---

[1] In seipso totus teres atque rotundus.

Lie down obscure like other folks
Below the lash of snarlers' jokes.
Their faction is five-hundred odds;
For every coxcomb lends them rods,
And sneers as learnedly as they,
Like females o'er their morning tea.

You say, the Muse will not contain,
And write you must, or break a vein.
Then, if you find the terms too hard,
No longer my advice regard:
But raise your fancy on the wing.
The Irish senate's praises sing;
How jealous of the nation's freedom,
And for corruptions, how they weed 'em;
How each the public good pursues,
How far their hearts from private views;
Make all true patriots up to shoeboys
Huzza their brethren at the Blue-boys.[1]
Thus grown a member of the club,
No longer dread the rage of Grub.

How oft am I for rhyme to seek!
To dress a thought, I toil a week:
And then how thankful to the town
If all my pains will earn a crown!
Whilst every critic can devour
My work and me in half an hour.
Would men of genius cease to write,
The rogues must die for want and spite;
Must die for want of food and raiment,
If scandal did not find them payment.
How cheerfully the hawkers cry
"A satire," and the gentry buy!
While my hard-laboured poem pines
Unsold upon the printer's lines.

A genius in the reverend gown
Must ever keep its owner down;
'Tis an unnatural conjunction,
And spoils the credit of the function.
Round all your brethren cast your eyes;
Point out the surest men to rise.
That club of candidates in black,
The least deserving of the pack,
Aspiring, factious, fierce, and loud,
With grace and learning unendowed,
Can turn their hands to every job,
The fittest tools to work for Bob;[2]

---

[1] The Irish parliament sat at the Blue-boys' Hospital while the new parliament-house was building.   [2] Sir Robert Walpole.

Will sooner coin a thousand lies
Than suffer men of parts to rise.
They crowd about preferment's gate,
And press you down with all their weight.
For, as of old mathematicians
Were by the vulgar thought magicians,
So academic dull ale-drinkers
Pronounce all men of wit *freethinkers*.

   Wit, as the chief of virtue's friends,
Disdains to serve ignoble ends.
Observe what loads of stupid rhymes
Oppress us in corrupted times.
What pamphlets in a court's defence
Show reason, grammar, truth, or sense?
For, though the Muse delights in fiction,
She ne'er inspires against conviction.
Then keep your virtue still unmixed,
And let not faction come betwixt:
By party-steps no grandeur climb at,
Though it would make you England's primate.
First learn the science to be dull,—
You then may soon your conscience lull;
If not, however seated high,
Your genius in your face will fly.

   When Jove was from his teeming head
Of wit's fair goddess brought to bed,
There followed at his lying-in
For afterbirth a Sooterkin;
Which, as the nurse pursued to kill,
Attained by flight the Muses' hill;
There in the soil began to root,
And littered at Parnassus' foot.
From hence the critic vermin sprung,
With harpy claws and poisonous tongue,
Who fatten on poetic scraps,
Too cunning to be caught in traps.
Dame Nature, as the learned show,
Provides each animal its foe:
Hounds hunt the hare, the wily fox
Devours your geese, the wolf your flocks:
Thus Envy pleads a natural claim
To persecute the Muses' fame;
On poets in all times abusive,
From Homer down to Pope inclusive.

   Yet what avails it to complain?
You try to take revenge in vain.
A rat your utmost rage defies,
That safe behind the wainscot lies.

Say, did you ever know by sight
In cheese an individual mite?
Show me the same numeric flea
That bit your neck but yesterday:
You then may boldly go in quest
To find the Grub-street poets' nest;
What spunging-house in dread of jail
Receives them while they wait for bail;
What alley they are nestled in,
To flourish o'er a cup of gin:
Find the last garret where they lay,
Or cellar where they starve to-day.
Suppose you had them all trepanned,
With each a libel in his hand,
What punishment would you inflict?
Or call 'em rogues, or get 'em kicked?
These they have often tried before;
You but oblige 'em so much more:
Themselves would be the first to tell,
To make their trash the better sell.

    You have been libelled——Let us know
What fool officious told you so.
Will you regard the hawker's cries,
Who in his titles always lies?
Whate'er the noisy scoundrel says,
It *might* be something in your praise:
And praise bestowed on Grub-street rhymes
Would vex one more a thousand times.
Till critics blame, and judges praise,
The poet cannot claim his bays.
On me when dunces are satiric,
I take it for a panegyric.
Hated by fools, and fools to hate,—
Be that my motto, and my fate.

WHITSHED'S MOTTO ON HIS COACH.[1]

Libertas et natale solum.—Liberty and my native country.

"LIBERTAS et natale solum :
Fine words! I wonder where you stole 'em.
Could nothing but thy chief reproach
Serve for a motto on thy coach?"

    "But let me now the words translate.
Natale solum, my estate;

---

[1] Whitshed was the Chief Justice who acted against Swift in the affair of the letters by "M. B. Drapier."

My dear estate, how well I love it!
My tenants, if you doubt, will prove it:
They swear I am so kind and good
I hug them till I squeeze their blood.
Libertas bears a large import:
First, how to swagger in a court;
And, secondly, to show my fury
Against an uncomplying jury;
And, thirdly, 'tis a new invention
To favour Wood, and keep my pension;
And, fourthly, 'tis to play an odd trick,
Get the great seal, and turn out Brod'rick;
And, fifthly (you know whom I mean),
To humble that vexatious Dean;
And, sixthly, for my soul, to barter it,
For fifty times its worth, to Carteret."[1]

"Now, since your motto thus you construe,
I must confess you've spoken once true.
Libertas et natale solum:
You had good reason when you stole 'em."

DEATH AND DAPHNE.
TO AN AGREEABLE YOUNG LADY, BUT EXTREMELY LEAN.

DEATH went upon a solemn day
At Pluto's hall his court to pay.
The phantom, having humbly kissed
His grisly monarch's sooty fist,
Presented him the weekly bills
Of doctors, fevers, plagues, and pills.
Pluto, observing, since the peace,
The burial-article decrease,
And vexed to see affairs miscarry,
Declared in council Death must marry:
Vowed he no longer could support
Old bachelors about his court:
The interest of his realm had need
That Death should get a numerous breed;
Young *deathlings*, who, by practice made
Proficient in their father's trade,
With colonies might stock around
His large dominions underground.

A consult of coquets below
Was called to rig him out a beau.
From her own head Megæra takes
A periwig of twisted snakes;
Which in the nicest fashion curled

---

[1] Lord Carteret, Lord Lieutenant of Ireland.

(Like *toupets* of this upper world),
With flour of sulphur powdered well,
That graceful on his shoulders fell;
An adder of the sable kind,
In line direct, hung down behind.
The owl, the raven, and the bat,
Clubbed for a feather to his hat;
His coat, an usurer's velvet pall,
Bequeathed to Pluto, corpse and all.
But, loth his person to expose
Bare, like a carcase picked by crows,
A lawyer o'er his hands and face
Stuck artfully a parchment case.
No new-fluxed rake showed fairer skin,
Nor Phillis after lying in.
With snuff was filled his ebon box,
Of shin-bones rotted by the pox.
Nine spirits of blaspheming fops
With aconite anoint his chops:
And give him words of dreadful sounds,
"God damn his blood," and "blood and wounds."

   Thus furnished out, he sent his train
To take a house in Warwick Lane.
The faculty, his humble friends,
A complimental message sends:
Their president in scarlet gown
Harangued, and welcomed him to town.

   But Death had business to dispatch;
His mind was running on his match.
And, hearing much of Daphne's fame,
His Majesty of Terrors came,
Fine as a colonel of the guards,
To visit where she sat at cards.
She, as he came into the room,
Thought him Adonis in his bloom.
And now her heart with pleasure jumps;
She scarce remembers what is trumps;
For such a shape of skin and bone
Was never seen except her own:
Charmed with his eyes, and chin, and snout,
Her pocket-glass drew slily out;
And grew enamoured with her phiz,
As just the counterpart of his.
She darted many a private glance,
And freely made the first advance;
Was of her beauty grown so vain
She doubted not to win the swain;
Nothing, she thought, could sooner gain him
Than with her wit to entertain him.

She asked about her friends below;
This meagre fop, that battered beau:
Whether some late-departed toasts
Had got gallants among the ghosts :
If Chloe were a sharper still
As great as ever at quadrille—
(The ladies there must needs be rooks,
For cards, we know, are Pluto's books):
If Florimel had found her love,
For whom she hanged herself above :
How oft a week was kept a ball
By Proserpine at Pluto's hall.
She fancied those Elysian shades
The sweetest place for masquerades :
How pleasant, on the banks of Styx,
To troll it in a coach and six !

What pride a female heart inflames !
How endless are ambition's aims !
Cease, haughty nymph; the fates decree
Death must not be a spouse for thee:
For when, by chance, the meagre shade
Upon thy hand his finger laid,—
Thy hand as dry and cold as lead,—
His matrimonial spirit fled.
He felt about his heart a damp,
That quite extinguished Cupid's lamp.
Away the frighted spectre scuds,
And leaves my Lady in the suds.

LORD LANSDOWNE[1] (GEORGE GRANVILLE).

[George Granville, or Greenvill, born in 1667, was created Baron Lansdowne of Bideford in 1711, and died in 1735. He was a dramatist, miscellaneous writer, and politician, having held various offices, including the secretaryship at war. At the accession of George I., he, with other leaders of the Tory party, fell into disfavour ; and he suffered an imprisonment of several months in the Tower without being coerced into belying his principles].

LINES.

CHLOE'S the wonder of her sex.
  'Tis well her heart is tender;
How might such killing eyes perplex,
  With virtue to defend her !

But nature, graciously inclined
  With liberal hand to please us,
Has to her boundless beauty joined
  A boundless bent to ease us.

---

[1] Or "Landsdown," as the title is often written.

JOSEPH ADDISON.

[Born at Milton, Wilts, 11 May 1672; died in Holland House, London, 17 June 1719].

THE PLAY-HOUSE.

WHERE gentle Thames through stately channels glides,
And England's proud metropolis divides,
A lofty fabric does the sight invade,
And stretches o'er the waves a pompous shade;
Whence sudden shouts the neighbourhood surprise,
And thundering claps and dreadful hissings rise.
  Here thrifty Rich hires monarchs by the day,
And keeps his mercenary kings in pay;
With deep-mouthed actors fills the vacant scenes,
And rakes the stews for goddesses and queens.
Here the lewd punk, with crowns and sceptres graced,
Teaches her eyes a more majestic cast:
And hungry monarchs, with a numerous train
Of suppliant slaves, like Sancho, starve and reign.
  But enter in, my Muse; the stage survey,
And all its pomp and pageantry display;
Trapdoors and pitfalls form the unfaithful ground,
And magic walls encompass it around:
On either side maimed temples fill our eyes,
And, intermixed with brothel-houses, rise;
Disjointed palaces in order stand,
And groves, obedient to the mover's hand,
O'ershade the stage, and flourish at command.
A stamp makes broken towns and trees entire:
So, when Amphion struck the vocal lyre,
He saw the spacious circuit all around
With crowding woods and rising cities crowned.
But next the tiring-room survey, and see
False titles and promiscuous quality
Confus'dly swarm, from heroes and from queens
To those that swing in clouds and fill machines.
Their various characters they choose with art.
The frowning bully fits the tyrant's part:
Swoln cheeks and swaggering belly make an host;
Pale meagre looks and hollow voice, a ghost.
From careful brows and heavy downcast eyes,
Dull cits and thick-skulled aldermen arise;
The comic tone, inspired by Congreve, draws
At every word loud laughter and applause:
The whining dame continues as before,
Her character unchanged, and acts a whore.
Above the rest, the prince, with haughty stalks,
Magnificent in purple buskins walks:
The royal robes his awful shoulders grace,
Profuse of spangles and of copper lace.

Officious rascals, to his mighty thigh
Guiltless of blood, the unpointed weapon tie:
Then the gay glittering diadem put on,
Ponderous with brass, and starred with Bristol stone.
His royal consort next consults her glass,
And out of twenty boxes culls a face.
The whitening first her ghastly looks besmears,
All pale and wan the unfinished form appears;
Till on her cheeks the blushing purple glows,
And a false virgin-modesty bestows.
Her ruddy lips the deep vermilion dyes:
Length to her brows the pencil's art supplies,
And with black-bending arches shades her eyes.
Well pleased at length the picture she beholds,
And spots it o'er with artificial moles.
Her countenance complete, the beaux she warms
With looks not hers; and, spite of nature, charms.
Thus artfully their persons they disguise,
Till the last flourish bids the curtain rise.
The Prince then enters on the stage in state;
Behind, a guard of candle-snuffers wait.
There, swoln with empire, terrible and fierce,
He shakes the dome, and tears his lungs with verse.
His subjects tremble; the submissive pit
Wrapped up in silence and attention sit.
Till, freed at length, he lays aside the weight
Of public business and affairs of state;
Forgets his pomp, dead to ambition's fires,
And to some peaceful brandy-shop retires;
Where in full gills his anxious thoughts he drowns,
And quaffs away the care that waits on crowns.
   The Princess next her painted charms displays,
Where every look the pencil's art betrays;
The callow squire at distance feeds his eyes,
And silently, for paint and washes, dies.
But, if the youth behind the scenes retreat,
He sees the blended colours melt with heat,
And all the trickling beauty run in sweat.
The borrowed visage he admires no more,
And nauseates every charm he loved before:
So the famed spear, for double force renowned,
Applied the remedy that gave the wound.
In tedious lists 'twere endless to engage,
And draw at length the rabble of the stage;
Where one for twenty years has given alarms,
And called contending monarchs to their arms.
Another fills a more important post,
And rises, every other night, a ghost;
Through the cleft stage his mealy face he rears,
Then stalks along, groans thrice, and disappears.

Others, with swords and shields, the soldier's pride,
More than a thousand times have changed their side,
And in a thousand fatal battles died.
   Thus several persons several parts perform ;
Soft lovers whine, and blustering heroes storm ;
The stern exasperated tyrants rage,
Till the kind bowl of poison clears the stage.
Then honours vanish, and distinctions cease ;
Then, with reluctance, haughty queens undress ;
Heroes no more their fading laurels boast,
And mighty kings in private men are lost.
He whom such titles swelled, such power made proud,
To whom whole realms and vanquished nations bowed,
Throws off the gaudy plume, the purple train,
And in his own vile tatters stinks again.

JOHN PHILIPS.

[Born in 1676, died in 1708. He studied as a physician ; but his *Splendid Shilling* (a parody on the Miltonian style, and the earliest specimen of its class) achieved so much success as to turn his attention to literature instead. It was published in 1703. Other writings by Philips, now forgotten, were of a more ambitious kind : and an early death put a stop to a peculiarly daring project, a poem on the Last Day].

THE SPLENDID SHILLING.

" . . . . . . Sing, heavenly Muse !
Things unattempted yet, in prose or rhyme,"
A Shilling, Breeches, and Chimeras dire.

HAPPY the man who, void of cares and strife,
In silken or in leathern purse retains
A Splendid Shilling. He nor hears with pain
New oysters cried, nor sighs for cheerful ale ;
But with his friends, when nightly mists arise,
To Juniper's Magpie or Town-Hall [1] repairs :
Where, mindful of the nymph whose wanton eye
Transfixed his soul and kindled amorous flames,
Chloe or Phillis, he each circling glass
Wisheth her health, and joy, and equal love.
Meanwhile, he smokes, and laughs at merry tale,
Or pun ambiguous, or conundrum quaint.
But I, whom griping Penury surrounds,
And Hunger, sure attendant upon Want,
With scanty offals, and small acid tiff,
(Wretched repast !) my meagre corpse sustain :
Then solitary walk, or doze at home
In garret vile, and with a warming puff
Regale chilled fingers ; or, from tube as black

---

[1] Two noted alehouses at Oxford in 1700.

As winter-chimney or well-polished jet,
Exhale mundungus, ill-perfuming scent!
Not blacker tube, nor of a shorter size,
Smokes Cambro-Briton (versed in pedigree,
Sprung from Cadwallader and Arthur, kings
Full famous in romantic tale), when he
O'er many a craggy hill and barren cliff,
Upon a cargo of famed Cestrian cheese,
High overshadowing rides, with a design
To vend his wares, or at the Arvonian mart,
Or Maridunum, or the ancient town
Yclept Brechinia, or where Vaga's stream
Encircles Ariconium, fruitful soil!
Whence flow nectareous wines, that well may vie
With Massic, Setin, or renowned Falern.

   Thus while my joyless minutes tedious flow,
With looks demure and silent pace, a Dun,
Horrible monster hated by gods and men,
To my aërial citadel ascends.
With vocal heel thrice thundering at my gate,
With hideous accent thrice he calls; I know
The voice ill-boding, and the solemn sound.
What should I do? or whither turn? Amazed,
Confounded, to the dark recess I fly
Of wood-hole; straight my bristling hairs erect
Through sudden fear; a chilly sweat bedews
My shuddering limbs, and, wonderful to tell!
My tongue forgets her faculty of speech;
So horrible he seems! His faded brow,
Entrenched with many a frown, and conic beard,
And spreading band admired by modern saints,
Disastrous acts forebode; in his right hand
Long scrolls of paper solemnly he waves,
With characters and figures dire inscribed,
Grievous to mortal eyes; ye gods, avert
Such plagues from righteous men! Behind him stalks
Another monster, not unlike himself,
Sullen of aspect, by the vulgar called
A Catchpole, whose polluted hands the gods
With force incredible and magic charms
Erst have endued. If he his ample palm
Should haply on ill-fated shoulder lay
Of debtor, straight his body, to the touch
Obsequious, as whilom knights were wont,
To some enchanted castle is conveyed;
Where gates impregnable and coercive chains
In durance strict detain him, till, in form
Of money, Pallas sets the captive free.

   Beware, ye Debtors! when ye walk, beware,
Be circumspect; oft with insidious ken

The caitiff eyes your steps aloof, and oft
Lies perdu in a nook or gloomy cave,
Prompt to enchant some inadvertent wretch
With his unhallowed touch. So (poets sing)
Grimalkin, to domestic vermin sworn
An everlasting foe, with watchful eye
Lies nightly brooding o'er a chinky gap,
Protending her fell claws, to thoughtless mice
Sure ruin. So her disembowelled web
Arachne, in a hall or kitchen, spreads
Obvious to vagrant flies. She secret stands
Within her woven cell ; the humming prey,
Regardless of their fate, rush on the toils
Inextricable, nor will aught avail
Their arts, or arms, or shapes of lovely hue.
The wasp insidious, and the buzzing drone,
And butterfly, proud of expanded wings
Distinct with gold, entangled in her snares,
Useless resistance make. With eager strides,
She towering flies to her expected spoils ;
Then, with envenomed jaws, the vital blood
Drinks of reluctant foes, and to her cave
Their bulky carcasses triumphant drags.

  So pass my days. But, when nocturnal shades
This world envelop, and the inclement air
Persuades men to repel benumbing frosts
With pleasant wines, and crackling blaze of wood ;
Me, lonely sitting, nor the glimmering light
Of make-weight candle, nor the joyous talk
Of loving friend, delights. Distressed, forlorn,
Amidst the horrors of the tedious night,
Darkling I sigh, and feed with dismal thoughts
My anxious mind ; or sometimes mournful verse
Indite, and sing of groves and myrtle shades,
Or desperate lady near a purling stream,
Or lover pendent on a willow-tree.
Meanwhile I labour with eternal drought,
And restless wish and rave ; my parchèd throat
Finds no relief, nor heavy eyes repose.
But, if a slumber haply does invade
My weary limbs, my fancy's still awake,
Thoughtful of drink, and, eager, in a dream,
Tipples imaginary pots of ale, —
In vain ; awake I find the settled thirst
Still gnawing, and the pleasant phantom curse.

  Thus do I live, from pleasure quite debarred,
Nor taste the fruits that the sun's genial rays
Mature ; john-apple, nor the downy peach,
Nor walnut in rough-furrowed coat secure,
Nor medlar, fruit delicious in decay.

Afflictions great! yet greater still remain.
My galligaskins, that have long withstood
The winter's fury, and encroaching frosts,
By time subdued (what will not time subdue?)
An horrid chasm disclosed with orifice
Wide, discontinuous; at which the winds
Eurus and Auster, and the dreadful force
Of Boreas that congeals the Cronian waves,
Tumultuous enter with dire chilling blasts,
Portending agues. Thus a well-fraught ship
Long sailed secure, or through the Ægean deep,
Or the Ionian; till, cruising near
The Lilybean shore, with hideous crash
On Scylla or Charybdis (dangerous rocks!)
She strikes rebounding. Whence the shattered oak,
So fierce a shock unable to withstand,
Admits the sea. In at the gaping side
The crowding waves gush with impetuous rage,
Resistless, overwhelming; horrors seize
The mariners; Death in their eyes appears;
They stare, they lave, they pump, they swear, they pray.
Vain efforts! Still the battering waves rush in,
Implacable, till, deluged by the foam,
The ship sinks foundering in the vast abyss.

GEORGE JEFFREYS.

[Born in 1678, died in 1755. Wrote some dramatic pieces, and translated Vida's poem on Chess. Two of his Tragedies, *Edwin* and *Merope*, were brought on the stage].

A RIDDLE OF DEAN SWIFT'S, VERSIFIED.

You ask a story, not more strange than true;
Nor must I hide it from a friend like you.
Without disguise my wretched lot behold,
In all its train of circumstances told.
And, though perhaps what I shall first advance
May make the whole resemble a romance,
A solemn truth it is—no whim, nor jest;
Which, if you please, the Parson shall attest.

Know then, dear Sir, my present situation
Is in a small and sorry habitation,
Ill fitted-up and fenced; upon the waste,
Like other clay-built cottages, 'tis placed.
In this poor hut I breathe with care and pain;
And, what is harder, if I durst complain,
One minute's warning turns me out again.

Held by a sort of copy, it appears
An easy bargain for the first seven years:

For, free from rent, I only then resort,
As bound in duty, to the Manor-court;
There once a week, or more, to custom true,
My landlord claims the suit and service due.
The twenty following years require a rose
In annual payment to my worst of foes.
My next acknowledgment is stranger still;
For, soon or later, at my landlord's will,
Each third or second year, or oftener yet,
A tooth discharges my unwelcome debt;
And, when to answer more demands I fail,
A meagre catchpole hurries me to jail.
No miscreant so remorseless ever tore
Thy journals, Fog, or knocked at Franklin's door.

In days of old, on better terms than these
I might have occupied the premises,
Ere a false step my fond great-grandsire made,
Warped by a wheedling wife, their race betrayed.
An orchard to the Manor-house adjoined,
Rich in delicious fruits of every kind:
In robbing it the graceless pair were caught
By a bad neighbour, to their ruin taught:
For by that slip, without retrieve, was lost
A certain privilege they once could boast;
And, from the hour when they were turned adrift,
Their hapless line have made this woful shift.

However, rubbing onward as I may,
I spare no pains to patch my house of clay;
And keep it in a tenantable way.
A little kitchen serves to dress my fare,
Shaped like an oven, rather round than square:
My garrets, poorly furnished, I may load,
Perhaps too much, with lumber à-la-mode.
To this low state uncomfortably tied,
Well as I can for rent-day I provide;
That, when my term (as soon it must) shall cease,
My gracious Lord may sign a full release.

When I am ousted, a mean creeping race,
Doomed to succeed me, have secured the place;
Where they are sure to multiply amain,
Triumphant o'er their foe in Abchurch Lane.

Meanwhile this lodge, or call it what you please,
Has one snug hole, contrived for warmth and ease.
On the left side of my abode it lies,
And for my friends a resting-place supplies:
This to your use with pleasure I resign;
Yours is the lodging, while the house is mine.

THOMAS SHERIDAN.

[Dr. Sheridan, translator of Persius, and grandfather of Richard Brinsley Sheridan, was born in 1684, and died in 1738. He was a clergyman, and a friend of Swift. His heart was as light as his purse ; and he was perpetually punning, fiddling, or throwing off some jocular effusion. On the anniversary of the accession of the reigning King, George I., Sheridan, being then one of the chaplains to the Lord Lieutenant, preached from the text " sufficient for the day is the evil thereof." This cost him his chaplaincy].

DR. DELANY'S VILLA.

WOULD you that Delville I describe?
Believe me, sir, I will not gibe :
For who could be satirical
Upon a thing so very small?
   You scarce upon the borders enter,
Before you're at the very centre :
A single crow can make it night
When o'er your farm she takes her flight.
Yet, in this narrow compass, we
Observe a vast variety;
Both walks, walls, meadows, and parterres,
Windows and doors, and rooms and stairs,
And hills and dales, and woods and fields,
And hay and grass and corn it yields ;
All to your haggard brought so cheap in,
Without the mowing or the reaping :
A razor, though to say't I'm loth,
Would shave you and your meadows both.
   Though small's the farm, yet here's a house
Full large to entertain a mouse,
But where a rat is dreaded more
Than savage Calydonian boar ;
For, if it's entered by a rat,
There is no room to bring a cat.
   A little rivulet seems to steal
Down through a thing you call a vale,
Like tears adown a wrinkled cheek,
Like rain along a blade of leek :
And this you call your sweet Meander,
Which might be sucked up by a gander,
Could he but force his nether bill
To scoop the channel of the rill.
For sure you'd make a mighty clutter,
Were it as big as city gutter.
   Next come I to your kitchen garden,
Where one poor mouse would fare but hard in ;
And round this garden is a walk,
No longer than a tailor's chalk ;
Thus I compare what space is in it,—
A snail creeps round it in a minute.

One lettuce makes a shift to squeeze
Up through a tuft you call your trees :
And, once a year, a single rose
Peeps from the bud, but never blows.
In vain then you expect its bloom :
It cannot blow for want of room.
In short, in all your boasted seat,
There's nothing but yourself that's Great.

JOSEPH MITCHELL.

[Born in Scotland towards 1684; died in 1738. He was called "Sir Robert Walpole's poet," being one of that minister's dependents. Two volumes of his poems appeared in 1729].

THE CHARMS OF INDOLENCE.
DEDICATED TO A CERTAIN LAZY PEER.

THY charms, O sacred Indolence, I sing ;
Droop, yawning Muse, and moult thy sleepy wing.
Ye lolling powers (if any powers there be
Who loll supine), to you I bend my knee :
O'er my lean labour shed a vapoury breath,
And clog my numbers with a weight like death.
I feel the arrested wheels of meaning stand :
With poppy tinged, see ! see ! yon waving wand.
Morpheus, I own the influence of thy reign ;
A drowsy sloth creeps cold through every vein.
Furred, like the Muses' magistrate, I sit,
And nod superior in a dream of wit.
Action expires, in honour of my lays,
And mankind snores encomiums to my praise.

Hail, holy state of unalarmed repose !
Dear source of honest and substantial prose !
Thou blest asylum of man's wearied race !
Nature's dumb picture, with her solemn face !
How shall my pen, untired, thy praise pursue ?
Oh woe of living to have aught to do !
'Till the almighty fiat waκened life,
And wandering chaos rose in untried strife,
Till atoms jostled atoms in the deep,
Nature lay careless, in eternal sleep.
No whispering hope, no murmuring wish, possessed
A place in all the extended realms of rest.
The seeds of being undisturbed remained,
And indolence through space unbounded reigned.
Thence, lordly Sloth, thy high descent we trace ;
The world's less ancient than thy reverend race.
Antiquity's whole boast is on thy side,
That great foundation of the modern pride.

Thou wert grown old before the birth of man,
And reign'dst before formation's self began;
From thee creation took its new-born way,
When infant Nature smiled on opening day.
Now, winking, weary of the oppressive light,
It longs to be re-hushed in lulling night:
For each bold starter from thy powerful reign
Returns at length thy humble slave again.
Oh happy he who, conscious of thy sweets,
Safe to thy circling arms betimes retreats!
Raised on thy downy car, he shuns all strife,
And lolls along the thorny roads of life.
Indulgent dreams his slumbering senses please,
And his numbed spirits shrink to central ease.
Nor passion's conflicts his soft peace infest,
Nor danger rouses his unlistening rest.
Stretched in supine content, afloat, he lies,
And drives down time's slow stream, with unfixed eyes.
Lethargic influence bars the approach of pain,
And storms blow round him, and grow hoarse in vain.
Forgetfulness plays balmy round his head,
And halcyon fogs hang lambent o'er his bed.
O sovereign Sloth, to whom we quiet owe!
Nature's kind nurse! soft couch for weary woe!
Safe in thy arms the unbusied slumberer lies,
Lives without pain, and without sighing dies.
States rise or fall, his lot is still the same;
For he's above mischance who has no aim.

How curs'd the man who still is musing found!
His mill-horse soul forms one eternal round;
When wiser beasts lie lost in needful rest,
He, madman! wakes, to war on his own breast.
Thoughts dash on thoughts, as waves on waves increase,
And storms of his own raising wreck his peace.
Now, like swift coursers in the rapid race,
His spirits strain for speed; now, with slow pace,
The sinking soul, tired out, scarce limps along,
Sullen and sick with such extremes of wrong.
What art thou, life, if care corrodes thy span?
A gnawing worm! a bosom-hell to man!
If e'er distracting business proves my doom,
Thou, Indolence, to my deliverance come:
Distil thy healing balm, like softening oil,
And cure the ignoble malady of toil.
Thou, best physician! canst the sulphur find
That dries this itch of action on the mind.
Malice and lust, voracious birds of prey,
That outsoar reason, and our wishes sway,
Desire's wild seas, on which the wise are tossed,

By pilot Indolence are safely crossed.
Hushed in soft rest they quiet captives lie,
And, wanting nourishment, grow faint and die.
By thee, O sacred Indolence, the sons
Of honest Levi loll like lazy drones;
While battered hirelings drudge in saying prayer,
Thou tak'st sleek doctors to thy downy care.
Well dost thou help to form the double chin,
Dilate the paunch, and raise the reverend mien.
By thee with stol'n discourses they are pleased,
That we with worse may not be dully teased:
A happiness that laymen ought to prize
Who value time and would be counted wise.
From thee innumerable blessings flow.
What coffee-man does not thy virtues know?
Tobacconists and newsmongers revere
Thy lordly influence, with religious fear.
Chairs, coaches, games, the glory of a land,
Are all the labours of thy lazy hand.
The Excise, the Treasury, strengthened by thy aid,
Own thy great use and energy in trade.
Who does not taste the pleasures of thy reign?
Princes themselves are servants in thy train.

   Diogenes! thou venerable shade,
Thou wert by Indolence immortal made.
Thee most I envy of all human race;
E'en in a tub, thou held'st thy native grace;
Thy soul outsoared the vulgar flights of life,
And looked abroad, with scorn, at noise and strife.
To thy hooped palace no bold business pressed,
No thought usurped the kingdom of thy breast.
Thou to high-fated Alexander's face
Maintain'dst that ease was nobler far than place.
The insulted world before him bowed the knee:
Thou sat'st unmoved, more conqueror than he.

   Scarce, O ye advocates for wit's wild chase,
Can your long heads be reconciled to Grace:
In drowsy dullness deep devotion dwells,
But searchful care contented faith expels.
Did ever Indolence produce despair,
Or to rash wishes prompt the impatient heir?
When murmurings and rebellions shake a state,
Does love of rest, or action, animate?
When did two sleepers clash in murderous war,
Or love of ease draw wranglers to the bar?
O'er sea and land, the world's wide space around,
Poise every loss, and probe each aching wound;
Then say which most, or business or repose,
Worries our lives, and wakes us into woes.

What first gave talons to coercive law?
Small need to keep the indolent in awe!
Hatched we our South-Sea egg by want of thought?
Are jobbers' airy arts in slumber taught?
What state was ever bubbled out of sense
By good, unfeared, unmeaning Indolence?
Weigh and consider, now, which cause is best,
And, yawning, yield—There's happiness in rest.

   Oh how I pity those deluded fools,
Who drudge their days out in bewildering schools—
Who, seeking knowledge with assiduous strife,
Lose their long toil, and make a hell of life!
Grasping at shadows, they but beat the air,
And cloud the spirits they attempt to clear.
Jargon of tongues, perplexive terms of art,
And mazy maxims, but benight the heart.
No end, no pause, of painful search they know,
But, still proceeding, aggrandize their woe;
Their nakedness of soul with fig-leaves hide,
And wrap their conscious shame in veils of pride.
Erring, they toil some shadowy gleam to find,
And, wandering, feel their way, sublimely blind.
Learning in this,—in that scale, doubt—be laid;
And mark how pomp is by plain truth outweighed.

   Hereafter then, ye poring students, cease,
Nor maze your minds, nor break your chain of peace:
Make truce with leisure for awhile, and view
What empty nothings your desires pursue.
Remember, Adam's fatal itch to know
Was the first bitter spring of human woe:
Think how presumptuous 'tis for breathing clay
To tread Heaven's winding paths, and lose its way.
Think what short limits understanding boasts,
And shun the enticements of her shoaly coasts.
With Solomon, that prudent sage, and me,
From fruitless labour set your spirits free:
Bind up bold thought in slumber's silky chain,
Since all we act, and all we know, is vain.

JOHN GAY.

[Born at Barnstaple, Devonshire, in 1688, of an old but reduced family; died on 4th December 1732. His burlesque pastorals, *The Shepherd's Week*, following some dramatic and other works, obtained high popularity; greatly increased afterwards by his *Fables*, and above all by *The Beggar's Opera*, produced in 1727. Disappointed in some reasonably grounded claims to court-favour, Gay was domesticated, in his closing years, with the Duke and Duchess of Queensberry. He was of a remarkably good-natured, easy, attaching disposition].

THE LION, THE FOX, AND THE GEESE.

A LION, tired with state affairs,
Quite sick of pomp, and worn with cares,
Resolved, remote from noise and strife,
In peace to pass his latter life.
It was proclaimed; the day was set:
Behold the general council met.
The Fox was Viceroy named. The crowd
To the new regent humbly bowed.
Wolves, bears, and mighty tigers, bend,
And strive who most should condescend.
He straight assumes a solemn grace,
Collects his wisdom in his face.
The crowd admire his wit, his sense:
Each word hath weight and consequence.
The flatterer all his art displays:
He who hath power is sure of praise.
A Fox stepped forth before the rest,
And thus the servile throng addressed :—
  "How vast his talents, born to rule,
And trained in Virtue's honest school!
What clemency his temper sways!
How uncorrupt are all his ways!
Beneath his conduct and command,
Rapine shall cease to waste the land.
His brain hath stratagem and art;
Prudence and mercy rule his heart;
What blessings must attend the nation
Under this good administration!"
  He said. A Goose, who distant stood,
Harangued apart the cackling brood:
  "Whene'er I hear a knave commend,
He bids me shun his worthy friend.
What praise! what mighty commendation!
But 'twas a Fox who spoke the oration.
Foxes this government may prize
As gentle, plentiful, and wise;
If they enjoy the sweets, 'tis plain
We Geese must feel a tyrant reign.
What havoc now shall thin our race,
When every petty clerk in place,
To prove his taste and seem polite,
Will feed on Geese both noon and night!"

THE LION AND THE CUB.

How fond are men of rule and place,
Who court it from the mean and base!
These cannot bear an equal nigh,
But from superior merit fly.
They love the cellar's vulgar joke,
And lose their hours in ale and smoke:
There o'er some petty club preside;
So poor, so paltry is their pride!
Nay, even with fools whole nights will sit,
In hopes to be supreme in wit.
If these can read, to these I write,
To set their worth in truest light.

   A Lion-cub, of sordid mind,
Avoided all the lion kind;
Fond of applause, he sought the feasts
Of vulgar and ignoble beasts;
With asses all his time he spent,
Their club's perpetual president.
He caught their manners, looks, and airs:
An ass in everything but ears!
If e'er his highness meant a joke,
They grinned applause before he spoke;
But at each word what shouts of praise!
"Good gods! how natural he brays!"

   Elate with flattery and conceit,
He seeks his royal sire's retreat;
Forward and fond to show his parts,
His highness brays; the Lion starts.

   "Puppy, that curs'd vociferation
Betrays thy life and conversation:
Coxcombs, an ever noisy race,
Are trumpets of their own disgrace."

   "Why so severe?" the Cub replies;
"Our senate always held me wise."

   "How weak is pride!" returns the sire:
"All fools are vain when fools admire!
But know, what stupid asses prize
Lions and noble beasts despise."

THE RATCATCHER AND CATS.

The rats by night such mischief did,
Betty was every morning chid.
They undermined whole sides of bacon,
Her cheese was sapped, her tarts were taken;
Her pasties, fenced with thickest paste,
Were all demolished and laid waste.

She cursed the Cat for want of duty,
Who left her foes a constant booty.
   An engineer of noted skill
Engaged to stop the growing ill,
From room to room he now surveys
Their haunts, their works, their secret ways;
Finds where they scape an ambuscade,
And whence the nightly sally's made.
   An envious Cat from place to place,
Unseen, attends his silent pace.
She saw that, if his trade went on,
The purring race must be undone;
So, secretly removes his baits,
And every stratagem defeats.
   Again he sets the poisoned toils,
And Puss again the labour foils.
   "What foe (to frustrate my designs)
My schemes thus nightly countermines?"
Incensed he cries; "this very hour
The wretch shall bleed beneath my power."
   So said—a ponderous trap he brought,
And in the fact poor Puss was caught.
   "Smuggler," says he, "thou shalt be made
A victim to our loss of trade."
   The captive Cat, with piteous mews,
For pardon, life, and freedom, sues.
"A sister of the science spare;
One interest is our common care."
   "What insolence!" the man replied;
"Shall Cats with us the game divide?
Were all your interloping band
Extinguished, or expelled the land,
We Rat-catchers might raise our fees,
Sole guardians of a nation's cheese!"
   A Cat, who saw the lifted knife,
Thus spoke, and saved her sister's life;
   "In every age and clime, we see,
Two of a trade can ne'er agree.
Each hates his neighbour for encroaching.
Squire stigmatizes squire for poaching;
Beauties with beauties are in arms,
And scandal pelts each other's charms;
Kings, too, their neighbour kings dethrone,
In hope to make the world their own.
But let us limit our desires,
Nor war like beauties, kings, and squires;
For, though we both one prey pursue,
There's game enough for us and you."

THE OLD WOMAN AND HER CATS.

Who friendship with a knave hath made
Is judged a partner in the trade.
The matron who conducts abroad
A willing nymph is thought a bawd;
And, if a modest girl be seen
With one who cures a lover's spleen,
We guess her not extremely nice,
And only wish to know her price.
'Tis thus that on the choice of friends
Our good or evil name depends.
   A wrinkled Hag, of wicked fame,
Beside a little smoky flame
Sat hovering, pinched with age and frost:
Her shrivelled hand, with veins embossed,
Upon her knees her weight sustains,
While palsy shook her crazy brains.
She mumbles forth her backward prayers,
An untamed scold of fourscore years.
About her swarmed a numerous brood
Of Cats, who, lank with hunger, mewed.
   Teased with their cries, her choler grew,
And thus she sputtered: " Hence, ye crew!
Fool that I was to entertain
Such imps, such fiends, a hellish train!
Had ye been never housed and nursed,
I for a witch had ne'er been cursed.
To you I owe that crowds of boys
Worry me with eternal noise;
Straws laid across my pace retard,
The horse-shoe's nailed, each threshold's guard.
The stunted broom the wenches hide,
For fear that I should up and ride;
They stick with pins my bleeding seat,
And bid me show my secret teat."
   " To hear you prate would vex a saint;
Who hath most reason of complaint?"
Replies a Cat. " Let's come to proof;
Had we ne'er starved beneath your roof,
We had, like others of our race,
In credit lived as beasts of chase.
'Tis infamy to serve a hag;
Cats are thought imps, her broom a nag!
And boys against our lives combine,
Because, 'tis said, *your* cats have nine."

THE BUTTERFLY AND THE SNAIL.

All upstarts, insolent in place,
Remind us of their vulgar race.
  As, in the sunshine of the morn,
A Butterfly, but newly born,
Sat proudly perking on a rose,
With pert conceit his bosom glows.
His wings, all glorious to behold,
Bedropped with azure, jet, and gold,
Wide he displays; the spangled dew
Reflects his eyes and various hue.
  His now-forgotten friend, a Snail,
Beneath his house, with slimy trail
Crawls o'er the grass; whom when he spies,
In wrath he to the gardener cries:
  "What means yon peasant's daily toil,
From choking weeds to rid the soil?
Why wake you to the morning's care?
Why with new arts correct the year?
Why grows the peach with crimson hue,
And why the plum's inviting blue?
Were they to feast his taste designed,
That vermin of voracious kind?
Crush then the slow, the pilfering race;
So purge thy garden from disgrace."
  "What arrogance!" the Snail replied;
"How insolent is upstart pride!
Hadst thou not thus, with insult vain,
Provoked my patience to complain,
I had concealed thy meaner birth,
Nor traced thee to the scum of earth.
For scarce nine suns have waked the hours,
To swell the fruit, and paint the flowers,
Since I thy humbler life surveyed,
In base and sordid guise arrayed;
A hideous insect, vile, unclean,
You dragged a slow and noisome train;
And from your spider bowels drew
Foul film, and spun the dirty clue.
I own my humble life, good friend;
Snail was I born, and Snail shall end.
And what's a Butterfly? At best,
He's but a caterpillar, dressed;
And all thy race (a numerous seed)
Shall prove of caterpillar breed."

THE FOX AT THE POINT OF DEATH.

A Fox, in life's extreme decay,
Weak, sick, and faint, expiring lay:
All appetite had left his maw,
And age disarmed his mumbling jaw.
His numerous race around him stand
To learn their dying sire's command.
He raised his head with whining moan,
And thus was heard the feeble tone:
 "Ah sons! from evil ways depart:
My crimes lie heavy on my heart.
See! see! the murdered geese appear!
Why are those bleeding turkeys there?
Why all around this cackling train,
Who haunt my ears for chicken slain?"
 The hungry foxes round them stared,
And for the promised feast prepared.
 "Where, Sir, is all this dainty cheer?
Nor turkey, goose, nor hen, is here.
These are the phantoms of your brain,
And your sons lick their lips in vain."
 "O gluttons!" says the drooping sire,
"Restrain inordinate desire;
Your licorish taste you shall deplore
When peace of conscience is no more.
Does not the hound betray our pace,
And gins and guns destroy our race?
Thieves dread the searching eye of power,
And never feel the quiet hour.
Old age (which few of us shall know)
Now puts a period to my woe.
Would you true happiness attain,
Let honesty your passions rein;
So live in credit and esteem,
And the good name you lost redeem."
 "The counsel's good," a Fox replies,
"Could we perform what you advise.
Think what our ancestors have done;
A line of thieves from son to son:
To us descends the long disgrace,
And infamy hath marked our race.
Though we, like harmless sheep, should feed,
Honest in thought, in word, in deed,
Whatever hen-roost is decreased,
We shall be thought to share the feast.
The change shall never be believed:
A lost good name is ne'er retrieved."

"Nay, then," replies the feeble Fox,
"(But hark! I hear a hen that clocks)
Go, but be moderate in your food;—
A chicken too might do me good."

THE MASTIFF.

THOSE who in quarrels interpose
Must often wipe a bloody nose.
  A Mastiff of true English blood
Loved fighting better than his food.
When dogs were snarling for a bone,
He longed to make the war his own;
And often found, when two contend,
To interpose obtained his end.
He gloried in his limping pace;
The scars of honour seamed his face;
In every limb a gash appears,
And frequent fights retrenched his ears.
  As on a time he heard from far
Two dogs engaged in noisy war,
Away he scours and lays about him,
Resolved no fray should be without him.
  Forth from his yard a tanner flies,
And to the bold intruder cries;
"A cudgel shall correct your manners:
Whence sprung this cursed hate to tanners?
While on my dog you vent your spite,
Sirrah! 'tis me you dare not bite."
  To see the battle thus perplexed,
With equal rage a butcher vexed,
Hoarse-screaming from the circled crowd,
To the curs'd Mastiff cries aloud:
"Both Hockley-Hole and Marybone
The combats of my dog have known.
He ne'er, like bullies coward-hearted,
Attacks, in public to be parted.
Think not, rash fool, to share his fame;
Be his the honour or the shame."
  Thus said, they swore, and raved like thunder,
Then dragged their fastened dogs asunder;
While clubs and kicks from every side
Rebounded from the Mastiff's hide.
  All reeking now with sweat and blood,
Awhile the parted warriors stood,
Then poured upon the meddling foe;
Who, worried, howled and sprawled below.
He rose; and, limping from the fray,
By both sides mangled, sneaked away.

THE TURKEY AND THE ANT.

In other men we faults can spy,
And blame the mote that dims their eye:
Each little speck and blemish find,
To our own stronger errors blind.
   A Turkey, tired of common food,
Forsook the barn, and sought the wood:
Behind her ran an infant train,
Collecting here and there a grain.
"Draw near, my birds," the mother cries;
"This hill delicious fare supplies;
Behold, the busy Negro race!
See, millions blacken all the place!
Fear not. Like me with freedom eat;
An Ant is most delightful meat.
How bless'd, how envied, were our life,
Could we but scape the poulterer's knife!
But man, curs'd man, on Turkeys preys,
And Christmas shortens all our days:
Sometimes with oysters we combine,
Sometimes assist the savoury chine.
From the low peasant to the lord,
The Turkey smokes on every board.
Sure, men for gluttony are curs'd,—
Of the seven deadly sins the worst."
   An Ant, who climbed beyond her reach,
Thus answered from the neighbouring beech:
"Ere you remark another's sin,
Bid thy own conscience look within:
Control thy more voracious bill,
Nor, for a breakfast nations kill."

THE TWO MONKEYS.

The learned, full of inward pride,
The Fops of outward show deride;
The Fop, with learning at defiance,
Scoffs at the pedant and the science.
The Don, a formal solemn strutter,
Despises Monsieur's airs and flutter;
While Monsieur mocks the formal fool,
Who looks and speaks and walks by rule.
Britain, a medley of the twain,
As pert as France, as grave as Spain,
In fancy wiser than the rest,
Laughs at them both, of both the jest.
Is not the poet's chiming close
Censured by all the sons of prose?

While bards of quick imagination
Despise the sleepy prose narration.
Men laugh at Apes, *they* men contemn ;
For what are we but Apes to them ?
   Two Monkeys went to Southwark fair ;
No critics had a sourer air.
They forced their way through draggled folks,
Who gaped to catch Jack-pudding's jokes ;
Then took their tickets for the show,
And got, by chance, the foremost row.
To see their grave observing face
Provoked a laugh through all the place.
   "Brother," says Pug, and turned his head,
"The rabble's monstrously ill bred !"
   Now through the booth loud hisses ran;
Nor ended till the show began.
The tumbler whirls the flip-flap round,
With somersets he shakes the ground.
The cord beneath the dancer springs ;
Aloft in air the vaulter swings ;
Distorted now, now prone depends,
Now through his twisted arms ascends.
The crowd, in wonder and delight,
With clapping hands applaud the sight.
With smiles, quoth Pug, "If pranks like these
The giant Apes of reason please,
How would they wonder at our arts !
They must adore us for our parts.
High on the twig I've seen you cling,
Play, twist, and turn, in airy ring.
How can those clumsy things, like me,
Fly with a bound from tree to tree ?
But yet, by this applause, we find
These emulators of our kind
Discern our worth, our parts regard,
Who our mean mimics thus reward."
   "Brother," the grinning mate replies,
"In this I grant that man is wise.
While good example they pursue,
We must allow some praise is due ;
But, when they strain beyond their guide,
I laugh to scorn the mimic pride.
For how fantastic is the sight
To meet men always bolt upright,
Because we sometimes walk on two !
I hate the imitating crew."

THE MAN AND THE FLEA.

Whether on earth, in air, or main,
Sure every thing alive is vain.
  Does not the hawk all fowls survey,
As destined only for his prey?
And do not tyrants, prouder things,
Think men were born for slaves to kings?
  When the crab views the pearly strands,
Or Tagus bright with golden sands;
Or crawls beside the coral grove,
And hears the ocean roll above;
"Nature is too profuse," says he,
"Who gave all these to pleasure me!"
When bordering pinks and roses bloom,
And every garden breathes perfume;
When peaches glow with sunny dyes,
Like Laura's cheek when blushes rise;
When with huge figs the branches bend;
When clusters from the vine depend;
The snail looks round on flower and tree,
And cries, "All these were made for me!"
  "What dignity's in human nature!"
Says Man, the most conceited creature,
As from a cliff he cast his eye,
And viewed the sea and archèd sky.
The sun was sunk beneath the main;
The moon and all the starry train
Hung the vast vault of Heaven. The Man
His contemplation thus began:
  "When I behold this glorious show,
And the wide watery world below,
The scaly people of the main,
The beasts that range the wood or plain,
The wing'd inhabitants of air,
The day, the night, the various year,
And know all these by Heaven designed
As gifts to pleasure human-kind;
I cannot raise my worth too high;
Of what vast consequence am I!"
  "Not of the importance you suppose,"
Replies a Flea upon his nose.
"Be humble, learn thyself to scan:
Know, pride was never made for man.
'Tis vanity that swells thy mind.
What, heaven and earth for thee designed!
For thee! made only for our need,
That more important Fleas might feed!"

VERSES TO BE PLACED UNDER THE PICTURE OF SIR RICHARD BLACKMORE,
CONTAINING A COMPLETE CATALOGUE OF HIS WORKS.[1]

SEE who ne'er was nor will be half read,
Who first sang Arthur, then sang Alfred;
Praised great Eliza in God's anger,
Till all true Englishmen cried "Hang her!"
Mauled human wit in one thick satire;
Next in three books spoiled human nature;
Undid Creation at a jerk,
And of Redemption made damned work;
Then took his Muse at once, and dipped her
Full in the middle of the Scripture.
What wonders there the man grown old did!
Sternhold himself he out-Sternholded;
Made David seem so mad and freakish
All thought him just what thought King Achish;
No mortal read his Solomon
But judged Reboam his own son;
Moses he served as Moses Pharaoh,
And Deborah as she Sisèra;
Made Jeremy full sore to cry,
And Job himself curse God and die.
 What punishment all this must follow?
Shall Arthur use him like King Tollo?
Shall David as Uriah slay him?
Or dexterous Deborah Sisèra him?
Or shall Eliza lay a plot
To treat him like her sister Scot?
No, none of these; Heaven save his life,—
But send him, honest Job, thy wife!

A NEW SONG OF NEW SIMILES.

MY passion is as mustard strong;
 I sit all sober sad;
Drunk as a piper all day long,
 Or like a March-hare mad.

Round as a hoop the bumpers flow;
 I drink, yet can't forget her;
For, though as drunk as David's sow,
 I love her still the better.

Pert as a pear-monger I'd be,
 If Molly were but kind;
Cool as a cucumber, could see
 The rest of womankind.

---

[1] Blackmore, a versifier now remembered only by name, was the author of *King Arthur* (an epic), *The Creation*, &c. &c.

Like a stuck pig, I gaping stare,
  And eye her o'er and o'er;
Lean as a rake, with sighs and care,—
  Sleek as a mouse before.

Plump as a partridge was I known,
  And soft as silk my skin;
My cheeks as fat as butter grown,
  But as a goat now thin!

I, melancholy as a cat,
  Am kept awake to weep;
But she, insensible of that,
  Sound as a top can sleep.

Hard is her heart as flint or stone,
  She laughs to see me pale;
And merry as a grig is grown,
  And brisk as bottled ale.

The god of love, at her approach,
  Is busy as a bee;
Hearts, sound as any bell or roach,
  Are smit, and sigh like me.

Ah me! as thick as hops or hail
  The fine men crowd about her;
But soon as dead as a door-nail
  Shall I be, if without her.

Straight as my leg her shape appears:
  Oh were we joined together!
My heart would be scot-free from cares,
  And lighter than a feather.

As fine as fivepence is her mien,
  No drum was ever tighter;
Her glance is as the razor keen,
  And not the sun is brighter.

As soft as pap her kisses are,—
  Methinks I taste them yet;
Brown as a berry is her hair,
  Her eyes as black as jet.

As smooth as glass, as white as curds,
  Her pretty hand invites;
Sharp as her needle are her words,
  Her wit like pepper bites.

Brisk as a body-louse she trips,
  Clean as a penny dressed;
Sweet as a rose her breath and lips,
  Round as the globe her breast.

Full as an egg was I with glee,
    And happy as a king :
Good Lord ! how all men envied me !
    She loved like anything.

But false as hell, she, like the wind,
    Changed, as her sex must do :
Though seeming as the turtle kind,
    And like the gospel true.

If I and Molly could agree,
    Let who would take Peru !
Great as an Emperor should I be,
    And richer than a Jew.

Till you grow tender as a chick,
    I'm dull as any post ;
Let us like curs together stick,
    And warm as any toast.

You'll know me truer than a die,
    And wish me better speed,—
Flat as a flounder when I lie,
    And as a herring dead.

Sure as a gun she'll drop a tear,
    And sigh, perhaps, and wish,
When I am rotten as a pear,
    And mute as any fish.

LISLE.[1]

EURYDICE.

When Orpheus went down to the regions below,
    Which men are forbidden to see ;
He tuned up his lyre, as old histories show,
    To set his Eurydice free.

All hell was astonished a person so wise
    Should rashly endanger his life,
And venture so far ; but how vast their surprise
    When they heard that he came for his wife !

To find out a punishment due for his fault
    Old Pluto long puzzled his brain ;
But hell had not torments sufficient, he thought,—
    So he gave him his wife back again.

---

[1] I have looked in various books for any particulars about this writer, but without success. His *Eurydice* is given in Aikin's *Collection of English Songs* (edition 1810) : the first edition of which book was published in 1772. From a peculiarity of rhyming common at one time—"fault" with "thought"—I presume the poem may have been written at some such date as 1720 to 1750.

But pity succeeding soon vanquished his heart;
And, pleased with his playing so well,
He took her again in reward of his art,—
Such merit had music in hell.

SAMUEL WESLEY (JUNR.)

[See Samuel Wesley (Sen.), p. 154. The Rev. Samuel Wesley, Jun., was born towards 1692, and died in 1739. He was for many years an usher in Westminster School, and afterwards Head Master of Tiverton School. He was an extreme high Tory, and strongly disapproved of the religious movement promoted by his brother John].

ON THE SETTING-UP MR. BUTLER'S[1] MONUMENT IN WESTMINSTER ABBEY.

WHILE Butler, needy wretch, was yet alive,
No generous patron would a dinner give :
See him, when starved to death and turned to dust,
Presented with a monumental bust !
The poet's fate is here in emblem shown ;
He asked for bread, and he received a stone.

ADVICE TO ONE WHO WAS ABOUT TO WRITE, TO AVOID THE IMMORALITIES OF THE ANCIENT AND MODERN POETS.

IF e'er to writing you pretend,
Your utmost aim and study bend
The paths of virtue to befriend,
   However mean your ditty;
That, while your verse the reader draws
To reason's and religion's laws,
None e'er hereafter may have cause
   To curse your being witty.

No gods or weak or wicked feign ;
Where foolish blasphemy is plain,
But good to wire-draw from the strain
   The critic's art perplexes.
Make not a pious chief forego
A Princess he betrayed to woe,
Nor shepherd, unplatonic, show
   His fondness for Alexis.

With partial blindness to a side,
Extol not surly stoic pride,
When wild ambition's rapid tide
   Bursts nature's bonds asunder :

---

[1] Butler, the author of *Hudibras*.

Nor let a hero loud blaspheme,
Rave like a madman in a dream,
Till Jove himself affrighted seem,
    Not trusting to his thunder.

Nor choose the wanton Ode, to praise
Unbridled loves or thoughtless days,
In soft Epicurean lays ;
    A numerous melting lyric :
Nor satire that would lust chastise
With angry warmth and maxim wise,
Yet, loosely painting naked vice,
    Becomes its panegyric.

Nor jumbled atoms entertain
In the void spaces of your brain,—
Deny all gods, while Venus vain
    Stands without vesture painted:
Nor show the foul nocturnal scene
Of courts and revellings unclean,
Where never libertine had been
    Worse than the poet tainted.

Nor let luxuriant fancy rove
Through nature, and through art of love,
Skilled in smooth Elegy to move,
    Youth unexperienced firing :
Nor gods as brutes expose to view,
Nor monstrous crimes, nor lend a clue
To guide the guilty lover through
    The mazes of desiring.

Nor sparrow mourn, nor sue to kiss ;
Nor draw your fine-spun wit so nice
That thin-spread sense like nothing is,
    Or worse than nothing showing :
Nor spite in Epigram declare,
Pleasing the mob with lewdness bare,
Or flattery's pestilential air
    In ears of princes blowing.

Through modern Italy pass down
(In crimes inferior she to none),
Through France, her thoughts in lust alone
    Without reserve proclaiming :
Stay there who count it worth the while !
Let *us* deduce our useful style
To note the poets of our isle,
    And only spare the naming.

Sing not loose stories for the nonce,
Where mirth for bawdry ill atones,
Nor long-tongued wife of Bath, at once

On earth and heaven jesting:
Nor, while the main at virtue aims,
Insert, to soothe forbidden flames,
In a chaste work, a squire of dames,
   Or Paridell a-feasting.

Nor comic licence let us see,
Where all things sacred outraged be,
Where plots of mere adultery
   Fill the lascivious pages.
One only step can yet remain,
More frankly, shamelessly unclean.—
To bring it from behind the scene,
   And act it on the stages.

Nor make your tragic hero bold
Out-bully Capaneus of old,
While justling gods his rage behold,
   And tremble at his frowning.
Nor need'st thou vulgar wit display,
Acknowledged in dramatic way
Greatest and best; Oh spare the lay
   Of poor Ophelia drowning!

Nor dress your shame in courtly phrase,
Where artful breaks the fancy raise,
And ribaldry unnamed the lays
   Transparently is seen in:
Nor make it your peculiar pride
To strive to show what others hide,
To throw the fig-leaf quite aside;
   And scorn a double meaning.

Nor ever prostitute the Muse,
Malicious, mercenary, loose,
All faith, all parties, to abuse;
   Still changing, still to evil:
Make Maximin with heaven engage,
Blaspheming Sigismonda rage,
Draw scenes of lust in latest age,
   Apostle of the Devil.

Detest profaning holy writ,—
A rock where heathens *could* not split.
Old Jove more harmless charmed the pit,
   Of Plautus's creation,
Than when the adulterer was showed
With attributes of real God
But fools the means of grace allowed
   Pervert to their damnation.

Mingle not wit with treason rude,
To please the rebel multitude:

From poison intermixed with food
　What caution e'er can screen us?
Ne'er stoop to court a wanton smile;
Thy pious strains and lofty style,
Too light, let nor an Alma soil,
　Nor paltry dove of Venus.

Such plots deform the tuneful train,
Whilst they false glory would attain,
Or present mirth, or present gain,
　Unmindful of hereafter.
Do you mistaken ends despise,
Nor fear to fall, nor seek to rise,
Nor taint the good, nor grieve the wise,
　To tickle fools with laughter.

What though with ease you could aspire
To Virgil's art or Homer's fire,
If vice and lewdness breathes the lyre,
　If virtue it asperses?
Better with honest Quarles compose
Emblem that good intention shows,
Better be Bunyan in his prose,
　Or Sternhold in his verses.

MATTHEW GREEN.

[Born in 1696, died in 1737. An official in the London Custom-House, and author of the poem named *The Spleen*—which, like the rest of his compositions, was only published after his death].

AN EPIGRAM
ON THE REV. MR. LAURENCE EACHARD'S AND BISHOP GILBERT BURNET'S HISTORIES.

Gil's history appears to me
Political anatomy;
A case of skeletons well done,
And malefactors every one.
His sharp and strong incision-pen
Historically cuts-up men,
And does with lucid skill impart
Their inward ails of head and heart.
Laurence proceeds another way,
And well-dressed figures does display:
His characters are all in flesh,
Their hands are fair, their faces fresh;
And from his sweetening art derive
A better scent than when alive.
He wax-work made to please the sons
Whose fathers were Gil's skeletons.

THE SPARROW AND DIAMOND.

I LATELY saw what now I sing,
  Fair Lucia's hand displayed;
This finger graced a diamond ring,
  On that a sparrow played.

The feathered plaything she caressed,
  She stroked its head and wings;
And, while it nestled on her breast,
  She lisped the dearest things.

With chisel bill a spark ill set
  He loosened from the nest,
And swallowed down to grind his meat,
  The easier to digest.

She seized his bill with wild affright,
  Her diamond to descry:
'Twas gone! she sickened at the sight,
  Moaning her bird would die.

The tongue-tied knocker none might use,
  The curtains none undraw;
The footmen went without their shoes,
  The street was laid with straw.

The doctor used his oily art
  Of strong emetic kind;
The apothecary played his part,
  And engineered behind.

When physic ceased to spend its store
  To bring away the stone,
Dicky, like people when given o'er,
  Picks up when let alone.

His eyes dispelled their sickly dews,
  He pecked behind his wing;
Lucia, recovering at the news,
  Relapses for the ring.

Meanwhile within her beauteous breast
  Two different passions strove;
When avarice ended the contest,
  And triumphed over love.

Poor little, pretty, fluttering thing!
  Thy pains the sex display
Who only to repair a ring
  Could take thy life away!

Drive avarice from your breasts, ye fair,
  Monster of foulest mien;

Ye would not let it harbour there,
    Could but its form be seen.

It made a virgin put-on guile,
    Truth's image break her word,
A Lucia's face forbear to smile,
    A Venus kill her bird.

ROBERT DODSLEY.

[Born in 1703, died in 1774. A footman whose integrity, industry, and good sense, advanced him to the position of the leading English bookseller of his time. His first publication was named *The Muse in Livery;* followed by some plays—*The Toyshop* and *Cleone* were more especially successful—a very popular little volume entitled *The Economy of Human Life*, and other works, original or re-edited].

THE FOOTMAN.

AN EPISTLE TO MY FRIEND, MR. WRIGHT.

DEAR FRIEND,—Since I am now at leisure,
And in the country taking pleasure,
If it be worth your while to hear
A silly footman's business there,
I'll try to tell, in easy rhyme,
How I in London spend my time.

And first;—
As soon as laziness will let me,
I rise from bed, and down I set me
To cleaning glasses, knives, and plate,
And such-like dirty work as that,
Which (by the bye) is what I hate.
This done, with expeditious care,
To dress myself I straight prepare.
I clean my buckles, black my shoes,
Powder my wig, and brush my clothes,
Take off my beard, and wash my face;
And then I'm ready for the chace.

Down comes my lady's woman straight:
"Where's Robin?" "Here." "Pray take your hat,
And go—and go—and go—and go—;
And this—and that desire to know."
The charge received, away run I,
And here and there and yonder fly,
With services, and how-d'ye-does;
Then home return full-fraught with news.

Here some short time does interpose,
Till warm effluvias greet my nose,
Which from the spits and kettles fly,
Declaring dinner-time is nigh.

To lay the cloth I now prepare,
With uniformity and care;
In order knives and forks are laid,
With folded napkins, salt, and bread:
The side-boards glittering too appear,
With plate, and glass, and china-ware.
Then, ale, and beer, and wine decanted,
And all things ready which are wanted,
The smoking dishes enter in,
To stomachs sharp a grateful scene;
Which on the table being placed,
And some few ceremonies past,
They all sit down, and fall to eating,
Whilst I behind stand silent waiting.

This is the only pleasant hour
Which I have in the twenty-four;
For, whilst I unregarded stand,
With ready salver in my hand,
And seem to understand no more
Than just what's called for out to pour,
I hear and mark the courtly phrases,
And all the elegance that passes;
Disputes maintained without digression,
With ready wit and fine expression;
The laws of true politeness stated,
And what good-breeding is, debated:
Where all unanimous exclude
The vain coquet, the formal prude,
The ceremonious, and the rude,
The flattering, fawning, praising train,
The fluttering, empty, noisy, vain;
Detraction, smut, and what's profane.

This happy hour elapsed and gone,
The time of drinking tea comes on.
The kettle filled, the water boiled,
The cream provided, biscuits piled,
And lamp prepared, I straight engage
The Lilliputian equipage
Of dishes, saucers, spoons, and tongs,
And all the *et cætera* which thereto belongs.
Which, ranged in order and decorum,
I carry in and set before 'em;
Then pour or green or Bohea out,
And, as commanded, hand about.

This business over, presently
The hour of visiting draws nigh;
The chairmen straight prepare the chair,
A lighted flambeau I prepare;

And, orders given where to go,
We march along, and bustle through
The parting crowds, who all stand off
To give us room.   Oh how you'd laugh
To see me strut before a chair,
And with a sturdy voice and air
Crying—"By your leave, Sir; have a care!"
From place to place with speed we fly,
And rat-tatat the knockers cry.
"Pray is your lady, Sir, within?"
If "no," go on; if "yes," we enter in.

Then to the hall I guide my steps,
Amongst a crowd of brother skips,
Drinking small-beer, and talking smut,
And this fool's nonsense putting that fool's out:
Whilst oaths and peals of laughter meet,
And he who's loudest is the greatest wit.
But here amongst us the chief trade is
To rail against our Lords and Ladies:
To aggravate their smallest failings,
To expose their faults with saucy railings.
For my part, as I hate the practice,
And see in them how base and black 'tis,
To some bye place I therefore creep,
And sit me down, and feign to sleep;
And, could I with old Morpheus bargain,
'Twould save my ears much noise and jargon.

But down my Lady comes again,
And I'm released from my pain.
To some new place our steps we bend,
The tedious evening out to spend;
Sometimes, perhaps, to see the play,
Assembly, or the opera;
Then home and sup, and thus we end the day.

SOAME JENYNS.

[Born in 1704, died in 1787. Made some figure in fashion and in politics, and is now best remembered—and even that more by tradition than otherwise—as author of a poem on *The Art of Dancing*].

SONG.

When first I sought fair Cœlia's love,
   And every charm was new,
I swore by all the Gods above
   To be for ever true.

But long in vain did I adore,
   Long wept and sighed in vain;
Still she protested, vowed, and swore,
   She ne'er would ease my pain.

At last o'ercome she made me blest,
   And yielded all her charms;
And I forsook her when possessed,
   And fled to others' arms.

But let not this, dear Cœlia, now
   To rage thy breast incline;
For why, since you forget *your* vow,
   Should I remember mine?

HENRY FIELDING.

[Born at Sharpham near Glastonbury, 22 April 1707; died in Lisbon, 8 October 1754].

PLAIN TRUTH.

As Bathian Venus t'other day
Invited all the Gods to tea,
Her maids of honour, the Miss Graces
Attending duly in their places,
Their godships gave a loose to mirth,
As we at Buttering's here on earth.
   Minerva in her usual way
Rallied the daughter of the sea.
"Madam," said she, "your loved resort,
The city where you hold your court,
Is lately fallen from its duty,
And triumphs more in wit than beauty;
For here," she cried, "see here a poem——
'Tis Dalston's; you, Apollo, know him."
Little persuasion sure invites
Pallas to read what Dalston writes:
Nay, I have heard that in Parnassus
For truth a current whisper passes,

That Dalston sometimes has been known
To publish her words as his own.
  Minerva read, and every God
Approved—Jove gave the critic nod :
Apollo and the sacred Nine
Were charmed, and smiled at every line ;
And Mars, who little understood,
Swore, damn him if it was not good !
Venus alone sat all the while
Silent, nor deigned a single smile.
All were surprised : some thought her stupid :
Not so her confident squire Cupid ;
For well the little rogue discerned
At what his mother was concerned,
Yet not a word the urchin said,
But hid in Hebe's lap his head.
At length the rising choler broke
From Venus' lips,—and thus she spoke.
  "That poetry so crammed with wit,
Minerva, should your palate hit,
I wonder not, nor that some prudes
(For such there are above the clouds)
Should wish the prize of beauty torn
From her they view with envious scorn.
Me poets never please but when
Justice and truth direct their pen.
This Dalston—formerly I've known him ;
Henceforth for ever I disown him ;
For Homer's wit shall I despise
In him who writes with Homer's eyes.
A poem on the fairest fair
At Bath, and Betty's name not there !
Hath not this poet seen those glances
In which my wicked urchin dances ?
Nor that dear dimple where he treats
Himself with all Arabia's sweets ;
In whose soft down while he reposes,
In vain the lilies bloom, or roses,
To tempt him from a sweeter bed
Of fairer white or livelier red ?
Hath he not seen, when some kind gale
Has blown aside the cambric veil,
That seat of paradise, where Jove
Might pamper his almighty love ?
Our milky way less fair does show :
There summer's seen 'twixt hills of snow.
From her loved voice, whene'er she speaks,
What softness in each accent breaks !
And, when her dimpled smiles arise,
What sweetness sparkles in her eyes !

Can I then bear," enraged she said,
"Slights offered to my favourite maid,—
The nymph whom I decreed to be
The representative of me?"
    The Goddess ceased—the Gods all bowed,
Nor one the wicked bard avowed,
Who, while in beauty's praise he writ,
Dared Beauty's Goddess to omit:
For now their godships recollected
'Twas Venus' self he had neglected,
Who in her visits to this place
Had still worn Betty Dalston's face.

AN EPISTLE TO SIR ROBERT WALPOLE.

WHILE at the helm of State you ride,
Our nation's envy, and its pride;
While foreign Courts with wonder gaze,
And curse those counsels that they praise;
Would you not wonder, sir, to view
Your bard a greater man than you?
Which that he is you cannot doubt
When you have read the sequel out.

You know, great sir, that ancient fellows,
Philosophers and such folks, tell us
No great analogy between
Greatness and happiness is seen.
If then, as it might follow straight,
Wretched to be is to be great,
Forbid it, gods, that you should try
What 'tis to be so great as I!

The family that dines the latest
Is in our street esteemed the greatest;
But latest hours must surely fall
'Fore him who never dines at all.
Your taste in architect, you know,
Hath been admired by friend and foe;
But can your earthly domes compare
With all my castles—in the air?
We're often taught, it doth behove us
To think those greater who're above us;
Another instance of my glory,
Who live above you, twice two story,
And from my garret can look down
On the whole street of Arlington.

Greatness by poets still is painted
With many followers acquainted:

This, too, doth in my favour speak;
Your levee is but twice a week;
From mine I can exclude but one day,—
My door is quiet on a Sunday.

Nor in the manner of attendance
Doth your great bard claim less ascendance.
Familiar you to admiration
May be approached by all the nation;
While I, like the Mogul in Indo,
Am never seen but at my window.
If with my greatness you're offended,
The fault is easily amended;
For I'll come down, with wondrous ease,
Into whatever *place* you please.
I'm not ambitious; little matters
Will serve us great but humble creatures.

Suppose a secretary o' this isle,
Just to be doing with a while;
Admiral, general, judge, or bishop:
Or I can foreign treaties dish up.
If the good genius of the nation
Should call me to negotiation,
Tuscan and French are in my head,
Latin I write, and Greek—I read.
If you should ask what pleases best—
To get the most, and do the least;
What fittest for?—you know, I'm sure,
I'm fittest for—a sinecure.

LORD LYTTELTON (GEORGE LYTTELTON).

[George, son of Sir Thomas Lyttelton, Bart., was born in 1709, and died in 1773. In Parliament he acted as a member of the liberal opposition against Sir Robert Walpole, and became secretary to the Prince of Wales. He was afterwards in office as a Lord of the Treasury, and later as Chancellor of the Exchequer. On the dissolution, in 1759, of the ministry with which he acted, he was raised to the peerage. He wrote *Dialogues of the Dead*, and various other works; and as a poet is known chiefly by his monody on the death of his wife —his *first* wife, to whom he was tenderly attached. A second marriage proved unfortunate].

TO MISS LUCY FORTESCUE,[1]
ON HER PLEADING WANT OF TIME.

On Thames's bank, a gentle youth
For Lucy sighed with matchless truth,
   Even when he sighed in rhyme;
The lovely maid his flame returned,
And would with equal warmth have burned,
   But that she had not time.

---

[1] The lady whom Lyttelton afterwards married as his first wife.

Oft he repaired with eager feet
In secret shades this fair to meet
    Beneath the accustomed lime ;
She would have fondly met him there,
And healed with love each tender care,
    But that she had not time.

"It was not thus, inconstant maid,
You acted once" (the shepherd said),
    "When love was in its prime."
She grieved to hear him thus complain,
And would have writ to ease his pain,
    But that she had not time.

"How can you act so cold a part?
No crime of mine has changed your heart,
    If love be not a crime.
We soon must part for months, for years"—
She would have answered with her tears,
    But that she had not time.

JOHN BANCKS.

[Born in 1709, died in 1751. He was apprenticed to a weaver; but, having broken an arm, was obliged to leave this employment, and then set up a book-stall in Spitalfields. He next became a journeyman to a bookseller, and started a *Weaver's Miscellany*, which was successful, and launched him on a thriving career of authorship. A *Life of Christ*, often reprinted, was one of his works; also a *Critical Review of the Life of Oliver Cromwell*. Our specimen refers no doubt to the tribulations which Bancks used to endure from wind and cold, while in charge of his book-stall].

TO BOREAS.

Blow, Boreas, foe to human kind !
Blow, blustering, freezing, piercing wind !
Blow, that thy force I may rehearse,
While all my thoughts congeal to verse !

Blow, and the strongest proofs dispense
To every doubtful reader's sense !
But chiefly chill the critic's nose
Who dares the truths I sing oppose !

Where'er old hoary Winter's feared,
There thou with trembling art revered :
In thee the dreaded power remains
By which the snowy monarch reigns.

The leaves that beautified the trees,
And waved before a softer breeze,
Torn off by thee, are scattered round,
To wither on the rusty ground.

Where rapid rivers used to flow,
To glass the silent waters grow:
The mighty Volga feels thy force,
And Dwina stagnates in his course.

Even oozy Thames submits to thee;
Thames, like the neighbouring valleys, free!
Augusta's sons, in sportive mood,
Oft tread the surface of his flood.

To the proud Czar's terrific fleet,
Which half the nations fear to meet,
Thou dost thy strict injunctions give,
Nor can it stir without thy leave.

Thy presence on Britannia's plains
To chimney-corner drives her swains:
There thy severity they shun;
And thither I would gladly run!

But I (so Jove and Fate command,
Exposed to all thy rage must stand:
Condemned thy tyranny to bear,
Unpitied, half the tedious year!

Though close begirt with garments three,
Not garments can defend from thee;
Thy penetrating force will find
Or hole before, or slit behind.

In vain my hands my bosom hides;
In vain I shield them by my sides;
In vain exhale the warmer air
Which my too feeble lungs prepare.

In vain upon the distant tiles
The God of day indulgent smiles.
His influence I should never know,
But for the drops of melted snow.

The melted snow beneath my feet
Still makes thy empire more complete.
My aged shoes, not water-proof,
Admit those droppings of the roof.

Full in my face is always driven,
By thee, whate'er descends from heaven,
Or snow, or rain, or sleet, or hail;
Nor can the pent-house aught avail!

But hold! I feel my senses clog:
Down drops my Fancy, like a log:
Like thickening streams my numbers run,
And slowly drag the meaning on.

It stops ; it hardens in a trice !
Lo ! all converts to solid ice !
To prove thy power as much as needs,
Enough to freeze the wretch who reads.

WILLIAM WHITEHEAD.

[Born in 1715, died in 1785. Succeeded Cibber as Poet Laureate in 1757 — not without exciting many satirical protests from Churchill and others].

VARIETY.
A TALE FOR MARRIED PEOPLE.

A GENTLE maid, of rural breeding,
By Nature first, and then by reading,
Was filled with all those soft sensations
Which we restrain in near relations,
Lest future husbands should be jealous,
And think their wives too fond of fellows.

The morning sun beheld her rove,
A nymph, or goddess of the grove ;
At eve she paced the dewy lawn,
And called each clown she saw a faun ;
Then, scudding homeward, locked her door,
And turned some copious volume o'er.
For much she read ; and chiefly those
Great authors who in verse or prose,
Or something betwixt both, unwind
The secret springs which move the mind.
These much she read ; and thought she knew
The human heart's minutest clue ;
Yet shrewd observers still declare
(To show how shrewd observers are),
Though plays which breathed heroic flame,
And novels in profusion, came,
Imported fresh-and-fresh from France,
She only read the heart's romance.

The world, no doubt, was well enough
To smooth the manners of the rough ;
Might please the giddy and the vain,
Those tinselled slaves of folly's train :
But, for her part, the truest taste
She found was in retirement placed,
Where, as in verse it sweetly flows,
"On every thorn instruction grows."

Not that she wished to "be alone,"
As some affected prudes have done ;
She knew it was decreed on high
We should "increase and multiply ; "

And therefore, if kind Fate would grant
Her fondest wish, her only want,
A cottage with the man she loved
Was what her gentle heart approved;
In some delightful solitude
Where step profane might ne'er intrude,
But Hymen guard the sacred ground,
And virtuous Cupids hover round.
Not such as flutter on a fan
Round Crete's vile bull, or Leda's swan
(Who scatter myrtles, scatter roses,
And hold their fingers to their noses),
But simpering, mild, and innocent,
As angels on a monument.

Fate heard her prayer: a lover came,
Who felt, like her, the innoxious flame;
One who had trod, as well as she,
The flowery paths of poesy;
Had warmed himself with Milton's heat,
Could every line of Pope repeat,
Or chant, in Shenstone's tender strains,
"The lover's hopes," "the lover's pains."

Attentive to the charmer's tongue,
With him she thought no evening long;
With him she sauntered half the day;
And sometimes, in a laughing way,
Ran o'er the catalogue by rote
Of who might marry, and who not;
"Consider, sir, we're near relations"—
"I hope so, in our inclinations."—
In short, she looked, she blushed consent;
He grasped her hand, to church they went;
And every matron that was there,
With tongue so voluble and supple,
Said for her part, she must declare,
  She never saw a finer couple.
Oh halcyon days! 'Twas Nature's reign,
'Twas Tempe's vale, and Enna's plain;
The fields assumed unusual bloom,
And every zephyr breathed perfume;
The laughing sun with genial beams
Danced lightly on the exulting streams;
And the pale regent of the night
In dewy softness shed delight.
'Twas transport not to be expressed;
'Twas Paradise!—But mark the rest.

Two smiling springs had waked the flowers
That paint the meads, or fringe the bowers

(Ye lovers, lend your wondering ears,
Who count by months, and not by years):
Two smiling springs had chaplets wove
To crown their solitude and love:
When lo, they find, they can't tell how,
Their walks are not so pleasant now.
The seasons sure were changed; the place
Had, somehow, got a different face.
Some blast had struck the cheerful scene;
The lawns, the woods, were not so green.
The purling rill which murmured by,
And once was liquid harmony,
Became a sluggish reedy pool:
The days grew hot, the evenings cool.
The moon, with all the starry reign,
Were melancholy's silent train.
And then the tedious winter night—
They could not read by candle-light.

 Full oft, unknowing why they did,
They called in adventitious aid.
A faithful, favourite dog ('twas thus
With Tobit and Telemachus)
Amused their steps; and for a while
They viewed his gambols with a smile.
The kitten too was comical,—
She played so oddly with her tail,
Or in the glass was pleased to find
Another cat, and peeped behind.

 A courteous neighbour at the door
Was deemed intrusive noise no more:
For rural visits, now and then,
Are right, as men must live with men.
Then cousin Jenny, fresh from town,
 A new recruit, a dear delight,
Made many a heavy hour go down,
 At morn, at noon, at eve, at night:
Sure they could hear her jokes for ever,
She was so sprightly and so clever!

 Yet neighbours were not quite the thing;
What joy, alas! could converse bring
With awkward creatures bred at home?—
The dog grew dull, or troublesome;
The cat had spoiled the kitten's merit,
And, with her youth, had lost her spirit;
And jokes repeated o'er and o'er
Had quite exhausted Jenny's store.
—"And then, my dear, I can't abide
This always sauntering side by side."

"Enough!" he cries, "the reason's plain:
For causes never rack your brain.
Our neighbours are like other folks.
Skip's playful tricks, and Jenny's jokes,
Are still delightful, still would please,
Were we, my dear, ourselves at ease.
Look round, with an impartial eye,
On yonder fields, on yonder sky;
The azure cope, the flowers below,
With all their wonted colours glow.
The rill still murmurs; and the moon
Shines, as she did, a softer sun.
No change has made the seasons fail,
No comet brushed us with his tail.
The scene's the same, the same the weather—
We live, my dear, too much together."

Agreed. A rich old uncle dies,
And added wealth the means supplies.
With eager haste to town they flew,
Where all must please, for all was new.

But here, by strict poetic laws,
Description claims its proper pause.

The rosy morn had raised her head
From old Tithonus' saffron bed;
And embryo sunbeams from the east,
Half-choked, were struggling through the mist,
When forth advanced the gilded chaise;
The village crowded round to gaze.
The pert postilion, now promoted
From driving plough, and neatly booted,
His jacket, cap, and baldric on,
(As greater folks than he have done)
Looked round; and, with a coxcomb air,
Smacked loud his lash. The happy pair
Bowed graceful, from a separate door,
And Jenny, from the stool before.

Roll swift, ye wheels! To willing eyes
New objects every moment rise.
Each carriage passing on the road,
From the broad waggon's ponderous load
To the light car where mounted high
The giddy driver seems to fly,
Were themes for harmless satire fit,
And gave fresh force to Jenny's wit.
Whate'er occurred, 'twas all delightful,
No noise was harsh, no danger frightful.
The dash and splash through thick and thin,
The hairbreadth 'scapes, the bustling inn

(Where well-bred landlords were so ready
To welcome in the squire and lady),
Dirt, dust, and sun, they bore with ease,
Determined to be pleased, and please.

Now nearer town, and all agog,
They know dear London by its fog.
Bridges they cross, through lanes they wind,
Leave Hounslow's dangerous heath behind,
Through Brentford win a passage free
By roaring "Wilkes and Liberty!"
At Knightsbridge bless the shortening way,
Where Bays's troops in ambush lay,
O'er Piccadilly's pavement glide,
With palaces to grace its side,
Till Bond Street with its lamps ablaze
Concludes the journey of three days.

Why should we paint, in tedious song,
How every day, and all day long,
They drove at first with curious haste
Through Lud's vast town; or, as they passed
'Midst risings, fallings, and repairs,
Of streets on streets and squares on squares,
Describe how strong their wonder grew
At buildings—and at builders too?

Scarce less astonishment arose
At architects more fair than those—
Who built as high, as widely spread,
The enormous loads that clothed their head.
For British dames new follies love,
And, if they can't invent, improve.
Some with erect pagodas vie,
Some nod, like Pisa's tower, awry.
Medusa's snakes, with Pallas' crest,
Convolved, contorted, and compressed,
With intermingling trees and flowers,
And corn and grass and shepherds' bowers,
Stage above stage the turrets run,
Like pendent groves of Babylon,
Till nodding from the topmost wall
Otranto's plumes envelop all:
Whilst the black ewes who owned the hair
Feed harmless on, in pastures fair,
Unconscious that their tails perfume,
In scented curls, the drawing-room.

When Night her murky pinions spread,
And sober folks retire to bed,
To every public place they flew,
Where Jenny told them who was who.

Money was always at command,
And tripped with Pleasure hand in hand.
Money was equipage, was show,
Gallini's, Almack's, and Soho;
The *passe-partout* through every vein
Of dissipation's hydra reign.

   O London, thou prolific source,
Parent of vice, and folly's nurse!
Fruitful as Nile, thy copious springs
Spawn hourly births—and all with stings:
But happiest far the he or she,
   I know not which, that livelier dunce
Who first contrived the coterie,
   To crush domestic bliss at once,—
Then grinned, no doubt, amidst the dames,
As Nero fiddled to the flames.

   Of thee, Pantheon, let me speak
With reverence, though in numbers weak;
Thy beauties satire's frown beguile,—
We spare the follies for the pile.
Flounced, furbelowed, and tricked for show,
With lamps above and lamps below,
Thy charms even modern taste defied,
They could not spoil thee, though they tried.
Ah pity that Time's hasty wings
Must sweep thee off with vulgar things!
Let architects of humbler name
On frail materials build their fame;
Their noblest works the world might want;
Wyatt should build in adamant.

   But what are these to scenes which lie
Secreted from the vulgar eye,
And baffle all the powers of song?—
A brazen throat, an iron tongue
(Which poets wish for, when at length
Their subject soars above their strength),
Would shun the task. Our humbler Muse,
Who only reads the public news,
And idly utters what she gleans
From chronicles and magazines,
Recoiling feels her feeble fires,
And blushing to her shades retires.
Alas! she knows not how to treat
The finer follies of the great,
Where even, Democritus, thy sneer
Were vain as Heraclitus' tear.

   Suffice it that by just degrees
They reached all heights, and rose with ease;

For beauty wins its way, uncalled,
And ready dupes are ne'er black-balled.
Each gambling dame she knew, and he
Knew every shark of quality;
From the grave cautious few who live
On thoughtless youth, and living thrive,
To the light train who mimic France,
And the soft sons of *nonchalance*.
While Jenny, now no more of use,
Excuse succeeding to excuse,
Grew piqued, and prudently withdrew
To shilling whist and chicken loo.

   Advanced to fashion's wavering head,
They now, where once they followed, led;
Devised new systems of delight,
Abed all day, and up all night,
In different circles reigned supreme.
Wives copied her, and husbands him;
Till so divinely life ran on,
So separate, so quite *bon-ton*,
That, meeting in a public place,
They scarcely knew each other's face.

   At last they met, by his desire,
A *tête-à-tête* across the fire;
Looked in each other's face awhile,
With half a tear, and half a smile.
The ruddy health, which wont to grace
With manly glow his rural face,
Now scarce retained its faintest streak;
So sallow was his leathern cheek.
She, lank and pale and hollow-eyed,
With rouge had striven in vain to hide
What once was beauty, and repair
The rapine of the midnight air.

   Silence is eloquence, 'tis said.
Both wished to speak, both hung the head.
At length it burst.——"'Tis time," he cries,
"When tired of folly, to be wise.
Are you too tired?"—then checked a groan.
She wept consent, and he went on:

   "How delicate the married life!
You love your husband, I my wife.
Not even satiety could tame,
Nor dissipation quench, the flame.
True to the bias of our kind,
'Tis happiness we wish to find.
In rural scenes retired we sought

In vain the dear delicious draught;
Though blest with love's indulgent store,
We found we wanted something more.
'Twas company, 'twas friends to share
The bliss we languished to declare.
'Twas social converse, change of scene,
To soothe the sullen hour of spleen;
Short absences to wake desire,
And sweet regrets to fan the fire.
We left the lonesome place ; and found,
In dissipation's giddy round,
A thousand novelties to wake
The springs of life, and not to break.
As, from the nest not wandering far,
In light excursions through the air,
The feathered tenants of the grove
Around in mazy circles move,
Sip the cool springs that murmuring flow,
Or taste the blossom on the bough, —
We sported freely with the rest ;
And still, returning to the nest,
In easy mirth we chatted o'er
The trifles of the day before.
Behold us now, dissolving quite
In the full ocean of delight,
In pleasures every hour employ,
Immersed in all the world calls joy;
Our affluence easing the expense
Of splendour and magnificence ;
Our company, the exalted set
Of all that's gay, and all that's great :
Nor happy yet !—and where's the wonder ?—
We live, my dear, too much asunder."

  The moral of my tale is this,—
Variety's the soul of bliss ;
But such variety alone
As makes our home the more our own.
As from the heart's impelling power
The life-blood pours its genial store ;
Though taking each a various way,
The active streams meandering play
Through every artery, every vein,
All to the heart return again ;
From thence resume their new career,
But still return and centre there :
So real happiness below
Must from the heart sincerely flow ;
Nor, listening to the siren's song,
Must stray too far, or rest too long.

All human pleasures thither tend ;
Must there begin, and there must end ;
Must there recruit their languid force,
And gain fresh vigour from their source.

THOMAS GRAY.

[Born in London, 26 November 1716, son of a scrivener; died at Cambridge, 13 July 1771].

ON THE DEATH OF A FAVOURITE CAT,
DROWNED IN A TUB OF GOLD-FISHES.

'Twas on a lofty vase's side,
Where China's gayest art had dyed
　The azure flowers that blow,
Demurest of the tabby kind,
The pensive Selima, reclined,
　Gazed on the lake below.

Her conscious tail her joy declared ;
The fair round face, the snowy beard,
　The velvet of her paws,
Her coat that with the tortoise vies,
Her ears of jet, and emerald eyes,
　She saw, and purred applause.

Still had she gazed, but, 'midst the tide,
Two angel forms were seen to glide,
　The Genii of the stream :
Their scaly armour's Tyrian hue,
Through richest purple, to the view
　Betrayed a golden gleam.

The hapless nymph with wonder saw :
A whisker first, and then a claw,
　With many an ardent wish,
She stretched in vain to reach the prize :
What female heart can gold despise ?
　What Cat's averse to fish ?

Presumptuous maid ! with looks intent,
Again she stretched, again she bent,
　Nor knew the gulf between.
Malignant Fate sat by and smiled :
The slippery verge her feet beguiled ;
　She stumbled headlong in.

Eight times emerging from the flood,
She mewed to every watery god
　Some speedy aid to send.
No Dolphin came, no Nereid stirred,
Nor cruel Tom or Susan heard :
　A favourite has no friend !

From hence, ye Beauties ! undeceived,
Know one false step is ne'er retrieved,
And be with caution bold :
Not all that tempts your wandering eyes
And heedless hearts is lawful prize,
Nor all that glisters, gold.

BISHOP (WILLIAM) BARNARD.

[William Barnard, Bishop of Limerick, was born in 1727, and died in 1806. The verses which ensue arose from the following incident. "Dr. Barnard had asserted, in Dr. Johnson's presence, that men did not improve after the age of forty-five. 'That is not true, Sir,' said Johnson. 'You, who perhaps are forty-eight, may still improve, if you will try : I wish you would set about it. And I am afraid,' he added, ' there is great room for it.'" Johnson afterwards greatly regretted his rudeness to the Bishop; who took the insult in good part, wrote the following verses next day, and sent them to Sir Joshua Reynolds].

VERSES.

I LATELY thought no man alive
Could e'er improve past forty-five,
    And ventured to assert it.
The observation was not new,
But seemed to me so just and true
    That none could controvert it.

"No, sir," said Johnson, " 'tis not so ;
'Tis your mistake, and I can show
    An instance, if you doubt it.
You, who perhaps are forty-eight,
May still improve, 'tis not too late ;
    I wish you'd set about it."

Encouraged thus to mend my faults,
I turned his counsel in my thoughts,
    Which way I could apply it ;
Genius I knew was past my reach,
For who can learn what none can teach ?
    And wit—I could not buy it.

Then come, my friends, and try your skill ;
You may improve me if you will
    (My books are at a distance) :
With you I'll live and learn, and then
Instead of books I shall read men,
    So lend me your assistance.

Dear Knight of Plympton, teach me how
To suffer with unclouded brow,
    And smile serene as thine,
The jest uncouth and truth severe ;
Like thee to turn my deafest ear,
    And calmly drink my wine.

Thou say'st not only skill is gained,
But genius, too, may be attained,
    By studious imitation;
Thy temper mild, thy genius fine,
I'll study till I make them mine
    By constant meditation.

The art of pleasing teach me, Garrick,
Thou who reversest odes Pindaric
    A second time read o'er;
Oh could we read thee backwards too,
Last thirty years thou shouldst review,
    And charm us thirty more.

If I have thoughts and can't express 'em,
Gibbon shall teach me how to dress 'em
    In terms select and terse;
Jones, teach me modesty and Greek;
Smith, how to think; Burke, how to speak;
    And Beauclerk, to converse.

Let Johnson teach me how to place
In fairest light each borrowed grace.
    From him I'll learn to write:
Copy his free and easy style,
And, from the roughness of his file,
    Grow, like himself, polite.

THOMAS WARTON (JUNR.)

[Born at Basingstoke in 1728; died in Oxford in 1790. Celebrated as the author of the *History of English Poetry*. He took holy orders; and held the appointment of Professor of Poetry in Oxford, and afterwards of Camden Professor of History, and succeeded Whitehead as Poet Laureate, 1785].

THE PROGRESS OF DISCONTENT.

When, now mature in classic knowledge,
The joyful youth is sent to college,
His father comes, a vicar plain,
At Oxford bred in Anna's reign,
And thus, in form of humble suitor,
Bowing accosts a reverend tutor:
"Sir, I'm a Glostershire divine,
And this my eldest son of nine.
My wife's ambition and my own
Was that this child should wear a gown.
I'll warrant that his good behaviour
Will justify your future favour;
And, for his parts, to tell the truth,
My son's a very forward youth;
Has Horace all by heart—you'd wonder—
And mouths out Homer's Greek like thunder.

If you'd examine and admit him,
A scholarship would nicely fit him;
That he succeeds, 'tis ten to one;
Your vote and interest, Sir!"—'Tis done.

   Our pupil's hopes, though twice defeated,
Are with a scholarship completed:
A scholarship but half maintains,
And college rules are heavy chains:
In garret dark he smokes and puns,
A prey to discipline and duns;
And, now intent on new designs,
Sighs for a fellowship—and fines.

   When nine full tedious winters passed,
That utmost wish is crowned at last:
But, the rich prize no sooner got,
Again he quarrels with his lot:
"These fellowships are pretty things,—
We live indeed like petty kings:
But who can bear to waste his whole age
Amid the dulness of a college,
Debarred the common joys of life,
And that prime bliss, a loving wife?
Oh! what's a table richly spread,
Without a woman at its head?
Would some snug benefice but fall,
Ye feasts, ye dinners! farewell all!
To offices I'd bid adieu,
Of Dean, Vice-Proes,—of Bursar too;
Come, joys that rural quiet yields,
Come, tithes, and house, and fruitful fields!"

   Too fond of freedom and of ease
A patron's vanity to please,
Long time he watches, and by stealth,
Each frail incumbent's doubtful health.
At length, and in his fortieth year,
A living drops—two hundred clear!
With breast elate beyond expression,
He hurries down to take possession,
With raptures views the sweet retreat.
"What a convenient house! how neat!
For fuel here's sufficient wood:
Pray God the cellars may be good!
The garden—that must be new planned—
Shall these old-fashioned yew-trees stand?
O'er yonder vacant plot shall rise
The flowery shrub of thousand dyes:—
Yon wall, that feels the southern ray,
Shall blush with ruddy fruitage gay:

While thick beneath its aspect warm
O'er well-ranged hives the bees shall swarm,
From which, ere long, of golden gleam
Metheglin's luscious juice shall stream.
This awkward hut, o'ergrown with ivy,
We'll alter to a modern privy.
Up yon green slope of hazels trim,
An avenue so cool and dim
Shall to an arbour at the end,
In spite of gout, entice a friend.
My predecessor loved devotion—
But of a garden had no notion."

Continuing this fantastic farce on,
He now commences country parson.
To make his character entire,
He weds a cousin of the squire:
Not over-weighty in the purse,
But many doctors have done worse:
And, though she boasts no charms divine,
Yet she can carve and make birch wine.

Thus fixed, content he taps his barrel,
Exhorts his neighbours not to quarrel;
Finds his churchwardens have discerning
Both in good liquor and good learning;
With tithes his barns replete he sees,
And chuckles o'er his surplice-fees;
Studies to find out latent dues,
And regulates the state of pews;
Rides a sleek mare with purple housing,
To share the monthly club's carousing;
Of Oxford pranks facetious tells,
And—but on Sundays—hears no bells;
Sends presents of his choicest fruit,
And prunes himself each sapless shoot;
Plants cauliflowers, and boasts to rear
The earliest melons of the year;
Thinks alteration charming work is,
Keeps bantam cocks, and feeds his turkeys:
Builds in his copse a favourite bench,
And stores the pond with carp and tench.

But ah! too soon his thoughtless breast
By cares domestic is oppressed;
And a third butcher's bill and brewing
Threaten inevitable ruin:
For children fresh expenses get,
And Dicky now for school is fit.
"Why did I sell my college life,"
He cries, "for benefice and wife?

Return, ye days when endless pleasure
I found in reading, or in leisure !
When calm around the common room
I puffed my daily pipe's perfume ;
Rode for a stomach, and inspected,
At annual bottlings, corks selected :
And dined untaxed, untroubled, under
The portrait of our pious Founder !
When impositions were supplied
To light my pipe or soothe my pride !
No cares were then for forward peas,
A yearly-longing wife to please ;
My thoughts no christ'ning dinners crossed,
No children cried for buttered toast ;
And every night I went to bed
Without a modus in my head !"

Oh ! trifling head, and fickle-heart !
Chagrined at whatsoe'er thou art ;
A dupe to follies yet untried,
And sick of pleasures, scarce enjoyed !
Each prize possessed, thy transport ceases,
And in pursuit alone it pleases.

OLIVER GOLDSMITH.

[Born on 10th November 1728, at Pallas, Ireland, son of a clergyman ; died in London, 4 April 1774].

DESCRIPTION OF AN AUTHOR'S BEDCHAMBER.

WHERE the Red Lion, staring o'er the way,
Invites each passing stranger that can pay ;
Where Calvert's butt, and Parson's black champagne,
Regale the drabs and bloods of Drury Lane ;
There, in a lonely room, from bailiffs snug,
The Muse found Scroggen stretched beneath a rug.
A window patched with paper lent a ray,
That dimly showed the state in which he lay.
The sanded floor that grits beneath the tread,
The humid wall with paltry pictures spread,
The royal game of goose was there in view,
And the twelve rules the royal martyr drew ;
The Seasons, framed with listing, found a place,
And brave Prince William showed his lamp-black face.
The morn was cold.   He views with keen desire
The rusty grate unconscious of a fire :
With beer and milk arrears the frieze was scored,
And five cracked tea-cups dressed the chimney-board ;
A night-cap decked his brows instead of bay,
A cap by night—a stocking all the day.

JOHN CUNNINGHAM.

[Born in Dublin in 1729; died in 1773. Was an actor by profession; composed a farce named *Love in a Mist*, and various miscellaneous poems].

THE FOX AND THE CAT.

The fox and the cat, as they travelled one day,
With moral discourses cut shorter the way.
"'Tis great," says the Fox, "to make justice our guide!"
"How god-like is mercy!" Grimalkin replied.
   Whilst thus they proceeded, a wolf from the wood,
Impatient of hunger, and thirsting for blood,
Rushed forth—as he saw the dull shepherd asleep—
And seized for his supper an innocent sheep.
"In vain, wretched victim, for mercy you bleat;
When mutton's at hand," says the wolf, "I must eat."
   Grimalkin's astonished—the fox stood aghast—
To see the fell beast at his bloody repast.
"What a wretch!" says the cat, "'tis the vilest of brutes;
Does he feed upon flesh when there's herbage and roots?"
Cries the fox, "While our oaks give us acorns so good,
What a tyrant is this to spill innocent blood!"
   Well, onward they marched, and they moralized still,
Till they came where some poultry picked chaff by a mill.
Sly Reynard surveyed them with gluttonous eyes,
And made, spite of morals, a pullet his prize.
A mouse, too, that chanced from her covert to stray,
The greedy Grimalkin secured as her prey.
   A spider, that sat in her web on the wall,
Perceived the poor victims, and pitied their fall.
She cried, "Of such murders how guiltless am I!"
So ran to regale on a new-taken fly.

CHARLES CHURCHILL.

[Born in London, 1731; died at Boulogne, 4 November 1764. He entered the church, with very few qualifications for supporting the clerical character. His extreme liking for the theatre prompted his first published poem, *The Rosciad*, which excited great public attention and applause. Another popular topic, the English prejudice against Scotchmen, was embodied in a later satire, *The Prophecy of Famine, a Scots Pastoral*. Soon afterwards he discarded the clerical habit; and figured as a strong party-politician on the side of Wilkes, and as a man of pleasure. It was in visiting Wilkes in France that he caught the illness which brought him to an early grave. Churchill was a man of much generous impulse; and the reader can still enjoy the vigour of many passages in his poems, although their obsolete subject-matter, combined with their length, is a bar to general perusal now-a-days.]

THE JOURNEY.

(A FRAGMENT.)

Some of my friends (for friends I must suppose
All who, not daring to appear my foes,
Feign great good-will, and, not more full of spite
Than full of craft, under false colours fight)

Some of my friends (so lavishly I print)
As more in sorrow than in anger, hint
(Though that indeed will scarce admit a doubt)
That I shall run my stock of genius out,
My no great stock, and, publishing so fast,
Must needs become a bankrupt at the last.

"The husbandman, to spare a thankful soil,
Which, rich in disposition, pays his toil
More than a hundredfold, which swells his store
E'en to his wish, and makes his barns run o'er,
By long experience taught, who teaches best,
Foregoes his hopes awhile, and gives it rest.
The land, allowed its losses to repair,
Refreshed, and full in strength, delights to wear
A second youth, and to the farmer's eyes
Bids richer crops and double harvests rise.
Nor think this practice to the earth confined;
It reaches to the culture of the mind.
The mind of man craves rest, and cannot bear,
Though next in power to gods, continual care.
Genius himself (nor here let Genius frown)
Must, to ensure his vigour, be laid down,
And fallowed well; had Churchill known but this,
Which the most slight observer scarce could miss,
He might have flourished twenty years, or more,
Though now alas! poor man! worn out in four."

Recovered from the vanity of youth,
I feel, alas! this melancholy truth,
Thanks to each cordial, each advising friend;
And am, if not too late, resolved to mend,—
Resolved to give some respite to my pen,
Apply myself once more to books and men,
View what is present, what is past review,
And, my old stock exhausted, lay-in new.
For twice six moons (let winds, turned porters, bear
This oath to heaven) for twice six moons I swear,
No Muse shall tempt me with her siren lay,
Nor draw me from improvement's thorny way.
Verse I abjure, nor will forgive that friend
Who in my hearing shall a rhyme commend.

It cannot be!—Whether I will or no,
Such as they are, my thoughts in measure flow.
Convinced, determined, I in prose begin;
But, ere I write one sentence, verse creeps in,
And taints me through and through. By this good light!
In verse I talk by day, I dream by night;
If now and then I curse, my curses chime,
Nor can I pray unless I pray in rhyme.

E'en now I err, in spite of common sense,
And my confession doubles my offence.

   Rest then, my friends—spare, spare your precious breath,
And be your slumbers not less sound than death;
Perturbèd spirits, rest! nor thus appear
To waste your counsels in a spendthrift's ear.
On your grave lessons I cannot subsist,
Nor e'en in verse become economist.
Rest then, my friends, nor, hateful to my eyes,
Let envy, in the shape of pity, rise
To blast me ere my time; with patience wait.
'Tis no long interval: propitious fate
Shall glut your pride, and every son of phlegm
Find ample room to censure and condemn.
Read some three-hundred lines (no easy task;
But probably the last that I shall ask),
And give me up for ever; wait one hour,—
Nay not so much. Revenge is in your power,
And ye may cry, ere Time hath turned his glass,
"Lo! what we prophesied is come to pass."

   Let those who poetry in poems claim
Or not read this, or only read to blame;
Let those who are by fiction's charms enslaved
Return me thanks for half-a-crown well-saved;
Let those who love a little gall in rhyme
Postpone their purchase now, and call next time;
Let those who, void of nature, look for art,
Take up their money, and in peace depart;
Let those who energy of diction prize
For Billingsgate quit Flexney, and be wise.
Here is no lie, no gall, no art, no force;
Mean are the words, and such as come of course;
The subject not less simple than the lay,—
A plain, unlaboured journey of a day.

   Far from me now be every tuneful maid;
I neither ask nor can receive their aid.
Pegasus turned into a common hack,
Alone I jog, and keep the beaten track;
Nor would I have the sisters of the hill
Behold their bard in such a dishabille.
Absent, but only absent for a time,
Let them caress some dearer son of rhyme;
Let them, as far as decency permits,
Without suspicion, play the fool with wits,
'Gainst fools be guarded; 'tis a certain rule,—
Wits are safe things, there's danger in a fool.

   Let them, though modest, Gray more modest woo;
Let them with Mason bleat, and bray, and coo;

Let them with Franklin, proud of some small Greek,
Make Sophocles, disguised, in English speak;
Let them with Glover o'er Medea doze;
Let them with Dodsley wail Cleone's woes,
Whilst he, fine feeling creature, all in tears,
Melts as they melt, and weeps with weeping peers;
Let them with simple Whitehead, taught to creep
Silent and soft, lay Fontenelle asleep;
Let them with Browne contrive, no vulgar trick,
To cure the dead, and make the living sick;
Let them in charity to Murphy give
Some old French piece, that he may steal and live;
Let them with antic Foote subscriptions get,
And advertise a summer-house of wit.

Thus, or in any better way they please,
With these great men, or with great men like these,
Let them their appetite for laughter feed;
I on my journey all alone proceed.

If fashionable grown, and fond of power,
With humorous Scots let them disport the hour;
Let them dance, fairy-like, round Ossian's tomb;
Let them forge lies and histories for Hume;
Let them with Home, the very prince of verse,
Make something like a tragedy in Erse;
Under dark allegory's flimsy veil
Let them with Ogilvie spin out a tale
Of rueful length; let them plain things obscure,
Debase what's truly rich, and what is poor
Make poorer still by jargon most uncouth.
With every pert prim prettiness of youth
Born of false taste, with fancy (like a child
Not knowing what it cries for) running wild,
With bloated style, by affectation taught,
With much false colouring, and little thought,
With phrases strange, and dialect decreed
By reason never to have passed the Tweed,
With words, which nature meant each other's foe,
Forced to compound whether they will or no,—
With such materials, let them, if they will,
To prove at once their pleasantry and skill,
Build up a bard to war 'gainst common sense,
By way of compliment to Providence.
Let them with Armstrong, taking leave of sense,
Read musty lectures on benevolence,
Or con the pages of his gaping *Day*,
Where all his former fame was thrown away,
Where all but barren labour was forgot,
And the vain stiffness of a lettered Scot.

Let them with Armstrong pass the term of light,
But not one hour of darkness. When the night
Suspends this mortal coil, when memory wakes,
When for our past misdoings conscience takes
A deep revenge, when, by reflection led,
She draws his curtains, and looks comfort dead,
Let every Muse be gone ; in vain he turns,
And tries to pray for sleep ; an Ætna burns,
A more than Ætna, in his coward breast,
And guilt, with vengeance armed, forbids him rest.
Though soft as plumage from young Zephyr's wing,
His couch seems hard, and no relief can bring.
Ingratitude hath planted daggers there
No good man can deserve, no brave man bear.

   Thus, or in any better way they please,
With these great men, or with great men like
     these,
Let them their appetite for laughter feed ;
I on my journey all alone proceed.

JOHN WOLCOT.

[Born in 1738, died in 1819 : wrote under the pseudonym of "Peter Pindar." Began life as an apothecary ; took his degree as a physician, and went out to Jamaica, where he found it convenient to occupy a clerical living, and so took holy orders. He afterwards resumed practice as a physician in Cornwall and Devonshire, and won a name as a satirist—more especially in matters connected with fine art, literature, and politics : he had himself some skill as a draughtsman, and more especially as a musician. Wolcot made many enemies by his pen, and his general character was that of a selfish man : at the same time, he gladly fostered merit where he discerned it, and had friends whose good opinion he secured].

TO A FISH OF THE BROOKE.[1]

WHY flyest thou away with fear ?
Trust me, there's nought of danger near ;
   I have no wicked hooke
All covered with a snaring bait,
Alas, to tempt thee to thy fate,
   And dragge thee from the brooke.

O harmless tenant of the flood,
I do not wish to spill thy blood,
   For Nature unto thee
Perchance hath given a tender wife,
And children dear, to charm thy life,
   As she hath done for me.

---

[1] The reader will understand the antiquated spelling to be a "take-off" of Walton.

>   Enjoy thy stream, O harmless fish;
>   And, when an angler for his dish,
>   Through gluttony's vile sin,
>   Attempts, a wretch, to pull thee *out*,
>   God give thee strength, O gentle trout,
>   To pull the raskall *in!*

THE PILGRIMS AND THE PEAS.

A BRACE of sinners, for no good,
   Were ordered to the Virgin Mary's shrine,
Who at Loreto dwelt, in wax, stone, wood,
   And in a fair white wig looked wondrous fine.

Fifty long miles had those sad rogues to travel,
With something in their shoes much worse than gravel;
In short, their toes so gentle to amuse,
The priest had ordered peas into their shoes:

A nostrum, famous in old Popish times,
For purifying souls that stunk with crimes;
   A sort of apostolic salt,
That Popish parsons for its power exalt
For keeping souls of sinners sweet,
Just as our kitchen-salt keeps meat.

The knaves set off on the same day,
Peas in their shoes, to go and pray.
   But very different was their speed, I wot:
One of the sinners galloped on,
Light as a bullet from a gun;
   The other limped as if he had been shot.

One saw the Virgin soon—"*Peccavi*" cried—
   Had his soul whitewashed all so clever;
Then home again he nimbly hied,
   Made fit with saints above to live for ever.

In coming back, however, let me say,
He met his brother-rogue about half way,
Hobbling with outstretched hams and bended knees,
Damning the souls and bodies of the peas;
His eyes in tears, his cheeks and brow in sweat,
Deep sympathizing with his groaning feet.

"How now," the light-toed, white-washed pilgrim broke,
   "You lazy lubber!"
"Odds curse it!" cried the other, "'tis no joke;
My feet, once hard as any rock,
   Are now as soft as blubber.

"Excuse me, Virgin Mary, that I swear:
As for Loreto, I shall not go there;
No! to the Devil my sinful soul must go,
For hang me if I ha'n't lost every toe!"

"But, brother sinner, do explain
How 'tis that you are not in pain?
   What power hath worked a wonder for your toes?
Whilst I, just like a snail, am crawling,
Now swearing, now on saints devoutly bawling,
   Whilst not a rascal comes to ease my woes!

"How is't that *you* can like a greyhound go,
   As merry as if nought had happened, burn ye?"
"Why," cried the other, grinning, "you must know
That, just before I ventured on my journey,
   To walk a little more at ease
   I took the liberty to boil *my* peas."

THE SAILOR-BOY AT PRAYERS.

A GREAT Law Chief whom God nor demon scares,
Compelled to kneel and pray, who swore his prayers;
   The devil behind him pleased and grinning,—
Patting the angry lawyer on the shoulder,
Declaring nought was ever bolder,
   Admiring such a novel mode of sinning:—

Like this, a subject would be reckoned rare,
Which proves what blood-game infidels can dare;
Which to my memory brings a fact,
Which nothing but an English tar would act.

In ships of war, on Sundays, prayers are given;
For, though so wicked, sailors think of heaven,
   Particularly in a storm;
Where, if they find no brandy to get drunk,
Their souls are in a miserable funk.
   Then vow they to the Almighty to reform,
If in his goodness only once, once more,
He'll suffer them to clap a foot on shore.

In calms, indeed, or gentle airs,
They ne'er on week-days pester Heaven with prayers;
For 'tis amongst the Jacks a common saying,
"Where there's no danger, there's no need of praying."

One Sunday morning all were met
   To hear the parson preach and pray;
All but a boy, who, willing to forget
   That prayers were handing out, had stolen away;
And, thinking praying but a useless task,
Had crawled, to take a nap, into a cask.

The boy was soon found missing, and full soon
   The boatswain's cat sagacious smelt him out;
Gave him a clawing to some tune—
   This cat's a cousin-germane to the knout.

"Come out, you skulking dog," the boatswain cried,
  "And save your damned young sinful soul!"
He then the moral-mending cat applied,
  And turned him like a badger from his hole.

Sulky the boy marched on, and did not mind him,
  Although the boatswain flogging kept behind him:
"Flog," cried the boy, "flog—curse me, flog away!
I'll go—but mind—God damn me if I'll pray!"

BOZZY AND PIOZZI; OR, THE BRITISH BIOGRAPHERS.
A PAIR OF TOWN ECLOGUES.

THE ARGUMENT.

On the death of Dr. Johnson, a number of people, ambitious of being distinguished from the mute part of their species, set about relating and printing stories and bon-mots of that celebrated moralist.—Amongst the most zealous, though not the most enlightened, appeared Mr. Boswell and Madame Piozzi, the hero and heroine of our Eclogues.—They are supposed to have in contemplation the Life of Johnson; and, to prove their biographical abilities, appeal to Sir John Hawkins for his decision on their respective merits, by quotations from their printed anecdotes of the Doctor.—Sir John hears them with uncommon patience, and determines very properly on the pretensions of the contending parties.

PART I.

WHEN Johnson sought (as Shakspeare says) that bourn
From whence, alas! no travellers return,—
In humbler English, when the Doctor died,—
Apollo whimpered, and the Muses cried;
Parnassus moped for days, in business slack,
And like a hearse the hill was hung with black.
Minerva, sighing for her favourite son,
Pronounced, with lengthened face, the world undone;
Her owl, too, hooted in so loud a style
That people might have heard the bird a mile.
Jove wiped his eyes so red, and told his wife
He ne'er made Johnson's equal in his life;
And that 'twould be a long time first, if ever,
His art could form a fellow half so clever.
Venus, of all the little Loves the dam,
With all the Graces, sobbed for brother Sam:
Such were the heavenly howlings for his death
As if Dame Nature had resigned her breath.
Nor less sonorous was the grief, I ween,
Amidst the natives of our earthly scene:
From beggars to the great who hold the helm,
One Johnso-mania raged through all the realm.

"Who" (cried the world) "can match his prose or rhyme?
O'er wits of modern days he towers sublime!
An oak, wide spreading o'er the shrubs below,
That round his roots with puny foliage blow;
A pyramid, amidst some barren waste,
That frowns o'er huts, the sport of every blast:
A mighty Atlas, whose aspiring head
O'er distant regions casts an awful shade.
By kings and vagabonds his tales are told,
And every sentence glows, a grain of gold!
Blest who his philosophic phiz can take,
Catch even his weaknesses—his noddle's shake,
The lengthened lip of scorn, the forehead's scowl,
The louring eye's contempt and bear-like growl!
In vain the critics vent their toothless rage:
Mere sprats, that venture war with whales to wage!
Unmoved he stands, and feels their force no more
Than some huge rock amidst the watery roar,
That calmly bears the tumults of the deep,
And howling tempests that as well might sleep."

Strong, 'midst the Rambler's cronies, was the rage
To fill, with Sam's bon-mots and tales, the page:
Mere flies, that buzzed around his setting ray,
And bore a splendour on their wings away.
Thus round his orb the pygmy planets run,
And catch their little lustre from the sun.

At length, rushed forth two candidates for fame,—
A Scotchman one, and one a London dame:
That, by the emphatic Johnson, christened Bozzy;
This, by the bishop's license, Dame Piozzi;
Whose widowed name, by topers loved, was Thrale,
Bright in the annals of election-ale:
A name, by marriage, that gave up the ghost,
In poor Pedocchio[1]—no, Piozzi—lost!
Each seized, with ardour wild, the grey goose-quill:
Each sat, to work the intellectual mill,
That pecks of bran so coarse began to pour
To one small solitary grain of flour.

Forth rushed to light their books—but who should say
Which bore the palm of anecdote away?
This to decide, the rival wits agreed
Before Sir John their tales and jokes to read;
And let the knight's opinion in the strife
Declare the properest pen to write Sam's life.
Sir John, renowned for musical [2] palavers—

---

[1] The author was nearly committing a blunder. Fortunate indeed was his recollection, as *Pedocchio* signifies, in the Italian language, that most contemptible of all animals, a louse.   [2] Vide his *History of Music*.

The prince, the king, the emperor of quavers ;
Sharp in solfeggi, as the sharpest needle ;
Great in the noble art of tweedle-tweedle ;
Of Music's college formed to be a fellow,
Fit for Mus. D. or Mastro di Capella ;
Whose volume, though it here and there offends,
Boasts *German merit*—makes by bulk amends.
Superior, frowning o'er octavo wits,
High-placed, the venerable quarto sits,—
And duodecimos, ignoble scum,
Poor prostitutes to every vulgar thumb,—
Whilst, undefiled by literary rage,
He bears a spotless leaf from age to age.

 Like schoolboys, lo ! before a two-armed chair
That held the knight wise-judging, stood the pair.
Or like two ponies on the sporting-ground,
Prepared to gallop when the drum should sound,
The couple ranged—for victory both as keen
As for a tottering bishopric a dean,
Or patriot Burke for giving glorious bastings
To that intolerable fellow Hastings.
Thus with their songs contended Virgil's swains,
And made the valleys vocal with their strains,
 Before some greybeard swain, whose judgment ripe
 Gave goats for prizes to the prettiest pipe.

 " Alternately in anecdotes go on ;
But first begin *you*, madam," cried Sir John.—
The thankful dame low curt'sied to the chair,
And thus, for victory panting, read the Fair :

MADAME PIOZZI.

 Sam Johnson was of Michael Johnson born,
Whose shop of books did Lichfield town adorn :
Wrong-headed, stubborn as a haltered ram ;
In short, the model of our Hero Sam ;
Inclined to madness, too—for, when his shop
Fell down, for want of cash to buy a prop,
For fear the thieves might steal the vanished store,
He duly went each night, and locked the door !

BOZZY.

 Whilst Johnson was in Edinburgh, my wife,
To please his palate, studied for her life ;
With every rarity she filled her house,
And gave the doctor, for his dinner, grouse.

MADAME PIOZZI.

 Dear Doctor Johnson was in size an ox ;
And from his uncle Andrew learned to box,—

A man to wrestlers and to bruisers dear,
Who kept the ring in Smithfield a whole year.

BOZZY.

At supper, rose a dialogue on witches,
When Crosbie said there could not be such bitches;
And that 'twas blasphemy to think such hags
Could stir up storms, and on their broomstick nags
Gallop along the air with wondrous pace,
And boldly fly in God Almighty's face.
But Johnson answered him, "There might be witches—
Nought proved the non-existence of the bitches."

MADAME PIOZZI.

When Thrale, as nimble as a boy at school,
Jumped, though fatigued with hunting, o'er a stool,
The Doctor, proud the same grand feat to do,
His powers exerted, and jumped over too.
And, though he might a broken back bewail,
He scorned to be eclipsed by Mr. Thrale.

BOZZY.

At Ulinish, our friend, to pass the time,
Regaled us with his knowledges sublime:
Showed that all sorts of learning filled his nob,
And that in butchery he could bear a bob.
He sagely told us of the different feat
Employed to kill the animals we eat.
"An ox," says he, "in country and in town,
Is by the butchers constantly knocked down;
As for that lesser animal, a calf,
The knock is really not so strong by half;
The beast is only stunned: but, as for goats,
And sheep, and lambs—the butchers cut their throats.
Those fellows only want to keep them quiet,
Not choosing that the brutes should breed a riot."

MADAME PIOZZI.

When Johnson was a child, and swallowed pap,
'Twas in his mother's old maid Catharine's lap.
There, whilst he sat, he took in wondrous learning;
For much his bowels were for knowledge yearning;
There heard the story which we Britons brag on,
The story of St. George and eke the Dragon.

BOZZY.

When Foote his leg by some misfortune broke,
Says I to Johnson, all by way of joke,
"Sam, Sir, in Paragraph, will soon be clever,
And take off Peter better now than ever."

On which, says Johnson, without hesitation,
"George[1] will rejoice at Foote's depeditation."
On which, says I—a penetrating elf—
"Doctor, I'm sure you coined that word yourself."
On which he laughed, and said I had divined it;
For, *bonâ fide*, he had really coined it.
"And yet, of all the words I've coined," says he,
"My Dictionary, Sir, contains but three."

MADAME PIOZZI.

The doctor said, in literary matters
A Frenchman goes not deep—he only smatters;
Then asked, what could be hoped for from the dogs—
Fellows that lived eternally on frogs!

BOZZY.

In grave procession to St. Leonard's College,
Well stuffed with every sort of useful knowledge,
We stately walked, as soon as supper ended:
The landlord and the waiter both attended.
The landlord, skilled a piece of grease to handle,
Before us marched, and held a tallow candle:
A lantern (some famed Scotsman its creator)
With equal grace was carried by the waiter.
Next morning, from our beds we took a leap,
And found ourselves much better for our sleep.

MADAME PIOZZI.

In Lincolnshire, a lady showed our friend
A grotto that she wished him to commend.
Quoth she, "How cool, in summer, this abode!"
"Yes, Madam," answered Johnson, "for a toad."

BOZZY.

Between old Scalpa's rugged isle and Rasay's,
The wind was vastly boisterous in our faces:
'Twas glorious Johnson's figure to set sight on—
High in the boat, he looked a noble Triton!
But lo! to damp our pleasure fate concurs;
For Joe, the blockhead, lost his master's spurs.
This for the Rambler's temper was a *rubber*,
Who wondered Joseph could be such a lubber.

MADAME PIOZZI.

I asked him if he knocked Tom Osborn[2] down,
As such a tale was current through the town:—
Says I, "Do tell me, doctor, what befell."
"Why, dearest lady, there is nought to tell:

---

[1] George Faulkner, the printer at Dublin, taken off by Foote, under the character of Peter Paragraph.   [2] Bookseller.

I pondered on the properest mode to treat him—
The dog was impudent, and so I beat him.
Tom, like a fool, proclaimed his fancied wrongs ;
Others that I belaboured held their tongues."

Did any one that he was "happy" cry—
Johnson would tell him plumply, 'twas a lie.
A lady told him she was really so ;
On which he sternly answered, "Madam, no !
Sickly you are, and ugly—foolish, poor ;
And therefore can't be happy, I am sure.
'Twould make a fellow hang himself, whose ear
Were, from such creatures, forced such stuff to hear."

BOZZY.

Lo ! when we landed on the Isle of Mull,
The megrims got into the doctor's skull :
With such bad humours he began to fill
I thought he would not go to Icolmkill.
But lo ! those megrims (wonderful to utter !)
Were banished all by tea and bread and butter !

MADAME PIOZZI.

The doctor had a cat, and christened Hodge,
That at his house in Fleet Street used to lodge.
This Hodge grew old and sick, and used to wish
That all his dinners were composed of fish.
To please poor Hodge, the doctor, all so kind,
Went out, and bought him oysters to his mind.
This every day he did—nor asked black Frank,[1]
Who deemed himself of much too high a rank
With vulgar fish-fags to be forced to chat,
And purchase oysters for a mangy cat.

SIR JOHN.

For God's sake, stay each anecdotic scrap !
Let me draw breath, and take a trifling nap.
With one half-hour's refreshing slumber blest,
And Heaven's assistance, I may hear the rest.

Aside.]—What have I done, inform me, gracious Lord,
That thus my ears with nonsense should be bored ?
Oh ! if I do not in the trial die,
The devil and all his brimstone I defy !
No punishment in other worlds I fear ;
My crimes will all be expiated *here*.
Ah ! ten times happier was my lot of yore,
When, raised to consequence that all adore,
I sat, each session, king-like, in the chair,
Awed every rank, and made the million stare :

---

[1] Dr. Johnson's servant.

Lord-paramount o'er every justice riding;
In causes, with a Turkish sway, deciding!
Yes, like a noble bashaw of three tails,
I spread a fear and trembling through the jails!
Blest have I browbeaten each thief and strumpet,
And blasted on them like the last day's trumpet.
I know no paltry weakness of the soul—
No snivelling pity dares my deeds control :—
Ashamed, the weakness of my king I hear,
Who, childish, drops on every death a tear.
Return, return again, thou glorious hour
That to my grasp once gav'st my idol, power ;
When, at my feet, the humbled knaves would fall ;
The thundering Jupiter of Hicks's Hall!

 The knight thus finishing his speech so fair,
Sleep pulled him gently backwards in his chair ;
Oped wide the mouth that oft on jail-birds swore ;
Then raised his nasal organ to a roar
That actually surpassed in tone and grace
The grumbled ditties of his favourite bass.[1]

PART II.

 Now from his sleep the knight, affrighted, sprung,
Whilst on his ear the words of Johnson rung ;
For lo! in dreams, the surly Rambler rose,
And, wildly staring, seemed a man of woes.

 "Wake, Hawkins," growled the doctor, with a frown,
"And knock that fellow and that woman down!
Bid them with Johnson's life proceed no further—
Enough already they have dealt in murther !
Say to their tales that little truth belongs :
If fame they mean me—bid them hold their tongues.
In vain at glory gudgeon Boswell snaps ;
His mind's a paper-kite—composed of scraps ;
Just o'er the tops of chimneys formed to fly,
Not with a wing sublime to mount the sky.
Say to the dog his head's a downright drum,
Unequal to the History of Tom Thumb :
Nay, tell of anecdote that thirsty leech
He is not equal to a Tyburn speech.
For that Piozzi's wife, Sir John, exhort her
To draw her immortality from porter ;
Give up her anecdotical inditing,
And study housewifery instead of writing.
Bid her a poor biography suspend,
Nor crucify, through vanity, a friend.—

---

[1] The violoncello, on which the knight is a performer.

I know no business women have with learning:
I scorn, I hate, the mole-eyed, half-discerning:
Their wit but serves a husband's heart to rack,
And make eternal horsewhips for his back.—
Tell Peter Pindar, should you chance to meet him,
I like his genius—should be glad to greet him.
Yet let him know, crowned heads are sacred things,
And bid him reverence more the best of kings;[1]
Still on his Pegasus continue jogging,
And give that Boswell's back another flogging."

Such was the dream that waked the sleepy knight,
And oped again his eyes upon the light—
Who, mindless of old Johnson and his frown,
And stern commands to knock the couple down,
Resolved to keep the peace—and, in a tone
Not much unlike a mastiff o'er a bone,
He grumbled that, enabled by the nap,
He now could meet more biographic scrap.
Then, nodding with a *magistratic* air,
To further anecdote he called the Fair.

MADAME PIOZZI.

Dear Doctor Johnson loved a leg of pork,
And hearty on it would his grinders work:
He liked to eat it so much overdone
That one might shake the flesh from off the bone.
A veal-pie too, with sugar crammed and plums,
Was wondrous grateful to the doctor's gums.
Though used from morn to night on fruit to stuff,
He vowed his belly never had enough.

BOZZY.

One Thursday morn did Doctor Johnson wake,
And call out "Lanky! Lanky!" by mistake;
But recollecting—"Bozzy! Bozzy!" cried—
For in contractions Johnson took a pride!

MADAME PIOZZI.

Whene'er our friend would read in bed by night,
Poor Mr. Thrale and I were in a fright;
For, blinking on his book, too near the flame,
Lo! to the foretop of his wig it came,—
Burnt all the hairs away, both great and small,
Down to the very network, named the cawl.

---

[1] This is a strange and almost incredible speech from Johnson's mouth; as, not many years ago, when the age of a certain great personage became the subject of debate, the doctor broke in upon the conversation with the following question:—"Of what importance to the present company is his age? Of what importance would it have been to the world if he had never existed?"

BOZZY.

At Corrachatachin's, in hoggism sunk,
I got with punch, alas! confounded drunk.
Much was I vexed that I could not be quiet,
But like a stupid blockhead breed a riot.
I scarcely knew how 'twas I reeled to bed.
Next morn I waked with dreadful pains of head:
And terrors too that of my peace did rob me—
For much I feared the Moralist would *mob* me.
But, as I lay along, a heavy log,
The Doctor, entering, called me "drunken dog."
Then up rose I, with apostolic air,
And read in Dame M'Kinnon's book of prayer;
In hopes, for such a sin, to be forgiven—
And make, if possible, my peace with Heaven.
'Twas strange that in that volume of divinity
I oped the Twentieth Sunday after Trinity,
And read these words:—" Pray, be not drunk with wine,
Since drunkenness doth make a man a swine."
" Alas!" says I, "the sinner that I am!"
And, having made my speech, I took a dram.

MADAME PIOZZI.

One day, with spirits low and sorrow filled,
I told him I had got a cousin killed.
" My dear," quoth he, " for heaven's sake, hold your canting:
Were all your cousins killed, they'd not be wanting.
Though Death on each of them should set his mark —
Though every one were spitted like a lark,
Roasted, and given that dog there for a meal—
The loss of them the world would never feel.
Trust me, dear madam, all your dear relations
Are nits—are nothings, in the eye of nations."

Again, says I one day, "I do believe,
A good acquaintance that I have will grieve
To hear her friend hath lost a large estate."—
" Yes," answered he, " lament as much her fate
As did your horse (I freely will allow)
To hear of the miscarriage of your cow."

BOZZY.

At Enoch, at M'Queen's, we went to bed;
A coloured handkerchief wrapped Johnson's head:
He said, " God bless us both—good night!" and then
I, like a parish clerk, pronounced Amen!
My good companion soon by sleep was seized—
But I by lice and fleas was sadly teazed:

Methought a spider, with terrific claws,
Was striding from the wainscot to my jaws.
But slumber soon did every sense entrap;
And so I sunk into the sweetest nap.

MADAME PIOZZI.

Travelling in Wales, at dinner-time we got on
Where, at Leweny, lives Sir Robert Cotton.
At table, our great Moralist to please—
Says I, "Dear Doctor, a'nt these charming peas?"
Quoth he, (to contradict and *run his rig*)
"Madam, they possibly might please a pig."

BOZZY.

Of thatching well the Doctor knew the art,
And with his thrashing wisdom made us start:
Described the greatest secrets of the mint—
And made folks fancy that he had been in't.
Of hops and malt 'tis wondrous what he knew;
And well as any brewer he could brew.

MADAME PIOZZI.

In ghosts the Doctor strongly did believe,
And pinned his faith on many a liar's sleeve.
He said to Doctor Lawrence; "Sure I am,
I heard my poor dear mother call out 'Sam!'
I'm sure," said he, "that I can trust my ears:
And yet my mother had been dead for years."

BOZZY.

When young ('twas rather silly, I allow),
Much was I pleased to imitate a cow.
One time, at Drury-lane, with Doctor Blair,
My imitations made the playhouse stare.
So very charming was I in my roar
That both the galleries clapped, and cried "encore!"
Blessed by the general plaudit and the laugh—
I tried to be a jackass and a calf.
But who, alas! in all things can be great?
In short, I met a terrible defeat:
So vile I brayed and bellowed, I was hissed—
Yet all who knew me wondered that I missed.
Blair whispered me; "You've lost your credit now:
Stick, Boswell, for the future, to your cow."

MADAME PIOZZI.

For me, in Latin, Doctor Johnson wrote
Two lines upon Sir Joseph Banks's goat;
A goat that round the world, so curious, went—
A goat that now eats grass that grows in Kent.

BOZZY.

To Lord Monboddo a few lines I wrote,
And, by the servant Joseph, sent this note :—

"Thus far, my lord, from Edinburgh, my home,
With Mr. Samuel Johnson I am come :
This night, by us, must certainly be seen
The very handsome town of Aberdeen.
For thoughts of Johnson you'll be not applied to—
I know your lordship likes him less than I do.
So near we are—to part I can't tell how
Without so much as making you a bow.
Besides, the Rambler says, to see Monbodd,
He'd wander two whole miles out of the road :
Which shows that he admires (whoever rails)
The pen which proves that men are born with tails.
Hoping that, as to health, your lordship does well,
I am your servant at command, JAMES BOSWELL."

MADAME PIOZZI.

On Mr. Thrale's old hunter Johnson rode—
Who with prodigious pride the beast bestrode ;
And, as on Brighton Downs he dashed away,
Much was he pleased to hear a sportsman say
That at a chase he was as tight a hand
As e'er an ill-bred lubber in the land.

BOZZY.

One morning, Johnson, on the Isle of Mull,
Was of his politics excessive full :
Quoth he, "That Pulteney was a rogue, 'tis plain—
Besides, the fellow was a Whig in grain."
Then to his principles he gave a banging,
And swore no Whig was ever worth a hanging.
"'Tis wonderful," says he, "and makes one stare,
To think, the livery chose John Wilkes lord mayor :
A dog of whom the world could nurse no hopes—
Prompt to debauch their girls, and rob their shops."

MADAME PIOZZI.

Sir, I believe that anecdote a lie ;
But grant that Johnson said it—by the bye—
As Wilkes unhappily your friendship shared,
The dirty anecdote might well be spared.

BOZZY.

Madam, I stick to truth as much as you,
And damme if the story be not true.

What you have said of Johnson and the larks
As much the Rambler for a savage marks.
'Twas scandalous, even Candour must allow,
To give the history of the horse and cow.
Who but an enemy to Johnson's fame
Dared his vile prank at Lichfield playhouse name,
Where, without ceremony, he thought fit
To fling the man and chair into the pit?
Who would have registered a speech so odd
On the dead Stay-maker, and Doctor Dodd?

MADAME PIOZZI.

Sam Johnson's thrashing knowledge, and his thatching,
May be your own inimitable hatching.
Pray, of his wisdom can't you tell more news?
Could not he make a shirt, and cobble shoes?
Knit stockings, or ingenious take up stitches—
Draw teeth, dress wigs, or make a pair of breeches?
You prate too of his knowledge of the mint,
As if the Rambler really had been in't:—
Who knows but you will tell us (truth forsaking)
That each bad shilling is of Johnson's making,
His each vile sixpence that the world hath cheated,
And his the art that every guinea sweated?
About his brewing knowledge you will prate too,
Who scarcely knew a hop from a potatoe:
And, though of beer he joyed in hearty swigs,
I'd pit against his taste my husband's pigs.

BOZZY.

How could your folly tell, so void of truth,
That miserable story of the youth
Who, in your book, of Doctor Johnson begs
Most seriously to know if cats laid eggs?

MADAME PIOZZI.

Who told of Mrs. Montague the lie—
So palpable a falsehood?—Bozzy, fie!

BOZZY.

Who, maddening with an anecdotic itch,
Declared that Johnson called his mother "bitch"?

MADAME PIOZZI.

Who, from M'Donald's rage to save his snout,
Cut twenty lines of defamation out?

BOZZY.

Who would have said a word about Sam's wig,
Or told the story of the peas and pig?

Who would have told a tale so very flat,
Of Frank the Black, and Hodge the mangy cat?

MADAME PIOZZI.

Ecod! you're grown at once confounded tender—
Of Doctor Johnson's fame a fierce defender!
I'm sure *you*'ve mentioned many a pretty story
Not much redounding to the Doctor's glory.
Now, for a saint upon us you would palm him—
First murder the poor man, and then embalm him!

BOZZY.

And truly, madam, Johnson cannot boast—
By your acquaintance, he hath rather lost:
His character so shockingly you handle
You've sunk your comet to a farthing candle.
Your vanities contrived the sage to hitch in,
And bribed him with the run of all your kitchen.
Yet nought he bettered by his elevation:
Though beef he won—he lost his reputation.

MADAME PIOZZI.

One quarter of your book had Johnson read,
Fist-criticism had rattled round your head.
Yet let my satire not too far pursue—
It boasts *some* merit, give the Devil his due.
Where grocers and where pastry-cooks reside,
Thy book, with triumph, may indulge its pride;
Preach to the patty-pans sententious stuff—
And hug that idol of the nose, called snuff;
With all its stories cloves and ginger please,
And pour its wonders to a pound of cheese!

BOZZY.

Madam, your irony is wondrous fine!
Sense in each thought, and wit in every line!
Yet, madam, when the leaves of my poor book
Visit the grocer or the pastry-cook,
Yours, to enjoy of fame the just reward,
May aid the trunk-maker of Paul's Church-Yard.
In the same alehouses together used,
By the same fingers they may be abused.
The greasy snuffers yours perchance may wipe,
Whilst mine, high honoured, lights a toper's pipe.
The praise of Courteney my book's fame secures:
Now who the devil, madam, praises yours?

MADAME PIOZZI.

Thousands, you blockhead!—no one now can doubt it,
For not a soul in London is without it.

The folks were ready Cadell to devour,
Who sold the first edition in an hour :
So!—Courteney's praises save you—ah!—that squire
Deals (let me tell you) more in smoke than fire.

BOZZY.

Zounds! he has praised me in the sweetest line—

MADAME PIOZZI.

Ay! ay! the verse and subject equal shine
Few are the mouths that Courteney's wit rehearse—
Mere cork in politics, and lead in verse.

BOZZY.

Well, ma'am! since all that Johnson said or wrote
You hold so sacred—how have you forgot
To grant the wonder-hunting world a reading
Of Sam's Epistle just before your wedding ;
Beginning thus, in strains not formed to flatter :
"Madam, If that most ignominious matter
Be not concluded,"—
Farther shall I say?
No—your kind self may give it us, one day—
And justify your passion for the youth,
With all the charms of eloquence and truth.

MADAME PIOZZI.

What was my marriage, Sir, to you or him?
He tell me what to do!—A pretty whim!
He to propriety (the beast) exhort!
As well might elephants preside at court.
Lord! let the world to damn my match agree ;
Tell me, James Boswell, what's that world to me
The folks who paid respect to Mrs. Thrale,
Fed on her pork, poor souls! and swilled her ale,
May sicken at Piozzi, nine in ten—
Turn up the nose of scorn—good God! what then?
For me, the devil may fetch their souls so great ;
They keep their company, and I my meat.
When they, poor owls! shall beat their cage, a jail—
I, unconfined, shall spread my peacock tail ;
Free as the birds of air, enjoy my ease,
Choose my own food, and see what climes *I* please.
I suffer only—*if* I'm in the wrong.
So, now, you prating puppy, hold your tongue.

SIR JOHN.

For shame! for shame! for heaven's sake, pray be
    quiet—
Not Billingsgate exhibits such a riot.

Behold! for scandal you have made a feast,
And turned your idol, Johnson, to a beast.
'Tis plain the tales of ghosts are arrant lies,
Or instantaneously would Johnson's rise;
Make you both eat your paragraphs so evil;
And, for your treatment to him, play the devil.
Just like two Mohocks on the man you fall;
No murderer is worse served at Surgeons' Hall!
Instead of adding splendour to his name,
Your books are downright gibbets to his fame.
Of those your anecdotes—may I be cursed
If I can tell you which of them is worst.
You never with posterity can thrive—
'Tis by the Rambler's death alone you live;
Like wrens that (in some volume I have read)
Hatched by strange fortune in a horse's head.
Poor Sam was rather fainting in his glory,
But now his fame lies foully dead before ye:
Thus to some dying man (a frequent case)
Two doctors come and give the *coup de grace*.
Zounds madam, mind the duties of a wife,
And dream no more of Dr. Johnson's life.
A happy knowledge in a pie or pudding
Will more delight your friends than all your studying;
One cut from venison to the heart can speak
Stronger than ten quotations from the Greek;
One fat sirloin possesses more sublime
Than all the airy castles built by rhyme.
One nipperkin of *stingo* with a toast
Beats all the streams the Muses' fount can boast.
Yes, in one pint of porter, lo! my belly can
Find blisses not in all the floods of Helicon.
Enough those anecdotes your powers have shown;
Sam's life, dear ma'am, will only damn your own.
For thee, James Boswell, may the hand of fate
Arrest thy goose-quill, and confine thy prate;
Thy egotisms the world disgusted hears.
Then load with vanities no more our ears;
Like some lone puppy, yelping all night long,
That tires the very echoes with his tongue.
Yet, should it lie beyond the powers of fate
To stop thy pen, and still thy darling prate,
Oh be in solitude to live thy luck—
A chattering magpie on the Isle of Muck!

 Thus spoke the Judge; then, leaping from the
  chair,
He left, in consternation lost, the pair:—
Black Frank he sought, on anecdote to cram,
And vomit first a life of surly Sam.—

Shocked at the little manners of the knight,
The rivals marvelling marked his sudden flight;
Then to their pens and paper rushed the twain,
To kill the mangled Rambler o'er again.

A POETICAL, SUPPLICATING, MODEST, AND AFFECTING
EPISTLE TO THOSE LITERARY COLOSSUSES,
THE REVIEWERS.

"Carmine Di Superi placantur, carmine Manes."

FATHERS of wisdom, a poor wight befriend!
  Oh hear my simple prayer in simple lays:
In formâ pauperis behold I bend,
  And of your worships ask a little praise.

I am no cormorant for fame, d'ye see;
  I ask not *all* the laurel, but a sprig!
Then hear me, guardians of the sacred tree,
  And stick a leaf or two about my wig.

In sonnet, ode, and legendary tale,
  Soon will the press my tuneful works display;
Then do not damn 'em, and prevent the sale;
  And your petitioner shall ever pray.

My labours damned, the Muse with grief will groan—
  The censure dire my lantern jaws will rue!
Know, I have teeth and stomach like your own,
  And that I wish to eat as well as you.

I never said, like murderers in their dens,
  You secret met in cloud-capped garret high,
With hatchets, scalping-knives in shape of pens,
  To bid, like Mohocks, hapless authors die:

Nor said, in your Reviews, together strung,
  The limbs of butchered writers, cheek by jowl,
Looked like the legs of flies on cobwebs hung
  Before the hungry spider's dreary hole.

I ne'er declared that, frightful as the Blacks,
  In greasy flannel caps you met together,
With scarce a rag of shirt about your backs,
  Or coat or breeches to keep out the weather.

Heaven knows I'm innocent of all transgression
  Against your honours, men of classic fame!
I ne'er abused your critical profession,
  Whose dictum saves at once or damns a name.

I never questioned your profound of head,
    Nor vulgar called your wit, your manners coarse ;
Nor swore on butchered authors that you fed
    Like carrion crows upon a poor dead horse.

I never said that pedlar-like you sold
    Praise by the ounce or pound, like snuff or cheese ;
Too well I knew you silver scorned, and gold—
    Such dross a sage Reviewer seldom sees !

I never hinted that with half a crown
    Books have been sent you by the scribbling tribe ;
Which fee hath purchased pages of renown :
    No, for I knew you'd spurn the *paltry* bribe.

I ne'er averred you critics, to a man,
    For pence would swear an owl excelled the lark ;
Nor called a coward gang your grave Divan,
    That stabbed, like base assassins, in the dark.

I never praised, or blamed, an author's book,
    Until your wise opinions came abroad.
On these with holy reverence did I look :
    With you I praised, or blamed, so help me God !

The famed Longinus all the world must know ;
    The gape of wonder Aristarchus drew,
As well as Alexander's tutor, lo !
    All, all great critics, gentlemen, like you.

Did any ask me, " Pray, Sir, your opinion
    Of those Reviewers who so bold bestride
The world of learning, and, with proud dominion,
    High on the backs of crouching authors ride ?"

Quick have I answered, in a rage, "Odsblood !
    No works like theirs such criticism convey :
Not all the timber of Dodona's wood
    E'er poured more sterling oracle than they."

Did others cry, " Whate'er *their* brains indite
    Be sure is excellent—a partial crew !
With io pæans ushered to the light,
    And praised to folly in the next Review."

This was my answer to each snarling elf
    (My eyeballs filled with fire, my mouth with foam) :
"Zounds ! is not justice due to one's dear self?
    And should not charity begin at home ?"

Full often I've been questioned with a sneer—
    "Think you one could not bribe 'em?"—"Not a
        nation."
"A beef-steak, with a pot or two of beer,
    Might save a little volume from damnation."

Furious I've answered: "Lo! my Lord Carlisle
    Hath begged in vain a seat in Fame's old temple;
Though you applaud, their wisdoms will not smile;
    And what they disapprove is cursèd simple.

"Could gold succeed, enough the peer might raise,
    Whose wealth would buy the critics o'er and o'er:
'Tis merit only can command their praise,
    Witness the volumes of Miss Hannah More;

"The *Search for Happiness*, that beauteous song,
    Which all of us would give our ears to own;
The *Captive*, Percy, that, like mustard strong,
    Make our eyes weep, and understandings groan."

Hail, Bristol town! Bœotia now no more,
    Since Garrick's Sappho sings, though rather slowly!
All hail, Miss Hannah! worth at least a score,
    Ay, twenty score, of Chatterton and Rowley.

Men of prodigious parts are mostly shy;
    Great Newton's self this failing did inherit;
Thus, frequent, *you* avoid the public eye,
    And hide in lurking-holes a world of merit.

Yet oft your cautious modesties I see,
    When from your bower with bats you wing the dark:
And Sundays, when no catchpoles prowl for prey,
    On ether dining in St. James's Park.

Meek Sirs! in frays you choose not to appear,—
    A circumstance most natural to suppose;
And therefore hide your precious heads, for fear
    Some angry bard abused should pull your nose.

The world's loud plaudit, lo! you don't desire,
    Nor do you hastily on books decide;
But first at every coffee-house enquire
    How in its favour runs the public tide.

There Wisdom often with a critic wig,
    The face demure, knit brows, and forehead scowling,
I've seen o'er pamphlets, with importance big,
    Mousing for faults, or, if you'll have it, owling.

Herculean gentlemen! I dread your drubs;
  Pity the lifted whites of both my eyes!
Strung with new strength beneath your massy clubs,
  Alas! I shall not an Antæus rise.

Lo, like an elephant along the ground,
  Great Caliban, the giant Johnson stretched!
The British Roscius too your clubs confound,
  Whose fame the farthest of the stars hath reached.

If such so easy sink beneath your might,
  Ye gods! I may be done for in a trice:
Hurled by your rage to everlasting night—
  Cracked with that ease a beggar cracks his lice.

If, awful Sirs, you grant me my petition,
  With brother pamphlets shall my pamphlet shine;
And, should it chance to pass a first edition,
  In capitals shall stare your praise divine.

Quote from my work as much as e'er you please;
  For extracts, lo! I'll put no angry face on;
Nor fill a hungry lawyer's fist with fees,
  To trounce a bookseller, like furious Mason.[1]

Sage Sirs! if favour in your sight I find,
  If fame you grant, I'll bless each generous giver;
Wish you sound coats, good stomachs, masters kind,[2]
  Gallons of broth, and pounds of bullock's liver.

A LYRIC ODE.

The mean, the rancorous jealousies, that swell
  In some sad artists' souls, I do despise;
Instead of nobly striving to excel,
  You strive to pick out one the other's eyes.
To be a painter was Correggio's glory:—
His speech should flame in gold—"*Sono pittore.*"

But what, if truth were spoke, would be *your* speeches?
This—"We're a set of fame-sucking horse-leeches,
Without a blush the poorest scandal speaking—
Like cocks, for ever at each other beaking;
As if the globe we dwell on were so small
There really was not room enough for all."

    Young men!——
I do presume that one of you in ten
Hath kept a dog or two; and hath **remarked**
  That, when you have been comfortably **feeding**,

---

[1] The contest between Mr. Mason and a bookseller is generally known.
[2] The booksellers.

The curs, without one atom of court-breeding,
With watery jaws, have whined, and pawed, and barked;
　Showed anxiousness about the mutton-bone,
And 'stead of *your* mouth, wished it in their own;
And if you gave this bone to one or t'other,
Heavens! what a snarling, quarrelling, and pother!
This oft, perhaps, has touched you to the quick,
And made you teach good manners by a kick;
And, if the tumult was beyond all bearing,
A little bit of sweet emphatic swearing,—
An eloquence of wondrous use in wars
Amongst sea-captains and the brave Jack-tars.

Now tell me honestly—pray don't you find
Somewhat in Christians just of the same kind
　　That you experienced in the curs,
　　Causing your anger and demurs?
As, for example, when your mistress, Fame,
Wishing to celebrate a worthy name,
Takes up her trump to give the just applause,
　How have you, puppy-like, pawed, wished, and
　　　whined,
　　And growled, and cursed, and swore, and pined,
And longed to tear the trumpet from her jaws!
The dogs deserve their kicking to be sure;
But you! O fie, boys! go, and sin no more!

TO MYSELF.

O Thou! whose daring works sublime
Defy the rudest rage of Time,
Say!—for the world is with conjecture dizzy,
Did Mousehole give thee birth, or Mevagizzy?

Hail, Mevagizzy! what a town of note!
　Where boats, and men, and stinks, and trade, are
　　　stirring;
Where pilchards come in myriads to be caught;
　Pilchard! a thousand times as good's a herring!

Pilchard, the idol of the Popish nation!
Hail, little instrument of vast salvation!
Pilchard, I ween, a most soul-saving fish,
　On which the Catholics in Lent are crammed,—
Who, had they not, poor souls, this lucky dish,
　Would flesh eat, and be consequently damned.
Pilchards! whose bodies yield the fragrant oil,
And make the London lamps at midnight smile;
Which lamps, wide-spreading salutary light,

Beam on the wandering Beauties of the night,
And show each gentle youth their cheeks' deep roses,
And tell him whether they have eyes and noses.

Hail, Mousehole! birthplace of old Doll Pentreath,[1]
　　The last who jabbered Cornish—so says Daines,
Who bat-like haunted ruins, lane, and heath,
　　With Will-o'-Wisp, to brighten up his brains.

Daines, who a thousand miles unwearied trots,
For bones, brass farthings, ashes, and old pots,
　To prove that folks of old, like us, were made
With heads, eyes, hands, and toes, to drive a trade.

FAREWELL ODES (1786).[2]

I.

PETER, like famed Christina, queen of Sweden,
Who thought a wicked court was not an Eden,
This year resigns the laurel crown for ever!
　　What all the famed Academicians wish—
　　No more on painted fowl, and flesh, and fish,
He shows the world his carving skill so clever.
Brass, iron, woodwork, stone, in peace shall rest :—
"Thank God!" exclaim the works of Mr. West.

"Thank God!" the works of Loutherbourg exclaim—
For guns of critics no ignoble game—
"No longer now afraid of rhyming praters,
Shall we be christened tea-boards, varnished waiters!
No verse shall swear that ours are pasteboard rocks;
Our trees, brass wigs; and mops, our fleecy flocks."

"Thank heaven!" exclaims Rigaud, with sparkling eyes—
"Then shall my pictures in importance rise,
And fill each gaping mouth and eye with wonder."
　　　Monsieur Rigaud,
　　　It may be so.
To think thy stars have made so strange a blunder,
That bred to paint the genius of a glazier!
That spoiled, to make a dauber, a good brazier!
None but thy partial tongue (believe my lays)
Can dare stand forth the herald of thy praise :
Could Fame applaud, whose voice my verse reveres,
Justice should break her trump about her ears.

---

[1] A very old woman of Mousehole, supposed (falsely however) to have been the last who spoke the Cornish language.—The honourable antiquarian, Daines Barrington Esq., journeyed, some years since, from London to the Land's-end, to converse with this wrinkled yet delicious *morceau*.

[2] Concluding a series of criticisms in verse on the annual exhibitions of the Royal Academy.

"Thank Heaven!" cries Mr. Garvy; and "Thank God!"
Cries Mr. Copley, "that this Man of Ode
No more, barbarian-like, shall o'er us ride;
   No more, like beads in nasty order strung,
   And round the waist of this vile Mohock hung,
Shall academic scalps indulge his pride.

"No more hung up in this dread fellow's rhyme,
Which he most impudently calls sublime,
   Shall we, poor inoffensive souls,
   Appear just like so many moles,
Trapped in an orchard, garden, or a field;
   Which mole-catchers suspend on trees,
   To show their titles to their fees,—
Like doctors, paid too often for the killed."

Pleased that no more my verses shall annoy,
   Glad that my blister Odes shall cease their stinging,
Each wooden figure's mouth expands with joy—
   Hark! how they all break forth in singing!—

In boastful sounds the grinning artists cry;
   "Lo! Peter's hour of insolence is o'er:
His Muse is dead—his lyric pump is dry—
   His Odes, like stinking fish, not worth a groat a score.
Art thou then weak like us, thou snarling sniveller?
Art thou like one of us, thou lyric driveller?

"Our kings and queens in glory now shall lie,
   Each unmolested, sleeping in his frame;
Our ponds, our lakes, our oceans, earth, and sky,
   No longer, scouted, shall be put to shame.
No poet's rage shall root our stumps and stumplings,
And swear our clouds are flying apple-dumplings.
Fame shall proclaim how well our plum-trees bud,
And sound the merits of our marle and mud.

"Our oaks, our brushwood, and our lofty elms,
No jingling tyrant's wicked rage o'erwhelms,
   Now this vile feller is laid low:
In peace shall our stone-hedges sleep,
Our huts, our barns, our pigs and sheep,
   And wild fowl, from the eagle to the crow.

"They who shall see this Peter in the street
With fearless eye his front shall meet,
   And cry, 'Is this the man of keen remark?
Is this the wight?' shall be their taunting speech;
'A dog! who dared to snap each artist's breech,
   And bite Academicians like a shark!

"'He whose broad cleaver chopped the sons of paint;
Crushed like a marrowbone each lovely saint;
   Spared not the very clothes about their backs;
The little duck-winged cherubims abused,
That could not more inhumanly be used,
   Poor lambkins! had they fallen among the blacks;—
He, once so furious, soon shall want relief,
Staked through the body like a paltry thief.

"'How art thou fallen, O Cherokee!' they cry;
   'How art thou fallen!' the joyful roofs resound;
   'Hell shall thy body for a rogue surround;
And there for ever roasting mayst thou lie:
Like Dives, mayst thou stretch in fires along,
Refused one drop of drink to cool thy tongue!'"

Ye goodly gentlemen, repress your yell;
   Your hearty wishes for my health restrain;
For, if our *works* can put us into hell,
   Kind Sirs! we certainly shall meet again.
Nay, what is worse, I really don't know whether
We must not lodge in the same room together.

II.

A MODEST love of praise I do not blame—
But I abhor a *rape* on Mistress Fame.
Although the lady is exceeding chaste,
Young forward bullies seize her round the waist;
Swear, *nolens volens*, that she shall be kissed;
   And, though she vows she does not like 'em,
   Nay, threatens for their impudence to strike 'em,
The saucy rascals still persist.

Reader!—of images here's no confusion—
Thou therefore understand'st the bard's allusion.
But possibly thou hast a thickish head,
   And therefore no vast quantity of brain:—
Why then, my precious pig of lead,
   'Tis necessary to explain.

Some artists, if I so may call 'em,—
So ignorant, the foul fiend maul 'em,
Mere drivellers in the charming art,—
   Are vastly fond of being praised,
   Wish to the stars, like Blanchard,[1] to be raised:
And raised they should be, reader,—from a cart.

---

[1] The famous Aeronaut.

If disappointed in some Stentor's tongue,
Upon themselves they pour forth prose or song;
  Or buy it in some venal paper,
  And then heroically vapour.

What prigs to immortality aspire,
  Who stick their trash around the room!—
  Trash, meriting a very different doom,—
I mean the warmer regions of the fire.

Heaven knows that I am angered to the soul
  To find some blockheads of their works so vain—
So proud to see them hanging cheek by jowl
  With his [1] whose powers the art's high fame sustain.

To wondrous merit their pretension,
On such vicinity-suspension,
Brings to my mind a not unpleasant story,
Which, gentle readers, let me lay before ye.

A shabby fellow chanced one day to meet
The British Roscius in the street,
  Garrick, of whom our nation justly brags.
The fellow hugged him, with a kind embrace.
"Good Sir, I do not recollect your face,"
  Quoth Garrick. "No?" replied the man of rags.
"The boards of Drury you and I have trod
Full many a time together, I am sure."
"When?" with an oath cried Garrick; "for, by God,
I never saw that face of yours before!—
  What characters, I pray,
    Did you and I together play?"
"Lord!" quoth the fellow, "think not that I mock—
When you played Hamlet, Sir,—I played the cock."[2]

---

[1] The President Reynolds.   [2] In the Ghost Scene.

CHARLES MORRIS.

[Captain Morris was born in 1740, and died in 1832].

THE CONTRAST.

In London I never know what I'd be at,
Enraptured with this, and enchanted with that;
I'm wild with the sweets of variety's plan,
And Life seems a blessing too happy for man.

But the Country, Lord help me! sets all matters right,
So calm and composing from morning to night;
Oh! it settles the spirits when nothing is seen
But an ass on a common, a goose on a green.

In town if it rain, why it damps not our hope,
The eye has her choice, and the fancy her scope;
What harm though it pour whole nights or whole days?
It spoils not our prospects, or stops not our ways.

In the country what bliss, when it rains in the fields,
To live on the transports that shuttlecock yields;
Or go crawling from window to window, to see
A pig on a dunghill, or crow on a tree!

In London, if folks ill together are put,
A bore may be dropped, and a quiz may be cut;
We change without end; and if lazy or ill,
All wants are at hand, and all wishes at will.

In the country you're nailed, like a pale in the park,
To some *stick* of a neighbour that's crammed in the ark;
And 'tis odds, if you're hurt, or in fits tumble down,
You reach death ere the doctor can reach you from town.

In London how easy we visit and meet!
Gay pleasure's the theme, and sweet smiles are our treat:
Our morning's a round of good-humoured delight,
And we rattle, in comfort, to pleasure at night.

In the country, how sprightly our visits we make
Through ten miles of mud, for Formality's sake!
With the coachman in drink, and the moon in a fog,
And no thought in our head but a ditch or a bog.

In London the spirits are cheerful and light,
All places are gay and all faces are bright;
We've ever new joys, and, revived by each whim,
Each day on a fresh tide of pleasure we swim.

But how gay in the country! what summer delight
To be waiting for winter from morning to night!
Then the fret of impatience gives exquisite glee
To relish the sweet rural subjects we see.

In town we've no use for the skies overhead,
For when the sun rises then we go to bed;
And as to that old-fashioned virgin the moon,
She shines out of season, like satin in June.

In the country these planets delightfully glare
Just to show us the object we want isn't there;
Oh how cheering and gay, when their beauties arise,
To sit and gaze round with the tears in one's eyes!

But 'tis in the country alone we can find
That happy resource, that relief of the mind,
When, drove to despair, our last efforts we make,
And drag the old fish-pond, for novelty's sake:

Indeed I must own, 'tis a pleasure complete
To see ladies well draggled and wet in their feet;
But what is all that to the transport we feel
When we capture, in triumph, two toads and an eel?

I have heard, though, that love in a cottage is sweet,
When two hearts in one link of soft sympathy meet:
That's to come—for as yet I, alas! am a swain
Who require, I own it, more links to my chain.

Your magpies and stock-doves may flirt among trees,
And chatter their transports in groves, if they please:
But a house is much more to my taste than a tree,
And for groves, Oh! a good grove of chimneys for me!

In the country, if Cupid should find a man out,
The poor tortured victim mopes hopeless about;
But in London, thank Heaven! our peace is secure,
Where for one eye to kill there's a thousand to cure.

I know love's a devil, too subtle to spy,
That shoots through the soul from the beam of an eye;
But in London these devils so quick fly about
That a new devil still drives an old devil out.

In town let me live then, in town let me die,
For in truth I can't relish the country, not I!
If one must have a villa in summer to dwell,
Oh give me the sweet shady side of Pall Mall!

HANNAH MORE.

[Born at Stapleton, Gloucestershire, in 1745, daughter of a village schoolmaster; died at Clifton in 1833. The talents of Hannah excited attention at a very early age, and she set up a good day-school, and afterwards a boarding-school. Her first printed work was the drama entitled *The Search after Happiness*; this was followed by *Sacred Dramas, Strictures on the Modern System of Female Education,* and a number of other works having for the most part a directly religious or didactic object].

THE BAS BLEU; OR, CONVERSATION.

ADDRESSED TO MRS. VESEY.

The following trifle owes its birth and name to the mistake of a Foreigner of distinction, who gave the literal appellation of the *Bas-bleu* to a small party of friends who had been often called, by way of pleasantry, the *Blue Stockings.* These little Societies have been sometimes misrepresented. They were composed of persons distinguished, in general, for their rank, talents, or respectable character, who met frequently at Mrs. Vesey's and at a few other houses, for the sole purpose of conversation, and were different in no respect from other parties but that the company did not play at cards.

May the author be permitted to bear her grateful testimony (which will not be suspected of flattery now that most of the persons named in this Poem are gone down to the grave) to the many pleasant and instructive hours she had the honour to pass in this company; in which learning was as little disfigured by pedantry, good taste as little tinctured by affectation, and general conversation as little disgraced by calumny, levity, and the other censurable errors with which it is too commonly tainted, as has perhaps been known in any Society.

VESEY! of Verse the judge and friend!
A while my idle strain attend.
Not with the days of early Greece
I mean to ope my slender piece;
The rare Symposium to proclaim
Which crowned the Athenians' social name;
Or how Aspasia's parties shone,
The first *Bas-bleu* at Athens known;
Where Socrates unbending sat,
With Alcibiades in chat,
And Pericles vouchsafed to mix
Taste, wit, and mirth, with politics.
Nor need I stop my tale to show,
At least to readers such as you,
How all that Rome esteemed polite
Supped with Lucullus every night;
Lucullus, who, from Pontus come,
Brought conquests and brought cherries home.
Name but the suppers in the Apollo,
What classic images will follow!
How wit flew round, while each might take
Conchylia from the Lucrine lake;
And Attic salt, and Garum sauce,
And lettuce from the isle of Cos;
The first and last from Greece transplanted,—
Used here because the rhyme I wanted,

How pheasants' heads with cost collected,
And phenicopters, stood neglected,
To laugh at Scipio's lucky hit,
Pompey's bon-mot, or Cæsar's wit.
Intemperance, listening to the tale,
Forgot the mullet growing[1] stale;
And Admiration balanced hung
'Twixt peacocks' brains and Tully's tongue.
I shall not stop to dwell on these,
But be as epic as I please,
And plunge at once *in medias res.*
To prove the privilege I plead,
I'll quote some Greek I cannot read;
Stunned by Authority, you yield,
And I, not reason, keep the field.

   Long was Society o'er-run
By Whist, that desolating Hun;
Long did Quadrille[2] despotic sit,
That Vandal of colloquial wit;
And Conversation's setting light
Lay half obscured in Gothic night.
At length the mental shades decline;
Colloquial wit begins to shine;
Genius prevails, and Conversation
Emerges into *Reformation.*
The vanquished triple crown to you,
Boscawen sage, bright Montagu,
Divided fell; your cares in haste
Rescued the ravaged realms of Taste.
And Lyttelton's accomplished name,
And witty Pulteney, shared the fame;
The men not bound by pedant rules,
Nor ladies *Précieuses ridicules;*
For polished Walpole showed the way,
How Wits may be both learn'd and gay;
And Carter taught the female train
The deeply wise are never vain;
And she, who Shakspeare's wrongs redressed,
Proved that the brightest are the best.
This just deduction still they drew,
And well they practised what they knew.
Nor taste nor wit deserves applause,
Unless, still true to critic laws,
Good Sense, of faculties the best,
Inspire and regulate the rest.

---

[1] Seneca says, that in his time the Romans were arrived at such a pitch of luxury that the mullet was reckoned stale which did not die in the hands of the guest.
[2] A game at cards.

Oh how unlike the wit that fell,
Rambouillet, at thy quaint hotel;
Where point, and turn, and equivoque,
Distorted every word they spoke!
All so intolerably bright,
Plain Common Sense was put to flight;
Each speaker so ingenious ever,
'Twas tiresome to be quite so clever.
There twisted Wit forgot to please,
And Mode and Figure banished ease;
No votive altar smoked to thee,
Chaste Queen, divine Simplicity;
But forced Conceit which ever fails,
And stiff Antithesis, prevails.
Uneasy rivalry destroys
Society's unlaboured joys.
Nature, of stilts and fetters tired,
Impatient from the Wits retired;
Long time the exile houseless strayed,
Till Sévigné received the maid.

Though here she comes to bless our isle,
Not universal is her smile.
Muse! snatch the lyre which Cambridge strung,
When he the *empty ball-room* sung;
'Tis tuned above thy pitch, I doubt,
And thou no music wouldst draw out;
Yet in a lower note presume
To sing the full, dull Drawing-room.[1]

Where the dire *Circle* keeps its station,
Each common phrase is an oration;
And cracking fans, and whispering Misses,
Compose their Conversation blisses.
The Matron marks the goodly show,
While the tall daughter eyes the Beau—
The frigid Beau! Ah! luckless fair,
'Tis not for you that studied air;
Ah! not for you that sidelong glance,
And all that charming nonchalance;
Ah! not for you the three long hours
He worshipped the "Cosmetic powers;"
That finished head which breathes perfume,
And kills the nerves of half the room;
And all the murders meant to lie
In that large, languishing, grey eye.
Desist—less wild the attempt would be
To warm the snows of Rhodope.

---

[1] These grave and formal parties now scarcely exist, having been swallowed up in the reigning multitudinous assemblies.

Too cold to feel, too proud to feign,
For him you're wise and fair in vain;
In vain to charm him you intend,—
Self is his object, aim, and end.

   Chill shade of that affected Peer
Who dreaded Mirth, come safely here!
For here no vulgar joy effaces
Thy rage for polish, *ton*, and graces.
Cold Ceremony's leaden hand
Waves o'er the room her poppy wand.
Arrives the stranger; every guest
Conspires to torture the distressed.
At once they rise. So have I seen—
You guess the simile I mean;
Take what comparison you please,
The crowded streets, the swarming bees,
The pebbles on the shores that lie,
The stars which form the galaxy;
These serve to embellish what is said,
And show, besides, that one has read.
At once they rise—the astonished guest
Back in a corner slinks, distressed;
Scared at the many bowing round,
And shocked at her own voice's sound;
Forgot the thing she meant to say,
Her words, half uttered, die away,
In sweet oblivion down she sinks,
And of her next appointment thinks.
While her loud neighbour on the right
Boasts what she has to do to-night;
So very much, you'd swear her pride is
To match the labours of Alcides;
'Tis true, in hyperbolic measure,
She nobly calls her labours *Pleasure;*
In this, unlike Alcmena's son,
She never means they should be done.
Her fancy of no *limits* dreams,
No *ne plus ultra* stops her schemes;
Twelve! she'd have scorned the paltry round,
No pillars would have marked her bound;
Calpe and Abyla in vain
Had nodded cross the opposing main;
A circumnavigator she
On *Ton's* illimitable sea.

   We pass the pleasures vast and various
Of Routs, not social but gregarious;
Where high heroic self-denial
Sustains her self-inflicted trial.

Day labourers! what an easy life,
To feed ten children and a wife!
No—I may juster pity spare
For the *night* labourer's keener care;
And, pleased, to gentler scenes retreat,
Where *Conversation* holds her seat.

   Small were that art which would ensure
The Circle's boasted quadrature!
See Vesey's[1] plastic genius make
A circle every figure take;
Nay, shapes and forms which would defy
All science of Geometry;
Isosceles and Parallel,
Names hard to speak and hard to spell!
The enchantress waved her wand and spoke!
Her potent wand the Circle broke;
The social spirits hover round,
And bless the liberated ground.
Ask you what charms this gift dispense?
'Tis the strong spell of Common Sense.
Away dull Ceremony flew,
And with her bore Detraction too.

   Not only Geometric Art
Does this presiding power impart;
But chemists too, who want the essence
Which makes or mars all coalescence,
Of her the secret rare might get
How different kinds amalgamate:
And he who wilder studies chose,
Find here a new metempsychose;
How forms can other forms assume,
Within her Pythagoric room;
Or be, and stranger is the event,
The very things which Nature meant,
Nor strive, by art and affectation,
To cross their genuine destination.
Here sober Duchesses are seen,
Chaste Wits, and Critics void of spleen;
Physicians fraught with real science,
And Whigs and Tories in alliance;
Poets fulfilling Christian duties,
Just Lawyers, reasonable Beauties;
Bishops who preach, and Peers who pay,
And Countesses who seldom play;
Learn'd Antiquaries, who, from college,
Reject the rust and bring the knowledge;

---

[1] This amiable lady was remarkable for her talent in breaking the formality of a circle, by inviting her parties to form themselves into little separate groups.

And, hear it, age, believe it, youth,—
Polemics really seeking truth ;
And Travellers of that rare tribe
Who've *seen* the countries they describe ;
Who studied there, so strange their plan,
Not plants nor herbs alone, but man ;
(While Travellers of other notions
Scale mountain-tops, and traverse oceans,
As if, so much these themes engross,
The study of mankind was moss) ;
Ladies who point, nor think me partial,
An epigram as well as Martial,
Yet in all female worth succeed
As well as those who cannot read.

   Right pleasant were the task, I ween,
To name the groups which fill the scene.
But Rhyme's of such fastidious nature,
She proudly scorns all nomenclature ;
Nor grace our Northern names her lips,
Like Homer's catalogue of ships.

   Once—faithful Memory ! heave a sigh,—
Here Roscius gladdened every eye.
Why comes not Maro ?—Far from town,
He rears the urn to Taste, and Brown ;
Plants cypress round the tomb of Gray,
Or decks his *English Garden* gay ;
Whose mingled sweets exhale perfume,
And promise a perennial bloom.[1]
Here rigid Cato, awful Sage !
Bold Censor of a thoughtless age,
Once dealt his pointed moral round,
And not unheeded fell the sound ;
The Muse his honoured memory weeps,
For Cato now with Roscius sleeps.
Here once Hortensius[2] loved to sit,
Apostate now from social wit :
Ah ! why in wrangling senates waste
The noblest parts, the happiest taste ?
Why democratic thunders wield,
And quit the Muses' calmer field ?
Taste thou the gentler joys they give ;
With Horace and with Lælius live.

   Hail, Conversation, soothing power,
Sweet Goddess of the social hour !

---

   [1] ["Perennial," with a difference. Many readers of the present day may require to be informed that "Maro," author of *The English Garden*, was Mason. "Roscius" and "Cato" stand, I suppose, for Garrick and Johnson].

   [2] This was written in the year 1787, when Mr. Edmund Burke had joined the then opposition.

Not with more heart-felt warmth, at least,
Does Lælius bend, thy true High Priest,
Than I, the lowest of thy train,
These field-flowers bring to deck thy fane.
Who to thy shrine like him can haste,
With warmer zeal or purer taste?
Oh may thy worship long prevail,
And thy true votaries never fail!
Long may thy polished altars blaze
With wax-lights' undiminished rays!
Still be thy nightly offerings paid,
Libations large of lemonade!
On silver vases loaded, rise
The biscuits' ample sacrifice!
Nor be the milk-white streams forgot
Of thirst-assuaging, cool orgeat;
Rise, incense pure from fragrant Tea,
Delicious incense, worthy Thee!

Hail, Conversation, heavenly fair,
Thou bliss of life and balm of care!
Still may thy gentle reign extend,
And taste with wit and science blend.
Soft polisher of rugged man!
Refiner of the social plan!
For thee, best solace of his toil,
The sage consumes his midnight oil;
And keeps late vigils, to produce
Materials for thy future use,—
Calls forth the else neglected knowledge
Of School, of Travel, and of College.
If none behold, ah! wherefore fair?
Ah! wherefore wise, if none must hear?
Our intellectual ore must shine,
Not slumber idly in the mine.
Let Education's moral mint
The noblest images imprint;
Let Taste her curious touchstone hold,
To try if standard be the gold;
But 'tis thy commerce, Conversation,
Must give it use by circulation;
That noblest commerce of mankind,
Whose precious merchandise is Mind.

What stoic traveller would try
A sterile soil and parching sky,
Or dare the intemperate Northern zone,
If what he saw must ne'er be known?
For this he bids his home farewell;
The joy of seeing is to tell.

Trust me, he never would have stirred,
Were he forbid to speak a word;
And Curiosity would sleep,
If her own secrets she must keep.
The bliss of telling what is past
Becomes her rich reward at last.
Who'd mock at death, at danger smile,
To steal one peep at father Nile—
Who, at Palmyra risk his neck,
Or search the ruins of Balbec—
If these must hide old Nilus' fount,
Nor Libyan tales at home recount,
If those must sink their learned labour,
Nor with their ruins treat a neighbour?
Range—study—think—do all we can,
Colloquial pleasures are for man.

Yet not from low desire to shine
Does Genius toil in learning's mine;
Not to indulge in idle vision,
But strike new light by strong collision.
Of Conversation, wisdom's friend,
This is the object and the end,—
Of moral truth, man's proper science,
With sense and learning in alliance,
To search the depths, and thence produce
What tends to practice and to use.
And next in value we shall find
What mends the taste and forms the mind.
If high those truths in estimation
Whose search is crowned with demonstration,
To these assign no scanty praise,
Our taste which clear, our views which raise.
For, grant that mathematic truth
Best balances the mind of Youth,
Yet scarce the truth of Taste is found
To grow from principles less sound.

O'er books the mind inactive lies,
Books, the mind's food, not exercise!
Her vigorous wing she scarcely feels,
Till use the latent strength reveals.
Her slumbering energies called forth,
She rises, conscious of her worth;
And, at her new-found powers elated,
Thinks them not roused, but new-created.

Enlightened spirits! you who know
What charms from polished converse flow,
Speak, for you can, the pure delight
When kindling sympathies unite;

When correspondent tastes impart
Communion sweet from heart to heart.
You ne'er the cold gradations need
Which vulgar souls to union lead;
No dry discussion to unfold
The meaning caught ere well 'tis told.
In taste, in learning, wit, or science,
Still kindled souls demand alliance;
Each in the other joys to find
The image answering to his mind.
But sparks electric only strike
On souls electrical alike.
The flash of Intellect expires,
Unless it meet congenial fires:
The language to the Elect alone
Is, like the Mason's mystery, known;
In vain the unerring sign is made
To him who is not of the *Trade.*
What lively pleasure to divine
The thought implied, the hinted line,
To feel allusion's artful force,
And trace the image to its source!
Quick Memory blends her scattered rays,
Till Fancy kindles at the blaze;
The works of ages start to view,
And ancient wit elicits new.

But, wit and parts if thus we praise,
What nobler altars should we raise,
Those sacrifices could we see
Which Wit, O Virtue! makes to thee!
At once the rising thought to dash,
To quench at once the bursting flash,
The shining mischief to subdue,
And lose the praise, and pleasure too!
Though Venus' self, could you detect her,
Imbuing with her richest nectar
The thought unchaste—to check that
  thought,
To spurn a fame so dearly bought;
This is high Principle's control!
This is true continence of soul!
Blush, heroes, at your cheap renown,
A vanquished realm, a plundered town!
Your conquests were to gain a name,—
This conquest triumphs over Fame;
So pure its essence 'twere destroyed
If known, and if commended void.
Amidst the brightest truths believed,
Amidst the fairest deeds achieved,

Shall stand recorded and admired
That Virtue sunk what Wit inspired!

But let the lettered and the fair,
And chiefly let the Wit, beware;
You, whose warm spirits never fail,
Forgive the hint which ends my tale.
Oh shun the perils which attend
On wit, on warmth, and heed your Friend.
Though Science nursed you in her bowers,
Though Fancy crown your brow with flowers,
Each thought though bright Invention fill,
Though Attic bees each word distil;
Yet, if one gracious power refuse
Her gentle influence to infuse;
If she withhold her magic spell,
Nor in the social circle dwell;
In vain shall listening crowds approve,—
They'll praise you, but they will not love.
"What is this power you're loth to mention,
This charm, this witchcraft?"—'Tis Attention:
Mute Angel, yes; thy looks dispense
The silence of intelligence;
Thy graceful form I well discern,
In act to listen and to learn.
'Tis thou for talents shalt obtain
That pardon Wit would hope in vain.
Thy wondrous power, thy secret charm,
Shall Envy of her sting disarm.
Thy silent flattery soothes our spirit,
And we forgive eclipsing merit;
Our jealous souls no longer burn,
Nor hate thee, though thou shine in turn;
The sweet atonement screens the fault,
And love and praise are cheaply bought.

With mild complacency to hear,
Though somewhat long the tale appear,—
The dull relation to attend
Which mars the story you could mend;
'Tis more than wit, 'tis moral beauty,
'Tis pleasure rising out of duty.
Nor vainly think the time you waste,
When temper triumphs over taste.

CHARLES DIBDIN.

[Born at Dibden, Southampton, in 1745; died in London in 1814. In boyhood he was placed under the organist of Winchester Cathedral. Going afterwards to London, he wrote part of the music for *The Maid of the Mill*, and himself acted in that opera. *Love in a Village* and many other operas followed; in several, such as *The Waterman*, Dibdin wrote both words and music. In 1788 he appeared in a monodramatic entertainment of his own composition, named *The Whim of the Moment, or Nature in Little*. He finally retired on a government pension of £200, well earned by his thoroughly British and popular strains, but not long paid in full. The nautical turn which is so distinctive of Dibdin's songs was caught by him from a brother, a master of a merchant-vessel. One of the song-writer's sons, also named Charles, wrote many other ditties of similar character].

JACK AT THE OPERA.

AT Wapping I landed, and called to hail Mog;
    She had just shaped her course to the play:
Of two rums and one water I ordered my grog,
    And to speak her soon stood under weigh.
But the Haymarket I for old Drury mistook,
    Like a lubber so raw and so soft;
Half a George handed out, at the change did not look,
    Manned the ratlins, and went up aloft.

As I mounted to one of the uppermost tiers,
    With many a coxcomb and flirt,
Such a damnable squalling saluted my ears
    I thought there'd been somebody hurt;
But the devil a bit—'twas your outlandish rips
    Singing out with their lanterns of jaws;
You'd ha' swored you'd been taking of one of they trips
    'Mongst the Caffres or wild Catabaws.

"What's the play, Ma'am?" says I, to a good-natured tit.
    "The play! 'tis the *uproar*, you quiz."
"My timbers," cried I, "the right name on't you've hit,
    For the devil an uproar it is."
For they pipe and they squeal, now alow, now aloft;
    If it wa'nt for the petticoat gear,
With their squeaking so mollyish, tender, and soft,
    One should scarcely know ma'am from mounseer.

Next at kicking and dancing they took a long spell,
    All springing and bounding so neat,
And spessiously one curious Madamaselle,—
    Oh she daintily handled her feet!
But she hopped, and she sprawled, and she spun round so queer,
    'Twas, you see, rather oddish to me;
And so I sung out, "Pray be decent, my dear;
    Consider I'm just come from sea.

"'Taint an Englishman's taste to have none of these goes ;
　　So away to the playhouse I'll jog,
Leaving all your fine Bantums and Ma'am Parisoes,
　　For old Billy Shakspeare and Mog."
So I made for the theatre, and hailed my dear spouse ;
　　She smiled as she sawed me approach ;
And, when I'd shook hands and saluted her bows,
　　We to Wapping set sail in a coach.

ONE.

　　Up the Mediterranin,
　　　One day was explaining
　　The chaplain and I about poets and bards ;
　　　For I'm pretty disarning,
　　　And loves about larning
To know, and all notions that such things regards.
Then to hear him sing out 'bout the islands around,
Tell their outlandish names, call them all classic ground,
Where the old ancient poets all formerly messed,
And wrote about love and the girls they caressed ;
Swore they thought 'em all goddesses, creatures divine ;—
I thinks that he said each old gemman had nine.
　　　Cried I, "Well said, old ones !
　　　These poets were bold ones ;
But everything's vanity under the sun.
　　　Love's as good sport as any ;
　　　But nine's eight too many ;—
I have one worth all nine, and my Nancy's that one."

　　　Then we read, for their wishes,
　　　They turned to queer fishes,
To cocks and to bulls, in some verses they call
　　　Ovid Metaramorphus ;
　　　And one Mr. Orphus
Went to hell for his wife—but that's nothing at all.
Some figary each hour set these codgers agog ;
Old Nackron swigged off his allowance of grog ;
Master Jove had his fancies and fine falderals,—
What a devil that god was for following the gals !
But what makes the curisest part of their lives,
They were always a-chasing of other men's wives.
　　　What nonsense and folly !
　　　'Tis quite melancholy
That a man can't be blessed till his neighbour's undone ;
　　　Why, 'tis wicked to ax 'em !
　　　Take the world, that's my maxum,
So one be left me, and my Nancy that one.

Then we'd hot work between us
　　　'Bout Graces and Wenus,
With their fine red and white, and their eyes full of darts.
　　"To be sure, pretty faces
　　Be well in their places,
But, your reverence, in love there be such things as hearts!
'Tis unmanly to chatter behind people's back,
But 'tis pretty well known that the lady's a crack.
Besides, if these things about beauty be true,
That there is but one Wenus, why, I says there's two!
Say there is but one Nancy, you'll then not mistake,
For she's mine, and I'd sail the world round for her sake.
　　Then no further norations,
　　Or chatterifications,
Bout Wenus, and Graces, and such pretty fun,
　　That so runs in your fancy;—
　　Just see but my Nancy,
You'll find all their charms spliced together in one."

RICHARD BRINSLEY SHERIDAN.

[Born in Dublin, September 1751; died in London, 7 July 1816.]

ODE TO SCANDAL.

　"O THOU whose all-consoling power
　　Can calm each female breast,
Whose touch, in Spleen's most vapourish hour,
　　Can soothe our cares to rest:

　"Thee, I invoke! Great Genius, hear!
　　Pity a Lady's sighs!
Unless thy kind relief be near,
　　Poor Colvileia dies!

　"Haste thee then, and with thee bring
Many a little venomed sting,
Many a tale that no one knows
Of shall-be-nameless Belles and Beaux,
Just imported—curtain-lectures,
Winks and nods, and shrewd conjectures,
Unknown marriages, some twenty,
Private child-bed linen plenty;
And horns just fitted to some people's heads,
And certain powdered coats, and certain tumbled beds.

　"Teach me, powerful Genius, teach
　　Thine own mysterious art,
　Safe from Retaliation's reach
　　To throw Destruction's dart.

So shall my hand an altar raise
Sacred to thy transcendent praise,
And daily with assiduous care
Some grateful sacrifice prepare.

" The first informations
   Of lost reputations
As offerings to thee I'll consign ;
   And the earliest news
   Of surprised billets-doux
Shall constant be served at thy shrine.
   Intrigues by the score,
   Never heard of before,
Shall the sacrifice daily augment ;
   And by each Morning Post
   Some favourite toast
A victim to thee shall be sent.

" Heavens ! methinks I see thy train
Lightly tripping o'er the plain :
All the alphabet I view,
Stepping forwards two by two,—
Hush ! for as they coupled walk,
Sure I hear the letters talk !
Though, slowly whispering, half they smother
The well-concerted tales they tell of one another.
   ' Lord ! who'd have thought our cousin D.
   Could think of marrying Mrs. E.?
   True, I don't like such things to tell ;
   But, faith, I pity Mrs. L.,
   And, was I her, the bride to vex
   I would intrigue with Mr. X.
   But they do say that Charlotte U.,
   With Fanny M. and we know who,
   Occasioned all, for you must know
   They set their caps at Mr. O. ;
   And as he courted Mrs. E.,
   They thought, if she'd have cousin D.,
   That things might be by Colonel A.
   Just brought about in their own way.'
Oh ! how the pleasing style regales my ear : . . .
But what new forms are those which now appear?

   " See yonder in the thickest throng,
   Designing Envy stalks along,
      Big with malicious laughter :
   Fiction and Cunning swell her train,
   While stretching far behind,—in vain
      Poor Truth comes panting after !

"Now, now indeed, I burn with sacred fires,—
'Tis Scandal's self that every thought inspires!
I feel, all-potent Genius! now I feel
Thy working magic through each artery steal;
    Each moment to my prying eyes
    Some fresh-disfigured beauties rise;
    Each moment I perceive some flaw
    That e'en Ill-nature never saw.

"But hush! some airy whisperer hints,
    In accents wisely faint,
'Divine Cleora rather squints:
    Maria uses paint!

"'That though some fops of Cœlia prate,
    Yet be not hers the praise;
For, if she should be passing straight,
    Hem! she may thank her stays.

"'Each fool of Delia's figure talks,
    And celebrates her fame;
But, for my part, whene'er she walks,
    I vow I think she's lame.

"'And see Ma'am Harriet toss her head;
    Lawk! how the creature stares!
Well, well, thank Heavens, it can't be said
    I give myself such airs!'

"But soft!—what figure's this I now see come,
Whose awful form strikes even Scandal dumb?
Ah me! The blood forsakes my trembling cheek,
While sternly thus, methinks, I hear her speak:
    'Peace! snarling woman, peace,
    'Tis Candour bids thee cease:
Candour, at whose insulted name
Even thy face shall burn with shame.
    Too long I've silent seen
    The venom of thy spleen,
    Too long with secret pain
    Beheld black Scandal's reign.
    But now, with indignation stung,
    Justice demands my willing tongue,
And bids me drag the lurking fiend to light,
And hold the deeds of darkness up to sight.—
Look on this prospect; and if e'er thy brow
Can feel Compunction's sickening influence—now—

"'Mark yonder weeping maid,
    Sadly deserted, laid
    Beside that mournful willow:

   There, every day, in silent woe,
   She bids her tears incessant flow,
   And every night forlornly pining,
   Mute, on her lily hand reclining,
    Bedews her waking pillow.

" 'Sweet girl! she was once most enchantingly gay;
Each youth owned her charms, and acknowledged their sway.
No arts did she use to acquire every grace;
'Twas good humour alone that enlivened her face;
Pure nature had leave in her actions to speak;
The spirit of youth gave the blush to her cheek;
And her looks uninstructed her thoughts would impart,
For her eyes only flashed from the warmth of her heart.
Herself undesigning, no scheme she suspected;
Ne'er dreaming of ambush, defence she neglected.
With the youth that she loved, at the moon's silver hour,
In confidence tender, she stole to the bower.
There he hoped his designs to have basely obtained,
But she spurned at the insult her virtue sustained;
And he, in revenge for his baffled endeavour,
Gave a hint—'twas enough—she was ruined for ever!
A thousand kind females the story augmented;
Each day, grinning Envy additions invented,
Till insatiate Malice had gained all her ends,
Had robbed her of character—happiness—friends.
   And now, poor maid, alone,
   Shunned as a pest, she makes her moan,
   And, in unheard despair,
Yields, all resigned to soul-consuming Care;
   And oftentimes her maddening brain
   Turns with its feverish weight of pain,
   And then a thousand childish things
   The pretty mad one rudely sings.
    Or mute on the pathway she gazes,
    And weeps as she scatters her daisies;
   Or else, in a strain more distractedly loud,
    She chaunts the sad thoughts of her fancy,
   And shivers and sings of her cold shroud:'
    'Alas alas! poor Nancy!'
   'Nay, weep not now: 'tis now too late!
   Thy friendship might have stopped her fate.
Rather now hide thy head in conscious shame,
Thy tongue too blabbed the lie that damned her fame.
   Such are the triumphs Scandal claims,—
   Triumphs derived from ruined names:
   Such as to generous minds unknown,
   And honest minds would blush to own.
   Nor think, vain woman, while you sneer
   At others' faults, that you are clear.

No:—turn your back—you undergo
　　The malice you to others show;
And soon, by some malicious tale o'erthrown,
Like Nancy, fall, unpitied or unknown.'"

Oh! then, ye blooming fair, attend;
And take kind Candour for your friend;
　　Nor forfeit, for a mean delight,
　　That power o'er Man that's yours by right.

To Woman every charm was given
Designed by all-indulgent Heaven
　　　　To soften care;
For ye were formed to bless mankind,
To harmonize and soothe the mind:
　　　　Indeed, indeed, ye were.

But, when from those sweet lips we hear
Ill-nature's whisper, envy's sneer,
　　Your power that moment dies:
Each coxcomb makes your name his sport,
And fools, when angry, will retort
　　What men of sense despise.

Leave then such vain disputes as these,
And take a nobler road to please;
　　Let Candour guide your way;
So shall you daily conquests gain,
And captives, happy in your chain,
　　Be proud to own your sway.

THOMAS CHATTERTON.

[Born in Bristol, 20 November 1752; committed suicide in London, 25 August 1770].

FEBRUARY.

AN ELEGY.

BEGIN, my Muse, the imitative lay;
　Æonian doxies, sound the thrumming string;
Attempt no number of the plaintive Gray;
　Let me like midnight cats, or Collins, sing.

If, in the trammels of the doleful line,
　The bounding hail or drilling rain descend,
Come, brooding Melancholy, power divine,
　And every unformed mass of words amend.

Now the rough Goat withdraws his curling horns,
　And the cold Waterer twirls his circling mop:
Swift sudden anguish darts through altering corns,
　And the spruce mercer trembles in his shop.

Now infant authors, maddening for renown,
    Extend the plume, and hum about the stage,
Procure a benefit, amuse the town,
    And proudly glitter in a title-page.

Now, wrapped in ninefold fur, his squeamish Grace
    Defies the fury of the howling storm;
And, whilst the tempest whistles round his face,
    Exults to find his mantled carcase warm.

Now rumbling coaches furious drive along,
    Full of the majesty of city dames,
Whose jewels, sparkling in the gaudy throng,
    Raise strange emotions and invidious flames.

Now Merit, happy in the calm of place,
    To mortals as a Highlander appears,
And, conscious of the excellence of lace,
    With spreading frogs and gleaming spangles glares:

Whilst Envy, on a tripod seated nigh,
    In form a shoe-boy, daubs the valued fruit,
And, darting lightnings from his vengeful eye,
    Raves about Wilkes, and politics, and Bute.

Now Barry, taller than a grenadier,
    Dwindles into a stripling of eighteen;
Or, sabled in Othello, breaks the ear,
    Exerts his voice, and totters to the scene.

Now Foote, a looking-glass for all mankind,
    Applies his wax to personal defects;
But leaves untouched the image of the mind;—
    His art no mental quality reflects.

Now Drury's potent king extorts applause,
    And pit, box, gallery, echo "How divine!"
Whilst, versed in all the drama's mystic laws,
    His graceful action saves the wooden line.

Now—but what further can the Muses sing?
    Now dropping particles of water fall;
Now vapours, riding on the north wind's wing,
    With transitory darkness shadow all.

Alas! how joyless the descriptive theme
    When sorrow on the writer's quiet preys,
And, like a mouse in Cheshire cheese supreme,
    Devours the substance of the lessening bays!

Come, February, lend thy darkest sky,—
    There teach the wintered Muse with clouds to soar:
Come, February, lift the number high;
    Let the sharp strain like wind through alleys roar.

Ye channels, wandering through the spacious street,
   In hollow murmurs roll the dirt along,
With inundations wet the sabled feet,
   Whilst gouts, responsive, join the elegiac song.

Ye damsels fair, whose silver voices shrill
   Sound through meandering folds of Echo's horn,
Let the sweet cry of liberty be still,
   No more let smoking cakes awake the morn.

O Winter! put away thy snowy pride;
   O Spring! neglect the cowslip and the bell;
O Summer! throw thy pears and plums aside;
   O Autumn! bid the grape with poison'swell:—

The pensioned muse of Johnson is no more!
   Drowned in a butt of wine his genius lies.
Earth, Ocean, Heaven, the wondrous loss deplore;
   The dregs of Nature with her glory dies.

What iron Stoic can suppress the tear?
   What sour reviewer read with vacant eye?
What bard but decks his literary bier?—
   Alas! I cannot sing—I howl—I cry!

GEORGE CRABBE.

[Born at Aldborough, Suffolk, 24 December 1754; died at Trowbridge, Wilts, 3 February 1832. The father of Crabbe was a collector of salt-duties—a poor man with a large family. Crabbe, after picking up some smattering of knowledge, was apprenticed to an apothecary; and continued for awhile, with little encouragement, to act as a druggist and country practitioner. In 1780 he boldly broke with this course of life, and came to London as a literary adventurer: one poem of his, *Inebriety*, had already been published in Ipswich some years before. In London he issued *The Candidate*; which was successful, but, through the failure of his bookseller, brought no profit to the author. In desperation he applied at a venture to the statesman Burke for assistance; was kindly received; and eventually enabled to take holy orders. He became rector of Muston, Leicestershire, and finally of Trowbridge; where he had once served with an apothecary, and had fallen in love with the lady, Miss Elmy, whom he married. *The Village*, *The Parish Register*, *The Borough*, and *Tales of the Hall*, are among his leading poems. Crabbe was a man of solid worth, upright and tender. The same qualities shine in his writings, which are masterpieces of sound strong sense, full of observation, shrewdness, and knowledge of character, chiefly in the lower or the middle ranks of life. They transfer into the domain of narrative some of the sententious decorum, castigating truth, and literary propriety, of the didactic school of the eighteenth century. Of course, some poetic readers will demur to a form of poetry which is not based on ideal perceptions, and does not afford any imaginative medium of conciliation between life and beauty—or scarcely any, allowance being made for descriptive passages of uncommon force, not unfrequently recurring: yet even these readers can, on other grounds, peruse Crabbe with no little gratification.]

THE DUMB ORATORS: OR, THE BENEFIT OF SOCIETY.

THAT all men would be cowards if they dare
Some men, we know, have courage to declare;
And this the life of many a hero shows,

That, like the tide, man's courage ebbs and flows.
With friends and gay companions round them, then
Men boldly speak, and have the hearts of men;
Who, with opponents seated, miss the aid
Of kind applauding looks, and grow afraid.
Like timid travellers in the night, they fear
The assault of foes, when not a friend is near.

In contest mighty, and of conquest proud,
Was Justice Bolt, impetuous, warm, and loud;
His fame, his prowess, all the country knew,
And disputants, with one so fierce, were few.
He was a younger son, for law designed,
With dauntless look and persevering mind;
While yet a clerk, for disputation famed,
No efforts tired him, and no conflicts tamed.
Scarcely he bade his master's desk adieu,
When both his brothers from the world withdrew.
An ample fortune he from them possessed,
And was with saving care and prudence blest.
Now would he go and to the country give
Example how an English squire should live;
How bounteous, yet how frugal, man may be,
By a well-ordered hospitality.
He would the rights of all so well maintain
That none should idle be, and none complain.

All this and more he purposed—and what man
Could do he did to realize his plan:
But time convinced him that we cannot keep
A breed of reasoners like a flock of sheep;
For they, so far from following as we lead,
Make that a cause why they will not proceed.
Man will not follow where a rule is shown,
But loves to take a method of his own:
Explain the way with all your care and skill,
This will he quit, if but to prove he will.—
Yet had our Justice honour—and the crowd,
Awed by his presence, their respect avowed.

In later years he found his heart incline,
More than in youth, to generous food and wine;
But no indulgence checked the powerful love
He felt to teach, to argue, and reprove.

Meetings, or public calls, he never missed—
To dictate often, always to assist.
Oft he the clergy joined, and not a cause
Pertained to them but he could quote the laws;
He upon tithes and residence displayed
A fund of knowledge for the hearer's aid;

And could on glebe and farming, wool and grain,
A long discourse, without a pause, maintain.

To his experience and his native sense
He joined a bold imperious eloquence ;
The grave, stern look of men informed and wise,
A full command of feature, heart, and eyes,
An awe-compelling frown, and fear-inspiring size.
When at the table, not a guest was seen
With appetite so lingering or so keen ;
But, when the outer man no more required,
The inner waked, and he was man inspired.
His subjects then were those a subject true
Presents in fairest form to public view ;
Of church and state, of law, with mighty strength
Of words he spoke, in speech of mighty length.
And now, into the vale of years declined,
He hides too little of the monarch-mind.
He kindles anger by untimely jokes,
And opposition by contempt provokes ;
Mirth he suppresses by his awful frown,
And humble spirits, by disdain, keeps down ;
Blamed by the mild, approved by the severe,
The prudent fly him, and the valiant fear.
For overbearing is his proud discourse,
And overwhelming of his voice the force :
And overpowering is he when he shows
What floats upon a mind that always overflows.

This ready man at every meeting rose,
Something to hint, determine, or propose ;
And grew so fond of teaching that he taught
Those who instruction needed not or sought.
Happy our hero when he could excite
Some thoughtless talker to the wordy fight.
Let him a subject at his pleasure choose,
Physic or law, religion or the muse ;
On all such themes he was prepared to shine,—
Physician, poet, lawyer, and divine.
Hemmed in by some tough argument, borne down
By press of language and the awful frown,
In vain for mercy shall the culprit plead ;
His crime is past, and sentence must proceed :
Ah suffering man ! have patience, bear thy woes—
For lo ! the clock—at ten the Justice goes.

This powerful man, on business, or to please
A curious taste, or weary grown of ease,
On a long journey travelled many a mile
Westward, and halted midway in our isle ;

Content to view a city large and fair,
Though none had notice what a man was there!

Silent two days, he then began to long
Again to try a voice so loud and strong ;
To give his favourite topics some new grace,
And gain some glory in such distant place ;
To reap some present pleasure, and to sow
Seeds of fair fame, in after-time to grow :
" Here will men say, 'We heard, at such an hour,
The best of speakers—wonderful his power.'"

Enquiry made, he found that day would meet
A learned club, and in the very street.
Knowledge to gain and give was the design ;
To speak, to hearken, to debate, and dine.
This pleased our traveller, for he felt his force
In either way, to eat or to discourse.

Nothing more easy than to gain access
To men like these, with his polite address.
So he succeeded, and first looked around,
To view his objects and to take his ground ;
And therefore silent chose awhile to sit,
Then enter boldly by some lucky hit ;
Some observation keen or stroke severe,
To cause some wonder or excite some fear.

Now, dinner past, no longer he suppressed
His strong dislike to be a silent guest ;
Subjects and words were now at his command—
When disappointment frowned on all he planned.
For, hark !—he heard amazed, on every side,
His church insulted and her priests belied ;
The laws reviled, the ruling power abused,
The land derided, and its foes excused.
He heard and pondered—What, to men so vile,
Should be his language ?—For his threatening style
They were too many ;—if his speech were meek,
They would despise such poor attempts to speak.
At other times with every word at will,
He now sat lost, perplexed, astonished, still.

Here were Socinians, Deists, and indeed
All who, as foes to England's church, agreed ;
But still with creeds unlike, and some without a creed.
Here, too, fierce friends of liberty he saw,
Who owned no prince and who obey no law.
There were reformers of each different sort,
Foes to the laws, the priesthood, and the court ;
Some on their favourite plans alone intent,

Some purely angry and malevolent.
The rash were proud to blame their country's laws ;
The vain, to seem supporters of a cause ;
One called for change, that he would dread to see ;
Another sighed for Gallic liberty ;
And numbers joining with the forward crew,
For no one reason—but that numbers do.

"How," said the Justice, "can this trouble rise,
This shame and pain, from creatures I despise?"
And Conscience answered—"The prevailing cause
Is thy delight in listening to applause.
Here, thou art seated with a tribe who spurn
Thy favourite themes, and into laughter turn
Thy fears and wishes. Silent and obscure,
Thyself, shalt thou the long harangue endure ;
And learn, by feeling, what it is to force
On thy unwilling friends the long discourse.
What though thy thoughts be just, and these, it seems,
Are traitors' projects, idiots' empty schemes,
Yet minds, like bodies, crammed, reject their food,
Nor will be forced and tortured for their good."

At length, a sharp, shrewd, sallow man arose,
And begged he briefly might his mind disclose ;
It was his duty, in these worst of times,
To inform the governed of their rulers' crimes.
This pleasant subject to attend, they each
Prepared to listen, and forbore to teach.

Then, voluble and fierce, the wordy man
Through a long chain of favourite horrors ran :—
First, of the Church, from whose enslaving power,
He was delivered, and he blessed the hour.
Bishops and deans and prebendaries all,
He said, were cattle fattening in the stall.
Slothful and pursy, insolent and mean,
Were every bishop, prebendary, dean,
And wealthy rector : curates, poorly paid,
Were only dull ;—he would not them upbraid.

From priests he turned to canons, creeds, and prayers,
Rubrics and rules, and all our Church affairs ;
Churches themselves, desk, pulpit, altar, all
The Justice reverenced—and pronounced their fall.

Then from religion Hammond turned his view,
To give our Rulers the correction due ;
Not one wise action had these triflers planned ;
There was, it seemed, no wisdom in the land,
Save in this patriot tribe, who meet at times
To show the statesman's errors and his crimes.

Now here was Justice Bolt compelled to sit,
To hear the deist's scorn, the rebel's wit,
The fact mis-stated, the envenomed lie;
And, staring spell-bound, made not one reply.

Then were our Laws abused—and, with the laws,
All who prepare, defend, or judge a cause.
"We have no lawyer whom a man can trust,"
Proceeded Hammond—"*if* the laws were just;
But they are evil; 'tis the savage state
Is only good, and ours sophisticate!
See the free creatures in their woods and plains,
Where without laws each happy monarch reigns,
King of himself—while we a number dread,
By slaves commanded and by dunces led.
Oh let the name with either state agree—
Savage our own we'll name, and civil theirs shall be."

The silent Justice still astonished sat,
And wondered much whom he was gazing at.
Twice he essayed to speak—but, in a cough,
The faint, indignant, dying speech went off.
"But who is this?" thought he—"a demon vile,
With wicked meaning and a vulgar style:
Hammond they call him: they can give the name
Of man to devils.—Why am I so tame?
Why crush I not the viper?"—Fear replied,
"Watch him awhile, and let his strength be tried;
He will be foiled, if man; but, if his aid
Be from beneath, 'tis well to be afraid."

"We are called free!" said Hammond—"doleful times,
When rulers add their insult to their crimes!
For, should our scorn expose each powerful vice,
It would be libel, and we pay the price."

Thus with licentious words the man went on,
Proving that liberty of speech was gone;
That all were slaves—nor had we better chance
For better times than as allies to France.

Loud groaned the Stranger. Why, he must relate;
And owned,—In sorrow for his country's fate.
"Nay, she were safe," the ready man replied,
"Might patriots rule her, and could reasoners guide.
When all to vote, to speak, to teach, are free,
Whate'er their creeds or their opinions be;
When books of statutes are consumed in flames,
And courts and copyholds are empty names;
Then will be times of joy—but, ere they come,
Havock and war and blood must be our doom."

The man here paused—then loudly for Reform
He called, and hailed the prospect of the storm;
The wholesome blast, the fertilizing flood—
Peace gained by tumult, plenty bought with blood.
Sharp means, he owned; but, when the land's disease
Asks cure complete, no medicines are like these.
Our Justice now, more led by fear than rage,
Saw it in vain with madness to engage;
With imps of darkness no man seeks to fight,
Knaves to instruct, or set deceivers right.
Then, as the daring speech denounced these woes,
Sick at the soul, the grieving Guest arose;
Quick on the board his ready cash he threw,
And from the demons to his closet flew.
There when secured, he prayed with earnest zeal
That all they wished these patriot-souls might feel.
"Let them to France, their darling country, haste,
And all the comforts of a Frenchman taste.
Let them his safety, freedom, pleasure know,
Feel all their rulers on the land bestow;
And be at length dismissed by one unerring blow,—
Not hacked and hewed by one afraid to strike,
But shorn by that which shears all men alike.
Nor, as in Britain, let them curse delay
Of law; but, borne without a form away,
Suspected, tried, condemned, and carted, in a day.
Oh let them taste what they so much approve,
These strong fierce freedoms of the land they love!"

Home came our hero, to forget no more
The fear he felt, and ever must deplore:
For, though he quickly joined his friends again,
And could with decent force his themes maintain,
Still it occurred that, in a luckless time,
He failed to fight with heresy and crime.
It was observed his words were not so strong,
His tones so powerful, his harangues so long,
As in old times—for he would often drop
The lofty look, and of a sudden stop;
When Conscience whispered that he once was still,
And let the wicked triumph at their will;
And therefore now, when not a foe was near,
He had no right so valiant to appear.

Some years had passed, and he perceived his fears
Yield to the spirit of his earlier years—
When at a meeting, with his friends beside,
He saw an object that awaked his pride.
His shame, wrath, vengeance, indignation—all
Man's harsher feelings did that sight recall.

For lo ! beneath him fixed, our Man of Law
That lawless man, the Foe of Order, saw ;
Once feared, now scorned ; once dreaded, now abhorred ;
A wordy man, and evil every word.
Again he gazed—" It is," said he, " the same ;
Caught and secure : his master owes him shame."
So thought our hero, who each instant found
His courage rising, from the numbers round.

As when a felon has escaped and fled,
So long that law conceives the culprit dead,
And back recalled her myrmidons, intent
On some new game, and with a stronger scent ;
Till she beholds him in a place where none
Could have conceived the culprit would have gone ;
There he sits upright in his seat, secure,
As one whose conscience is correct and pure ;
This rouses anger for the old offence,
And scorn for all such seeming and pretence :—
So on this Hammond looked our hero bold,
Remembering well that vile offence of old.
And now he saw the rebel dared to intrude
Among the pure, the loyal, and the good ;
The crime provoked his wrath, the folly stirred his blood.
Nor wonder was it if so strange a sight
Caused joy with vengeance, terror with delight.
Terror like this a tiger might create ;
A joy like that, to see his captive state,
At once to know his force, and then decree his fate.

Hammond, much praised by numerous friends, was come
To read his lectures, so admired at home ;
Historic lectures, where he loved to mix
His free plain hints on modern politics.
Here he had heard that numbers had design,
Their business finished, to sit down and dine ;
This gave him pleasure, for he judged it right
To show by day that he could speak at night.
Rash the design—for he perceived, too late,
Not one approving friend beside him sate ;
The greater number whom he traced around
Were men in black, and he conceived they frowned.
" I will not speak," he thought ; " no pearls of mine
Shall be presented to this herd of swine."
Not this availed him when he cast his eye
On Justice Bolt ; he could not fight, nor fly.
He saw a man to whom he gave the pain
Which now he felt must be returned again ;
His conscience told him with what keen delight
He, at that time, enjoyed a stranger's fright ;

That stranger now befriended,—he alone,
For all his insult, friendless, to atone ;
Now he could feel it cruel that a heart
Should be distressed, and none to take its part.
" Though one by one," said Pride, " I would defy
Much greater men, yet, meeting every eye,
I do confess a fear—but he will pass me by."

Vain hope ! the Justice saw the foe's distress,
With exultation he could not suppress,
He felt the fish was hooked—and so forbore,
In playful spite, to draw it to the shore.
Hammond looked round again ; but none were near,
With friendly smile to still his growing fear ;
But all above him seemed a solemn row
Of priests and deacons, so they seemed below.
He wondered who his right-hand man might be—
Vicar of Holt cum Uppingham was he ;
And who the man of that dark frown possessed—
Rector of Bradley and of Barton-west ;
" A pluralist," he growled—but checked the word,
That warfare might not, by his zeal, be stirred.

But now began the man above to show
Fierce looks and threatenings to the man below ;
Who had some thoughts his peace by flight to seek—
But how then lecture, if he dared not speak ?

Now as the Justice for the war prepared,
He seemed just then to question if he dared :
" He may resist, although his power be small,
And, growing desperate, may defy us all.
One dog attack, and he prepares for flight
Resist another, and he strives to bite ;
Nor can I say if this rebellious cur
Will fly for safety, or will scorn to stir."
Alarmed by this, he lashed his soul to rage,
Burned with strong shame, and hurried to engage.

As a male turkey straggling on the green,
When by fierce harriers, terriers, mongrels, seen,
He feels the insult of the noisy train
And skulks aside, though moved by much disdain ;
But when that turkey, at his own barn-door,
Sees one poor straying puppy and no more
(A foolish puppy who had left the pack,
Thoughtless what foe was threatening at his back),
He moves about, as ship prepared to sail,
He hoists his proud rotundity of tail,
The half-sealed eyes and changeful neck he shows,
Where, in its quickening colours, vengeance glows ;

From red to blue the pendent wattles turn,
Blue mixed with red, as matches when they burn;
And thus the intruding snarler to oppose,
Urged by enkindling wrath, he gobbling goes :—
So looked our hero in his wrath. His cheeks
Flushed with fresh fires, and glowed in tingling streaks;
His breath, by passion's force awhile restrained,
Like a stopped current greater force regained;
So spoke, so looked he, every eye and ear
Were fixed to view him, or were turned to hear.

"My friends, you know me; you can witness all
How, urged by passion, I restrain my gall;
And every motive to revenge withstand—
Save when I hear abused my native land.
Is it not known, agreed, confirmed, confessed,
That, of all people, we are governed best?
We have the force of monarchies; are free
As the most proud republicans can be;
And have those prudent counsels that arise
In grave and cautious aristocracies.
And live there those, in such all-glorious state,
Traitors protected in the land they hate?
Rebels, still warring with the laws that give
To them subsistence?—Yes, such wretches live.
Ours is a Church reformed, and now no more
Is aught for man to mend or to restore;
'Tis pure in doctrines, 'tis correct in creeds,
Has nought redundant, and it nothing needs.
No evil is therein—no wrinkle, spot,
Stain, blame, or blemish :—I affirm there's not.
All this you know—now mark what once befell;
With grief I bore it, and with shame I tell.
I was entrapped—yes, so it came to pass,
'Mid heathen rebels, a tumultuous class;
Each to his country bore a hellish mind,
Each like his neighbour was of cursed kind.
The land that nursed them they blasphemed; the laws,
Their sovereign's glory, and their country's cause;
And who their mouth, their master-fiend, and who
Rebellion's oracle?————You, caitiff, you!"

He spoke, and standing stretched his mighty arm,
And fixed the Man of Words, as by a charm.

"How raved that railer! Sure some hellish power
Restrained my tongue in that delirious hour,
Or I had hurled the shame and vengeance due
On him, the guide of that infuriate crew.
But to mine eyes such dreadful looks appeared,
Such mingled yell of lying words I heard,

That I conceived around were demons all,
And, till I fled the house, I feared its fall.
Oh ! could our country from our coasts expel
Such foes,—to nourish those who wish her well !
This her mild laws forbid, but we may still
From us eject them by our sovereign will ;
This let us do."—He said ; and then began
A gentler feeling for the silent man ;
Even in our hero's mighty soul arose
A touch of pity for experienced woes.
But this was transient, and with angry eye
He sternly looked, and paused for a reply.

   'Twas then the Man of many Words would speak—
But, in his trial, had them all to seek :
To find a friend he looked the circle round,
But joy or scorn in every feature found.
He sipped his wine, but in those times of dread
Wine only adds confusion to the head ;
In doubt he reasoned with himself—" And how
Harangue at night, if I be silent now ?"
From pride, and praise received, he sought to draw
Courage to speak, but still remained the awe.
One moment rose he with a forced disdain,
And then, abashed, sunk sadly down again ;
While in our hero's glance he seemed to read,
" Slave and insurgent ! what hast thou to plead ?"

   By desperation urged, he now began :
" I seek no favour—I—the rights of man
Claim ; and I—nay !—but give me leave—and I
Insist—a man—that is—and in reply
I speak."—Alas ! each new attempt was vain :
Confused he stood, he sate, he rose again ;
At length he growled defiance, sought the door,
Cursed the whole synod, and was seen no more.

   " Laud we," said Justice Bolt, " the Powers above :
Thus could our speech the sturdiest foe remove."
Exulting now he gained new strength of fame,
And lost all feelings of defeat and shame.
" He dared not strive, you witnessed—dared not lift
His voice, nor drive at his accursèd drift :
So all shall tremble, wretches who oppose
Our Church or State—thus be it to our foes."

   He spoke, and, seated with his former air,
Looked his full self, and filled his ample chair ;
Took one full bumper to each favourite cause,
And dwelt all night on politics and laws,
With high applauding voice, that gained him high applause.

THE WIDOW.

Harriet at school was very much the same
As other misses; and so home she came,
Like other ladies, there to live and learn,
To wait her season, and to take her turn.

Their husbands maids as priests their livings gain;
The best, they find, are hardest to obtain.
On those that offer both awhile debate—
"I need not take it, it is not so late;
Better will come if we will longer stay,
And strive to put ourselves in fortune's way."
And thus they wait, till many years are past,
For what comes slowly—but it comes at last.

Harriet was wedded,—but it must be said,
The vowed obedience was not duly paid.
Hers was an easy man,—it gave him pain
To hear a lady murmur and complain.
He was a merchant, whom his father made
Rich in the gains of a successful trade:
A lot more pleasant, or a view more fair,
Has seldom fallen to a youthful pair.

But what is faultless in a world like this?
In every station something seems amiss:
The lady, married, found the house too small—
"Two shabby parlours, and that ugly hall!
Had we a cottage somewhere, and could meet
One's friends and favourites in one's snug retreat,
Or only join a single room to these,
It would be living something at our ease,
And have one's self, at home, the comfort that one sees."

Such powers of reason, and of mind such strength,
Fought with man's fear, and they prevailed at length:
The room was built,—and Harriet did not know
A prettier dwelling, either high or low.
But Harriet loved such conquests, loved to plead
With her reluctant man, and to succeed;
It was such pleasure to prevail o'er one
Who would oppose the thing that still was done,
Who never gained the race, but yet would groan and run.

But there were times when love and pity gave
Whatever thoughtless vanity could crave.
She now the carriage chose with freshest name,
And was in quite a fever till it came.
But can a carriage be alone enjoyed?
The pleasure not partaken is destroyed;
"I must have some good creature to attend
On morning visits as a kind of friend."

A courteous maiden then was found to sit
Beside the lady, for her purpose fit,
Who had been trained in all the soothing ways
And servile duties from her early days;
One who had never from her childhood known
A wish fulfilled, a purpose of her own.
Her part it was to sit beside the dame,
And give relief in every want that came;
To soothe the pride, to watch the varying look,
And bow in silence to the dumb rebuke.

This supple being strove with all her skill
To draw her master's to her lady's will;
For they were like the magnet and the steel,
At times so distant that they could not feel;
Then would she gently move them, till she saw
That to each other they began to draw;
And then would leave them, sure on her return
In Harriet's joy her conquest to discern.

She was a mother now, and grieved to find
The nursery-window caught the eastern wind.
What could she do, with fears like these oppressed?
She built a room all windowed to the west;
For sure in one so dull, so bleak, so old,
She and her children must expire with cold.
Meantime the husband murmured.—So he might;
She would be judged by Cousins—Was it right?

Water was near them; and, her mind afloat,
The lady saw a cottage and a boat,
And thought what sweet excursions they might make,
How they might sail, what neighbours they might take,
And nicely would she deck the lodge upon the lake.

She now prevailed by habit; had her will,
And found her patient husband sad and still.
Yet this displeased; she gained, indeed, the prize,
But not the pleasure of her victories.
Was she a child to be indulged? He knew
She would have right, but would have reason too.

Now came the time when in her husband's face
Care, and concern, and caution, she could trace.
His troubled features gloom and sadness bore;
Less he resisted, but he suffered more;
His nerves were shook like hers; in him her grief
Had much of sympathy, but no relief.

She could no longer read, and therefore kept
A girl to give her stories while she wept;

Better for Lady Julia's woes to cry
Than have her own for ever in her eye.
Her husband grieved, and o'er his spirits came
Gloom ; and disease attacked his slender frame ;
He felt a loathing for the wretched state
Of his concerns, so sad, so complicate ;
Grief and confusion seized him in the day,
And the night passed in agony away.
" My ruin comes ! " was his awakening thought ;
And vainly through the day was comfort sought.
" There, take my all ! " he said, and in his dream
Heard the door bolted, and his children scream.
And he was right, for not a day arose
That he exclaimed not, " Will it never close ? "
" Would it were come ! "—but still he shifted on,
Till health, and hope, and life's fair views, were gone.

Fretful herself, he of his wife in vain
For comfort sought.—He would be well again ;
Time would disorders of such nature heal.
Oh if he felt what she was doomed to feel !
Such sleepless nights ! such broken rest ! her frame
Racked with diseases that she could not name !
With pangs like hers no other was oppressed !—
Weeping, she said, and sighed herself to rest.

The suffering husband looked the world around,
And saw no friend : on him misfortune frowned ;
Him self-reproach tormented.   Sorely tried
By threats he mourned, and by disease he died.

As weak as wailing infancy or age,
How could the widow with the world engage ?
Fortune not now the means of comfort gave,
Yet all her comforts Harriet wept to have.

" My helpless babes," she said, " will nothing know ; "
Yet not a single lesson would bestow.
Her debts would overwhelm her, that was sure ;
But one privation would she not endure.
" We shall want bread ! the thing is past a doubt."—
" Then part with Cousins ! "—" Can I do without ? "—
" Dismiss your servants ! "—" Spare me them, I pray ! "—
" At least your carriage ! "—" What will people say ? "—
" That useless boat, that folly on the lake ! "—
" Oh ! but what cry and scandal will it make ! "

It was so hard on her, who not a thing
Had done such mischief on their heads to bring ;
This was her comfort, this she would declare,
And then slept soundly on her pillowed chair.

When not asleep, how restless was the soul,
Above advice, exempted from control;
For ever begging all to be sincere,
And never willing any truth to hear.
A yellow paleness o'er her visage spread,
Her fears augmented as her comforts fled;
Views dark and dismal to her mind appeared,
And death she sometimes wooed, and always feared.

Among the clerks there was a thoughtful one,
Who still believed that something might be done;
All in his view was not so sunk and lost
But of a trial things would pay the cost.
He judged the widow, and he saw the way
In which her husband suffered her to stray.
He saw entangled and perplexed affairs,
And Time's sure hand at work on their repairs;
Children he saw, but nothing could he see
Why he might nor their careful father be;
And, looking keenly round him, he believed
That what was lost might quickly be retrieved.

Now thought our clerk—"I must not mention love,—
That she at least must seem to disapprove;
But I must fear of poverty enforce,
And then consent will be a thing of course."

"Madam!" said he, "with sorrow I relate,
That our affairs are in a dreadful state;
I called on all our friends, and they declared
They dared not meddle—not a creature dared.
But still our perseverance chance may aid,
And, though I'm puzzled, I am not afraid.
If you, dear lady, will attention give
To me, the credit of the house shall live.
Do not, I pray you, my proposal blame;
It is my wish to guard your husband's fame,
And ease your trouble; then your cares resign
To my discretion—and, in short, be mine."

"Yours! O my stars!—Your goodness, sir, deserves
My grateful thanks—take pity on my nerves;
I shake and tremble at a thing so new,
And fear 'tis what a lady should not do;
And then to marry upon ruin's brink
In all this hurry—what will people think?"

"Nay, there's against us neither rule nor law,
And people's thinking is not worth a straw;
Those who are prudent have too much to do
With their own cares to think of me and you;

And those who are not are so poor a race
That what they utter can be no disgrace.—
Come! let us now embark when time and tide
Invite to sea; in happy hour decide;
If yet we linger, both are sure to fail,
The turning waters and the varying gale.
Trust me, our vessel shall be ably steered,
Nor will I quit her till the rocks are cleared."

Allured and frightened, softened and afraid,
The widow doubted, pondered, and obeyed.
So were they wedded, and the careful man
His reformation instantly began;
Began his state with vigour to reform,
And made a calm by laughing at the storm.

The attendant-maiden he dismissed—for why?
She might on him and love like his rely,
She needed none to form her children's mind,—
That duty nature to *her* care assigned.
In vain she mourned, it was her health he prized,
And hence enforced the measures he advised.
She wanted air; and walking, she was told,
Was safe, was pleasant!—he the carriage sold.
He found a tenant who agreed to take
The boat and cottage on the useless lake;
The house itself had now superfluous room,
And a rich lodger was induced to come.

The lady wondered at the sudden change,
That yet was pleasant, that was very strange.
When every deed by her desire was done,
She had no day of comfort—no, not one.
When nothing moved or stopped at her request,
Her heart had comfort, and her temper rest;
For all was done with kindness,—most polite
Was her new lord, and she confessed it right;
For now she found that she could gaily live
On what the chance of common life could give:
And her sick mind was cured of every ill,
By finding no compliance with her will;
For, when she saw that her desires were vain,
She wisely thought it foolish to complain.

Born for her man, she gave a gentle sigh
To her lost power, and grieved not to comply;
Within, without, the face of things improved,
And all in order and subjection moved.
As wealth increased, ambition now began
To swell the soul of the aspiring man;

In some few years he thought to purchase land,
And build a seat that hope and fancy planned;
To this a name his youthful bride should give!
Harriet, of course, not many years would live.
Then he would farm, and every soil should show
The tree that best upon the place would grow.
He would, moreover, on the Bench debate
On sundry questions—when a magistrate;
Would talk of all that to the state belongs,
The rich man's duties, and the poor man's wrongs;
He would with favourites of the people rank,
And him the weak and the oppressed should thank.

'Tis true those children, orphans then, would need
Help in a world of trouble to succeed;
And they should have it.—He should then possess
All that man needs for earthly happiness.

"Proud words, and vain!" said Doctor Young; and proud
They are; and vain, were by our clerk allowed;
For, while he dreamed, there came both pain and cough,
And fever never tamed, and bore him off;
Young as he was, and planning schemes to live
With more delight than man's success can give;
Building a mansion in his fancy vast,
Beyond the Gothic pride of ages past!
While this was planned, but ere a place was sought,
The timber seasoned, or the quarry wrought,
Came Death's dread summons, and the man was laid
In the poor house the simple sexton made.

But he had time for thought when he was ill,
And made his lady an indulgent will.
'Tis said he gave, in parting, his advice,
"It is sufficient to be married twice:"
To which she answered, as 'tis said again,
"There's none will have you if you're poor and plain;
And, if you're rich and handsome, there is none
Will take refusal—let the point alone."

Be this or true or false, it is her praise
She mourned correctly all the mourning days.
But grieve she did not; for the canker grief
Soils the complexion, and is beauty's thief;
Nothing, indeed, so much will discompose
Our public mourning as our private woes.
When tender thoughts a widow's bosom probe,
She thinks not then how graceful sits the robe;
But our nice widow looked to every fold,
And every eye its beauty might behold.

It was becoming; she composed her face,
She looked serenely, and she mourned with grace.

Some months were passed, but yet there wanted three
Of the full time when widows wives may be;
One trying year, and then the mind is freed,
And man may to the vacant throne succeed.

There was a tenant—he, to wit, who hired
That cot and lake that were so much admired;
A man of spirit, one who doubtless meant,
Though he delayed awhile, to pay his rent.
The widow's riches gave her much delight,
And some her claims, and she resolved to write :—
He knew her grievous loss, how every care
Devolved on her, who had indeed her share;
She had no doubt of him,—but was as sure
As that she breathed her money was secure;
But she had made a rash and idle vow
To claim her dues, and she must keep it now :
So if it suited——
            And for this there came
A civil answer to the gentle dame :
Within the letter were excuses, thanks,
And clean bank-paper from the best of banks;
There were condolence, consolation, praise,
With some slight hints of danger in delays.
With these good things were others from the lake,
Perch that were wished to salmon for her sake,
And compliment as sweet as new-born hope could make.

This led to friendly visits, social calls,
And much discourse of races, rambles, balls;
But all in proper bounds, and not a word
Before its time—the man was not absurd,
Nor was he cold; but, when she might expect,
A letter came, and one to this effect :—

That, if his eyes had not his love conveyed,
They had their master shamefully betrayed;
But she must know the flame, *that* he was sure,
Nor she could doubt would long as life endure.
Both were in widowed state, and both possessed
Of ample means to make their union blest.
That she had been confined he knew for truth,
And begged her to have pity on her youth;
Youth, he would say, and he desired his wife
To have the comforts of an easy life :
She loved a carriage, loved a decent seat
To which they might at certain times retreat.

Servants indeed were sorrows,—yet a few
They still must add, and do as others do:
She too would some attendant damsel need,
To hear, to speak, to travel, or to read.
In short, the man his remedies assigned
For his foreknown diseases in the mind:—
First, he presumed that in a nervous case
Nothing was better than a change of a place:
He added, too,—'Twas well that he could prove
That his was pure, disinterested love;
Not as when lawyers couple house and land
In such a way as none can understand;
No! thanks to Him that every good supplied,
He had enough, and wanted nought beside!
Merit was all.—
    Well! now, she would protest,
This was a letter prettily expressed!
To every female friend away she flew
To ask advice, and say "What shall I do?"
She kissed her children,—and she said, with tears,
"I wonder what is best for you, my dears?
How can I, darlings, to your good attend
Without the help of some experienced friend,
Who will protect us all, or, injured, will defend?"

The Widow then asked counsel of her heart,—
In vain, for that had nothing to impart;
But yet, with that (or something) for her guide,
She to her swain thus guardedly replied:—

She must believe he was sincere, for why
Should one who needed nothing deign to lie?
But, though she could and did his truth admit,
She could not praise him for his taste a bit.
And yet men's tastes were various, she confessed,
And none could prove his own to be the best.
It was a vast concern, including all
That we can happiness or comfort call;
And yet she found that those who waited long
Before their choice had often chosen wrong.
Nothing, indeed, could for her loss atone,
But 'twas the greater that she lived alone.
She too had means, and therefore what the use
Of more, that still more trouble would produce?
And pleasure too, she owned, as well as care,—
Of which, at present, she had not her share.
The things he offered, she must needs confess,
They were all women's wishes, more or less;
But were expensive; though a man of sense
Would by his prudence lighten the expense.

Prudent he was, but made a sad mistake
When he proposed her faded face to take;
And yet, 'tis said, there's beauty that will last
When the rose withers and the bloom be past.

One thing displeased her,—that he could suppose
He might so soon his purposes disclose;
Yet had she hints of such intent before,
And would excuse him if he wrote no more.
What would the world?—and yet she judged them fools
Who let the world's suggestions be their rules.
What would her friends?—Yet in her own affairs
It was *her* business to decide, not theirs.
"Adieu! then, sir," she added; "thus you find
The changeless purpose of a steady mind,
In one now left alone, but to her fate resigned."

The marriage followed; and the experienced dame
Considered what the conduct that became
A thrice-devoted lady.—She confessed
That when indulged she was but more distressed;
And, by her second husband when controlled,
Her life was pleasant, though her love was cold;
"Then let me yield," she said, and with a sigh;
"Let me to wrong submit, with right comply."
Alas! obedience may mistake, and they
Who reason not will err when they obey;
And fated was the gentle dame to find
Her duty wrong, and her obedience blind.

The man was kind, but would have no dispute;
His love and kindness both were absolute.
She needed not her wishes to express
To one who urged her on to happiness;
For this he took her to the lakes and seas,
To mines and mountains; nor allowed her ease;—
She must be pleased, he said, and he must live to please.

He hurried north and south, and east and west;
When age required, they would have time to rest:
He in the richest dress her form arrayed,
And cared not what he promised, what he paid;
She should share all his pleasures as her own,
And see whatever could be sought or shown.

This run of pleasure for a time she bore,
And then affirmed that she could taste no more;
She loved it while its nature it retained,
But, made a duty, it displeased and pained.
"Have we not means?" the joyous husband cried.
"But I am wearied out," the wife replied.

'Wearied with pleasure! Thing till now unheard!—
Are all that sweeten trouble to be feared?
'Tis but the sameness tires you,—cross the seas,
And let us taste the world's varieties.
'Tis said, in Paris that a man may live
In all the luxuries a world can give,
And in a space confined to narrow bound
All the enjoyments of our life are found.
There we may eat and drink, may dance and dress,
And in its very essence joy possess;
May see a moving crowd of lovely dames,
May win a fortune at your favourite games;
May hear the sounds that ravish human sense,
And all without receding foot from thence."

 The conquered wife, resistless and afraid,
To the strong call a sad obedience paid.

 As we an infant, in its pain, with sweets
Loved once, now loathed, torment him till he eats,
Who on the authors of his new distress
Looks trembling with disgusted weariness,
So Harriet felt, so looked, and seemed to say,
"Oh for a day of rest, a holiday!"

 At length, her courage rising with her fear,
She said, "Our pleasures may be bought too dear!"

 To this he answered—"Dearest! from thy heart
Bid every fear of evil times depart.
I ever trusted in the trying hour
To my good stars, and felt the ruling power.
When Want drew nigh, his threatening speed was stopped;
Some virgin aunt, some childless uncle, dropped.
In all his threats I sought expedients new,
And my last, best resource was found in you."

 Silent and sad the wife beheld her doom,
And sat her down to see the ruin come,
And meet the ills that rise where money fails,—
Debts, threats, and duns, bills, bailiffs, writs, and jails.

 These was she spared; ere yet by want oppressed,
Came one more fierce than bailiff in arrest.
Amid a scene where Pleasure never came,
Though never ceased the mention of his name,
The husband's heated blood received the breath
Of strong disease, that bore him to his death.

 Her all collected,—whether great or small
The sum, I know not, but collected all,—

The widowed lady to her cot retired,
And there she lives delighted and admired:
Civil to all, compliant and polite,
Disposed to think "whatever is is right:"
She wears the widow's weeds, she gives the widow's mite.
At home awhile, she in the autumn finds
The sea an object for reflecting minds,
And change for tender spirits; there she reads,
And weeps in comfort in her graceful weeds.

What gives our tale its moral? Here we find
That wives like this are not for rule designed,
Nor yet for blind submission. Happy they
Who, while they feel it pleasant to obey,
Have yet a kind companion at their side
Who in their journey will his power divide,
Or yield the reins, and bid the lady guide;
Then points the wonders of the way, and makes
The duty pleasant that she undertakes.
He shows her objects as they move along,
And gently rules the movements that are wrong;
He tells her all the skilful driver's art,
And smiles to see how well she acts her part;
Nor praise denies to courage or to skill,
In using power that he resumes at will.

WILLIAM BLAKE.

[Born in London, 28 November[1] 1757; died there, 12 August 1827. This would be an inappropriate place for giving any account of the supernal mystic —designer, painter, engraver, poet, and seer. Indeed, to include him at all in a volume of Humorous Poetry requires almost an apology; the quaintness and freakish quality (not unmingled with a deep sense) of the following slight compositions may however furnish such apology, if needed].

THE LITTLE VAGABOND.

DEAR mother, dear mother, the Church is cold;
But the Alehouse is healthy, and pleasant, and warm.
Besides, I can tell where I am used well;
The poor parsons with wind like a blown bladder swell.

But, if at the Church they would give us some ale,
And a pleasant fire our souls to regale,
We'd sing and we'd pray all the livelong day,
Nor ever once wish from the Church to stray.

---

[1] This is the date given in the *Life of Blake* by Gilchrist, and elsewhere. A MS. which I have seen, belonging to Mr. Tatham who knew Blake in his closing years, says "20 November," and I am not sure but that this may be right.

Then the Parson might preach, and drink, and sing,
And we'd be as happy as birds in the spring;
And modest Dame Lurch, who is always at church,
Would not have bandy children, nor fasting, nor birch.

And God, like a father, rejoicing to see
His children as pleasant and happy as He,
Would have no more quarrel with the Devil or the barrel,
But kiss him, and give him both drink and apparel.

ORATOR PRIG.

I asked of my dear friend orator Prig:
"What's the first part of oratory?" He said: "A great wig."
"And what is the second?" Then, dancing a jig
And bowing profoundly, he said: "A great wig."
"And what is the third?" Then he snored like a pig,
And, puffing his cheeks out, replied: "A great wig."—
So, if to a painter the question you push,
"What's the first part of painting?" he'll say: "A paint-brush."
"And what is the second?" With most modest blush,
He'll smile like a cherub, and say: "A paint-brush."
"And what is the third?" He'll bow like a rush,
With a leer in his eye, and reply: "A paint-brush."
Perhaps this is all a painter can want:
But look yonder,—that house is the house of Rembrandt.

GEORGE COLMAN (JUNR.)

[Born 21 October 1762, died 26 October 1836. Author of *The Poor Gentleman, The Iron Chest, The Heir at Law,* and numerous plays that have held a high position on the stage; also of *Broad Grins,* and other humorous compositions in verse. He was a theatrical manager, and Examiner of Plays for several years. His father, George Colman the elder, was also a writer of a similar class; *The Clandestine Marriage* (written by him and Garrick jointly) being one of his chief productions].

THE NEWCASTLE APOTHECARY.

A man, in many a country town, we know,
  Professes openly with Death to wrestle;
Entering the field against the grimly foe,
  Armed with a mortar and a pestle.

Yet some affirm no enemies they are;
  But meet just like prize-fighters in a fair,
  Who first shake hands before they box,
  Then give each other plaguy knocks,
With all the love and kindness of a brother:
  So, many a suffering patient saith,
Though the Apothecary fights with Death,
  Still they're sworn friends to one another.

A member of this Æsculapian line
    Lived at Newcastle-upon-Tyne:
      No man could better gild a pill,
        Or make a bill,
    Or mix a draught, or bleed, or blister,
    Or draw a tooth out of your head,
    Or chatter scandal by your bed,
      Or give a clyster.

Of occupations these were *quantum suff.*:
Yet still he thought the list not long enough,
    And therefore midwifery he chose to pin to't.
      This balanced things:—for, if he hurled
      A few score mortals from the world,
    He made amends by bringing others into't.

His fame full six miles round the country ran;
    In short, in reputation he was *solus*
All the old women called him "a fine man!"
      His name was Bolus.

    Benjamin Bolus, though in trade
(Which oftentimes will genius fetter),
    Read works of fancy, it is said,
And cultivated the *Belles-Lettres.*

    And why should this be thought so odd?
Can't men have taste who cure a phthisic?
    Of poetry though patron-god,
Apollo patronizes physic.

Bolus loved verse;—and took so much delight in't
That his prescriptions he resolved to write in't.

No opportunity he e'er let pass
    Of writing the directions on his labels
    In dapper couplets,—like Gay's Fables;
Or rather like the lines in Hudibras.

Apothecary's verse! And where's the treason?
  'Tis simply honest dealing:—not a crime;
When patients swallow physic without reason,
  It is but fair to give a little rhyme.

He had a patient lying at death's door,
Some three miles from the town,—it might be four;
To whom, one evening, Bolus sent an article,
In Pharmacy, that's called cathartical,
      And on the label of the stuff
      He wrote this verse;

Which, one would think, was clear enough,
   And terse :—
  "*When taken,
  To be well shaken.*"

Next morning, early, Bolus rose;
And to the patient's house he goes,
   Upon his pad,
Who a vile trick of stumbling had.
It was, indeed, a very sorry hack;
   But that's of course:
For what's expected from a horse
With an Apothecary on his back?
Bolus arrived ; and gave a doubtful tap,
Between a single and a double rap.

   Knocks of this kind
Are given by gentlemen who teach to dance,
  By fiddlers, and by opera-singers :
One loud, and then a little one behind ;
  As if the knocker fell, by chance,
   Out of their fingers.

The servant lets him in, with dismal face,
  Long as a courtier's out of place—
   Portending some disaster.
John's countenance as rueful looked, and grim,
As if the Apothecary had physicked him,
   And not his master.
 "Well, how's the patient?" Bolus said.
   John shook his head.
 "Indeed !—hum ! ha !—that's very odd !
 He took the draught?" John gave a nod.
 "Well,—how?—what then?—speak out, you dunce !"
 "Why, then," says John, "we *shook* him once."
 "Shook him! How?" Bolus stammered out.
   "We jolted him about."
 "Zounds ! Shake a patient, man !—a shake won't do."
  "No, Sir,—and so we gave him *two*."
   "Two shakes ! od's curse !
  'Twould make the patient worse."
 "It did so, Sir !—and so a third we tried."
 "Well, and what then?"—"Then, Sir, my master died !"

ROBERT BLOOMFIELD.

[Born at Honington, Suffolk, 1766; died in 1823. He was the son of a tailor; worked at first with a farmer, and afterwards as a shoemaker. Having a turn for verse, he published some compositions in a newspaper; and next wrote *The Farmer's Boy*, a poem of some length which ran through various editions. He tried one or two occupations, as a change from shoemaking, but without commercial success, and at last his sight failed almost entirely].

THE HORKEY.[1]

A PROVINCIAL BALLAD.

WHAT gossips prattled in the sun,
   Who talked him fairly down,
Up, memory ! tell ; 'tis Suffolk fun,
   And lingo of their own.

Ah ! Judie Twitchet ! though thou'rt dead,
   With thee the tale begins ;
For still seems thrumming in my head
   The rattling of thy pins.

Thou Queen of knitters ! for a ball
   Of worsted was thy pride ;
With dangling stockings great and small,
   And world of clack beside !

"We did so laugh ; the moon shone bright ;
   More fun you never knew ;
'Twas Farmer Cheerum's Horkey night,
   And I, and Grace, and Sue——

"But bring a stool, sit round about,—
   And boys, be quiet, pray ;
And let me tell my story out ;
   'Twas sich a merry day !

"The butcher whistled at the door,
   And brought a load of meat ;
Boys rubbed their hands, and cried 'there's more,'
   Dogs wagged their tails to see't.

---

[1] In Suffolk husbandry the man who (whether by merit or by sufferance I know not) goes foremost through the harvest with the scythe or the sickle is honoured with the title of '*Lord*,' and at the Horkey, or harvest-home feast, collects what he can, for himself and brethren, from the farmers and visitors, to make a "frolic" afterwards, called "the largess spending." By way of returning thanks, though perhaps formerly of much more or of different signification, they immediately leave the seat of festivity, and with a very long and repeated shout of "a largess," the number of shouts being regulated by the sums given, seem to wish to make themselves heard by the people of the surrounding farms. And, before they rejoin the company within, the pranks and the jollity I have endeavoured to describe usually take place.

"On went the boilers till the hake [1]
    Had much ado to bear 'em;
The magpie talked for talking sake,
    Birds sung;—but who could hear 'em?

"Creak went the jack; the cats were scared,
    We had not time to heed 'em;
The owd hins cackled in the yard,
    For we forgot to feed 'em!

"Yet 'twas not I, as I may say,
    Because as how, d'ye see,
I only helped there for the day;
    They couldn't lay't to me.

"Now Mrs. Cheerum's best lace cap
    Was mounted on her head;
Guests at the door began to rap,
    And now the cloth was spread.

"Then clatter went the earthen plates—
    'Mind, Judie,' was the cry;
I could have cop't [2] them at their pates;
    'Trenchers for me,' said I,—

"'That look so clean upon the ledge,
    And never mind a fall,
Nor never turn a sharp knife's edge;—
    But fashion rules us all.'

"Home came the jovial Horkey load,
    Last of the whole year's crop;
And Grace amongst the green boughs rode
    Right plump upon the top.

"This way and that the waggon reeled,
    And never queen rode higher;
Her cheeks were coloured in the field,
    And ours before the fire.

"The laughing harvest-folks, and John,
    Came in and looked askew;
'Twas my red face that set them on,
    And then they leered at Sue.

"And Farmer Cheerum went, good man,
    And broached the Horkey beer;
And sich a mort [3] of folks began
    To eat up our good cheer.

---

[1] A sliding pot-hook.   [2] Thrown.   [3] Such a number.

"Says he, 'Thank God for what's before us ;
  That thus we meet again ;'
The mingling voices, like a chorus,
  Joined cheerfully, 'Amen.'—

"Welcome and plenty, there they found 'em ;
  The ribs of beef grew light ;
And puddings—till the boys got round 'em,
  And then they vanished quite.

"Now all the guests, with Farmer Crouder,
  Began to prate of corn ;
And we found out they talked the louder,
  The oftener passed the horn.

"Out came the nuts ; we set a-cracking,
  The ale came round our way ;
By gom, we women fell a-clacking
  As loud again as they.

"John sung 'Old Benbow' loud and strong,
  And I, 'The Constant Swain ;'
'Cheer up, my Lads,' was Simon's song,
  'We'll conquer them again.'

"Now twelve o'clock was drawing nigh,
  And all in merry cue ;
I knocked the cask : 'O ho !' said I,
  'We've almost conquered you.'

"My Lord begged round, and held his hat ;—
  Says Farmer Gruff, says he,
'There's many a Lord, Sam, I know that,
  Has begged as well as thee.'

"Bump in his hat the shillings tumbled
  All round among the folks ;
Laugh if you wool,' said Sam, and mumbled,
  'You pay for all your jokes.'

"Joint stock, you know, among the men,
  To drink at their own charges ;
So up they got full drive, and then
  Went out to halloo largess.

"And sure enough the noise they made !—
  —But let me mind my tale ;
We followed them, we wor'nt afraid,
  We had all been drinking ale.

"As they stood hallooing back to back,
    We, lightly as a feather,
Went sideling round, and in a crack
    Had pinned their coats together.

"'Twas near upon't as light as noon;
    'A largess,' on the hill,
They shouted to the full round moon,—
    I think I hear 'em still!

"But when they found the trick, my stars!
    They well knew who to blame;
Our giggles turned to ha ha ha's,
    And arter us they came.

"Grace by the tumbril made a squat,
    Then ran as Sam came by;
They said she could not run for fat,—
    I know she did not try.

"Sue round the neathouse [1] squalling ran,
    Where Simon scarcely dare;
He stopped,—for he's a fearful man——
    'By gom there's suffen [2] there!

"And off set John, with all his might,
    To chase me down the yard,
Till I was nearly graned [3] outright;
    He hugged so woundly hard.

"Still they kept up the race and laugh,
    And round the house we flew;
But hark ye! the best fun by half
    Was Simon arter Sue.

"She cared not, dark nor light, not she;
    So, near the dairy door
She passed a clean white hog, you see,
    They'd kilt the day before.

"High on the spirket [4] there it hung,—
    'Now Susie—what can save ye?'
Round the cold pig his arms he flung,
    And cried 'Ah! here I have ye!'

"The farmers heard what Simon said,
    And what a noise! good lack!
Some almost laughed themselves to dead,
    And others clapped his back.

---

[1] Cow-house.   [2] Something.   [3] Strangled.   [4] An iron hook.

"We all at once began to tell
  What fun we had abroad;
But Simon stood our jeers right well;
  —He fell asleep and snored.

"Then in his button-hole upright
  Did Farmer Crouder put
A slip of paper twisted tight,
  And held the candle to't.

"It smoked, and smoked, beneath his nose,
  The harmless blaze crept higher;
Till with a vengeance up he rose,
  'Grace, Judie, Sue! fire, fire!'

"The clock struck one—some talked of parting,
  Some said it was a sin,
And hitched their chairs;—but those for starting
  Now let the moonlight in.

"Owd women, loitering for the nonce,[1]
  Stood praising the fine weather;
The menfolks took the hint at once
  To kiss them all together.

"And out ran every soul beside,
  A shanny-pated[2] crew;
Owd folks could neither run nor hide,
  So some ketched one, some tew.

"They skriggled[3] and began to scold,
  But laughing got the master;
Some quackling[4] cried, 'let go your hold;'
  The farmers held the faster.

"All innocent, that I'll be sworn,
  There wor'nt a bit of sorrow;
And women, if their gowns *are* torn,
  Can mend them on the morrow.

"Our shadows helter skelter danced
  About the moonlight ground;
The wondering sheep, as on we pranced,
  Got up and gazed around.

"And well they might—till Farmer Cheerum
  Now with a hearty glee
Bade all good morn as he came near 'em,
  And then to bed went he.

---

[1] For the purpose.   [2] Giddy, thoughtless.
[3] To struggle quick.   [4] Choking.

"Then off we strolled this way and that,
    With merry voices ringing;
And Echo answered us right pat,
    As home we rambled singing.

"For, when we laughed, it laughed again,
    And to our own doors followed.
'Yo ho!' we cried; 'Yo ho!' so plain
    The misty meadow hallooed.

That's all my tale, and all the fun;
    Come, turn your wheels about;
My worsted, see!—that's nicely done,
    Just held my story out!"

Poor Judie!—Thus Time knits or spins
    The worsted from Life's ball!
Death stopped thy tales, and stopped thy pins,
    —And so he'll serve us all.

RICHARD ALFRED MILLIKIN.

[Born in the county of Cork, 1767; died in 1815. Was an attorney in Cork, but not very zealous in his profession, having more taste for literature and for drawing. He had some reputation as an amateur artist, and was active in founding a Society for the Promotion of the Fine Arts in Cork. He published *The Riverside*, a blank-verse poem, in 1807. One of his compositions was the famous song, *The Groves of Blarney*.

THE FAIR MAID OF PASSAGE.[1]

O FAIR maid of Passage,
    As plump as a sassage,
And as mild as a kitten,
    Those eyes in your face!—
    Yerrah! pity my case,
For poor Dermuid is smitten!
    Far softer nor silk,
    And more white than new milk,
Oh your lily-white hand is;
    Your lips red as cherries,
    And your eyes like blackberries,
And you're straight as a wand is!

    Your talk is so quare,
    And your sweet curly hair,
Is as black as the devil;
    And your breath is as sweet, too,
    As any potatoe,
Or orange from Seville.

---

[1] Passage is the town now named Queenstown, Cork.

When dressed in her boddice
She trips like a goddess,
So nimble, so frisky;
One kiss from her cheek,
'Tis so soft and so sleek
That 'twould warm me like whisky.

So I sobs and I pine,
And I grunts like a swine,
Because you're so cruel;
No rest can I take,
All asleep or awake,
But I dreams of my jewel.
Your hate, then, give over,
Nor Dermuid, your lover,
So cruelly handle;
Or, faith, Dermuid must die,
Like a pig in a stye,
Or the snuff of a candle.

SIMON QUIN.[1]

THE TOWN OF PASSAGE.

THE town of Passage is neat and spacious,
All situated upon the sea;
The ships a-floating, and the youths a-boating,
With their cotton coats on each summer's day.
'Tis there you'd see, both night and morning,
The men of war, with fresh-flowing sails;
The bould lieutenants, and the tars so jolly,
All steering for Cork in a hackney chaise.

'Tis there's a stature drawn after nature,
A leaping from the mud upon the dry land;
A lion or a leopard, or some fierce creature,
With a Reading-made-easy all in his hand.[2]
There's a rendez-vous house for each bould hero
For to take on, whose heart beats high;
The colours a-drooping, and the children's rockets
All pinned across it, hanging out to dry.

'Tis there's a Strand too, that's decked with oar-weeds,
And tender gob-stones[3] and mussel-shells;
And there's skeehories,[4] and what still more is,
A comely fresh-flowing water rill.

---

[1] I am unable to give any particulars concerning this writer. His poem is inserted in Crofton Croker's *Popular Songs of Ireland*, 1839: it appears to be the first form of a ballad which has been retouched by various hands, and has been popular under all.

[2] The figure-head of an old ship.   [3] Round pebbles.   [4] Hawthorn berries.

'Tis there the ladies, when break of day is,
   And tender lovers, do often pelt ;
Some a-airing and some a-bathing,
   All mother-naked, to enjoy their health.

And there's a ferry-boat that's quite convenient,
   Where man and horses do take a ride ;
'Tis there in clover you may pass over
   To Carrigaloe on the other side.
There may be seen O ! the sweet Marino,[1]
   With its trees so green O ! and fruit so red ;
Brave White Point, and right fornent it
   The Giant's Stairs, and sweet Horse's Head.

There's a house of lodgings at one Molly Bowen's,
   Where often goes in one Simon Quin ;
Oh ! 'tis there without a coat on, you'd hear her grope on
   The door to open, to let him in.
Then straight up stairs one pair of windows,
   With but the slates betwixt him and the sky ;
Oh 'tis there till morning the fleas all swarming
   Do keep him warm in where he does lie.

MATTHEW GREGORY LEWIS.

[Born in London in 1773, son of a West-India planter, and deputy-secretary in the War-Office ; died in the Gulf of Florida, July 1818. Lewis was partly educated in Germany, which may have served to develop his peculiar taste for the horrible, supernatural, and grotesque. His first work was the once highly celebrated romance of *The Monk*, published in 1795 : hence his ordinary nickname "Monk Lewis." *Tales of Terror, Tales of Wonder*, and other volumes in verse and in prose, followed : his play of *The Castle Spectre* was a conspicuous public success. Lewis entered parliament, but soon retired thence. He was a man of fashion, of a volatile mercurial nature, which, along with his very diminutive stature, exposed him to some ridicule. At the same time, he was truly good-hearted, and in many respects estimable : Walter Scott has termed him " one of the kindest and best creatures that ever lived." He took two voyages to the West Indies, in 1815 and 1817, to look after his property there, and partly to assure himself that the slaves upon his estates received humane treatment. It was on returning from the second of these voyages that he died at sea, of a fever. At first it was rumoured that his philanthropic feelings had cost him his life : one of his slaves was said to have given him poison, in order to hasten the emancipation which, as announced by Lewis himself, would be accorded to all of them on the occurrence of his death].

GRIM, KING OF THE GHOSTS; OR, THE DANCE OF DEATH.

A CHURCHYARD TALE.

" WHY, how now, old sexton ? why shake you with dread ?
   Why haunt you this street, where you're sure to catch cold ?
Full warm is your blanket, full snug is your bed !
   And long since, by the steeple-chimes, twelve has been told."

---

[1] The seat of Savage French, Esq., on the Great Island.

" Tom Tap, on this night my retreat you'll approve,
 For my churchyard will swarm with its shroud-covered hosts;
Who will tell, with loud shriek, that resentment and love
 Still nip the cold heart of Grim, King of the Ghosts.

" One eve, as the fiend wandered through the thick gloom,
 Towards my newly-tiled cot he directed his sight;
And, casting a glance in my little back-room,
 Gazed on Nancy, my daughter, with wanton delight.

" Yet Nancy was proud, and disdainful was she,
 In affection's fond speech she'd no pleasure or joy;
And vainly he sued, though he knelt at her knee,
 Bob Brisket, so comely, the young butcher's boy!

" ' For you, dearest Nancy, I've oft been a thief,
 Yet my theft it was venial, a theft if it be;
For who could have eyes, and not see you loved beef?
 Or who see a steak and not steal it for thee?

" ' Remember, dear beauty, dead flesh cannot feel;
 With frowns you my heart and its passion requite;
Yet oft have I seen you, when hungry at meal,
 On a dead bullock's heart gaze with tender delight.

" ' When you dress it for dinner, so hard and so tough,
 I wish the employ your stern breast would improve;
And, the dead bullock's heart while with onions you stuff,
 You would stuff your own heart, cruel virgin, with love.'

" ' Young rascal! presum'st thou, with butcher-like phrase,
 To foul stinking onions *my* love to compare,
Who have set Wick, the candle-man, all in a blaze,
 And Alderman Paunch, who has since been the Mayor?

" ' You bid me remember dead flesh cannot feel?
 Then I vow, by my father's old pickaxe and spade,
Till some prince from the tombs shall behave so genteel
 As to ask me to wed, I'll continue a maid!

" ' Nor him will I wed, till (these terms must he own)
 Of my two first commands the performance he boasts.'—
Straight, instead of a footman, a deep-pealing groan
 Announced the approach of Grim, King of the Ghosts!

" No flesh had the spectre, his skeleton skull
 Was loosely wrapped round with a brown shrivelled skin;
His bones, 'stead of marrow, of maggots were full,
 And the worms they crawled out, and the worms they crawled in.

" His shoes they were coffins, his dim eye revealed
    The gleam of a grave-lamp with vapours oppressed ;
And a dark crimson necklace of blood-drops congealed
    Reflected each bone that jagged out of his breast.

" In a hoarse hollow whisper—' Thy beauties,' he cried,
    ' Have drawn up a spirit to give thee a kiss ;
No butcher shall call thee, proud Nancy, his bride ;
    The grim King of Spectres demands thee for his.

" ' My name frightens infants, my word raises ghosts,
    My tread wakes the echoes which breathe through the aisle ;
And lo ! here stands the Prince of the Churchyard, who boasts
    The will to perform thy commands, for a smile.'

" He said, and he kissed her : she packed up her clothes,
    And straight they eloped through the window with joy ;
Yet long in her ears rang the curses and oaths
    Which growled at his rival the gruff butcher's boy.

" At the charnel-house palace soon Nancy arrived,
    When the fiend, with a grin which her soul did appal,
Exclaimed—' I must warn my pale subjects I'm wived,
    And bid them prepare a grand supper and ball !'—

" Thrice swifter than thought on his heel round he turns,
    Three capers he cut, and then motionless stood ;
Then on cards, made of dead men's skin, Nancy discerns
    His lank fingers to scrawl invitations in blood.

" His quill was a wind-pipe, his ink-horn a skull,
    A blade-bone his pen-knife, a tooth was his seal ;
Soon he ordered the cards, in a voice deep and dull,
    To haste and invite all his friends to the meal.

" Away flew the cards to the south and the north,
    Away flew the cards to the east and the west ;
Straight with groans, from their tombs, the pale spectres stalked
        forth,
    In deadly apparel and shrouding-sheets dressed.

" And quickly scared Nancy, with anxious affright,
    Hears the tramp of a steed, and a knock at the gate ;
On an hell-horse so gaunt 'twas a grim ghastly sprite,
    On a pillion behind a she-skeleton sate !

" The poor maiden she thought 'twas a dream or a trance,
    While the guests they assembled gigantic and tall ;
Each sprite asked a skeleton lady to dance,
    And King Grim with fair Nancy now opened the ball.

" Pale spectres send music from dark vaults above,
 Withered legs, 'stead of drum-sticks, they brandish on high ;
Grinning ghosts, sheeted spirits, skipping skeletons, move,
 While hoarse whispers and rattling of bones shake the sky.

" With their pliable joints the Scotch steps they do well,
 Nancy's hand with their cold clammy fingers they squeeze ;
Now sudden, appalled, the maid hears a death-bell,
 And straight dark and dismal the supper she sees !

" A tomb was the table : now each took his seat,
 Every sprite next his partner so pale and so wan.
Soon as ceased was the rattling of skeleton feet,
 The clattering of jaw-bones directly began.

" Of dead aldermen's fat the mould candles were made,
 Stuck in sockets of bone they gleamed dimly and blue ;
Their dishes were scutcheons, and corses decayed
 Were the viands that glutted this ravenous crew !

" Through the nostrils of skulls their blood-liquor they pour,
 The black draught in the heads of young infants they quaff.
The vice-president rose, with his jaws dripping gore,
 And addressed the pale damsel with horrible laugh.

" ' Feast, Queen of the Ghosts ! the repast do not scorn ;
 Feast, Queen of the Ghosts ! I perceive thou hast food ;
To-morrow again shall we feast, for at noon
 Shall we feast on thy flesh, shall we drink of thy blood.'—

" Then cold as a cucumber Nancy she grew ;
 Her proud stomach came down, and she blared, and she cried,
' Oh tell me, dear Grim, does that spectre speak true,
 And will you not save from his clutches your bride ? '

" ' Vain your grief, silly maid ; when the matin-bells ring,
 The bond becomes due which long since did I sign ;
For she who at night weds the grizzly Ghost King
 Next morn must be dressed for his subjects to dine.'—

" ' In silks and in satins for *you* I'll be dressed ;
 My soft tender limbs let *their* fangs never crunch.' "—
' Fair Nancy, yon ghosts, should I grant your request,
 Instead of at dinner would eat you at lunch ! '—

" ' But vain, ghostly King, is your cunning and guile ;
 That bond must be void which you never can pay ;
Lo ! I ne'er will be yours, till, to purchase my smile,
 My two first commands (as you swore) you obey.'

" ' Well say'st thou, fair Nancy ; thy wishes impart ;
   But think not to puzzle Grim, King of the Ghosts.'
" Straight she turns o'er each difficult task in her heart,
   And—' I've found out a poser,' exultingly boasts.

" ' You vowed that no *butcher* should call me his bride.
   That this vow you fulfil my first asking shall be ;
And, since so many maids in your clutches have died,
   Than yourself show a *bloodier butcher*,'—said she.

" Then shrill scream the spectres ; the charnel-house gloom
   Swift lightnings disperse, and the palace destroy ;
Again Nancy stood in the little back-room,
   And again at her knee knelt the young butcher's boy !

" ' I'll have done with dead husbands,' she Brisket bespeaks ;
   ' I'll now take a live one, so fetch me a ring ! '—
And when pressed to her lips were his red beefin cheeks,
   She loved him much more than the shrivelled Ghost King.

" No longer his steaks and his cutlets she spurns,
   No longer he fears his grim rival's pale band ;
Yet still when the famed *first of April* returns,
   The sprites rise in squadrons, and Nancy demand.

" This informs you, Tom Tap, why to-night I remove,
   For I dread the approach of the shroud-covered hosts,
Who tell, with loud shriek, that resentment and love
   Still nip the cold heart of Grim, King of the Ghosts ! "

ROBERT SOUTHEY.

[Born in Bristol, the son of a linen-draper, 4 October 1774 ; died, 21 March 1843. In the opening years of the French Revolution, Southey was a free-thinker in both politics and religion ; but this phase of feeling soon passed, and he became as doggedly conservative in his own person as he was pertinaciously virulent against thinkers of a different school. To name Byron and Shelley is, at the present day, to reduce Southey almost to a condition of ignominy. This is a fitting retribution. Nevertheless the literary enquirer will discover Southey to have been a man of marked ability, with much ambition and variety of aim as a poet, and some vocation too, if *aptitude* could be regarded as *faculty* in poetic matters : and, along with these merits as a man of letters, the uniform testimony of those who knew him establishes Southey's sterling personal qualities. He settled at Greta, near Keswick, Cumberland, towards 1804 ; and succeeded Pye as Poet Laureate in 1813].

TO A GOOSE.

IF thou didst feed on western plains of yore ;
Or waddle wide with flat and flabby feet
Over some Cambrian mountain's plashy moor ;
Or find in farmer's yard a safe retreat
From gipsy thieves, and foxes sly and fleet ;
If thy great quills, by lawyer guided, trace
Deeds big with ruin to some wretched race,

Or love-sick poet's sonnet, sad and sweet,
  Wailing the rigour of his lady fair;
Or if, the drudge of housemaid's daily toil,
  Cobwebs and dust thy pinions white besoil,
Departed Goose! I neither know nor care.
But this I know, that we pronounced thee fine,
Seasoned with sage and onions, and port wine.

THE POET RELATES HOW HE STOLE A LOCK OF DELIA'S HAIR, AND HER ANGER.

OH! be the day accurst that gave me birth!
  Ye seas, to swallow me, in kindness rise!
Fall on me, mountains! and thou, merciful earth,
  Open, and hide me from my Delia's eyes!

Let universal chaos now return,
  Now let the central fires their prison burst,
And earth and heaven and air and ocean burn—
  For Delia frowns—she frowns, and I am curst!

Oh! I could dare the fury of the fight,
  Where hostile millions sought my single life;
Would storm volcano batteries with delight,
  And grapple with grim death in glorious strife.

Oh! I could brave the bolts of angry Jove,
  When ceaseless lightnings fire the midnight skies;
What is his wrath to that of her I love?
  What is his lightning to my Delia's eyes?

Go, fatal lock! I cast thee to the wind;
  Ye serpent curls, ye poison-tendrils, go!
Would I could tear thy memory from my mind,
  Accursed lock,—thou cause of all my woe!

Seize the curst curls, ye Furies, as they fly!
  Demons of darkness, guard the infernal roll,
That thence your cruel vengeance, when I die,
  May knit the knots of torture for my soul.

Last night,—Oh hear me, Heaven, and grant my prayer!
  The book of fate before thy suppliant lay,
And let me from its ample records tear
  Only the single page of yesterday.

Or let me meet old Time upon his flight,
  And I will stop him on his restless way:
Omnipotent in Love's resistless might,
  I'll force him back the road of yesterday.

Last night, as o'er the page of love's despair
  My Delia bent deliciously to grieve,
I stood a treacherous loiterer by her chair,
  And drew the fatal scissors from my sleeve;

And would that at that instant o'er my thread
  The shears of Atropos had opened then,
And, when I reft the lock from Delia's head,
  Had cut me sudden from the sons of men!

She heard the scissors that fair lock divide;
  And, whilst my heart with transport panted big,
She cast a fury frown on me, and cried,
  "You stupid Puppy,—you have spoiled my wig!"

EPISTLE TO ALLAN CUNNINGHAM.

WELL, Heaven be thanked! friend Allan, here I am,
Once more to that dear dwelling-place returned
Where I have passed the whole mid stage of life,
Not idly, certes; not unworthily,—
So let me hope: where Time upon my head
Hath laid his frore and monitory hand;
And when this poor frail earthly tabernacle
Shall be dissolved,—it matters not how soon
Or late, in God's good time,—where I would fain
Be gathered to my children, earth to earth.

  Needless it were to say how willingly
I bade the huge metropolis farewell,
Its din, and dust, and dirt, and smoke, and smut,
Thames water, paviour's ground, and London sky;
Weary of hurried days and restless nights,
Watchmen, whose office is to murder sleep
When sleep might else have weighed one's eyelids down,
Rattle of carriages, and roll of carts,
And tramp of iron hoofs; and worse than all
(Confusion being worse confounded then
With coachmen's quarrels and with footmen's shouts)
My next-door neighbours, in a street not yet
Macadamized, (me miserable!) *at home;*
For then had we from midnight until morn
House-quakes, street-thunders, and door-batteries.
O Government! in thy wisdom and thy want,
Tax knockers;—in compassion to the sick,
And those whose sober habits are not yet
Inverted, topsy-turvying night and day,
Tax them more heavily than thou hast charged
Armorial bearings and bepowdered pates.

And thou, O Michael, ever to be praised,
Angelic among Taylors, for thy laws
Antifuliginous, extend those laws
Till every chimney its own smoke consume,
And give thenceforth thy dinners unlampooned.
Escaping from all this, the very whirl
Of mail-coach wheels bound outward from Lad-lane
Was peace and quietness. Three hundred miles
Of homeward way seemed to the body rest,
And to the mind repose.
     Donne[1] did not hate
More perfectly that city. Not for all
Its social, all its intellectual joys,—
Which having touched, I may not condescend
To name aught else the Demon of the place
Might for his lure hold forth,—not even for these
Would I forego gardens and green-field walks,
And hedge-row trees, and stiles, and shady lanes,
And orchards, were such ordinary scenes
Alone to me accessible as those
Wherein I learnt in infancy to love
The sights and sounds of nature;—wholesome sights
Gladdening the eye that they refresh ; and sounds
Which, when from life and happiness they spring,
Bear with them to the yet unhardened heart
A sense that thrills its chords of sympathy;
Or, when proceeding from insensate things,
Give to tranquillity a voice wherewith
To woo the ear and win the soul attuned.—
Oh not for all that London might bestow
Would I renounce the genial influences
And thoughts and feelings to be found where'er
We breathe beneath the open sky, and see
Earth's liberal bosom. Judge then by thyself,
Allan, true child of Scotland,—thou who art
So oft in spirit on thy native hills,
And yonder Solway shores,—a poet thou,
Judge by thyself how strong the ties which bind
A poet to his home; when,—making thus
Large recompense for all that haply else
Might seem perversely or unkindly done,—
Fortune hath set his happy habitacle
Among the ancient hills, near mountain-streams
And lakes pellucid, in a land sublime
And lovely as those regions of Romance

---

[1] This poet begins his second Satire thus:—
 "Sir, though (I thank God for it) I do hate
 Perfectly all this town, yet there's one state
 In all ill things so excellently best
 That hate towards them breeds pity towards the rest."

Where his young fancy in his day-dreams roamed,
Expatiating in forests wild and wide,
Loëgrian, or of dearest Faery-land.

   Yet, Allan, of the cup of social joy
No man drinks freelier, nor with heartier thirst,
Nor keener relish, where I see around
Faces which I have known and loved so long
That, when he prints a dream upon my brain,
Dan Morpheus takes them for his readiest types.
And therefore in that loathed metropolis
Time measured out to me some golden hours.
They were not leaden-footed while the clay
Beneath the patient touch of Chantrey's hand
Grew to the semblance of my lineaments.
Lit up in memory's landscape, like green spots
Of sunshine, are the mornings when in talk
With him and thee, and Bedford (my true friend
Of forty years), I saw the work proceed,
Subject the while myself to no restraint,
But pleasurably in frank discourse engaged:
Pleased too, and with no unbecoming pride,
To think this countenance, such as it is,
So oft by rascally mislikeness wronged,
Should faithfully, to those who in his works
Have seen the inner man pourtrayed, be shown,
And in enduring marble should partake
Of our great sculptor's immortality.

   I have been libelled, Allan, as thou knowest,
Through all degrees of calumny; but they
Who fix one's name for public sale beneath
A set of features slanderously unlike
Are the worst libellers. Against the wrong
Which *they* inflict Time hath no remedy.
Injuries there are which Time redresseth best,
Being more sure in judgment, though perhaps
Slower in process even, than the court
Where Justice, tortoise-footed and mole-eyed,
Sleeps undisturbed, fanned by the lulling wings
Of harpies at their prey. We soon live down
Evil or good report, if undeserved.
Let then the dogs of Faction bark and bay,
Its bloodhounds, savaged by a cross of wolf,
Its full-bred kennel from the Blatant-beast;
And from my lady's gay veranda let
Her pampered lap-dog with his fetid breath
In bold bravado join, and snap and growl,
With petulant consequentialness elate,
There in his imbecility at once

Ridiculous and safe; though all give cry,
Whiggery's sleek spaniels, and its lurchers lean,
Its poodles by unlucky training marred,
Mongrel and cur and bob-tail, let them yelp
Till weariness and hoarseness shall at length
Silence the noisy pack; meantime be sure
I will not stoop for stones to cast among them.
The foumarts and the skunks may be secure
In their own scent; and, for that viler swarm,
The vermin of the press, both those that skip,
And those that creep and crawl, I do not catch
And pin them for exposure on the page,—
Their filth is their defence.
      But I appeal
Against the limner's and the graver's wrong;
Their evil works survive them. Bilderdijk
Whom I am privileged to call my friend,
Suffering by graphic libels in like wise,
Gave his wrath vent in verse. Would I could give
The life and spirit of his vigorous Dutch,
As his dear consort hath transfused *my* strains
Into her native speech, and made them known
On Rhine and Yssel, and rich Amstel's banks,
And wheresoe'er the voice of Vondel still
Is heard, and still Antonides and Hooft
Are living agencies, and Father Cats,
The household poet, teacheth in his songs
The love of all things lovely, all things pure:
Best poet, who delights the cheerful mind
Of childhood, stores with moral strength the heart
Of youth, with wisdom maketh mid-life rich,
And fills with quiet tears the eyes of age.

  Hear then in English rhyme how Bilderdijk
Describes his wicked portraits, one by one.

"A madman who from Bedlam hath broke loose:
 An honest fellow of the numskull race;
And pappyer-headed still, a very goose
 Staring with eyes aghast and vacant face;
A Frenchman who would mirthfully display
 On some poor idiot his malicious wit;
And lastly one who, trained up in the way
 Of worldly craft, hath not forsaken it,
But hath served Mammon with his whole intent,
 A thing of Nature's worst materials made,
Low-minded, stupid, base, and insolent.
 I, I, a poet, have been thus pourtrayed.
Can ye believe that my true effigy
 Among these vile varieties is found?

What thought, or line, or word, hath fallen from me
  In all my numerous works whereon to ground
The opprobrious notion? Safely I may smile
  At these, acknowledging no likeness here.
But worse is yet to come ; so, soft awhile !
  For now in potter's earth must I appear,
And in such workmanship that, sooth to say,
  Humanity disowns the imitation,
And the dolt image is not worth its clay.
  Then comes there one who will to admiration
In plastic wax my perfect face present ;
  And what of his performance comes at last ?
Folly itself in every lineament !
  Its consequential features overcast
With the coxcombical and shallow laugh
  Of one who would for condescension hide,
Yet in his best behaviour can but half
  Suppress, the scornfulness of empty pride."

"And who is Bilderdijk?" methinks thou sayest ;
A ready question ; yet which, trust me, Allan,
Would not be asked, had not the curse that came
From Babel clipped the wings of Poetry.
Napoleon asked him once with cold fixed look,
"Art thou then in the world of letters known ?"
"I have deserved to be," the Hollander
Replied, meeting that proud imperial look
With calm and proper confidence, and eye
As little wont to turn away abashed
Before a mortal presence. He is one
Who hath received upon his constant breast
The sharpest arrows of adversity ;
Whom not the clamours of the multitude,
Demanding in their madness and their might
Iniquitous things, could shake in his firm mind ;
Nor the strong hand of instant tyranny
From the straight path of duty turn aside ;
But who in public troubles, in the wreck
Of his own fortunes, in proscription, exile,
Want, obloquy, ingratitude, neglect,
And what severer trials Providence
Sometimes inflicteth, chastening whom it loves,
In all, through all, and over all, hath borne
An equal heart, as resolute toward
The world as humbly and religiously
Beneath his heavenly Father's rod resigned.
Right-minded, happy-minded, righteous man,
True lover of his country and his kind ;
In knowledge and in inexhaustive stores
Of native genius rich ; philosopher,

Poet, and sage. The language of a state
Inferior in illustrious deeds to none,
But circumscribed by narrow bounds, and now
Sinking in irrecoverable decline,
Hath pent within its sphere a name wherewith
Europe should else have rung from side to side.

 Such, Allan, is the Hollander to whom
Esteem and admiration have attached
My soul, not less than pre-consent of mind,
And gratitude for benefits, when, being
A stranger, sick, and in a foreign land,
He took me like a brother to his house,
And ministered to me, and made a time
Which had been wearisome and careful else
So pleasurable that in my kalendar
There are no whiter days. 'Twill be a joy
For us to meet in heaven, though we should look
Upon each other's earthly face no more.
—This is this world's complexion! " cheerful thoughts
Bring sad thoughts to the mind," and these again
Give place to calm content, and steadfast hope,
And happy faith assured.—Return we now,
With such transition as our daily life
Imposes in its wholesome discipline,
To a lighter strain ; and, from the gallery
Of the Dutch poet's mis-resemblances,
Pass into mine ; where I shall show thee, Allan,
Such an array of villainous visages
That, if among them all there were but one
Which as a likeness could be proved upon me,
It were enough to make me in mere shame
Take up an alias, and forswear myself.

 Whom have we first ? A dainty gentleman,
His sleepy eyes half-closed, and countenance
To no expression stronger than might suit
A simper capable of being moved :
Sawney and sentimental ; with an air
So lack-thought and so lackadaisical
You might suppose the volume in his hand
Must needs be Zimmermann on Solitude.

 Then comes a jovial landlord, who hath made it
Part of his trade to be the shoeing-horn
For his commercial customers. Good Bacchus
Hath not a thirstier votary. Many a pipe
Of Porto's vintage hath contributed
To give his cheeks that deep carmine engrained,
And many a runlet of right Nantes, I ween,

Hath suffered percolation through that trunk,
Leaving behind it in the boozy eyes
A swoln and red suffusion, glazed and dim.

Our next is in the evangelical line,
A leaden-visaged specimen; demure,
Because he hath put on his Sunday's face;
Dull by formation, by complexion sad,
By bile, opinions, and dyspepsy, sour.
One of the sons of Jack,—I know not which,
For Jack hath a most numerous progeny,—
Made up for Mr. Colburn's Magazine,
This pleasant composite; a bust supplied
The features; look, expression, character,
Are of the artist's fancy and free grace.
Such was that fellow's birth and parentage.
The rascal proved prolific; one of his breed,
By Docteur Pichot introduced in France,
Passes for Monsieur Sooté; and another—
An uglier miscreant too—the brothers Schumann,
And their most cruel copper-scratcher Zschoch,
From Zwickau sent abroad through Germany.
I wish the Schumen and the copper-scratcher
No worse misfortune for their recompence
Than to encounter such a cut-throat face
In the Black Forest or the Odenwald.

And now is there a third derivative
From Mr. Colburn's composite, which late
The Arch-Pirate Galignani hath prefixed,
A spurious portrait to a faithless life,
And bearing lyingly the libelled name
Of Lawrence, impudently there insculpt.

The bust that was the innocent forefather
To all this base abominable brood
I blame not, Allan. 'Twas the work of Smith,
A modest, mild, ingenious man; and errs,
Where erring, only because over-true,
Too close a likeness for similitude;
Fixing to every part and lineament
Its separate character, and missing thus
That which results from all.
      Sir Smug comes next;
Allan, I own Sir Smug! I recognise
That visage with its dull sobriety.
I see it duly as the day returns,
When at the looking-glass with lathered chin
And razor-weaponed hand I sit, the face
Composed and apprehensively intent

X

Upon the necessary operation
About to be performed, with touch, alas,
Not always confident of hair-breadth skill.
Even in such sober sadness, and constrained
Composure cold, the faithful Painter's eye
Had fixed me like a spell, and I could feel
My features stiffen as he glanced upon them.
And yet he was a man whom I loved dearly,
My fellow-traveller, my familiar friend,
My household guest. But, when he looked upon me,
Anxious to exercise his excellent art,
The countenance he knew so thoroughly
Was gone, and in its stead there sate Sir Smug.

  Under the graver's hand, Sir Smug became
Sir Smouch,—a son of Abraham. Now albeit
Far rather would I trace my lineage thence
Than with the oldest line of Peers or Kings
Claim consanguinity, that cast of features
Would ill accord with me, who, in all forms
Of pork (baked, roasted, toasted, boiled, or broiled,
Fresh, salted, pickled, seasoned, moist or dry,
Whether ham, bacon, sausage, souse, or brawn,
Leg, bladebone, baldrib, griskin, chine, or chop),
Profess myself a genuine Philopig.

  It was, however, as a Jew whose portion
Had fallen unto him in a goodly land
Of loans, of omnium, and of three per cents,
That Messrs. Percy of the Anecdote-firm
Presented me unto their customers.
Poor Smouch endured a worse judaization
Under another hand. In this next stage
He is on trial at the Old Bailey, charged
With dealing in base coin. That he is guilty
No Judge or Jury could have half a doubt
When they saw the culprit's face; and he himself,
As you may plainly see, is comforted
By thinking he has just contrived to keep
Out of rope's reach, and will come off this time
For transportation.   Stand thou forth for trial,
Now, William Darton, of the Society
Of Friends called Quakers; thou who in 4th month
Of the year 24, on Holborn Hill,
At No. 58, didst wilfully,
Falsely, and knowing it was falsely done,
Publish upon a card, as Robert Southey's,
A face which might be just as like Tom Fool's,
Or John or Richard Any-body-else's!

What had I done to thee, thou William Darton,
That thou shouldst for the lucre of base gain,
Yea, for the sake of filthy fourpences,
Palm on my countrymen that face for mine?
O William Darton, let the Yearly Meeting
Deal with thee for that falseness! All the rest
Are traceable; Smug's Hebrew family;
The German who might properly adorn
A gibbet or a wheel, and Monsieur Sooté,
Sons of Fitzbust the Evangelical;—
I recognize all these unlikenesses,
Spurious abominations though they be,
Each filiated on some original;
But thou, Friend Darton (and observe me, man,
Only in courtesy, and *quasi* Quaker,
I call thee Friend) hadst no original;
No likeness or unlikeness, *silhouette*,
Outline, or plaster, representing me,
Whereon to form thy misrepresentation.
If I guess rightly at the pedigree
Of thy bad groatsworth, thou didst get a barber
To personate my injured Laureateship;
An advertising barber,—one who keeps
A bear, and, when he puts to death poor Bruin,
Sells his grease, fresh as from the carcass cut,
Pro bono publico, the price per pound
Twelve shillings and no more. From such a barber,
O unfriend Darton! was that portrait made,
I think, or peradventure from his block.

Next comes a minion worthy to be set
In a wooden frame; and here I might invoke
Avenging Nemesis, if I did not feel
Just now God Cynthius pluck me by the ear.
But, Allan, in what shape God Cynthius comes,
And wherefore he admonisheth me thus,
Nor thou nor I will tell the world; hereafter
The commentators, my Malones and Reids,
May if they can. For in my gallery
Though there remaineth undescribed good store,
Yet " of enough enough, and now no more"
(As honest old George Gascoigne said of yore);
Save only a last couplet to express
That I am always truly yours,
                       R. S.

Keswick, August 1828.

THE PIOUS PAINTER.

The legend of the Pious Painter is related in the *Pia Hilaria* of Gazæus; but the Pious Poet has omitted the second part of the story, though it rests upon quite as good authority as the first. It is to be found in the *Fabliaux* of Le Grand.

THE FIRST PART.

THERE once was a painter in Catholic days,
    Like Job who eschewed all evil.
Still on his Madonnas the curious may gaze
With applause and with pleasure: but chiefly his praise
    And delight was in painting the Devil.

They were Angels, compared to the devils he drew,
    Who besieged poor St. Anthony's cell;
Such burning hot eyes, such a furnace-like hue!
And round them a sulphurous colouring he threw,
    That their breath seemed of brimstone to smell.

And now had the artist a picture begun;
    'Twas over the Virgin's church-door;
She stood on the Dragon embracing her Son.
Many Devils already the artist had done,
    But this must out-do all before.

The Old Dragon's imps, as they fled through the air,
    At seeing it paused on the wing;
For he had the likeness so just to a hair
That they came, as Apollyon himself had been there,
    To pay their respects to their King.

Every child at beholding it trembled with dread,
    And screamed as he turned away quick.
Not an old woman saw it but, raising her head,
Dropped a bead, made a cross on her wrinkles, and said,
    "Lord keep me from ugly Old Nick!"

What the Painter so earnestly thought on by day
    He sometimes would dream of by night.
But once he was startled as sleeping he lay;
'Twas no fancy, no dream, he could plainly survey
    That the Devil himself was in sight.

"You rascally dauber!" old Beelzebub cries,
    "Take heed how you wrong me again!
Though your caricatures for myself I despise,
Make me handsomer now in the multitude's eyes,
    Or see if I threaten in vain!"

Now the Painter was bold, and religious beside,
    And on faith he had certain reliance;
So carefully he the grim countenance eyed,
And thanked him for sitting, with Catholic pride,
    And sturdily bade him defiance.

Betimes in the morning the Painter arose;
    He is ready as soon as 'tis light.
Every look, every line, every feature, he knows;
'Tis fresh in his eye; to his labour he goes,
    And he has the old Wicked One quite.

Happy man! he is sure the resemblance can't fail;
    The tip of the nose is like fire,
There's his grin and his fangs, and his dragon-like mail,
And the very identical curl of his tail,—
    So that nothing is left to desire.

He looks and retouches again with delight;
    'Tis a portrait complete to his mind;
And, exulting again and again at the sight,
He looks round for applause,—and he sees with affright
    The Original standing behind.

"Fool! Idiot!" old Beelzebub grinned as he spoke,
    And stamped on the scaffold in ire.
The Painter grew pale, for he knew it no joke;
'Twas a terrible height, and the scaffolding broke,—
    The Devil could wish it no higher.

"Help—help! Blessed Mary!" he cried in alarm,
    As the scaffold sunk under his feet.
From the canvas the Virgin extended her arm;
She caught the good Painter, she saved him from harm;
    There were hundreds who saw in the street.

The Old Dragon fled when the wonder he spied,
    And cursed his own fruitless endeavour;
While the Painter called after, his rage to deride,
Shook his pallet and brushes in triumph, and cried,
    "I'll paint thee more ugly than ever!"

THE SECOND PART.

The Painter so pious all praise had acquired
    For defying the malice of Hell;
The Monks the unerring resemblance admired;
Not a Lady lived near but her portrait desired
    From a hand that succeeded so well.

One there was to be painted the number among,
   Of features most fair to behold ;
The country around of fair Marguerite rung ;
Marguerite she was lovely and lively and young,
   Her husband was ugly and old.

O Painter, avoid her ! O Painter, take care,
   For Satan is watchful for you !
Take heed lest you fall in the Wicked One's snare ;
The net is made ready, O Painter, beware
   Of Satan and Marguerite too !

She seats herself now, now she lifts up her head,
   On the artist she fixes her eyes ;
The colours are ready, the canvas is spread,
He lays on the white, and he lays on the red,
   And the features of beauty arise.

He is come to her eyes, eyes so bright and so blue !
   There's a look which he cannot express ;—
His colours are dull to their quick-sparkling hue ;
More and more on the lady he fixes his view,
   On the canvas he looks less and less.

In vain he retouches, her eyes sparkle more,
   And that look which fair Marguerite gave !
Many Devils the Artist had painted of yore,
But he never had tried a live Angel before,
   St. Anthony help him and save !

He yielded, alas ! for the truth must be told,
   To the Woman, the Tempter, and Fate.
It was settled the Lady, so fair to behold,
Should elope from her Husband so ugly and old,
   With the Painter so pious of late.

Now Satan exults in his vengeance complete ;
   To the Husband he makes the scheme known.
Night comes, and the lovers impatiently meet ;
Together they fly, they are seized in the street,
   And in prison the Painter is thrown.

With Repentance, his only companion, he lies,
   And a dismal companion is she !
On a sudden he saw the Old Enemy rise ;
"Now, you villainous dauber !" Sir Beelzebub cries,
   "You are paid for your insults to me !

"But my tender heart you may easily move
   If to what I propose you agree ;
That picture,—be just ! the resemblance improve ;
Make a handsomer portrait ; your chains I'll remove,
   And you shall this instant be free."

Overjoyed, the conditions so easy he hears;
  "I'll make you quite handsome!" he said.
He said, and his chain on the Devil appears;
Released from his prison, released from his fears,
  The Painter is snug in his bed.

At morn he arises, composes his look,
  And proceeds to his work as before.
The people beheld him, the culprit they took;
They thought that the Painter his prison had broke,
  And to prison they led him once more.

They open the dungeon;—behold in his place
  In the corner old Beelzebub lay;
He smirks and he smiles and he leers with a grace,
That the Painter might catch all the charms of his face,
  Then vanished in lightning away.

Quoth the Painter; "I trust you'll suspect me no more,
  Since you find my assertions were true.
But I'll alter the picture above the Church-door,
For he never vouchsafed me a sitting before,
  And I must give the Devil his due."

ST. ROMUALD.

ONE day, it matters not to know
  How many hundred years ago,
  A Frenchman stopped at an inn door:
The Landlord came to welcome him, and cha
      Of this and that,
For he had seen the Traveller there before.

    "Doth holy Romuald dwell
          Still in his cell?"
The Traveller asked; "or is the old man dead?"
    "No; he has left his loving flock, and we
    So great a Christian never more shall see,"
The Landlord answered, and he shook his head.
      "Ah, Sir! we knew his worth!
If ever there did live a saint on earth!—
Why, Sir, he always used to wear a shirt
    For thirty days, all seasons, day and night;
    Good man, he knew it was not right
For Dust and Ashes to fall out with Dirt!
And then he only hung it out in the rain,
      And put it on again.

"There has been perilous work
With him and the Devil there in yonder cell;
For Satan used to maul him like a Turk.
    There they would sometimes fight
        All through a winter's night,
        From sunset until morn,—
He with a cross, the Devil with his horn;
The Devil spitting fire with might and main
Enough to make St. Michael half afraid:
He splashing holy water till he made
        His red hide hiss again,
And the hot vapour filled the smoking cell.
    This was so common that his face became
    All black and yellow with the brimstone flame,—
And then he smelt,—O Lord! how he did smell!

"Then, Sir! to see how he would mortify
    The flesh! If any one had dainty fare,
        Good man, he would come there,
And look at all the delicate things, and cry,
        'O Belly, Belly,
You would be gormandizing now, I know;
        But it shall not be so!—
Home to your bread and water—home, I tell ye!'"

"But," quoth the Traveller, "wherefore did he leave
A flock that knew his saintly worth so well?"
"Why," said the Landlord, "Sir, it so befell
        He heard unluckily of our intent
To do him a great honour: and, you know,
He was not covetous of fame below,
And so by stealth one night away he went."

"What might this honour be?" the Traveller cried.
        "Why, Sir," the Host replied,
"We thought perhaps that he might one day leave us;
        And then, should strangers have
            The good man's grave,
A loss like that would naturally grieve us,
For he'll be made a Saint of, to be sure.
Therefore we thought it prudent to secure
        His relics while we might;
And so we meant to strangle him one night."

CHARLES LAMB.

[Born in London, 18 February 1775; died at Edmonton, 27 December 1834.]

A FAREWELL TO TOBACCO.

MAY the Babylonish curse
Straight confound my stammering verse
If I can a passage see
In this word-perplexity,
Or a fit expression find,
Or a language to my mind
(Still the phrase is wide or scant),
To take leave of thee, Great Plant!
Or in any terms relate
Half my love, or half my hate:
For I hate yet love thee so
That, whichever thing I show,
The plain truth will seem to be
A constrained hyperbole,
And the passion to proceed
More from a mistress than a weed.

Sooty retainer to the vine,
Bacchus' black servant, negro fine;
Sorcerer that mak'st us dote upon
Thy begrimed complexion,
And, for thy pernicious sake,
More and greater oaths to break
Than reclaimèd lovers take
'Gainst women: thou thy siege dost lay
Much, too, in the female way,
While thou suck'st the labouring breath
Faster than kisses, or than death.

Thou in such a cloud dost bind us
That our worst foes cannot find us,
And ill fortune that would thwart us
Shoots at rovers, shooting at us;
While each man, through thy heightening steam,
Does like a smoking Etna seem,
And all about us does express
(Fancy and wit in richest dress)
A Sicilian fruitfulness.

Thou through such a mist dost show us
That our best friends do not know us,
And, for those allowèd features
Due to reasonable creatures,
Liken'st us to fell Chimeras,
Monsters that who see us fear us;
Worse than Cerberus or Geryon,
Or, who first loved a cloud, Ixion.

Bacchus we know, and we allow
His tipsy rites. But what art thou,
That but by reflex canst show
What his deity can do,
As the false Egyptian spell
Aped the true Hebrew miracle?
Some few vapours thou mayst raise
The weak brain may serve to amaze,
But to the reins and nobler heart
Canst nor life nor heat impart.

Brother of Bacchus, later born,
The old world was sure forlorn
Wanting thee, that aidest more
The god's victories than before
All his panthers, and the brawls
Of his piping Bacchanals.
These, as stale, we disallow,
Or judge of *thee* meant: only thou
His true Indian conquest art;
And, for ivy round his dart,
The reformèd god now weaves
A finer thyrsus of thy leaves.

Scent to match thy rich perfume
Chemic art did ne'er presume
Through her quaint alembic strain,
None so sovereign to the brain;
Nature, that did in thee excel,
Framed again no second smell.
Roses, violets, but toys
For the smaller sort of boys,
Or for greener damsels meant;
Thou art the only manly scent.

Stinking'st of the stinking kind,
Filth of the mouth and fog of the mind,
Africa, that brags her foison,
Breeds no such prodigious poison.
Henbane, nightshade, both together,
Hemlock, aconite——

                    Nay, rather,
Plant divine, of rarest virtue;
Blisters on the tongue would hurt you!
'Twas but in a sort I blamed thee;
None e'er prospered who defamed thee.
Irony all, and feigned abuse,
Such as perplexèd lovers use
At a need, when, in despair
To paint forth their fairest fair,

Or in part but to express
That exceeding comeliness
Which their fancies doth so strike,
They borrow language of dislike;
And, instead of Dearest Miss,
Jewel, Honey, Sweetheart, Bliss,
And those forms of old admiring,
Call her Cockatrice and Siren,
Basilisk, and all that's evil,
Witch, Hyena, Mermaid, Devil,
Ethiop, Wench, and Blackamoor,
Monkey, Ape, and twenty more;
Friendly Traitress, loving Foe;—
Not that she is truly so,
But no other way they know
A contentment to express
Borders so upon excess
That they do not rightly wot
Whether it be pain or not.
Or as men constrained to part
With what's nearest to their heart,
While their sorrow's at the height,
Lose discrimination quite,
And their hasty wrath let fall,
To appease their frantic gall,
On the darling thing whatever
Whence they feel it death to sever,
Though it be, as they, perforce,
Guiltless of the sad divorce.

    For I must (nor let it grieve thee,
Friendliest of plants, that I must) leave thee.
For thy sake, Tobacco, I
Would do anything but die,
And but seek to extend my days
Long enough to sing thy praise.
But, as she who once hath been
A king's consort is a queen
Ever after, nor will bate
Any title of her state,
Though a widow or divorced,
So I, from thy converse forced,
The old name and style retain,
A right Katherine of Spain;
And a seat, too, 'mongst the joys
Of the blest Tobacco Boys.
Where, though I, by sour physician,
Am debarred the full fruition
Of thy favours, I may catch
Some collateral sweets, and snatch

Sidelong odours, that give life
Like glances from a neighbour's wife;
And still live in the by-places
And the suburbs of thy graces,
And in thy borders take delight,
An unconquered Canaanite.

JAMES SMITH.

[Born in 1775, son of the solicitor to the Board of Ordnance; died on 24th December 1839. Smith, who succeeded to his father's legal business, was a highly genial and estimable specimen of the man about town—witty, pleasant, and kind-hearted. He wrote very generally in conjunction with his younger brother Horace: thus was produced *Horace in London*, and afterwards (1812) the more famous *Rejected Addresses*, from which our extracts are taken.* He was a great sufferer from gout in his later years.—The reader should understand (if indeed any explanation is needed on the point) that, Drury Lane Theatre having been burned down, the Directors offered a premium for the best poetical address to be spoken at the opening of the re-edified structure: the Smiths seized hold of this idea, concocted addresses in the several styles, not a little burlesqued, of various leading writers of the day; and published the collection under the name of *Rejected Addresses*, to the huge amusement of the public].

THE BABY'S DEBUT.
BY W. WORDSWORTH.

Spoken in the character of Nancy Lake, a girl eight years of age, who is drawn upon the stage in a child's chaise, by Samuel Hughes, her uncle's porter.

My brother Jack was nine in May,
And I was eight on new-year's-day;
  So in Kate Wilson's shop
Papa (he's my papa and Jack's)
Bought me, last week, a doll of wax,
  And brother Jack a top.

Jack's in the pouts, and this it is,—
He thinks mine came to more than his;
  So to my drawer he goes,
Takes out the doll, and oh my stars!
He pokes her head between the bars,
  And melts off half her nose!

Quite cross, a bit of string I beg,
And tie it to his peg-top's peg,
  And bang, with might and main,
Its head against the parlour door:
Off flies the head, and hits the floor,
  And breaks a window pane.

This made him cry with rage and spite:
Well, let him cry, it serves him right.
  A pretty thing, forsooth!
If he's to melt, all scalding hot,
Half my doll's nose, and I am not
  To draw his peg-top's tooth!

Aunt Hannah heard the window break,
And cried, " O naughty Nancy Lake,
   Thus to distress your aunt:
No Drury Lane for you to-day!"
And while papa said, "Pooh, she may!"
   Mamma said, "No, she shan't!"

Well, after many a sad reproach,
They got into a hackney coach,
   And trotted down the street.
I saw them go: one horse was blind,
The tails of both hung down behind,
   Their shoes were on their feet.

The chaise in which poor brother Bill
Used to be drawn to Pentonville
   Stood in the lumber-room:
I wiped the dust from off the top,
While Molly mopped it with a mop,
   And brushed it with a broom.

My uncle's porter, Samuel Hughes,
Came in at six to black the shoes
   (I always talk to Sam):
So what does he but takes and drags
Me in the chaise along the flags,
   And leaves me where I am?

My father's walls are made of brick,
But not so tall, and not so thick,
   As these; and, goodness me!
My father's beams are made of wood,
But never, never half so good
   As these that now I see.

What a large floor! 'tis like a town!
The carpet, when they lay it down,
   Won't hide it, I'll be bound;
And there's a row of lamps! my eye!
How they do blaze! I wonder why
   They keep them on the ground.

At first I caught hold of the wing,
And kept away; but Mr. Thing-
   umbob, the prompter man,
Gave with his hand my chaise a shove,
And said, "Go on, my pretty love,—
   Speak to 'em, little Nan.

"You've only got to curtsey, whisper, hold your chin up, laugh and lisp,
   And then you're sure to take:

I've known the day when brats not quite
Thirteen got fifty pounds a night;
  Then why not Nancy Lake?"

But while I'm speaking, where's papa?
And where's my aunt? and where's mamma?
  Where's Jack? Oh there they sit!
They smile, they nod; I'll go my ways,
And order round poor Billy's chaise,
  To join them in the pit.

And now, good gentlefolks, I go
To join mamma, and see the show;
  So, bidding you adieu,
I curtsey, like a pretty miss,
And, if you'll blow to me a kiss,
  I'll blow a kiss to you.
              [*Blows kiss, and exit.*

THE THEATRE.

BY THE REV. GEORGE CRABBE.

'TIS sweet to view, from half-past five to six,
Our long wax-candles, with short cotton wicks,
Touched by the lamplighter's Promethean art,
Start into light, and make the lighter start;
To see red Phœbus through the gallery pane
Tinge with his beam the beams of Drury Lane,
While gradual parties fill our widened pit,
And gape, and gaze, and wonder, ere they sit.

  At first, while vacant seats give choice and ease,
Distant or near, they settle where they please;
But, when the multitude contracts the span,
And seats are rare, they settle where they can.

  Now the full benches, to late comers, doom
No room for standing, miscalled *standing-room*.

  Hark! the check-taker moody silence breaks,
And bawling "Pit full," gives the check he takes;
Yet onward still the gathering numbers cram,
Contending crowders shout the frequent "damn,"
And all is bustle, squeeze, row, jabbering, and jam.

  See to their desks Apollo's sons repair;
Swift rides the rosin o'er the horse's hair;
In unison their various tones to tune
Murmurs the hautboy, growls the hoarse bassoon;

In soft vibration sighs the whispering lute,
Tang goes the harpischord, too-too the flute,
Brays the loud trumpet, squeaks the fiddle sharp,
Winds the French horn, and twangs the tingling harp ;
Till, like great Jove, the leader, figuring in,
Attunes to order the chaotic din.
Now all seems hushed—but no, one fiddle will
Give, half-ashamed, a tiny flourish still.
Foiled in his crash, the leader of the clan
Reproves with frowns the dilatory man ;
Then on his candlestick thrice taps his bow,
Nods a new signal, and away they go.
Perchance while pit and gallery cry "Hats off,"
And awed consumption checks his chided cough,
Some giggling daughter of the Queen of Love
Drops, reft of pin, her play-bill from above ;
Like Icarus, while laughing galleries clap,
Soars, ducks, and dives in air, the printed scrap ;
But, wiser far than he, combustion fears,
And, as it flies, eludes the chandeliers ;
Till sinking gradual, with repeated twirl,
It settles, curling, on a fiddler's curl ;
Who from his powdered pate the intruder strikes,
And, for mere malice, sticks it on the spikes.

Say, why these Babel strains from Babel tongues?
Who's that calls "Silence" with such leathern lungs?
He who, in quest of quiet, "silence" hoots,
Is apt to make the hubbub he imputes.

What various swains our motley walls contain !
Fashion from Moorfields, honour from Chick Lane ;
Bankers from Paper Buildings here resort,
Bankrupts from Golden Square and Riches Court ;
From the Haymarket canting rogues in grain,
Culls from the Poultry, sots from Water Lane ;
The lottery cormorant, the auction shark,
The full-price master, and the half-price clerk ;
Boys who long linger at the gallery door,
With pence twice five, they want but two-pence more,—
Till some Samaritan the two-pence spares,
And sends them jumping up the gallery stairs.

Critics we boast who ne'er their malice baulk,
But talk their minds,—we wish they'd mind their talk ;
Big-worded bullies, who by quarrels live,
Who give the lie, and tell the lie they give ;
Jews from St. Mary Axe, for jobs so wary
That for old clothes they'd even axe St. Mary ;
And bucks with pockets empty as their pate,

Lax in their gaiters, laxer in their gait,
Who oft, when we our house lock up, carouse
With tippling tipstaves in a lock-up house.

Yet here, as elsewhere, chance can joy bestow,
Where scowling fortune seemed to threaten woe.

John Richard William Alexander Dwyer
Was footman to Justinian Stubbs, Esquire;
But, when John Dwyer listed in the Blues,
Emanuel Jennings polished Stubbs's shoes.

Emanuel Jennings brought his youngest boy
Up as a corn-cutter, a safe employ;
In Holywell Street, St. Pancras, he was bred
(At number twenty-seven, it is said,
Facing the pump, and near the Granby's Head).
He would have bound him to some shop in town,
But with a premium he could not come down.
Pat was the urchin's name, a red-haired youth,
Fonder of purl and skittle-grounds than truth.

Silence, ye gods!—to keep your tongues in awe,
The Muse shall tell an accident she saw.

Pat Jennings in the upper gallery sat,
But, leaning forward, Jennings lost his hat;
Down from the gallery the beaver flew,
And spurned the one to settle in the two.
How shall he act? Pay at the gallery door
Two shillings for what cost, when new, but four?
Or till half-price, to save his shilling, wait,
And gain his hat again at half-past eight?
Now, while his fears anticipate a thief,
John Mullins whispers, "Take my handkerchief."
"Thank you," cries Pat, "but one won't make a line."
"Take mine," cried Wilson; and cried Stokes, "Take mine."
A motley cable soon Pat Jennings ties,
Where Spitalfields with real India vies.
Like Iris' bow, down darts the painted hue,
Starred, striped, and spotted, yellow, red, and blue,
Old calico, torn silk, and muslin new.
George Green below, with palpitating hand,
Loops the last kerchief to the beaver's band.
Upsoars the prize; the youth, with joy unfeigned,
Regained the felt, and felt what he regained,—
While to the applauding galleries grateful Pat
Made a low bow, and touched the ransomed hat.

HORACE SMITH.

[Brother of the preceding; born towards 1779, died on 12th July 1849. Was a stockbroker by profession, and a man of a fine loveable nature, truly generous. Shelley has sketched him:
"Wit and sense,
Virtue and human knowledge, all that might
Make this dull world a business of delight,
Are all combined in Horace Smith."
He wrote *Brambletye House*, and some other novels].

LOYAL EFFUSION.[1]
BY W. T. FITZGERALD.

HAIL, glorious edifice, stupendous work!
God bless the Regent and the Duke of York!

Ye Muses! by whose aid I cried down Fox,
Grant me in Drury-Lane a private box,
Where I may loll, cry Bravo, and profess
The boundless powers of England's glorious press;
While Afric's sons exclaim, from shore to shore,
"Quashee ma boo! the slave-trade is no more!"

In fair Arabia (happy once, now stony,
Since ruined by that arch apostate, Boney)
A phœnix late was caught: the Arab host
Long pondered, part would boil it, part would roast:
But while they ponder, up the pot-lid flies;
Fledged, beaked, and clawed, alive, they see him rise
To heaven, and caw defiance in the skies.
So Drury, first in roasting flames consumed,
Then by old renters to hot water doomed,
By Wyatt's trowel patted, plump and sleek,
Soars without wings, and caws without a beak.
Gallia's stern despot shall in vain advance
From Paris, the metropolis of France;
By this day month the monster shall not gain
A foot of land in Portugal or Spain.
See Wellington in Salamanca's field
Forces his favourite general to yield,
Breaks through his lines, and leaves his boasted Marmont
Expiring on the plain without his arm on:
Madrid he enters at the cannon's mouth,
And then the villages still further south.
Base Buonaparte, filled with deadly ire,
Sets, one by one, our playhouses on fire.
Some years ago he pounced with deadly glee on
The Opera House, then burnt down the Pantheon;
Nay, still unsated, in a coat of flames

---

[1] This poem, and the three next ensuing, are from the *Rejected Addresses*: not so *The Jester Condemned to Death.*

Next at Millbank he crossed the river Thames:
Thy hatch, O Halfpenny! passed in a trice,
Boiled some black pitch, and burnt down Astley's twice;
Then buzzing on through æther with a vile hum,
Turned to the left hand, fronting the Asylum,
And burnt the Royal Circus in a hurry,—
('Twas called the Circus then, but now the Surry.)

 Who burnt (confound his soul!) the houses twain
Of Covent Garden and of Drury-Lane?
Who, while the British squadron lay off Cork,
(God bless the Regent and the Duke of York)
With a foul earthquake ravaged the Caraccas,
And raised the price of dry goods and tobaccos?
Who makes the quartern loaf and Luddites rise?
Who fills the butchers' shops with large blue flies?
Who thought in flames St. James's court to pinch?
Who burnt the wardrobe of poor Lady Finch?
Why he who, forging for this isle a yoke,
Reminds me of a line I lately spoke,
"The tree of freedom is the British oak."

 Bless every man possessed of aught to give;
Long may Long Tilney Wellesley Long Pole live;
God bless the army, bless their coats of scarlet,
God bless the navy, bless the Princess Charlotte,
God bless the guards, though worsted Gallia scoff,
And bless their pig-tails, though they're now cut off;
And oh, in Downing-Street should old Nick revel,
England's prime minister, then bless the Devil!

A TALE OF DRURY LANE.
BY WALTER SCOTT.

To be spoken by Mr. Kemble in a suit of the Black Prince's Armour, borrowed from the Tower.

 SURVEY this shield all bossy bright;
These cuisses twain behold;
Look on my form in armour dight
 Of steel inlaid with gold.
My knees are stiff in iron buckles,
Stiff spikes of steel protect my knuckles.
These once belonged to Sable Prince,
Who never did in battle wince;
With valour tart as pungent quince,
 He slew the vaunting Gaul.
Rest there awhile, my bearded lance,
While from green curtain I advance
To yon foot-lights, no trivial dance,
And tell the town what sad mischance
 Did Drury Lane befall.

THE NIGHT.

On fair Augusta's towers and trees
Flitted the silent midnight breeze,
Curling the foliage as it passed,
Which from the moon-tipped plumage cast
A spangled light like dancing spray,
Then reassumed its still array:
When, as night's lamp unclouded hung,
And down its full effulgence flung,
It shed such soft and balmy power
That cot and castle, hall and bower,
And spire and dome and turret-height,
Appeared to slumber in the light.
From Henry's chapel, Rufus' hall,
To Savoy, Temple, and St. Paul,
From Knightsbridge, Pancras, Camden Town,
To Redriff, Shadwell, Horselydown,
No voice was heard, no eye unclosed,
But all in deepest sleep reposed.
They might have thought who gazed around,
Amid a silence so profound
  It made the senses thrill,
That 'twas no place inhabited,
But some vast city of the dead,
  All was so hushed and still.

THE BURNING.

As Chaos, which, by heavenly doom,
Had slept in everlasting gloom,
Started with terror and surprise
When light first flashed upon her eyes;
So London's sons in night-cap woke,
  In bed-gown woke her dames,
For shouts were heard 'mid fire and smoke,
And twice ten hundred voices spoke,
  "The Playhouse is in flames!"
And lo! where Catherine Street extends,
A fiery tail its lustre lends
  To every window-pane;
Blushes each spout in Martlet Court,
And Barbican, moth-eaten fort,
And Covent Garden kennels sport
  A bright ensanguined drain.
Meux's new brewhouse shows the light,
Rowland Hill's chapel, and the height
  Where patent shot they sell.
The Tennis Court, so fair and tall,
Partakes the ray with Surgeons' Hall,

The ticket-porter's house of call,
Old Bedlam, close by London Wall,
Wright's shrimp and oyster shop withal,
    And Richardson's Hotel.

Nor these alone, but far and wide,
Across the Thames's gleaming tide,
To distant fields the blaze was borne,
And daisy white and hoary thorn
In borrowed lustre seemed to sham
The rose or red sweet-Wil-li-am.
  To those who on the hills around
  Beheld the flames from Drury's mound
As from a lofty altar rise
  It seemed that nations did conspire
  To offer to the god of fire
Some vast stupendous sacrifice !
The summoned firemen woke at call,
And hied them to their stations all.
Starting from short and broken snooze,
Each sought his ponderous hobnailed shoes ;
But first his worsted hosen plied.
Plush breeches next, in crimson dyed,
    His nether bulk embraced;
Then jacket thick of red or blue,
Whose massy shoulder gave to view
The badge of each respective crew,
    In tin or copper traced.
The engines thundered through the street,
Fire-hook, pipe, bucket, all complete ;
And torches glared, and clattering feet
    Along the pavement paced.

And one, the leader of the band,
From Charing Cross along the Strand,
Like stag by beagles hunted hard,
Ran till he stopped at Vin'gar Yard.
The burning badge his shoulder bore,
The belt and oil-skin hat he wore,
The cane he had his men to bang,
Showed foreman of the British gang.
His name was Higginbottom. Now
'Tis meet that I should tell you how
    The others came in view.
The Hand-in-Hand the race begun,
Then came the Phœnix and the Sun,
The Exchange, where old insurers run,
    The Eagle, where the new.
With these came Rumford, Bumford, Cole,
Robins from Hockley in the Hole,
Lawson and Dawson, cheek by jowl,

Crump from St. Giles's Pound:
Whitford and Mitford joined the train,
Huggins and Muggins from Chick Lane,
And Clutterbuck, who got a sprain
    Before the plug was found.
Hobson and Jobson did not sleep;
But ah! no trophy could they reap,
For both were in the donjon keep
    Of Bridewell's gloomy mound!

E'en Higginbottom now was posed,
For sadder scene was ne'er disclosed.
Without, within, in hideous show,
Devouring flames resistless glow,
And blazing rafters downward go,
And never halloo "heads below!"
    Nor notice give at all.
The firemen, terrified, are slow
To bid the pumping torrent flow,
    For fear the roof should fall.
Back, Robins, bac ! Crump, stand aloof!
Whitford, keep near the walls!
Huggins, regard your own behoof,—
For lo! the blazing rocking roof
    Down, down in thunder falls!

An awful pause succeeds the stroke;
And o'er the ruins volumed smoke,
Rolling around its pitchy shroud,
Concealed them from the astonished crowd.
At length the mist awhile was cleared;
When lo! amid the wreck upreared,
Gradual a moving head appeared,
    And Eagle firemen knew
'Twas Joseph Muggins, name revered,
    The foreman of their crew.
Loud shouted all in signs of woe,
"A Muggins to the rescue, ho!"
    And poured the hissing tide:
Meanwhile the Muggins fought amain,
And strove and struggled all in vain,
For rallying but to fall again,
    He tottered, sunk, and died!

Did none attempt, before he fell,
To succour one they loved so well?
Yes, Higginbottom did aspire
(His fireman's soul was all on fire)
    His brother chief to save;
But ah! his reckless generous ire
    Served but to share his grave!

Mid blazing beams and scalding streams,
Through fire and smoke he dauntless broke,
    Where Muggins broke before.
But sulphury stench and boiling drench,
Destroying sight, o'erwhelmed him quite,—
    He sunk to rise no more.
Still o'er his head, while Fate he braved,
His whizzing water-pipe he waved;
"Whitford and Mitford, ply your pumps,—
You, Clutterbuck, come, stir your stumps,—
Why are you in such doleful dumps?
A fireman, and afraid of bumps!
What are they feared on? fools! 'od rot 'em!"
Were the last words of Higginbottom.

THE REVIVAL.

Peace to his soul! New prospects bloom,
And toil rebuilds what fires consume!
"Eat we and drink we," be our ditty,
"Joy to the managing committee."
Eat we and drink we; join to rum
Roast beef and pudding of the plum.
Forth from thy nook, John Horner, come,
With bread of ginger brown thy thumb,
    For this is Drury's gay day:
Roll, roll thy hoop, and twirl thy tops,
And buy, to glad thy smiling chops,
Crisp parliament with lollypops,
    And fingers of the lady.

Didst mark how toiled the busy train
From morn to eve, till Drury Lane
Leaped like a roebuck from the plain?
Ropes rose and sunk, and rose again,
    And nimble workmen trod.
To realize bold Wyatt's plan,
Rushed many a howling Irishman;
Loud clattered many a porter-can,
And many a ragamuffin clan,
    With trowel and with hod.

Drury revives! her rounded pate
Is blue, is heavenly blue, with slate;
She "wings the midway air" elate,
    As magpie, crow, or chough;
White paint her modish visage smears,
Yellow and pointed are her ears.
No pendent portico appears
Dangling beneath, for Whitbread's shears
    Have cut the bauble off.

Yes, she exalts her stately head;
And, but that solid bulk outspread
Opposed you on your onward tread,
And posts and pillars warranted
That all was true that Wyatt said,
You might have deemed her walls so thick
Were not composed of stone or brick,—
But all a phantom, all a trick
Of brain disturbed and fancy-sick,
So high she soars, so vast, so quick.

DRURY'S DIRGE.

BY LAURA MATILDA.

BALMY Zephyrs lightly flitting,
   Shade me with your azure wing;
On Parnassus' summit sitting,
   Aid me, Clio, while I sing.

Softly slept the dome of Drury
   O'er the empyreal crest,
When Alecto's sister-fury
   Softly slumbering sunk to rest.

Lo! from Lemnos limping lamely,
   Lags the lowly Lord of Fire;
Cytherea yielding tamely
   To the Cyclops dark and dire.

Clouds of amber, dreams of gladness,
   Dulcet joys and sports of youth,
Soon must yield to haughty sadness;
   Mercy holds the veil to Truth.

See, Erostratus the second
   Fires again Diana's fane;
By the Fates from Orcus beckoned,
   Clouds envelop Drury Lane.

Lurid smoke and frank suspicion
   Hand in hand reluctant dance:
While the God fulfils his mission,
   Chivalry, resign thy lance!

Hark! the engines blandly thunder,
   Fleecy clouds dishevelled lie,
And the firemen, mute with wonder,
   On the son of Saturn cry.

See the bird of Ammon sailing
    Perches on the engine's peak,
And, the Eagle firemen hailing,
    Soothes them with its bickering beak.

Juno saw, and, mad with malice,
    Lost the prize that Paris gave;
Jealousy's ensanguined chalice
    Mantling pours the orient wave.

Pan beheld Patroclus dying,
    Nox to Niobe was turned;
From Busiris Bacchus flying
    Saw his Semele inurned.

Thus fell Drury's lofty glory,
    Levelled with the shuddering stones;
Mars, with tresses black and gory,
    Drinks the dew of pearly groans.

Hark! what soft Æolian numbers
    Gem the blushes of the morn;
Break, Amphion, break your slumbers,
    Nature's ringlets deck the thorn.

Ha! I hear the strain erratic
    Dimly glance from pole to pole,
Raptures sweet and dreams ecstatic
    Fire my everlasting soul.

Where is Cupid's crimson motion?
    Billowy ecstacy of woe,
Bear me straight, meandering ocean,
    Where the stagnant torrents flow.

Blood in every vein is gushing,
    Vixen vengeance lulls my heart,
See, the Gorgon gang is rushing!
    Never, never let us part!

ARCHITECTURAL ATOMS.

TRANSLATED BY DR. B.

To be recited by the Translator's Son.

AWAY, fond dupes! who, smit with sacred lore,
Mosaic dreams in Genesis explore,
Dote with Copernicus, or darkling stray
With Newton, Ptolemy, or Tycho Brahe:
To you I sing not, for I sing of truth,

Primæval systems, and creation's youth;
Such as of old, with magic wisdom fraught,
Inspired Lucretius to the Latians taught.

   I sing how casual bricks, in airy climb,
Encountered casual horse-hair, casual lime;
How rafters, borne through wondering clouds elate,
Kissed in their slope blue elemental slate,
Clasped solid beams in chance-directed fury,
And gave to birth our renovated Drury.

   Thee, son of Jove, whose sceptre was confessed
Where fair Æolia springs from Tethys' breast:
Thence on Olympus 'mid Celestials placed,
God of the Winds and Æther's boundless waste,
Thee I invoke! Oh puff my bold design,
Prompt the bright thought, and swell the harmonious
    line;
Uphold my pinions, and my verse inspire
With Winsor's patent gas, or wind of fire,
In whose pure blaze thy embryo form enrolled
The dark enlightens, and enchafes the cold.

   But, while I court thy gifts, be mine to shun
The deprecated prize Ulysses won;
Who, sailing homeward from thy breezy shore,
The prisoned Winds in skins of parchment bore.—
Speeds the fleet bark, till o'er the billowy green
The azure heights of Ithaca are seen;
But, while with favouring gales her way she wins,
His curious comrades ope the mystic skins:
When lo! the rescued Winds, with boisterous sweep,
Roar to the clouds, and lash the rocking deep:
Heaves the smote vessel in the howling blast,
Splits the stretched sail, and cracks the tottering mast.
Launched on a plank, the buoyant hero rides
Where ebon Afric stems the sable tides,
While his ducked comrades o'er the ocean fly,
And sleep not in the whole skins they untie.

   So, when to raise the wind some lawyer tries,
Mysterious skins of parchment meet our eyes.
On speeds the smiling suit; "Pleas of our Lord
The King" shine jetty on the wide record.
Nods the prunellaed bar, attorneys smile,
And siren jurors flatter to beguile;
Till stripped—nonsuited—he is doomed to toss
In legal shipwreck and redeemless loss;
Lucky if, like Ulysses, he can keep
His head above the waters of the deep.

Æolian monarch! Emperor of Puffs!
We modern sailors dread not thy rebuffs;
See, to thy golden shore promiscuous come
Quacks for the lame, the blind, the deaf, the dumb;
Fools are their bankers—a prolific line,
And every mortal malady's a mine.
Each sly Sangrado, with his poisonous pill,
Flies to the printer's devil with his bill,
Whose Midas touch can gild his ass's ears,
And load a knave with folly's rich arrears.
And lo! a second miracle is thine,
For sloe-juiced water stands transformed to wine.
Where Day and Martin's patent blacking rolled,
Burst from the vase Pactolian streams of gold;
Laugh the sly wizards glorying in their stealth,
Quit the black art, and loll in lazy wealth.
See, Britain's Algerines, the Lottery fry,
Win annual tribute by the annual lie.
Aided by thee. . . . But whither do I stray?
Court, city, borough, own thy sovereign sway:
An age of puffs the age of gold succeeds,
And windy bubbles are the spawn it breeds.

If such thy power, Oh hear the Muse's prayer!
Swell thy loud lungs, and wave thy wings of air;
Spread, viewless giant, all thy arms of mist
Like windmill sails to bring the poet grist,
As erst thy roaring son with eddying gale
Whirled Orithyia from her native vale.
So, while Lucretian wonders I rehearse,
Augusta's sons shall patronize my verse.

I sing of Atoms, whose creative brain,
With eddying impulse, built new Drury Lane;
Not to the labours of subservient man,
To no young Wyatt, appertains the plan;
We mortals stalk, like horses in a mill,
Impassive media of Atomic will.
Ye stare! Then truth's broad talisman discern—
Tis Demonstration speaks.—Attend and learn!

From floating elements in chaos hurled,
Self-formed of atoms, sprang the infant world.
No great First Cause inspired the happy plot,
But all was matter, and no matter what.
Atoms, attracted by some law occult,
Settling in spheres, the globe was the result;
Pure child of Chance, which still directs the ball,
As rotatory atoms rise or fall.
In æther launched, the peopled bubble floats,
A mass of particles and confluent motes;

So nicely poised that, if one atom flings
Its weight away, aloft the planet springs,
And wings its course through realms of boundless space,
Outstripping comets in eccentric race.
Add but one atom more, it sinks outright
Down to the realms of Tartarus and night.
What waters melt, or scorching fires consume,
In different forms their being reassume ;
Hence can no change arise, except in name,
For weight and substance ever are the same.

Thus, with the flames that from old Drury rise,
Its elements primæval sought the skies ;
There pendulous to wait the happy hour
When new attractions should restore their power.
So, in this procreant theatre elate,
Echoes unborn their future life await ;
Here embryo sounds in æther lie concealed,
Like words in northern atmosphere congealed.
Here many a fœtus-laugh and half-encore
Clings to the roof, or creeps along the floor.
By puffs concipient, some in æther flit,
And soar in bravos from the thundering pit ;
Some forth on ticket-nights from tradesmen break,
To mar the actor they design to make ;
While some this mortal life abortive miss,
Crushed by a groan, or strangled by a hiss.
So, when "dog's-meat" re-echoes through the streets,
Rush sympathetic dogs from their retreats,
Beam with bright blaze their supplicating eyes,
Sink their hind-legs, ascend their joyful cries ;
Each, wild with hope, and maddening to prevail,
Points the pleased ear, and wags the expectant tail.

Ye fallen bricks, in Drury's fire calcined,—
Since doomed to slumber, couched upon the wind,—
Sweet was the hour when, tempted by your freaks,
Congenial trowels smoothed your yellow cheeks.
Float dulcet serenades upon the ear,
Bends every atom from its ruddy sphere,
Twinkles each eye, and, peeping from its veil,
Marks in the adverse crowd its destined male.
The oblong beauties clap their hands of grit,
And brick-dust titterings on the breezes flit ;
Then down they rush in amatory race,
Their dusty bridegrooms eager to embrace.
Some choose old lovers, some decide for new ;
But each, when fixed, is to her station true.
Thus various bricks are made as tastes invite
The red, the grey, the dingy, or the white.

Perhaps some half-baked rover, frank and free,
To alien beauty bends the lawless knee;
But, of unhallowed fascination sick,
Soon quits his Cyprian for his married brick.
The Dido atom calls and scolds in vain;
No crisp Æneas soothes the widow's pain.

So in Cheapside, what time Aurora peeps,
A mingled noise of dustmen, milk, and sweeps,
Falls on the housemaid's ear; amazed she stands,
Then opes the door with cinder-sabled hands,
And "matches" calls. The dustman, bubbled flat,
Thinks 'tis for him, and doffs his fan-tailed hat;
The milkman, whom her second cries assail,
With sudden sink, unyokes the clinking pail.
Now, louder grown, by turns she screams and weeps;
Alas! her screaming only brings the sweeps.
Sweeps but put out—she wants to raise a flame,
And calls for matches, but 'tis still the same.
Atoms and housemaids! mark the moral true,—
If once ye go astray, no match for you!

As atoms in one mass united mix,
So bricks attraction feel for kindred bricks.
Some in the cellar view, perchance, on high,
Fair chimney chums on beds of mortar lie;
Enamoured of the sympathetic clod,
Leaps the red bridegroom to the labourer's hod,
And up the ladder bears the workman, taught
To think he bears the bricks—mistaken thought!
A proof behold—if near the top they find
The nymphs or broken-cornered or unkind,
Back to the bottom leaping with a bound,
They bear their bleeding carriers to the ground.

So, legends tell, along the lofty hill
Paced the twin heroes, gallant Jack and Jill;
On trudged the Gemini to reach the rail
That shields the well's top from the expectant pail,
When ah! Jack falls; and, rolling in the rear,
Jill feels the attraction of his kindred sphere;
Head over heels begins his toppling track,
Throws sympathetic somersets with Jack,
And at the mountain's base bobs plump against him,
   whack!

Ye living atoms who unconscious sit,
Jumbled by chance in gallery, box, and pit,
For you no Peter opes the fabled door,
No churlish Charon plies the shadowy oar;—

Breathe but a space, and Boreas' casual sweep
Shall bear your scattered corses o'er the deep,
To gorge the greedy elements, and mix
With water, marl and clay, and stones and sticks;
While, charged with fancied souls, sticks, stones, and clay,
Shall take your seats, and hiss or clap the play.

O happy age when convert Christians read
No sacred writings but the Pagan creed!
O happy age when, spurning Newton's dreams,
Our poet's sons recite Lucretian themes,
Abjure the idle systems of their youth,
And turn again to atoms and to truth!
O happier still when England's dauntless dames,
Awed by no chaste alarms, no latent shames,
The bard's fourth book unblushingly peruse,
And learn the rampant lessons of the stews!

All hail, Lucretius, renovated sage!
Unfold the modest mystics of thy page;
Return no more to thy sepulchral shelf,
But live, kind bard,—that I may live myself!

THE JESTER CONDEMNED TO DEATH.

ONE of the Kings of Scanderoon
    A Royal Jester
Had in his train; a gross buffoon,
    Who used to pester
The Court with tricks inopportune,
Venting on the highest folks his
Scurvy pleasantries and hoaxes.

It needs some sense to play the fool,
    Which wholesome rule
Occurred not to our jackanapes,
    Who consequently found his freaks
Lead to innumerable scrapes,
    And quite as many kicks and tweaks,
Which only seemed to make him faster
Try the patience of his master.

Some sin, at last, beyond all measure,
Incurred the desperate displeasure
    Of his serene and raging Highness.
Whether he twitched his most revered
    And sacred beard,
Or had intruded on the shyness
Of the Seraglio, or let fly

An epigram at royalty,
None knows :—his sin was an occult one.
But records tell us that the Sultan,
Meaning to terrify the knave,
  Exclaimed—"'Tis time to stop that breath ;
Thy doom is sealed :—presumptuous slave !
  Thou stand'st condemned to certain death.
Silence, base rebel !—no replying !—
  But such is my indulgence still
That, of my own free grace and will,
I leave to thee the mode of dying."

"Thy royal will be done—'tis just,"
Replied the wretch, and kissed the dust.
  "Since, my last moments to assuage,
Your Majesty's humane decree
Has deigned to leave the choice to me,
  I'll die, so please you, of old age !"

PATRICK O'KELLY.

[The earliest trace I find of this writer is the publication, in 1808, of his *Poems on the Giant's Causeway and Killarney, with other Miscellanies*. He published another volume of verse in 1824, and is mentioned as having met Sir Walter Scott at Limerick in 1825. His worldly circumstances must then have been the reverse of flourishing, for he borrowed five shillings of the Scottish poet. He was "a scarecrow figure," and seems to have been well known as an eccentric humourist, naturally amenable to banter].

THE DONERAILE LITANY.

Alas ! how dismal is my tale !—
I lost my watch in Doneraile ;
My Dublin watch, my chain and seal,
Pilfered at once in Doneraile.

May fire and brimstone never fail
To fall in showers on Doneraile ;
May all the leading fiends assail
The thieving town of Doneraile.

As lightnings flash across the vale,
So down to hell with Doneraile ;
The fate of Pompey at Pharsale,
Be that the curse of Doneraile.

May beef or mutton, lamb or veal,
Be never found in Doneraile ;
But garlic-soup and scurvy kail
Be still the food for Doneraile.

And forward as the creeping snail
The industry be of Doneraile ;
May Heaven a chosen curse entail
On rigid, rotten Doneraile.

May sun and moon for ever fail
To beam their lights in Doneraile;
May every pestilential gale
Blast that curst spot called Doneraile.

May no sweet cuckoo, thrush, or quail,
Be ever heard in Doneraile;
May patriots, kings, and commonweal,
Despise and harass Doneraile.

May every Post, Gazette, and Mail,
Sad tidings bring of Doneraile;
May loudest thunders ring a peal
To blind and deafen Doneraile.

May vengeance fall at head and tail,
From north to south, at Doneraile;
May profit light, and tardy sale,
Still damp the trade of Doneraile.

May Fame resound a dismal tale
Whene'er she lights on Doneraile;
May Egypt's plagues at once prevail,
To thin the knaves of Doneraile.

May frost and snow, and sleet and hail,
Benumb each joint in Doneraile;
May wolves and bloodhounds trace and trail
The cursed crew of Doneraile.

May Oscar, with his fiery flail,
To atoms thresh all Doneraile;
May every mischief, fresh and stale,
Abide henceforth in Doneraile.

May all, from Belfast to Kinsale,
Scoff, curse, and damn you, Doneraile;
May neither flour nor oatenmeal
Be found or known in Doneraile.

May want and woe each joy curtail
That e'er was known in Doneraile;
May no one coffin want a nail
That wraps a rogue in Doneraile.

May all the thieves that rob and steal
The gallows meet in Doneraile;
May all the sons of Granaweal
Blush at the thieves of Doneraile.

May mischief, big as Norway whale,
O'erwhelm the knaves of Doneraile;
May curses, wholesale and retail,
Pour with full force on Doneraile.

May every transport wont to sail
A convict bring from Doneraile;
May every churn and milking-pail
Fall dry to staves in Doneraile.

May cold and hunger still congeal
The stagnant blood of Doneraile;
May every hour new woes reveal
That hell reserves for Doneraile.

May every chosen ill prevail
O'er all the imps of Doneraile;
May no one wish or prayer avail
To soothe the woes of Doneraile.

May the Inquisition straight impale
The rapparees of Doneraile;
May Charon's boat triumphant sail,
Completely manned, from Doneraile.

Oh may my couplets never fail
To find a curse for Doneraile;
And may grim Pluto's inner jail
For ever groan with Doneraile!

ORLANDO THOMAS DOBBIN.

[The Rev. Dr. Dobbin, a clergyman of the Anglo-Irish Church, was born in the County of Armagh in 1807. Along with various original writings, he has published, with a translation, Diodati's *De Christo Græce loquente*, and the *Codex Montfortianus*].

MY MANX MINX.

ALL the Bard's rhymes, and all his inks,
Will scarce pourtray the Proteus—MINX:

Nor artist brush with brightest tincts
Of Fancy's rainbow picture MINX.

The child of Man and beast: a sphinx
Of noble rearing: that is MINX.

With paw of leopard, eye of lynx,
And spring of tiger, such is MINX.

She's playful, harmless: Mousie thinks:
But dreadful earnest's artful MINX.

Seems *nonchalante*, and bobs, and blinks:
Ma foi, toute autre chose is MINX.

Dormitat Homer oft: *her* winks
Are rare: no "nid-nid-noddin"—MINX.

Aye "takkin notes" of holes and chinks:
A slee and pawky body's MINX.

An Abbess of Misrule: she slinks
From no malfeasance: wilful MINX.

(Law:)—*Ne quid nim. of neighbour's trinks:*
She's always nimming: roguish MINX.

With reels of silk, thread, wool, plays rinks:
Tossing and tangling: tricksy MINX.

Loves frisks, curvets, and highest jinks:
Frolic's own daughter, merry MINX.

As high-born dame in idlesse sinks,
So idleth *fa-niente* MINX.

A pert, coquettish, flirting finks:
Has fifty beaux at once: vain MINX.

On window-sill, in sunshine, prinks
Her dainty paws and fur: neat MINX.

Simplex munditiis, all the sminks
And smears of sluthood shuns spruce MINX.

Soprani trill their tink-a-tinks:
My *prima cat=atrice*'s MINX.

Horns blare, drums beat, and cymbal clinks:
No *mewsic* equals mews of MINX.

His richest creams, nectareous drinks,
Her master sets aside for MINX.

From human cares and snares he shrinks,
To spend serener hours with MINX.

The Dean's rare taste in his precincts
Pets wild ducks: I pet wilder MINX.

Of the CAT world the pink of pinks
Is tailless, peerless, *schönste* MINX.

'Es ἀεί twinned, the Bard enlinks
The names for ever: OTHO,[1] MINX.

---

[1] O. THO. D.

A DITHYRAMB ON CATS.

Confound the Cats! All Cats—alway—
Cats of all colours, black, white, grey;
By night a nuisance and by day—
    Confound the Cats!

Confound their saucy-looking whiskers!
Confound them whether staid or friskers!
Confound their midnight squeally discourse!
    Confound the Cats!

Confound their roof-ridge caterwaulings—
Their spittings, hissings, skirlings, squallings,
And their still more lugubrious miaulings—
    Confound the Cats!

Confound all Cats! Whate'er the fashion—
Persian, Manx, Maltese, or Circassian,
The sleek young Kit, or skinny passé one—
    Confound the Cats!

Confound the Cats! Yet Egypt loved 'em,
With balsams and with unguents stuffed 'em,
And then within Grand Pyramids shoved 'em—
    Confound the Cats!

Not Puss in Boots, of fairy scribe,
Which charmed my youth, could ever bribe
My heart to love that claw-armed tribe:
    Confound the Cats!

Sly Pussies lap their milky food,
Seeming a harmless playful brood—
Yet nurse a tiger's thirst for blood.
    Confound the Cats!

My Tenny—that's her name—is black,
Soft, shining, furry is her back;
But she has griffin's claws, alack!
    Confound the Cats!

Confound the blackamoorish sinner!
Of waifs and strays the strenuous winner,
Purveying "small deer" for her dinner—
    Confound the Cats!

While other game abound in plenties,
And young soft mice are caught in twenties,
Song-birds should still be tabooed dainties—
    Confound the Cats!

O Tenny, Tenny, arch-deceiver!
Assassin, Fenian, filch and reiver!
How wilt, when tried, thy soul deliver?
    Confound the Cats!

The Judge's charge—a Robin's—read,
Twelve honest Robins' verdict said,
A Robin Ketch will hang thee dead,—
          Confound the Cats!

Laid in unblest abysmal tomb,
Resurgam none—a cat-acomb—
Thou'lt rot in Paris, Memphis, Rome—
          Confound the Cats!

Would, Richard Whittington! you'd ta'en
Your "turn again" through my domain,
And shipped a cargo off for Spain!
          Confound the Cats!

'Twould have saved Robin—cheeriest fellow!
With pipe so clear, and soul so mellow,
Amongst his mates a regular swell, Oh
          Confound the Cats!

In scarlet vest and breeches grey,
He looked the gentleman so gay—
His nut-brown coat, a cut-away.
          Confound the Cats!

Puss eyed him plump and debonnair,—
Compassion cried in vain "Oh spare!"—
And trussed his gentle carcase there:
          Confound the Cats!

Cat *venit, vidit, vicit* Rob,
A Cæsarlike and summary job,
Without one quick compunctious throb.
          Confound the Cats!

Swooned Queen Robina at his rape;
While her Lord Chamberlain bade drape
All Robindom with deepest crape.
          Confound the Cats!

"Confound the Cats," she cried sob-sobbing,
"Who took their hard and hungry gob in
My royal spouse—my peerless Robin!
          Ah me, sweet Robin!

"O feline and felonious breed!
My true love's red breast—Ah foul deed!—
To cause with redder red to bleed,
          Dear murdered Robin!

"The bagpipes drone fu' sad and sairlie,
Aye liltin' 'Wae's me for Prince Charlie;'
My heart responds, Wae's me for rarely
          Gifted Prince Robin!

"O early lost and long adored!
My dhilka tookra, my soul's lord!
Thy virtues how shall I record,
    My noble Robin?

"Victoria builds her Alberteum,
As Caria's Queen her Mausoleum;
I'll raise, I vow, my Robineum
    For Consort Robin!

"*Ad Viduarum nexa choream,
Extruam, in majorem gloriam
Robini, propriam In Memoriam.*
    O loved—lost—Robin!"

Her grief we share :—confound the brutes
Who turn sweet warblers into mutes,
And clothe their mates in mourning-suits—
    Confound the Cats!

O one-tailed Cats, remorseless crew!
Did all Garotters meet their due,
A nine-tailed Cat would harry you—
    Confound the Cats!

When Thetis dipped her bantling stout
In Styx, she pulled him quickly out
By the heel—whence came Achilles' gout:
    Confound the Cats!

Far different guerdon thou shouldst win,
Tenny! for thine enormous sin;
No heel I'd hold, but plump thee in :
    Confound the Cats!

O utinam the watery strife
Absorbed the last Cat's last ninth life,
Nor left one thread for Fate's sharp knife!
    Confound the Cats!

Were the Cat-world one-necked, as Nero
Wished all mankind a one-necked hero,
"Off with his head!" I'd ring out clear, Oh
    Confound the Cats!

But hush, my soul, bereavement-riven!
Bow to the dark behest of Heaven—
In this round world there may be even
    Needs-be for Cats!

POEMS BY UNKNOWN WRITERS.

WOMEN.[1]

WOMEN, women, love of women,
Makè bare purse with some men!
Some be nice as a nunne hen,
    Yit all they be nat so.
Some be lewd, some all be shrewed,—[2]
    Go shrews where they go.

Some be wise, and some be fond,
And some be tame, I understond,
And some can take bread of a man's hond,
    Yit all they be nat so.

Some will be drunken as a mouse;
Some be crooked, and will hurt a louse;
And some be fair, and good in a house;
    Yit all be nat so:
For some be lewd, and some be shrewed,—
    Go shrew wheresoever ye go.

Some can prate withouten hire,
And some make debate in every shire,
And some checkmate with oure sire,
    Yit all they be nat so.
Some be lewd, and some be shrewed,
    Go where they go.

Some be brown, and some be white,
And some be tender as a tripe,
And some of them be cherry-ripe,
    Yit all they be nat so.
Some be lewd, and some be shrewed,
    Go where they go.

---

[1] The date of this poem may be towards 1460. I have seen three several versions of it. Two of them are nearly alike, and are here substantially reproduced. From the other, which differs considerably, I have taken the stanza which appears third in the present reprint.
[2] Curst, hateful.

Some of them be true of love
Beneath the girdle but not above,
And in a hood above can chove;
   Yit all they be nat so.
Some be lewd, and some be shrewed,
   Go where they go.

Some can whister, and some can cry;
Some can flatter, and some can lie;
And some can set the moke awry;
   Yit all they do nat so.
Some be lewd, and some be shrewed,
   Go where they go.

He that made this song full good
Came of the north and the southern blood,
And somewhat kine[1] to Robin Hood;
   Yit all we be nat so.
Some be lewd, and some be shrewed,
   Go where they go;
Some be lewd and some be shrewed,
   Go where they go.

A GOOD MEDICINE FOR SORE EYNE.[2]

For a man that is almost blind,
Let him go barehead all day again the wind,
   Till the sun be set;
And than wrap him in a cloak,
And put him in a house full of smoke,
And look that every hole be well shet.
And, whan his eyes begin to rope,
Fill hem full of brimstone and soap,
   And hyll[3] him well and warm.
And, if he be not, by the next moon,
As well at midnight as at noon,
   I shall lese my right arm.

TRUST IN WOMEN.

When these things following be done to our intent,
   Than put women in trust and confident.

When nettles in winter bring forth roses red,
   And all manner of thorn-trees bear figs naturally,
   And geese bear pearls in every mead,
      And laurel bear cherries abundantly,
      And oaks bear dates very plenteously,

---

[1] Kin.
[2] Date towards 1480: so also for the two poems that follow next.
[3] Cover.

    And kisks give of honey superfluence,
      Than put women in trust and confidence.

When box bear paper in every lond and town,
    And thistles bear berries in every place,
And pikes have naturally feathers in their crown,
    And bulls of the sea sing a good bass,
    And men be the ships fishes do trace,
    And in women be found no insipience,
      Than put hem in trust and confidence.

When whitings do walk forests to chase harts,
And herrings their horns in forests boldly blow,
    And marmsats morn in moors and in lakes,
And gurnards shoot rooks out of a cross-bow,
And goslings hunt the wolf to overthrow,
And sprats bear spears in armes of defence,
      Than put women in trust and confidence.

When swine be cunning in all points of music,
    And asses be doctors of every science,
    And cats do heal men be practising of physic,
    And buzzards to scripture gif ony credence,
And marchans buy with horn, instead of groats and pence,
    And pyes be made poets for their eloquence,
      Than put women in trust and confidence.

When sparrows build churches on a heighth,
    And wrens carry secks[1] onto the mill,
And curlews carry timber houses to dighth,[2]
    And fomalls bear butter to market to sell,
    And woodcocks wear woodknives cranes to kill,
And greenfinches to goslings do obedience,
      Than put women in trust and confidence.

When crowves take sarmon[3] in woods and parks,
    And be take with swifts and snails,
And camels in the air take swallows and larks,
And mice move mountains with wagging of their tails,
    And shipmen take a ryd instead of sails,
    And when wifes to their husbands do no offence,
      Than put women in trust and confidence.

When hantlopes surmounts eagles in flight,
    And swans be swifter than hawks of the tower,
    And wrens set gos-hawks be force and might,
    And muskets make vergece of crabbes sour,
    And ships sail on dry lond, syll gyfe flower,[4]
And apes in Westminster gif judgment and sentence,
      Than put women in trust and confidence.

---

    [1] Sacks.   [2] Construct.   [3] Salmon.
[4] I don't understand these three words—not to speak of some few others *passim*.

GOSSIP MINE.[1]

I will you tell a full good sport,
How gossips gather them on a sort,
Their sick bodies for to comfort,
When they meet in a lane or street.

But I dare not, for their displeasance,
Tell of these matters half the substance;
But yet somewhat of their governance,
As far as I dare, I will declare.

"Good gossip mine, where have ye be?
It is so long sith I you see!
Where is the best wine? Tell you me:
Can you aught tell full well."

"I know a draught of merry-go-down,—
The best it is in all this town:
But yet would I not, for my gown,
My husband it wist,—ye may me trust.

"Call forth your gossips by and by,—
Elinore, Joan, and Margery,
Margaret, Alice, and Cecily;
For they will come, both all and some.

"And each of them will somewhat bring,—
Goose, pig, or capon's wing,
Pasties of pigeons, or some such thing:
For a gallon of wine they will not wring.

"Go before be twain and twain,
Wisely, that ye be not seen;
For I must home—and come again—
To wit, I wis, where my husband is.

"A stripe or two God might send me,
If my husband might here see me."
"She that is afeard, let her flee!"
Quod Alice than: "I dread no man!"

"Now be we in tavern set;
A draught of the best let him fett,
To bring our husbands out of debt;
For we will spend till God more send."

---

[1] Of this poem I have seen two versions. On the whole, I think the one here printed is superior in touches of character and manners. The other differs in arrangement and in numerous details, and devotes some stanzas to an incident which does not appear at all in our version—namely, the summoning of a harper for the diversion of the "merry wives."

Each of them brought forth their dish :
Some brought flesh, and some fish.
Quod Margaret meek : " Now, with a wish,
I would Anne were here—she would make us cheer."

" How say you, gossips ? Is this wine good ?"
" That it is," quod Elinore, " by the rood !
It cherisheth the heart, and comfort the blood ;
Such junkets among shall make us live long."

" Anne, bid fill a pot of muscadel,
For of all wines I love it well.
Sweet wines keep my body in hele :
If I had of it nought, I should take great thought.

" How look ye, gossip, at the board's end ?
Not merry, gossip ? God it amend !
All shall be well, else God it defend :
Be merry and glad, and sit not so sad."

" Would God I had done after your counsèl !
For my husband is so fell
He beateth me like the devil of hell ;
And, the more I cry, the less mercy."

Alice with a loud voice spake than :
" I wis," she said, " little good he can
That beateth or striketh ony woman,
And specially his wife :—God give him short live !"

Margaret meek said : " So mote I thrife,
I know no man that is alife
That give me two strokes but he shall have fife :
I am not afeard, though I have no beard."

One cast down her shot, and went her way.
" Gossip," quod Elinore, " what did she pay ?"
" Not but a penny." " Lo therefore I say
She shall be no more of our lore.

" Such guests we may have enow
That will not for their shot allow.
With whom come she ? Gossip, with you ?"
" Nay," quod Joan, " I come alone."

" Now reckon our shot, and go we hence.
What ! cost it each of us but three pence ?
Pardie ! this is but a small expense
For such a sort, and all but sport.

" Turn down the street where ye come out,
And we will compass round-about."
" Gossip," quod Anne, " what needeth that doubt ?
Your husbands be pleased when ye be reised.

"Whatsoever ony man think,
We come for nought but for good drink.
Now let us go home and wink;
For it may be seen where we have been."

From the tavern be they all gone;
And everich of hem showeth her wisdom,
And there she telleth her husband anon
    She had been at the church.[1]

This is the thought that gossips take;
Once in the week merry will they make,
And all small drink they will forsake,
But wine of the best shall han no rest.

Some be at the tavern once in a week,
And so be some every day eke,
Or else they will groan and make them sick;
For things used will not be refused.

How say you, women, is it not so?
Yes surely, and that ye well know:
And therefore let us drink all a-row,
And of our singing make a good ending.

Now fill the cup, and drink to me,
And than shall we good fellows be:—
And of this talking leave will we,
And speak then good of women.

JOLLY GOOD ALE AND OLD. [2]

Back and side, go bare, go bare!
  Both hand and foot, go cold!
But, belly, God send thee good ale enough,
  Whether it be new or old!

    But-if that I
    May have truly
Good ale my bellyful,
    I shall look like one,
    By sweet Saint John,
Were shorn against the wool.
    Thouth I go bare,
    Take you no care,
I am nothing cold,
    I stuff my skin
    So full within
Of jolly good ale and old.

---

[1] This neat touch comes from the second version of the poem.
[2] The date of this chant may be somewhere towards 1540.

> I cannot eat
> But little meat,
> My stomach is not good;
> But sure I think
> That I could drink
> With him that wear'th an hood.
> Drink is my life,
> Although my wife
> Sometime do chide and scold:
> Yet spare I not
> To ply the pot
> Of jolly good ale and old.
> Back and side &c.
>
> I love no roast,
> But a brown toast,
> Or a crab in the fire;
> A little bread
> Shall do me stead,—
> Much bread I never desire.
> Nor frost nor snow,
> Nor wind, I trow,
> Can hurt me if it wold;
> I am so wrapped
> Within and lapped
> With jolly good ale and old.
> Back and side &c.
>
> I care right nought,
> I take no thought
> For clothes to keep me warm:
> Have I good drink,
> I surely think
> Nothing can do me harm.
> For truly than
> I fear no man,
> Be he never so bold,
> When I am armed
> And throughly warmed
> With jolly good ale and old.
> Back and side &c.
>
> But now and than
> I curse and ban,
> They make their ale so small:
> God give them care,
> And evil to fare,—
> They strye[1] the malt and all!
> Such peevish pew—
> I tell you true—

---

[1] Destroy, ruin, spoil.

  Not for a crown of gold
   There cometh one sip
   Within my lip,
Whether it be new or old.
Back and side &c.

  Good ale and strong
   Mak'th me among
Full jocund and full light,
  That oft I sleep,
  And take no keep,
From morning until night.
  Then start I up,
  And flee to the cup;
The right way on I hold
  My thirst to staunch;
  I fill my paunch
With jolly good ale and old.
Back and side &c.

  And Kitt, my wife,
  That as her life
Loveth well good ale to seek,
  Full oft drinketh she,
  That ye may see
The tears run down her cheek.
  Then doth she troll
  To me the bowl,
As a good malt-worm shold,—
  And say: "Sweetheart,
  I have take my part
Of jolly good ale and old."
Back and side &c.

  They that do drink
  Till they nod and wink,
Even as good fellows should do,
  They shall not miss
  To have the bliss
That good ale hath brought them to.
  And all poor souls
  That scour black bowls,
And them hath lustily trolled,
  God save the lives
  Of them and their wives,
Whether they be young or old!
Back and side &c.

AS IT BEFELL ONE SATURDAY.[1]

As it befell one Saturday at noon,
   As I went up Scotland gate,
I heard one to another say,
   "John a' Bagilie hath lost his mate."

At Eaton Water I wash my hands—
   For tickling[2] tears I could scarce see:
I lifted up my lily-white hands:
   "O Katty Whitworth, God be with thee!

"There is none but you and I, sweetheart,
   No lookers-on we can allow:
Your lips they be so sugared sweet
   I must do more than kiss you now!

"Farewell, my love, my leave I take:
   Though against my will, it must be so:
No marvel all this moan I make:
   Whom I love best I must forego!

"If that thou wilt Scotland forsake,
   And come into fair England with me,
Both kith and kin I will forsake,
   Bonny sweet wench, to go with thee."

There was two men, they loved a lass:
   The one of them he was a Scot,
The other was an Englishman—
   The name of him I have quite forgot.

As I went up Kelsall wood,
   And up that bank that was so stair,[3]
I looked over my left shoulder,
   Where I was wont to see my dear.

"There is sixteen in thy father's house:
   Fifteen of them against me be:
Not one of them to take my part,
   But only thou, pretty Kattye."

The young man walkèd home again,
   As time of night thereto moves:
The fair maid called him back again,
   And gave to him a sweet pair of gloves.

---

[1] This is a specimen of the compositions termed "Tom-a-Bedlams," common and popular towards the beginning of the seventeenth century. The fun of them consists in their perpetual incongruities or irrelevancies.
[2] Probably a mis-writing for "trickling:" or the change *may* be intentional.
[3] Steer, steep.

"Thy father hath silver and gold enough,
   Silver and gold to maintain thee ;
But as for that I do not care,
   So that thou wilt my true love be."

"When I was young and in my youth,
   Then could I have lovers two or three:
Now I am old, and count the hours,
   And fain would do—but it will not be."

"Upon your lips my leave I take,
   Desiring you to be my friend,
And grant me love for love again,
   For why, my life is at an end.

"My mother, Kate, hath sent for me,
   And needly her I must obey.
I weigh not of thy constancy
   When I am fled and gone away.

"I weep, I wail, I wring my hands,
   I sob, I sigh, I make heavy cheer !
No marvel all this moan I make,
   For why, alas ! I have lost my dear !"

MARK MORE,[1] FOOL.

To pass the time thereas I went,
   A history there I chanced to read.—
Whereas Salomon reignèd king,
   He did many a worthy deed,
And many statutes he caused to be made :
   And this was one amongst the rest plain—
It was felony to any one that found aught was lost,
   And would not restore it to the owner again.

So then there was a rich merchant :
   As he rode to a market-town,
It was his chance to lose his purse :
   He said there was in it a hundred pound.
A proclamation he caused to be made,
   Whosoever could find the same again
Should give it him again without all doubt,
   And he should have for twenty pound his pain.

So then there was a silly poor man
   Had two sheep's pells upon his back to sell,
And, going to the market-town,
   He found the purse, and liked it well.
He took it up into his hand,
   And needs see what was in it he wold :
But the same he could not understand—
   For why, there was nothing in it but gold.

The rich man he pursued him soon.
   " Thou whoreson villain ! " quoth he then,
" I think it is thou that has found my purse,
   And wilt thou not give it me again ? "
" Good sir," said he, " I found such a purse—
   The truth full soon it shall be known.
You shall have it again, it's never the worse,
   But pay me my safety that is mine own."

" Let me see what's in the purse," said the merchant.
   " Found thou a hundred pound and no more ?
Thou whoreson villain ! thou hast paid thyself !
   For in my purse was full six score.
It's best my purse to me thou restore,
   Or before the king thou shalt be brought."
" I warrant," quoth he, " when I come the king before,
   He'll not reward me again with nought."

Then they led him towards the king :
   And, as they led him on the way,

---

[1] Mr. Furnivall, who edited this piece from the Percy MS., supposes "More" to represent Morio, or μωρός, a blockhead.

And there met him a gallant knight,
   And with him was his lady gay.
With tugging and lugging this poor man,
   His leather skins began to crack:
The gelding was wanton the lady rode on,
   And threw her down beside his back.

Then to the earth she got a thwack
   (No hurt in the world the poor man did mean),
To the ground he cast the lady there;
   On a stub she dang out one of her een.
The knight would needs upon him have been.
" Nay," said the merchant, " I pray you, sir, stay:
   I have a action against him already:
He shall be brought to the king, and hanged this day."

Then they led him towards the king;
   But the poor man liked not their leading well,
And, coming near to the seaside,
   He thought to be drowned or save himself.
And, as he lope into the sea,
   No harm to no man he did wot;
But there he light upon two fishermen:
   With the leap he broke one of their necks in a boat.

The other would needs upon him have been.
   " Nay," said the merchant, " I pray thee now stay:
We have two actions against him already:
   He shall be carried to the king, and hanged this day."
Then they led him bound before the king,
   Where he sate in a gallery gay.
" My liege," said the merchant, "we have brought such a villain
   As came not before you this many a day.

" For it was my chance to lose my purse,
   And in it there was full six score:
And now the villain will not give it me again,
   Except that he had twenty pound more."
" I cut[1] I have a worse match than that," said the knight,
   " For I know not what the villain did mean:
He caused my gelding to cast my lady;
   On a stub she hath dang out one of her een."

" But I have the worst match of all," said the fisher,
   For I may sigh and say God wot!
He lope at me and my brother upon the seas:
   With the leap he hath broken my brother's neck in a boat."

---

[1] Say.

The king he turned him round-about,
  Being well advised of everything :—
Quoth he : "Never since I can remember,
  Came three such matters since I was king."

Then Mark More, fool, being by,
  "How now, brother Salomon?" then quoth he.
Gif you will not give judgment of these three matters,
  I pray you, return them o'er to me."
"With all my heart," quoth Salomon to him ;
  "Take you the judgment of them as yet ;
For never came matters me before
  That fainer of I would be quit."

"Well," quoth Mark, "we have these three men here,
  And every one hath put up a bill.
But, poor man, come nither to me :
  Let's hear what tale thou canst tell for thyself."
"Why, my lord," quoth he, "as touching this merchant,—
  As he rode to a market-town,
It was his chance to lose his purse :
  He said there was in it a hundred pound.

"A proclamation he caused to be made,
  Whosoever could find the same again plain
Should give it him again without all doubt,
  And he should have twenty pound for his pain.
And it was my chance to find that purse,
  And gladly to him I would it restore :
But now he would reward me with nothing,
  But challengeth in his purse twenty pound more."

"Hast thou any witness of that?" said my lord Mark :
  "I pray thee, fellow, tell me round."
"Yes, my lord, here's his owne man
  That carried the message from town to town."
The man was called before them all ;
  And said it was a hundred pound plain,
And that his master would give twenty pound
  To any would give him his purse again.

"I had forgotten twenty pound," said the merchant,
  "Give me leave for myself to say."
"Nay," said Mark, "thou challengeth more than thine own :
  Therefore with the poor fellow the purse shall stay.
And this shall be my judgment straight :—
  Thou shalt follow each day by the heeles plain
Till thou have found such another purse with him,
  And then keep it thyself, and ne'er give it him again."

"Marry! our gods forbot," said the merchant,
  "That ever so bad should be my share!

How should I find a hundred pound of him
 That hath not a hundred pence to spare?
Rather I'll give him twenty pound more;
 And with that he hath let him stay."
"Marry! render us down the money," said Mark,
 "So may thou chance go quietly away.—

"Fellow, how hinderedst thou the knight?
 Thou must make him amends here, I mean.
It's against law and right:
 His lady she hath lost one of her een."
"Why, my lord, as they led me towards the king,
 For fear lest I should lost my trattle,
These leather skins you see me bring,
 With tugging and lugging, began to rattle.

"The gelding was wanton the lady rode upon:
 No hurt in the world, my lord, I did mean:
To the ground he cast that lady there,
 And on a stub she dang out one of her een."
"Fellow," quoth Mark, "hath thy wife two eyes?
 I pray thee," quoth he, "tell me then."
"Yes, my lord—a good honest poor woman,
 That for her living takes great pain."

"Why, then, this shall be my judgment straight,
 Though thou perhaps may think it strange:
Thy wife with two eyes, his lady hath but one,
 As thou hast dressed her, with him thou'st change."
"Marry, our gods forbot," then said the knight,
 "That ever so bad should be my shame!
I had rather give him a hundred pound
 Than to be troubled with his dunnish dame!"

"Marry! tender us down the money," said Mark,
 "So may thou be gone within a while."—
But the fisher, for fear he should have been called,
 He ran away a quarter of a mile.
"I pray you, call him again," quoth Mark,
 "Gif he be within sight;
For never came matter me before
 But every man should have his right."

They called the fisher back again.
 "How now, fellow? why didst not stay?"
"My lord," quoth he, "I have a great way home,
 And fain I would be gone my way."
"But, fellow, how hinderedst thou this fisher?
 I pray thee," quoth Mark, "to us tell."
"My lord, as I came near the easide,
 I thought either to be drowned or save myself.

"And as I lope into the sea—
  No harm to no man I did wot—
There I light upon this fisher's brother :
  With a leap I broke his neck in a boat."
"Fisher," quoth Mark, "knowest thou where the boat
    stood?
Thou'st set her again in the selfsame stead,
And thou'st leap at him as he did at thy brother,
And so thou may quit thy brother's dead."

"Marry, gods forbot," then said the fisher,
  "That ever so bad should be my luck !
If I leap at him as he did at my brother,
  I'st either be drowned, or break my neck.
Rather I'll give him twenty pound,
  An. I would, my lord, I had ne'er come hither."
"Marry, tender us down the money," said Mark,
  "And you shall be packing all three together."

The poor man he was well content,
  And very well pleased of everything :
He said he would ne'er take great care
  How oft he came before the king.—
These other three could never agree,
  But every one fell out with other ;
And said they would ne'er come more to the king
  While he was in company with Mark his brother.

THE POOR MAN AND THE KING.[1]

It was a poor man, he dwelled in Kent ;
He paid our King five pound of rent.

And there is a lawyer dwelt him by ;
  A fault in his lease, God wot, he hath found :
"And all was for falling of five ash-trees
  To build me a house of my own good ground.

"I bid him let me and my ground alone ;
  To cease his self, if he was willing,
And pick no vantages out of my lease :
  And he seemed a good fellow, I would give him forty
    shilling.

---

[1] "This," says Mr. Furnivall, "is a Kent version of the ballad which Martin Parker issued as a Northumberland one in 1640, with the title *The King and a Poor Northern Man.*" In this latter much altered form, the poem has passed as Parker's own composition, but perhaps not correctly so : it is to be found in Mr. W. C. Hazlitt's *Early Popular Poetry.*

"Forty shilling nor forty ponnd
  Would not agree this lawyer and me,
Without I would give him of my farm-ground,
  And stand to his good courtesy."

He said—Nay, by his fay, that he would not do,
  For wife and children would make mad wark;
But, and he would let him and his ground alone—
  He seemed a good fellow,—he would give him five mark.

He said—Nay, by his fay, that he would not do,
  For five good ash-trees that he fell.
"Then I'll do as neighbours have put me in head
  I'll make a submission to the King myself."

By that he had gone a day's journey,
  One of his neighbours he did spy.
"Neighbour, how far off have I to our King?
  I am going towards him as fast as I can hie."

"Alas to-day," said his neighbour,
  "It's for you I make all this moan.
You may talk of that time enough
  By that ten days' journey you have gone."

But, when he came to London Street,
  For an host-house he did call.
He lay so long o' the tother morning asleep
  That the court was removed to Windsor Hall.

"Arise, my guest, you have great need;
  You have lien too long even by a great while:
The court is removed to Windsor this morning;
  He is further off to seek by twenty mile."

"Alack to-day!" quoth the poor man,
  "I think not [1] your King at me got wit:
Had he knowen of my coming,
  I think he would have tarried yet."

"He foled not for you," then said his host;
  "But hie you to Windsor as fast as you may;
And all your costs and your charges
  Have you no doubt but the King will pay."

He hath gotten a grey russet gown on his back,
  And a hood well buckled under his chin,
And a long staff upon his neck,
  And he is to Windsor to our King.

---

[1] This "not" (which is my interpolation) seems needed to reconcile the sense of line 2 with that of lines 3 and 4.

So, when he came to Windsor Hall,
   The gates were shut as he there stood.
He knocked and poled with a great long staff:
   The porter had thought he had been wood.

He knocked again with might and main:
   Says, "Hey ho! is our King within?"—
With that he proffered a great reward,
   A single penny, to let him come in.

"I thank you, sir," quoth the porter then;
   "The reward is so great I cannot say nay.
There is a nobleman standing by:
   First I'll go hear what he will say."

The nobleman then came to the gates,
   And asked him what his business might be.
"Nay, soft," quoth the fellow; "I tell thee not yet,
   Before I do the King himself see.

"It was told me ere I came from home
   That gentlemen's hounds eaten arrands by the way,
And poor cur-dogs may eat mine:
   Therefore I mean my own arrands to say."
"But and thou come in," says the porter then,
   "Thy bumble-staff behind we must stay."

"Beshrew thee, liar!" then said the poor man;
   "Then may thou term me a fool, or a worse.
I know not what bankrouts be about our King
   For lack of money would take my purse."

"Hold him back," then said the nobleman,
   "And more of his speech we will have soon.
I'll see how he can answer the matter,
   As soon as the match at bowls is done."

The porter took the poor man by the hand,
   And led him before the nobleman.
He kneelèd down upon his knees,
   And these words to him said then:—

   And you be sir King," then said the poor man,
     "You are the goodliest fellow that ever I see:
You have so many jingles-jangles about ye
   I never see man wear but ye."

"I am not the King," the nobleman said,
   "Although I wear now a proud coat."
"And you be not King, and you'll bring me to him,
   For your reward I'll give you a groat."

"I thank you, sir," said the nobleman;
  "Your reward is so great I cannot say nay.
I'll first go know our King's pleasure :
  Till I come again be sure that you stay."

"Here is such a staying," said the poor man,
  "I think the King's better here than in our countrie :
I could have gone to farmost nook in the house,
  Neither lad nor man to have troubled me."

The nobleman went before our King,
  So well he knew his courtesy.
"There is one of the rankest clowns at your gates
  That ever Englishman did see.

"He calls them knaves your highness keep ;
  Withal he calls them somewhat worse.
He dare not come in without a long staff :
  He's feared lest some bankrout should pick his purse."

"Let him come in," then said our king ;
  "Let him come in, and his staff too.
We'll see how we can answer every matter,
  Now the match at bowls is do."

The nobleman took the poor man by the hand,
  And led him through chambers and galleries high.
'What does our king with so many empty houses,
  And gars them not filled with corn and hay?"

And, as they went through one alley,
  The nobleman soon the king did spy.
"Yond is the king," the nobleman said :
  "Look thee, good fellow, yond he goes by."

"Belike he is some unthrift," said the poor man,
  "And he hath made some of his clothes away."
"Now hold thy tongue," said the nobleman,
  "And take good heed what thou dost say."
(The weather it was exceeding hot,
  And our king had laid some of his clothes away).

And, when the nobleman came before our king,
  So well he knew his courtesy,
The poor man followed after him,—
  Gave a nod with his head, and a beck with his knee.

"And if you be the king," then said the poor man,
  "As I can hardly think you be,
This goodly fellow that brought me hither
  Seems liker to be a king than ye."

"I am the king, and the king indeed :
  Let me thy matter understand."
Then the poor man fell down on his knees.
  'I am your tenant on your own good land ;

"And there is a lawyer dwells me by,
  A fault in my lease, God wot, he hath found ;
And all is for felling of five ash-trees,
  To build me a house in my own good ground.

"I bade him let me and my ground alone,
  And cease himself, if that he was willing,
And pick no vantage out of my lease ;
  He seemed a good fellow, I would give him forty shilling.

"Forty shilling nor forty pound
  Would not agree this lawyer and me,
Without I would give him of my farm-ground,
  And stand to his good courtesy.

"I said, nay, by fay, that would I not do,
  For wife and children would make mad wark ;
And he would let me and my ground alone,
  He seemed a good fellow, I would give him five mark."

"But hast thou thy lease e'en thee upon,
  Or canst thou show to me thy deed ?"
He pulled it forth of his bosom,
  And says : "Here, my liege, if you can read."

"What if I cannot ?" then says our king :
  "Good fellow, to me what hast thou to say ?"
"I have a boy at home, but thirteen year old,
  Will read it as fale gast as young [1] by the way."

"I can never get these knots loose," then said our king :
  He gave it a gentleman stood him hard by.
"That's a proud horse," then said the poor man,
  "That will not carry his own proventy.

"And ye paid me five shillings rent, as I do ye,
  I would not be too proud to loose a knot :
But give it me again, and I'll loose it for ye,
  So that in my rent you'll bate me a groat."

An old man took this lease in his hand,
  And the king's majesty stood so.
"I'll warrant thee, poor man, and thy ground,
  If thou had fallen five ashes moe."

---

[1] The meaning of "as fale gast as young" is unknown to me : I suspect a misprint—or rather a miswriting in the MS. printed from. "Will read it *as fast as going* by the way" would seem to be a natural expression; equivalent to "will read it as fast as he can run."

"Alas to-day!" then said the poor man.—
  "Now hold your tongue, and trouble not me."—
"He that troubles *me* this day with this matter
  Cares neither for your warrants, you, nor me."

"I'll make thee attachment, fool," he says,
  "That all that sees it shall take thy part.
Until he have paid thee a hundred pound,
  Thou'st tie him to a tree that he cannot start."

"I thank you, sir," said the poor man then.
  "About this matter as you have been willing,
And seemed to do the best you can,
  With all my heart I'll give you a shilling."

"A plague on thy knave's heart!" then said our king:
  "This money on my skin lies so cold!"
He flang it into the king's bosom,
  Because in his hand he would it not hold.

The king callèd his treasurer;
  Says: "Count me down a hundred pound—
Since he hath spent money by the way—
  To bring him home to his own good ground."

When the hundred pound was counted,
  To receive it the poor man was willing.
"If I had thought you had had so much silver and gold,
  You should not have had my good shilling."

The lawyer came to welcome him
  When he came home upon a Sundày.
"Where have you been, neighbour?" he says:
  "Methinks you have been long away."

"I have been at the king," the poor man said.—
  "And what the devil didst thou do there?
Could not our neighbours have agreed us,
  But thou must go so far from here?"

"There could no neighbours have agreed thee and me,
  Nor half so well have pleased my heart.
Until thou have paid me a hundred pound,
  I'll tie thee to a tree, thou cannot start."

When the hundred pound was counted,
  To receive it the poor man was most willing:
And for the pains in the law he had taken
  He would not give him again one shilling.

God send all lawyers thus well served—
  Then may poor farmers live in ease!
God bless and save our noble king,
  And send us all to live in peace!

SONGS OF SHEPHERDS.

Songs of shepherds, rustical roundelays,
   Framed on fancies, whistled on reeds,
Songs to solace young nymphs upon holidays,
   Are too unworthy for wonderful deeds.
Phœbus Ismenius,[1] or wingèd Cyllenius
   His lofty genius, may seem to declare,
In verse better coined and voice more refined,
   How stars divined once hunted the hare.

Stars enamoured with pastimes Olympical,
   Stars and planets that beautiful shone,
Would no longer that earthly men only shall
   Swim in pleasures, and they but look on.
Round about horned Lucina they swarmed;
   And her informed how minded they were,
Each god and goddess, to take human bodies,
   As lords and ladies, to follow the hare.

Chaste Diana applauded the motion ;
   And pale Proserpina sate in her place,—
Lights the welkin, and governs the ocean,
   Whilst she conducted her nephews in chase.
And, by her example, her father, to trample
   The cold and ample earth, leaveth the air ;
Neptune, the water,—the wine, Liber Pater,—
   And Mars, the slaughter,—to follow the hare.

Light young Cupid was horsed upon Pegasus,
   Borrowed of Muses with kisses and prayers:
Strong Alcides, upon cloudy Caucasus,
   Mounts a centaur that proudly him bears:
Postilion of the sky, light-heelèd Mercury
   Makes his courser fly fleet as the air:
Yellow Apollo the kennel doth follow,
   With whoop and hallo after the hare.

Hymen ushers the ladies :—Astræa,
   That just took hands with Minerva the bold ;
Ceres the brown with the bright Cytheræa,
   Thetis the wanton, Bellona the old,
Shamefaced Aurora with subtle Pandora,
   And May with Flora, did company bear.
Juno was stated too high to be mated,
   But oh she hated not hunting the hare!

---

[1] One copy of the poem gives "Aeminius;" another gives "ingenious." The former word seems to be meaningless, and the latter unmeaning. I substitute, at a guess, "Ismenius," which is one of the known appellations of Phœbus. The various texts of this composition are very inaccurate.

Drowned Narcissus, from his metamorphosis
  Raised with Echo, new manhood did take:
Snoring Somnus upstarted in Cimmeris—
  That this thousand years was not awake—
To see clubfooted old Mulciber booted,
  And Pan promoted on Chiron's mare.
Proud Faunus pouted, proud Æolus shouted,
  And Momus flouted,—but followed the hare.

Deep Melampus and cunning Ichnobates,
  Nappy and Tigre and Harpy, the skies
Rends with roaring; whilst hunter-like Hercules
  Sounds the plentiful horn to their cries.
Till—with varieties to solace their pieties—
  The weary Deities reposed them where
We shepherds were seated, the whilst we repeated
  What we conceited of their hunting the hare.

Young Amyntas supposed the gods came to breathe,
  After some battle, themselves on the ground.
Thyrsis thought the stars came to dwell here beneath,
  And that hereafter the world would go round.
Corydon aged, with Phillis engagèd,
  Was much enragèd with jealous despair:
But fury vaded, and he was persuaded,
  When I thus applauded their hunting the hare:—

"Stars but shadows were, state were but sorrow,—
  That no motion, nor that no delight:
Joys are jovial, delight is the marrow
  Of life, and action the apple of light.
Pleasure depends upon no other ends,
  But freely lends to each virtue a share:
Only is measure the jewel of treasure:
  Of pleasure the treasure is hunting the hare!"

Four broad bowls to the Olympical rector
  That Troy-borne eagle does bring on his knee:[1]
Jove to Phœbus carouses in nectar,
  And he to Hermes, and Hermes to me:
Wherewith infused, I piped, and I mused
  In verse unused this sport to declare.
Oh that the rouse of Jove round as his sphere may move!
  Health to all that love hunting the hare!

---

[1] The poet seems to have hesitated here between introducing the eagle, or Ganymede, on the scene: and a very jumbled line is the result.

ROBIN GOODFELLOW.[1]

From Oberon, in fairy-land,
  The king of ghosts and shadows there,
Mad Robin I, at his command,
  Am sent to view the night-sports here.
    What revel rout
    Is kept about,
In every corner where I go,
    I will o'ersee,
    And merry be,
And make good sport with ho ho ho!

More swift than lightning can I fly
  About this airy welkin soon,
And in a minute's space descry
  Each thing that's done below the moon.
    There's not a hag
    Or ghost shall wag,
Or cry, 'ware goblins! where I go,
    But Robin I
    Their feats will spy,
And send them home with ho ho ho!

Whene'er such wanderers I meet,
  As from their night-sports they trudge home,
With counterfeiting voice I greet,
  And call them on with me to roam:
    Through woods, through lakes;
    Through bogs, through brakes;
Or else, unseen, with them I go,
    All in the nick,
    To play some trick,
And frolic it with ho ho ho!

Sometimes I meet them like a man,
  Sometimes an ox, sometimes a hound;
And to a horse I turn me can,
  To trip and trot about them round.
    But, if to ride
    My back they stride,
More swift than wind away I go,
    O'er hedge and lands,
    Through pools and ponds,
I hurry, laughing ho ho ho!

When lads and lasses merry be,
  With possets and with junkets fine,
Unseen of all the company,
  I eat their cakes and sip their wine:

---

[1] This poem has sometimes been attributed to Ben Jonson.

  And to make sport
  I puff and snort;
And out the candles I do blow:
  The maids I kiss,
  They shriek—" Who's this?"
I answer nought but ho ho ho!

Yet now and then, the maids to please,
 At midnight I card up their wool;
And, while they sleep and take their ease,
 With wheel to threads their flax I pull.
  I grind at mill
  Their malt up still;
I dress their hemp; I spin their tow;
  If any wake,
  And would me take,
I wend me, laughing ho ho ho!

When house or hearth doth sluttish lie,
 I pinch the maidens black and blue;
The bed-clothes from the bed pull I,
 And lay them naked all to view.
  'Twixt sleep and wake,
  I do them take,
And on the key-cold floor them throw;
  If out they cry,
  Then forth I fly,
And loudly laugh out ho ho ho!

When any need to borrow aught,
 We lend them what they do require;
And, for the use, demand we nought;
 Our own is all we do desire.
  If to repay
  They do delay,
Abroad amongst them then I go,
  And night by night
  I them affright,
With pinchings, dreams, and ho ho ho!

When lazy queans have nought to do,
 But study how to cog and lie,
To make debate and mischief too
 'Twixt one another secretly:
  I mark their gloze,
  And it disclose
To them whom they have wrongèd so:
  When I have done,
  I get me gone,
And leave them scolding, ho ho ho!

When men do traps and engines set
　In loop-holes, where the vermin creep
Who from their folds and houses get
　Their ducks and geese and lambs and sheep;
　　I spy the gin,
　　And enter in,
　And seem a vermin taken so;
　　But, when they there
　　Approach me near,
　I leap out laughing ho ho ho!

By wells and rills and meadows green,
　We nightly dance our heyday guise;
And to our fairy king and queen,
　We chant our moonlight minstrelsies.
　　When larks 'gin sing,
　　Away we fling;
　And babes new-born steal as we go;
　　And elf in bed
　　We leave instead,
　And wend us laughing ho ho ho!

From hag-bred Merlin's time, have I
　Thus nightly revelled to and fro;
And for my pranks men call me by
　The name of Robin Goodfellow.
　　Fiends, ghosts, and sprites,
　　Who haunt the nights,
　The hags and goblins, do me know;
　　And beldames old
　　My feats have told,—
　So *Vale, vale;* ho ho ho!

THE SONG OF THE BEGGAR.

I AM a rogue and a stout one,
　A most courageous drinker;
I do excel, 'tis known full well,
　The Ratter, Tom, and Tinker.
　　Still do I cry, "Good your worship,
　　　good Sir,
　　　Bestow one small denire, Sir;"
　And bravely at the boozing-ken
　　I'll booze it all in beer, Sir.

If a bung be got by the high law,
　Then straight I do attend them;
For, if hue and cry do follow, I
　A wrong way soon do send them.
　　Still do I cry, &c.

Ten miles unto a market
  I run to meet a miser;
Then in a throng I nip his bung,
  And the party ne'er the wiser.
    Still do I cry, &c.

My dainty Dals, my Doxies,
  Whene'er they see me lacking,
Without delay, poor wretches, they
  Will set their duds a-packing.
    Still do I cry, &c.

I pay for what I call for,
  And so perforce it must be;
For as yet I can not know the man
  Nor hostess that will trust me.
    Still do I cry, &c.

If any give me lodging,
  A courteous knave they find me;
For in their bed, alive or dead,
  I leave some lice behind me.
    Still do I cry, &c.

If a gentry coe be coming,
  Then straight (it is our fashion)
My leg I tie close to my thigh,
  To move him to compassion.
    Still do I cry, &c.

My doublet-sleeve hangs empty;
  And, for to beg the bolder
For meat and drink, mine arm I shrink,
  Up close unto my shoulder.
    Still do I cry, &c.

If a coach I hear be rumbling,
  To my crutches then I hie me;
For, being lame, it is a shame
  Such gallants should deny me.
    Still do I cry, &c.

With a seeming bursten belly,
  I look like one half dead, Sir;
Or else I beg with a wooden leg,
  And a night-cap on my head, Sir.
    Still do I cry, &c.

In winter-time stark naked
  I come into some city;
Then every man that spare them can
  Will give me clothes for pity.
    Still do I cry, &c.

If from out the Low-country
  I hear a captain's name, Sir,
Then straight I swear I have been there,
  And so in fight came lame, Sir.
    Still do I cry, &c.

My dog in a string doth lead me,
  When in the town I go, Sir;
For to the blind all men are kind,
  And will their alms bestow, Sir.
    Still do I cry, &c.

With switches sometimes stand I
  In the bottom of a hill, Sir;
There those men which do want a switch
  Some money give me still, Sir.
    Still do I cry, &c.

"Come buy, come buy, a horn-book!
  Who buys my pins or needles?"
In cities I these things do cry
  Oft-times to scape the beadles.
    Still do I cry, &c.

In Paul's church by a pillar
  Sometimes you see me stand, Sir,
With a writ that shows what care and woes
  I passed by sea and land, Sir.
    Still do I cry, &c.

Now blame me not for boasting
  And bragging thus alone, Sir;
For myself I will be praising still,
  For neighbours have I none, Sir.
    Which makes me cry, "Good your
      worship, good Sir,
    Bestow one small denire, Sir;"
    And bravely then at the boozing-ken
    I'll booze it all in beer, Sir.

A NEW-YEAR'S GIFT FOR SHREWS.

Who marrieth a wife upon a Monday,
If she will not be good upon a Tuesday,
Let him go to the wood upon a Wednesday,
And cut him a cudgel upon the Thursday,
And pay her soundly upon a Friday:
And she mend not, the divil take her a' Saturday:
Then he may eat his meat in peace on the Sunday.

LINES ON A PRINTING OFFICE.

THE world's a printing-house. Our words, our thoughts,
　　Our deeds, are characters of several sizes.
Each soul is a compos'tor, of whose faults
　　The Levites are correctors ; Heaven revises.
Death is the common press ; from whence being driven,
We're gathered sheet by sheet, and bound for heaven.

THE MAY-POLE.

COME, lasses and lads, take leave of your dads,
　　And away to the may-pole hie ;
For every he has got him a she,
　　And the minstrel's standing by ;
For Willie has gotten his Jill,
　　And Johnny has got his Joan,
To jig it, jig it, jig it,
　　Jig it up and down.

"Strike up," says Wat. "Agreed," says Kate,
　　"And I prithee, fiddler, play."
"Content," says Hodge, and so says Madge,
　　For this is a holiday.
Then every man did put
　　His hat off to his lass,
And every girl did curchy,
　　Curchy, curchy on the grass.

"Begin," says Hal. "Aye, aye," says Mall,
　　"We'll lead up *Packington's Pound.*"
"No, no," says Noll, and so says Doll,
　　"We'll first have *Sellenger's Round.*"
Then every man began
　　To foot it round about ;
And every girl did jet it,
　　Jet it, jet it, in and out.

"You're out," says Dick. "'Tis a lie," says Nick ;
　　"The fiddler played it false."
"'Tis true," says Hugh, and so says Sue,
　　And so says nimble Alice.
The fiddler then began
　　To play the tune again ;
And every girl did trip it, trip it,
　　Trip it to the men.

"Let's kiss," says Jane.[1] "Content," says Nan,
  And so says every she.
"How many?" says Batt. "Why three," says Matt,
  "For that's a maiden's fee."
But they, instead of three,
  Did give them half a score;
And they in kindness gave 'em, gave 'em,
  Gave 'em as many more.

Then after an hour they went to a bower,
  And played for ale and cakes;
And kisses, too;—until they were due,
  The lasses kept the stakes.
The girls did then begin
  To quarrel with the men;
And bid 'em take their kisses back,
  And give them their own again.

Yet there they sate, until it was late,
  And tired the fiddler quite,
With singing and playing, without any paying,
  From morning unto night.
They told the fiddler then
  They'd pay him for his play;
And each a two-pence, two-pence,
  Gave him, and went away.

"Good night," says Harry; "Good night," says Mary;
  "Good night," says Dolly to John;
"Good night," says Sue; "Good night," says Hugh;
  "Good night," says every one.
Some walked, and some did run,
  Some loitered on the way;
And bound themselves with love-knots, love-knots,
  To meet the next holiday.

THERE WAS AN OLD MAN CAME OVER THE LEA.

THERE was an old man came over the Lea;
Ha-ha-ha-ha! but I won't have he.
    He came over the Lea,
    A-courting to me,
With his grey beard newly shaven.

My mother she bid me open the door:
    I opened the door,
    And he fell on the floor.

---

[1] Some copies say "Pan," and this reading has not been without its defender. I can hardly suppose "Pan" to be right: but surely it ought to be a male name of some sort—probably "Dan."

My mother she bid me set him a stool:
   I set him a stool,
   And he looked like a fool.

My mother she bid me give him some beer:
   I gave him some beer,
   And he thought it good cheer.

My mother she bid me cut him some bread:
   I cut him some bread,
   And I threw't at his head.

My mother she bid me light him to bed:
   I lit him to bed,
   And wished he were dead.

My mother she bid me tell him to rise:
   I told him to rise,
   And he opened his eyes.

My mother she bid me take him to church:
   I took him to church,
   And left him in the lurch,
With his grey beard newly shaven.

THE NEW LITANY.

FROM an extempore prayer and a godly ditty,
From the churlish government of a city,
From the power of a country committee,
          Libera nos, Domine.

From the Turk, the Pope, and the Scottish nation,
From being governed by proclamation,
And from an old Protestant, quite out of fashion,
          Libera nos, Domine.

From meddling with those that are out of our reaches,
From a fighting priest, and a soldier that preaches,
From an ignoramus that writes, and a woman that teaches,
          Libera nos, Domine.

From the doctrine of deposing of a king,
From the *Directory*,[1] or any such thing,
From a fine new marriage without a ring,
          Libera nos, Domine.

---

[1] The Directory for the Public Worship of God, ordered by the Assembly of Divines at Westminster in 1644, to supersede the Book of Common Prayer.

From a city that yields at the first summons,
From plundering goods, either man or woman's,
Or having to do with the House of Commons,
    Libera nos, Domine.

From a stumbling horse that tumbles o'er and o'er,
From ushering a lady, or walking before,
From an English-Irish rebel, newly come o'er,[1]
    Libera nos, Domine.

From compounding, or hanging in a silken halter,
From oaths and covenants, and being pounded in a mortar,
From contributions, or free-quarter,
    Libera nos, Domine.

From mouldy bread and musty beer,
From a holiday's fast, and a Friday's cheer,
From a brotherhood, and a she-cavalier,
    Libera nos, Domine.

From Nick Neuter, for you and for *you*,
From Thomas Turn-coat that will never prove true,
From a reverend Rabbi that's worse than a Jew,
    Libera nos, Domine.

From a country justice that still looks big,
From swallowing up the Italian fig,
Or learning of the Scottish jig,
    Libera nos, Domine.

From being taken in a disguise,
From believing of the printed lies,
From the Devil and from the Excise,[2]
    Libera nos, Domine.

From a broken pate with a pint pot
For fighting for I know not what,
And from a friend as false as a Scot,
    Libera nos, Domine.

From one that speaks no sense, yet talks all that he can,
From an old woman and a Parliament man,
From an Anabaptist and a Presbyter man,
    Libera nos, Domine.

From Irish rebels and Welsh hubub-men,
From Independents and their tub-men,
From sheriffs' bailiffs and their club-men,
    Libera nos, Domine.

---

[1] The Earl of Thomond.
[2] The Excise was first introduced by the Long Parliament.

From one that cares not what he saith,
From trusting one that never pay'th,
From a private preacher and a public faith,
    Libera nos, Domine.

From a vapouring horse and a Roundhead in buff,
From roaring Jack Cavee, with money little enough,
From beads and such idolatrous stuff,
    Libera nos, Domine.

From holy days, and all that's holy,
From may-poles and fiddlers, and all that's jolly,
From Latin or learning, since that is folly,
    Libera nos, Domine.

And now to make an end of all,
I wish the Roundheads had a fall,
Or else were hanged in Goldsmiths' Hall!
 Amen.
    Benedicat Dominus.

THE CLEAN CONTRARY WAY;

OR, COLONEL VENNE'S ENCOURAGEMENT TO HIS SOLDIERS.

Fight on, brave soldiers, for the cause,—
 Fear not the Cavaliers;
Their threatenings are as senseless as
 Our jealousies and fears.
'Tis you must perfect this great work,
 And all malignants slay;
You must bring back the King again
 The clean contrary way.

'Tis for religion that you fight,
 And for the kingdom's good,
By robbing churches, plundering them,
 And shedding guiltless blood.
Down with the orthodoxal train;
 All loyal subjects slay;
When these are gone, we shall be blest
 The clean contrary way.

When Charles we have made bankrupt,
 Of power and crown bereft him,
And all his loyal subjects slain,
 And none but rebels left him;
When we have beggared all the land,
 And sent our trunks away,
We'll make him then a glorious prince
 The clean contrary way.

'Tis to preserve his Majesty
  That we against him fight,
Nor ever are we beaten back,
  Because our cause is right:
If any make a scruple at
  Our Declarations, say,—
"Who fight for us fight for the King"
  (The clean contrary way).

At Keinton, Brainsford, Plymouth, York,
  And divers places more,
What victories we saints obtain,
  The like ne'er seen before!
How often we Prince Rupert killed,
  And bravely won the day!
The wicked Cavaliers did run
  The clean contrary way.

The true religion we maintain;
  The kingdom's peace and plenty;
The privilege of Parliament,
  Not known to one and twenty;
The ancient fundamental laws;
  And teach men to obey
Their lawful sovereign;—and all these
  The clean contrary way.

We subjects' liberties preserve
  By imprisonment and plunder,
And do enrich ourselves and state
  By keeping th' wicked under.
We must preserve mechanics now
  To lectorize and pray;
By them the gospel is advanced
  The clean contrary way.

And, though the King be much misled
  By that malignant crew,
He'll find us honest at the last,
  Give all of us our due.
For we do wisely plot, and plot
  Rebellion to allay;
He sees we stand for peace and truth
  The clean contrary way.

The public faith shall save our souls
  And our good works together;
And ships shall save our lives, that stay
  Only for wind and weather:
But, when our faith and works fall down
  And all our hopes decay,
Our acts will bear us up to heaven
  The clean contrary way.

THE ANARCHY;
OR, THE BLEST REFORMATION SINCE 1640.

Now that, thanks to the powers below,
    We have e'en done out our do,
The mitre is down, and so is the crown,
    And with them the coronet too;
Come clowns, and come boys, come hober-de-hoys,
    Come females of each degree;
Stretch your throats, bring in your votes,
    And make good the anarchy.
And "thus it shall go," says Alice;
    "Nay, thus it shall go," says Amy;
"Nay, thus it shall go," says Taffie, "I trow;"
    "Nay, thus it shall go," says Jamy.

Ah! but the truth, good people all,
    The truth is such a thing;
For it would undo both Church and State too,
    And cut the throat of our King.
Yet not the spirit, nor the new light,
    Can make this point so clear
But thou must bring out, thou deified rout,
    What thing this truth is, and where.
Speak Abraham, speak Kester, speak Judith, speak Hester,
    Speak tag and rag, short coat and long;
Truth's the spell made us rebel,
    And murder and plunder, ding-dong.
"Sure I have the truth," says Numph;
    "Nay, I ha' the truth," says Clemme;
"Nay, I ha' the truth," says Reverend Ruth;
    "Nay, I ha' the truth," says Nem.

Well, let the truth be where it will,
    We're sure all else is ours;
Yet these divisions in our religions
    May chance abate our powers.
Then let's agree on some one way,
    It skills not much how true;
Take Prynne and his clubs, or Say and his tubs,
    Or any sect old or new.
The devil's i' the pack if choice you can lack,—
    We're fourscore religions strong;
Take your choice, the major voice
    Shall carry it, right or wrong.
"Then we'll be of this," says Megg,
    "Nay, we'll be of that," says Tibb;
"Nay, we'll be of all," says pitiful Paul;
    "Nay, we'll be of none," says Gibb.

Neighbours and friends, pray one word more,
  There's something yet behind ;
And, wise though you be, you do not well see
  In which door sits the wind.
As for religion (to speak right,
  And in the House's sense),
The matter is all one to have any or none,
  If 'twere not for the pretence.
But herein doth lurk the key of the work,—
  Even to dispose of the crown
Dexteriously, and, as may be,
  For our behoof and your own.
"Then let's ha' king Charles," says George ;
"Nay, let's have his son," says Hugh ;
"Nay, let's have none," says Jabbering Joan ;
"Nay, let's be all kings," says Prue.

Oh we shall have (if we go on
  In plunder, excise, and blood)
But few folk and poor to domineer o'er,
  And that will not be so good.
Then let's resolve on some new way,
  Some new and happy course ;
The country's grown sad, the city horn-mad,
  And both the Houses are worse.
The synod hath writ, the general hath spit,
  And both to like purposes too ;
Religion, laws, the truth, the cause,
  Are talked of, but nothing we do.
"Come, come, shall's ha' peace?" says Nell ;
"No, no, but we won't," says Madge ;
"But I say we will," says fiery-faced Phil ;
"We will and we won't," says Hodge.

Thus from the rout who can expect
  Aught but division?
Since unity doth with monarchy
  Begin and end in one.
If then, when all is thought their own,
  And lies at their behest,
These popular pates reap nought but debates
  From that many round-headed beast ;
Come, Royalists, then, do you play the men,
  And, Cavaliers, give the word ;
Now let us see at what you would be,
  And whether you can accord.
" A health to King Charles," says Tom ;
" Up with it," says Ralph, like a man ;
" God bless him," says Doll ; " and raise him," says Moll ;
" And send him his own !" says Nan.

Now for these prudent things that sit
   Without end and to none,
And their committees, that towns and cities
   Fill with confusion ;
For the bold troops of sectaries,
   The Scots and their partakers,
Our new British states, Colonel Burges and his mates,
   The covenant and its makers ;
For all these we'll pray, and in such a way
   As, if it might granted be,
Jack and Gill, Matt and Will,
   And all the world would agree.
"A plague take them all!" says Bess ;
   "And a pestilence too!" says Margery :
"The devil!" says Dick ; "And his dam, too!" says Nick ;
   "Amen! and Amen!" say I.

JOAN'S ALE WAS NEW.

THERE were six jovial tradesmen,
   And they all set down to drinking,
   For they were a jovial crew ;
They sat themselves down to be merry,
And they called for a bottle of sherry.
"You're welcome as the hills," says Nolly,
   "While Joan's ale is new, brave boys,
   While Joan's ale is new."

The first that came in was a soldier,
With his firelock over his shoulder ;
Sure no one could be bolder,
   And a long broad-sword he drew :
He swore he would fight for England's ground,
Before the nation should be run down ;
He boldly drank their healths all round,
   While Joan's ale was new.

The next that came in was a hatter,
Sure no one could be blacker,
And he began to chatter,
   Among the jovial crew :
He threw his hat upon the ground,
And swore every man should spend his pound,
And boldly drank their healths all round,
   While Joan's ale was new.

The next that came in was a dyer,
And he sat himself down by the fire,
For it was his heart's desire
   To drink with the jovial crew :

He told the landlord to his face
The chimney-corner should be his place,
And there he'd sit and dye his face,
    While Joan's ale was new.

The next that came in was a tinker,
And he was no small-beer drinker,
And he was no strong-ale shrinker,
    Among the jovial crew:
For his brass nails were made of metal,
And he swore he'd go and mend a kettle.
Good heart! how his hammer and nails did rattle,
    When Joan's ale was new!

The next that came in was a tailor,
With his bodkin, shears, and thimble;
He swore he would be nimble
    Among the jovial crew:
They sat and they called for ale so stout,
Till the poor tailor was almost broke,
And was forced to go and pawn his coat,
    While Joan's ale was new.

The next that came in was a ragman,
With his rag-bag over his shoulder;
Sure no one could be bolder
    Among the jovial crew.
They sat and called for pots and glasses,
Till they were all as drunk as asses,
And burnt the old ragman's bag to ashes,
    While Joan's ale was new.

THE REFORMATION.[1]

Tell me not of Lords and laws,
    Rules or reformation;
All that's done not worth two straws
    To the welfare of the nation;
If men in power do rant it still,
And give no reason but their will
    For all their domination;
Or, if they do an act that's just,
'Tis not because they would, but must,
To gratify some party's lust.

All our expense of blood and purse
    Has yet produced no profit;
Men are still as bad or worse,
    And will, whate'er comes of it.

---

[1] This has been ascribed to Butler—I believe, without any reason.

We've shuffled out and shuffled in
The person, but retain the sin,
  To make our game the surer;
Yet, spite of all our pains and skill,
The knaves all in the pack are still,
And ever were, and ever will,
  Though something now demurer.

And it can never be but so,
  Since knaves are still in fashion;
Men of souls so base and low,
  Mere bigots of the nation;
Whose designs are power and wealth,
At which, by rapine, power, and stealth,
  Audaciously they vent're ye
They lay their consciences aside,
And turn with every wind and tide,
Puffed on by ignorance and pride,
  And all to look like gentry.

Crimes are not punished 'cause they're crimes,
  But 'cause they're low and little.
Mean men for mean faults in these times
  Make satisfaction to a tittle;
While those in office and in power
Boldly the underlings devour,—
  Our cobweb laws can't hold 'em;
They sell for many a thousand crown
Things which were never yet their own;
And this is law and custom grown,
  'Cause those do judge who sold 'em.

Brothers still with brothers brawl,
  And for trifles sue 'em;
For two pronouns that spoil all,
  Contentious *meum* and *tuum*.
The wary lawyer buys and builds,
While the client sells his fields
  To sacrifice his fury;
And, when he thinks to obtain his right,
He's baffled off or beaten quite
By the judge's will or lawyer's sleight,
  Or ignorance of the jury.

See the tradesman how he thrives
  With perpetual trouble:
How he cheats and how he strives,
  His estate to enlarge and double;
Extort, oppress, grind, and encroach,
To be a squire and keep a coach,
  And to be one o' the quorum,

Who may with his brother worships sit,
And judge, without law, fear, or wit,
Poor petty thieves that nothing get,
    And yet are brought before 'em.

And his way to get all this
    Is mere dissimulation;
No factious lecture does he miss,
    And scape no schism that's in fashion:
But, with short hair and shining shoes,
He with two pens and note-book goes,
    And winks and writes at random;
Thence with short meal and tedious grace,
In a loud tone and public place,
Sings wisdom's hymns, that trot and pace
    As if Goliah scanned 'em.

But, when Death begins his threats,
    And his conscience struggles
To call to mind his former cheats,
    Then at Heaven he turns and juggles:
And out of all's ill-gotten store
He gives a dribbling to the poor,
    An hospital or school-house;
And the suborned priest for his hire
Quite frees him from the infernal fire,
And places him in the angels' choir:
    Thus these Jack-puddings fool us!

All he gets by his pains, i' the close,
    Is that he died worth so much;
Which he on his doubtful seed bestows,
    That neither care nor know much.
Then fortune's favourite, his heir,
Bred base and ignorant and bare,
    Is blown up like a bubble:
Who, wondering at's own sudden rise,
By pride, simplicity, and vice,
Falls to his sports, drink, drabs, and dice,
    And makes all fly like stubble.

And the Church, the other twin
    Whose mad zeal enraged us,
Is not purified a pin
    By all those broils in which they engaged us.
We our wives turned out of doors,
And took in concubines and whores,
    To make an alteration.
Our pulpitors are proud and bold;
They their own wills and factions hold,
And sell salvation still for gold;—
    And here's our *reformation!*

'Tis a madness then to make
  Thriving our employment,
And lucre love for lucre's sake,
  Since we've possession, not enjoyment.
Let the times run on their course,
For oppression makes them worse,—
  We ne'er shall better find 'em;
Let grandees wealth and power engross,
And honour too,—while we sit close,
And laugh, and take our plenteous dose
  Of sack, and never mind 'em.

THE SALE OF REBELLION'S HOUSEHOLD STUFF.

Rebellion hath broken up house,
  And hath left me old lumber to sell;
Come hither and take your choice,
  I'll promise to use you well.
Will you buy the old Speaker's chair?
  Which was warm and easy to sit in,
And oft has been cleaned, I declare,
  Whereas it was fouler than fitting.
    Says old Simon the King,
    Says old Simon the King,
With his ale-dropped hose, and his Malmsey nose,
  Sing, hey ding, ding-a-ding, ding.

Will you buy any bacon flitches,
  The fattest that ever were spent?
They're the sides of the old committees
  Fed up in the Long Parliament.
Here's a pair of bellows and tongs,
  And for a small matter I'll sell ye 'em;
They are made of the presbyter's lungs,
  To blow up the coals of rebellion.
    Says old Simon, &c.

I had thought to have given them once
  To some blacksmith for his forge;
But, now I have considered on't,
  They are consecrate to the Church.
So I'll give them unto some choir;
  They will make the big organs roar,
And the little pipes to squeak higher
  Than ever they could before.
    Says old Simon, &c.

Here's a couple of stools for sale,
  One's square, and t'other is round;

Betwixt them both, the tail
   Of the Rump fell down to the ground.
Will you buy the State's council-table,
   Which was made of the good wain-Scot?
The frame was a tottering Babel,
   To uphold th' Independent plot.
     Says old Simon, &c.

Here's the besom of Reformation,
   Which should have made clean the floor;
But it swept the wealth out of the nation,
   And left us dirt good store.
Will you buy the State's spinning-wheel,
   Which spun for the roper's trade?
But better it had stood still,
   For now it has spun a fair thread.
     Says old Simon, &c.

Here's a glyster-pipe well tried,
   Which was made of a butcher's stump,
And has been safely applied
   To cure the colds of the Rump.
Here's a lump of pilgrim's-salve,
   Which once was a justice of peace
Who Noll and the devil did serve,—
   But now it is come to this!
     Says old Simon, &c.

Here's a roll of the State's tobacco,
   If any good fellow will take it;
No Virginia had e'er such a smack-o,
   And I'll tell you how they did make it:
'Tis th' Engagement and Covenant cooked
   Up with the abjuration-oath,
And many of them that have took't
   Complain it was foul in the mouth.
     Says old Simon, &c.

Yet the ashes may happily serve
   To cure the scab of the nation,
Whene'er't has an itch to swerve
   To rebellion by innovation.
A lantern here is to be bought;
   The like was scarce ever gotten,
For many plots it has found out
   Before they ever were thought on.
     Says old Simon, &c.

Will you buy the Rump's great saddle,
   With which it jockeyed the nation?
And here is the bit and the bridle,
   And curb of dissimulation;

And here's the trunk-hose of the Rump,
    And their fair dissembling cloak;
And a Presbyterian jump,
    With an Independent smock.
        Says old Simon, &c.

Will you buy a conscience oft turned,
    Which served the High Court of Justice,
And stretched until England it mourned?—
    But hell will buy that, if the worst is.
Here's Joan Cromwell's kitchen-stuff tub,
    Wherein is the fat of the Rumpers,
With which old Noll's horns she did rub
    When he was got drunk with false bumpers.
        Says old Simon, &c.

Here's the purse of the public faith;
    Here's the model of the Sequestration,
When the old wives upon their good troth
    Lent thimbles to ruin the nation.
Here's Dick Cromwell's Protectorship,
    And here are Lambert's commissions,
And here is Hugh Peters his scrip,
    Crammed with tumultuous petitions.
        Says old Simon, &c.

And here are old Noll's brewing-vessels,
    And here are his dray and his flings;
Here are Hewson's[1] awl and his bristles,
    With diverse other odd things.
And what is the price doth belong
    To all these matters before ye?
I'll sell them all for an old song,
    And so I do end my story.
        Says old Simon, &c.

THE DEVIL'S PROGRESS ON EARTH; OR, HUGGLE DUGGLE.[2]

FRIAR BACON walks again,
    And Doctor Faustus too;
Proserpine and Pluto,
    And many a goblin crew.
With that, a merry devil
    To make the airing vowed;
Huggle Duggle, Ha! ha! ha!
    The Devil laughed aloud.

---

[1] Colonel Hewson, originally a shoemaker.
[2] This savage stroke of grotesque humour was no doubt the model for the poem of like subject written by Southey and Coleridge, and thence for those of Shelley and Byron.

Why think you that he laughed?
  Forsooth he came from court;
And there amongst the gallants
  Had spied such pretty sport;
There was such cunning juggling,
  And ladies gone so proud;
Huggle Duggle, Ha! ha! ha!
  The Devil laughed aloud.

With that into the city
  Away the Devil went;
To view the merchants' dealings
  It was his full intent:
And there along the brave Exchange
  He crept into the crowd.
Huggle Duggle, Ha! ha! ba!
  The Devil laughed aloud.

He went into the city,
  To see all there was well.
Their scales were false, their weights were light,
  Their conscience fit for hell;
And Pandars chosen magistrates,
  And Puritans allowed.
Huggle Duggle, Ha! ha! ha!
  The Devil laughed aloud.

With that unto the country
  Away the Devil goeth;
For there is all plain dealing,
  For that the Devil knoweth.
But the rich man reaps the gains
  For which the poor man ploughed.
Huggle Duggle, Ha! ha! ha!
  The Devil laughed aloud.

With that the Devil in haste
  Took post away to hell,
And called his fellow furies,
  And told them all on earth was well:
That falsehood there did flourish,
  Plain dealing was in a cloud.
    Huggle Duggle, Ha! ha! ha!
  The devils laughed aloud.

THE DESPONDING WHIG.[1]

When owls are stripped of their disguise,
    And wolves of shepherd's clothing,
Those birds and beasts that please our eyes
    Will then beget our loathing;
When foxes tremble in their holes
    At dangers that they see,
And those we think so wise prove fools,—
    Then low, boys, down go we.

If those designs abortive prove
    We've been so long in hatching,
And cunning knaves are forced to move
    From home for fear of catching;
The rabble soon will change their tone
    When our intrigues they see,
And cry "God save the Church and Throne!"
    Then low, boys, down go we.

The weaver then no more must leave
    His loom, and turn a preacher,
Nor with his cant poor fools deceive
    To make himself the richer.
Our leaders soon would disappear
    If such a change should be,
Our scribblers too would stink for fear,—
    Then low, boys, down go we.

No canvisars would dare to show
    Their postures and grimaces,
Or prophesy what they never knew,
    By dint of ugly faces;
But shove the tumbler through the town,
    And quickly banished be,
For none must teach without a gown;
    Then low, boys, down go we.

If such unhappy days should come,
    Our virtue, moderation,
Would surely be repaid us home
    With double compensation;
For, as we never could forgive,
    I fear we then should see
That what we lent we must receive,—
    Then low, boys, down go we.

Should honest brethren once discern
    Our knaveries, they'd disown us,

---

[1] Modelled partly on Quarles's chant, "Hey then up go we," p. 100.

And bubbled fools more wit should learn,—
　The Lord have mercy on us!
Let's guard against that evil day,
　Lest such a time should be,
And tackers should come into play,—
　Then low, boys, down go we.

Though hitherto we've played our parts
　Like wary cunning foxes,
And gained the common people's hearts
　By broaching heterodoxies,—
But they're as fickle as the winds,
　With nothing long agree,
And, when they change their wavering minds,
　Then low, boys, down go we.

Let's preach and pray, but spit our gall
　On those that do oppose us,
And cant of grace, in spite of all
　The shame the Devil owes us:
The just, the loyal, and the wise,
　With us shall Papists be,
For if the *High Church* once should rise,
　Then, *Low Church*, down go we.

THE CAMERONIAN CAT.

THERE was a Cameronian cat
　Was hunting for a prey,
And in the house she catched a mouse
　Upon the Sabbath-day.

The Whig, being offended
　At such an act profane,
Laid by his book, the cat he took,
　And bound her in a chain.

"Thou damned, thou cursed creature!
　This deed so dark with thee!
Think'st thou to bring to hell below
　My holy wife and me?

"Assure thyself that for the deed
　Thou blood for blood shalt pay,
For killing of the Lord's own mouse
　Upon the Sabbath-day."

The presbyter laid by the book,
  And earnestly he prayed
That the great sin the cat had done
  Might not on him be laid.

And straight to execution
  Poor pussy she was drawn,
And high hanged up upon a tree—
  The preacher sung a psalm.

And, when the work was ended,
  They thought the cat near dead;
She gave a paw, and then a mew,
  And stretchèd out her head.

"Thy name," said he, "shall certainly
  A beacon still remain,
A terror unto evil ones
  For evermore, Amen."

TITUS OATES IN THE PILLORY.

BEHOLD the hero, who has done all this,
In a small "triumph" stand, such as it is.
A kind of an "ovation" only?—True.
But those for bloodless victories are due;
His were not such. He merits more than "eggs":
Let him in "triumph" swing, and ease his legs.

COSMELIA.

COSMELIA'S charms inspire my lays;
  Who, young in nature's scorn,
Blooms in the winter of her days
  Like Glastonbury thorn.

Cosmelia, cruel at three score
  (Like bards in modern plays),
Four acts of life passed guiltless o'er,
  But in the fifth she slays.

If e'er, impatient for the bliss,
  Within her arms you fall,
The plastered fair returns the kiss,
  Like Thisbe, through a wall.

PHILLIDA FLOUTS ME.

Oh what a pain is love!
   How shall I bear it?
She will unconstant prove,
   I greatly fear it.
She so torments my mind
   That my strength faileth,
And wavers with the wind,
   As a ship that saileth.
Please her the best I may,
She looks another way;
Alack and well-a-day!
          Phillida flouts me!

All the fair yesterday
   She did pass by me;
She looked another way,
   And would not spy me.
I wooed her for to dine,
   But could not get her:
Will had her to the wine;
   He might entreat her.
With Daniel she did dance;
On me she looked askance!
Oh thrice unhappy chance!
          Phillida flouts me!

Fair maid! be not so coy,
   Do not disdain me;
I am my mother's joy,—
   Sweet! entertain me!
She'll give me, when she dies,
   All that is fitting;
Her poultry and her bees,
   And her geese sitting;
A pair of mattress-beds,
And a bagful of shreds;
And yet, for all this goods,
          Phillida flouts me!

She hath a clout of mine,
   Wrought with good Coventry,
Which she keeps for a sign
   Of my fidelity.
But i' faith, if she flinch,
   She shall not wear it;
To Tib, my t'other wench,
   I mean to bear it.

And yet it grieves my heart
So soon from her to part!
Death strikes me with his dart!
   Phillida flouts me!

Thou shalt eat curds and cream,
 All the year lasting;
And drink the crystal stream,
 Pleasant in tasting:
Wigge and whey, while thou burst,
 And bramble-berry,
Pie-lid and pastry-crust,
 Pears, plums, and cherry;
Thy raiment shall be thin,
Made of a weaven skin;—
Yet all not worth a pin!
   Phillida flouts me!

Fair maidens, have a care,
 And in time take me;
I can have those as fair,
 If you forsake me.
For Doll the dairy-maid
 Laughed on me lately,
And wanton Winifred
 Favours me greatly.
One throws milk on my clothes,
T'other plays with my nose:
What wanton signs are those!
   Phillida flouts me!

I cannot work and sleep
 All at a season;
Love wounds my heart so deep,
 Without all reason.
I 'gin to pine away
 With grief and sorrow,
Like to a fatted beast
 Penned in a meadow.
I shall be dead, I fear,
Within this thousand year,
And all for very fear
   Phillida flouts me!

ONE DENIAL.

WHAT! put off with one denial,
And not make a second trial?
You might see my eyes consenting,
All about me was relenting;
Women, obliged to dwell in forms,
Forgive the youth that boldly storms.
Lovers, when you sigh and languish,
When you tell us of your anguish,
To the nymph you'll be more pleasing
When those sorrows you are easing;
We love to try how far men dare,
And never wish the foe should spare.

AN ECHO SONG.

"If I address the Echo yonder
What will its answer be, I wonder?"
     "I wonder!"

"Oh wondrous Echo! Tell me, bless 'ee,
Am I for marriage or celibacy?"
     "Silly Bessy!"

"If then to win the maid I try,
Shall I find her a property?"
     "A proper tie!"

"If neither being grave nor funny
Will win this maid to matrimony?"
     "Try money!"

"If I should try to gain her heart,
Shall I go plain, or rather smart?"
     "Smart!"

"She mayn't love dress, and I again, then,
May come too smart, and she'll complain then."
     "Come plain then."

"Then if to marry me I teaze her,
What will she say if that should please her?
     "Please, sir!"

"When cross nor good words can appease her,
What if such naughty whims should seize her?"
     "You'd see, sir!"

"When wed, she'll change, for Love's no sticker,
And love her husband less than liquor!"
"Then lick her!"

"To leave me then I can't compel her,
Though every woman else excel her!"
"Sell her!"

CHLOE AND CŒLIA.

CHLOE brisk and gay appears,
  On purpose to invite;
Yet, when I press her, she, in tears,
  Denies her sole delight:

Whilst Cœlia, seeming shy and coy,
  To all her favours grants,
And secretly receives that joy
  Which others think she wants.

I would, but fear I never shall,
  With either fair agree;
For Cœlia will be kind to all,
  But Chloe won't to me.

GET UP AND BAR THE DOOR.

IT fell upon a Martinmas time,
  And a gay time it was then,
When our goodwife got puddings to make,
  And she boiled them in a pan.

The wind sae cauld blew south and north,
  And blew into the floor;
Quoth our goodman to our goodwife,
  "Get up and bar the door."

"My hand is in my hussy's skap,
  Goodman, as you may see;
An' it should na be barred this hundred year,
  It's no be barred, for me."

They made a paction 'tween them twa,
  They made it firm and sure,
That the first word whae'er should speak
  Should rise and bar the door.

Then by there came twa gentlemen,
    At twelve o'clock at night;
And they could neither see house nor hall,
    Nor coal nor candle-light.

"Now whether is this a rich man's house?
    Or whether is it a poor?"
But ne'er a word would ane o' them speak,
    For barring of the door.

And first they ate the white puddings,
    And then they ate the black;
Though muckle thought the goodwife to hersel',
    Yet ne'er a word she spak.

Then said the one unto the other;
    "Here man, take my knife;
Do ye tak aff the auld man's beard,
    And I'll kiss the goodwife.

"But there's nae water in the house,
    And what shall we do then?
What ails you at the pudding bree
    That boils into the pan?"

Oh up then started our goodman,
    An angry man was he;
"Will ye kiss my wife before my face,
    And sca'd me wi' pudding bree?"

Then up then started our goodwife,
    Gi'ed three skips on the floor;
"Goodman, you've spoken the foremost word!
    Get up and bar the door!"

NATURE AND FORTUNE.

NATURE and Fortune, blithe and gay,
    To pass an hour or two,
In frolic mood agreed to play
    At "What shall this man do?"

"Come, I'll be judge then," Fortune cries,
    "And therefore must be blind;"
Then whipped a napkin round her eyes,
    And tied it fast behind.

Nature had now prepared her list
  Of names on scraps of leather ;
Which rolled, she gave them each a twist,
  And hustled them together.

Thus mixed, whichever came to hand
  She very surely drew ;
Then bade her sister give command
  For what that man should do.

'Twould almost burst one's sides to hear
  What strange commands she gave ;
That Cibber should the laurel wear,
  And C——e an army have.

At length, when Stanhope's name was come,
  Dame Nature smiled, and cried ;
"Now tell me, sister, this man's doom,
  And what shall him betide."

"That man," said Fortune, "shall be one
  Blest both by you and me ;"—
"Nay, then," quoth Nature, "let's have done ;
  Sister, I'm sure you see."

AT CHURCH.

Last Sunday at St. James's prayers,
  The prince and princess by,
I, dressed in all my whale-bone airs,
  Sat in a closet nigh.
I bowed my knees, I held my book,
  Read all the answers o'er ;
But was perverted by a look
  Which pierced me from the door.
High thoughts of Heaven I came to use
  With the devoutest care ;
Which gay young Strephon made me lose,
  And all the raptures there.
He stood to hand me to my chair,
  And bowed with courtly grace ;
But whispered love into my ear,
  Too warm for that grave place.
"Love, love," said he, "by all adored,
  My tender heart has won."

But I grew peevish at the word,
And bade he would be gone.
He went quite out of sight, while I
A kinder answer meant;
Nor did I for my sins that day
By half so much repent.

KISSING.

As I went to the wake that is held on the green,
I met with young Phœbe, as blithe as a queen;
A form so divine might an anchorite move,
And I found (though a clown) I was smitten with love:
So I asked for a kiss, but she, blushing, replied,
"Indeed, gentle shepherd, you must be denied."

"Lovely Phœbe," says I, "don't affect to be shy,
I vow I will kiss you—here's nobody by."
"No matter for that," she replied, "'tis the same;
For know, silly shepherd, I value my fame;
So pray let me go, I shall surely be missed;
Besides, I'm resolved that I will not be kissed.

"Lord bless me!" I cried, "I'm surprised you refuse;
A few harmless kisses but serve to amuse;
The month it is May, and the season for love,
So come, my dear girl, to the wake let us rove."
"No, Damon," she cried, "I must first be your wife;
You then shall be welcome to kiss me for life."

"Well, come then," I cried, "to the church let us go,
But after, dear Phœbe must never say No."
"Do *you* prove but true," she replied, "you shall find
I'll ever be constant, good-humoured, and kind."
So I kiss when I please, for she ne'er says she won't;
And I kiss her so much that I wonder she don't.

THERE WAS AN OLD WOMAN.

There was an old woman, as I've heard tell,
She went to market her eggs for to sell;
She went to market all on a market-day;
And she fell asleep on the king's highway.

There came by a pedlar whose name was Stout,
He cut her petticoats all round about;
He cut her petticoats up to the knees,
Which made the old woman to shiver and freeze.

When this little woman first did wake,
She began to shiver, and she began to shake :
She began to wonder, and she began to cry,
"Lauk-a-mercy on me, this is none of I !

" But if it be I, as I do hope it be,
I've a little dog at home, and he'll know me ;
If it be I, he'll wag his little tail,
And if it be not I, he'll loudly bark and wail !"

Home went the little woman all in the dark ;
Up got the little dog, and he began to bark ;
He began to bark, so she began to cry,
"Lauk-a-mercy on me, this is none of I !"

THE MERRY MAN.

I AM a young fellow
Who loves to be mellow,
To drink and be merry is all my delight ;
I often get frisky
By tippling good whisky
With jovial companions from morning to night.
I never took pleasure
In hoarding up treasure ;
The sight of a miser I cannot endure,
Who always is griping,
And sharping, and biting,
And laying out schemes for to plunder the poor.
Ri fal-da-riddle lah, &c.

Of the beggarly miser
I am a despiser ;
The fruit of his labour he never enjoys ;
His heirs for his money,
Impatient of honey,
Are waiting, and hate him, while with it he toys.
His frame is complaining,
For want of sustaining ;
His limbs are decrepit from hunger and cold ;
Instead of good liquor,
To make his pulse quicker,
He's gloating and doating on that idol called gold,

As for me, while I'm able,
At the head of a table,
Set me down of good whisky a full water-stand,

Where each clever toper
May drink like the pope, or
May toast to his friends with a bumper in hand.
By the side of that jorum,
Like a Justice of Quorum,
I'll preside full of state in my holiday clothes;
In winter or summer,
With a rollicking rummer,
A pipe for to smoke, and a jug at my nose.

"Come, drawer, this spirit
Of yours has some merit.
Sweet piper, come squeeze up your leather and play;
And hand him the pitcher,
It makes music richer,"—
Thus we'll drink and carouse to the dawning of day.
I hold them but asses
Who wait to fill glasses,—
Such muddling and fuddling's unworthy of man;
It only is wasting
The time that is hasting,—
Commend me to those that will fugle the can.

When stopped in my toddy
By death seizing my body,
No crocodile tears shall be shed at my wake;
While there I am lying,
No counterfeit crying,
No moans, I desire, shall be made for my sake.
I've no taste for squalling,
Or old women's bawling,
Who string nonsense together and call it a keen,
Who only are selling
Their yelping and yelling
For some one perhaps that they never have seen.

But of whisky a cruiskeen
To fill up each loose skin,
Let all have to toast to my journey up-hill;
And three jolly pipers
To tune up for the swipers,
While each boy honestly swallows his fill.
Then a blackthorn cudgel
For each, should they grudge ill
To anoint one another, and none to control :
Nor let them be down-hearted
For him that's departed,
But end their disputes in a full-flowing bowl.
The next morning early,
When daylight 'tis fairly,

My trunk shall be nailed quite close to my back;
   Four stout lads so civil
   Will bear it up level,
Whilst I ride on their shoulders instead of a sack.
   Now let them all sing,
   And the valleys will ring,
Raising up a fine chorus, both gallant and brave;
   Then lay me down flat,
   Like a sieve-woman's hat,
And away goes the merry man into his grave.
           Ri fal-da-riddle lah, &c.

THE COURT OF ALDERMEN AT FISHMONGERS' HALL.

"Is that dace or perch?"
   Said Alderman Birch;
"I take it for herring,"
   Said Alderman Perring.
"This jack's very good,"
   Said Alderman Wood;
'But its bones might a man slay,"
   Said Alderman Ansley.
"I'll butter what I get,"
   Said Alderman Heygate.
Give me some stewed carp,"
   Said Alderman Thorp.
"The roe's dry as pith,"
   Said Alderman Smith.
"Don't cut so far down,"
   Said Alderman Brown:
But nearer the fin,"
   Said Alderman Glyn.
"I've finished, i' faith, man,"
   Said Alderman Waithman:
"And I too, i' fatkins,"
   Said Alderman Atkins.
"They've crimped this cod drolly,"
   Said Alderman Scholey;
"'Tis bruised at the ridges,"
   Said Alderman Brydges.
"Was it caught in a drag? Nay,"
   Said Alderman Magnay.
"'Twas brought by two men,"
   Said Alderman Ven-
   ables: "Yes, in a box,"
   Said Alderman Cox.
"They care not how *fur 'tis*,"
   Said Alderman Curtis—

"From air kept, and from sun,"
    Said Alderman Thompson;
"Packed neatly in straw,"
    Said Alderman Shaw:
"In ice got from Gunter,"
    Said Alderman Hunter.
"This ketchup is sour,"
    Said Alderman Flower;
"Then steep it in claret,"
    Said Alderman Garret.

AMERICAN WRITERS

JOHN QUINCY ADAMS.

[Born in 1767, died in 1848. President of the United States from 1825 to 1829. He wrote much in both verse and prose: his principal poetical composition, published in 1832, is named *Dermot MacMorrogh, or the Conquest of Ireland, an Historical Tale of the Twelfth Century, in Four Cantos*].

THE PLAGUE IN THE FOREST

TIME was when round the lion's den
   A peopled city raised its head;
'Twas not inhabited by men,
   But by four-footed beasts instead.
The lynx, the leopard, and the bear,
The tiger and the wolf, were there;
   The hoof-defended steed;
The bull, prepared with horns to gore;
The cat with claws, the tusky boar,
   And all the canine breed.

In social compact thus combined,
   Together dwelt the beasts of prey;
Their murderous weapons all resigned,
   And vowed each other not to slay.
Among them Reynard thrust his phiz;
Not hoof nor horn nor tusk was his,
   For warfare all unfit.
He whispered to the royal dunce,
And gained a settlement at once;
   His weapon was—his wit.

One summer, by some fatal spell,
   (Phœbus was peevish for some scoff)
The plague upon that city fell,
   And swept the beasts by thousands off.
The lion, as became his part,

Loved his own people from his heart;
   And, taking counsel sage,
His peerage summoned to advise,
And offer up a sacrifice
   To soothe Apollo's rage.

Quoth Lion, "We are sinners all;
   And even, it must be confessed,
If among sheep I chance to fall,
   I—I am guilty as the rest.
To me the sight of lamb is cursed;
It kindles in my throat a thirst,—
   I struggle to refrain,—
Poor innocent! his blood so sweet!
His flesh so delicate to eat!
   I find resistance vain.

"Now to be candid, I must own
   The sheep are weak and I am strong,
But, when we find ourselves alone,
   The sheep have never done me wrong.
And, since I purpose to reveal
All my offences, nor conceal
   One trespass from your view,
My appetite is made so keen
That with the sheep the time has been
   I took the shepherd too.

"Then let us all our sins confess,
   And whosesoe'er the blackest guilt,
To ease my people's deep distress,
   Let *his* atoning blood be spilt.
My own confession now you hear.
Should none of deeper dye appear,
   Your sentence freely give;
And, if on me should fall the lot,
Make me the victim on the spot,
   And let my people live."

The council with applauses rung,
   To hear the Codrus of the wood;
Though still some doubt suspended hung
   If he would make his promise good.
Quoth Reynard, "Since the world was made,
Was ever love like this displayed?
   Let us like subjects true
Swear, as before your feet we fall,
Sooner than you should die for all,
   We all will die for you.

"But please your majesty, I deem,
   Submissive to your royal grace,
You hold in far too high esteem
   That paltry, poltroon, sheepish race;
For oft, reflecting in the shade,
I ask myself why sheep were made
   By all-creating power:
And, howsoe'er I tax my mind,
This the sole reason I can find—
   For lions to devour.

"And as for eating now and then
   As well the shepherd as the sheep,—
How can that braggart breed of men
   Expect with you the peace to keep?
'Tis time their blustering boast to stem,
That all the world was made for them—
   And prove creation's plan;
Teach them by evidence profuse
That man was made for lions' use,
   Not lions made for man."

And now the noble peers begin,
   And, cheered with such examples bright,
Disclosing each his secret sin,
   Some midnight murder brought to light.
Reynard was counsel for them all;
No crime the assembly could appal,
   But *he* could botch with paint:
Hark, as his honeyed accents roll,
Each tiger is a gentle soul,
   Each bloodhound is a saint.

When each had told his tale in turn,
   The long-eared beast of burden came,
And meekly said, "My bowels yearn
   To make confession of my shame;
But I remember on a time
I passed, not thinking of a crime,
   A haystack on my way:
His lure some tempting devil spread,
I stretched across the fence my head,
   And cropped a lock of hay."

"Oh monster! villain!" Reynard cried—
   "No longer seek the victim, sire;
Nor why your subjects thus have died
   To expiate Apollo's ire."

The council with one voice decreed ;
  All joined to execrate the deed,—
  "What, steal another's grass !"
The blackest crime *their* lives could show
  Was washed as white as virgin snow ;
    The victim was—the Ass.

FITZ-GREENE HALLECK.

[Born in 1795, died in 1868. His maternal descent was from John Eliot, "the Apostle of the Indians." He engaged in business, acting for several years as agent to the great capitalist Astor.]

RED JACKET, A CHIEF OF THE INDIAN TRIBES, THE TUSCARORAS.

ON LOOKING AT HIS PORTRAIT BY WEIR.

COOPER, whose name is with his country's woven,
  First in her files, her Pioneer of mind—
A wanderer now in other climes, has proven
  His love for the young land he left behind ; [1]

And throned her in the senate-hall of nations,
  Robed like the deluge rainbow, heaven-wrought,
Magnificent as his own mind's creations,
  And beautiful as its green world of thought.

And, faithful to the Act of Congress, quoted
  As law authority, it passed nem. con. :
He writes that we are, as ourselves have voted,
  The most enlightened people ever known ;

That all our week is happy as a Sunday
  In Paris, full of song, and dance, and laugh ;
And that, from Orleans to the Bay of Fundy,
  There's not a bailiff or an epitaph.

And furthermore—in fifty years, or sooner,
  We shall export our poetry and wine ;
And our brave fleet, eight frigates and a schooner,
  Will sweep the seas from Zembla to the Line.

If he were with me, King of Tuscarora !
  Gazing, as I, upon thy portrait now,
In all its medalled, fringed, and beaded glory,
  Its eye's dark beauty, and its thoughtful brow—

Its brow, half martial and half diplomatic,
  Its eye, upsoaring like an eagle's wings ;
Well might he boast that we, the Democratic,
  Outrival Europe, even in our Kings !

---

[1] *Red Jacket* appeared originally in 1828, soon after the publication of J. Fenimore Cooper's *Notions of the Americans*.

For thou wast monarch born. Tradition's pages
    Tell not the planting of thy parent tree,
But that the forest tribes have bent for ages
    To thee, and to thy sires, the subject knee.

Thy name is princely :—if no poet's magic
    Could make Red Jacket grace an English rhyme,
Though some one with a genius for the tragic
    Hath introduced it in a pantomime,

Yet it is music in the language spoken
    Of thine own land, and on her herald roll ;
As bravely fought for, and as proud a token
    As Cœur de Lion's of a warrior's soul.

Thy garb—though Austria's bosom-star would frighten
    That medal pale, as diamonds the dark mine,
And George the Fourth wore, at his court at Brighton,
    A more becoming evening dress than thine ;

Yet 'tis a brave one, scorning wind and weather,
    And fitted for thy couch on field and flood,
As Rob Roy's tartan for the Highland heather,
    Or forest green for England's Robin Hood.

Is strength a monarch's merit, like a whaler's?
    Thou art as tall, as sinewy, and as strong,
As earth's first kings—the Argo's gallant sailors,
    Heroes in history, and gods in song.

Is beauty ?—Thine has with thy youth departed ;
    But the love-legends of thy manhood's years,
And she who perished, young and broken-hearted,
    Are—but I rhyme for smiles and not for tears.

Is eloquence ?—Her spell is thine that reaches
    The heart, and makes the wisest head its sport ;
And there's one rare, strange virtue in thy speeches,
    The secret of their mastery—they are short.

The monarch mind, the mystery of commanding,
    The birth-hour gift, the art Napoleon,
Of winning, fettering, moulding, wielding, banding
    The hearts of millions till they move as one :

Thou hast it. At thy bidding men have crowded
    The road to death as to a festival ;
And minstrels, at their sepulchres, have shrouded
    With banner-folds of glory the dark pall.

Who will believe? (Not I—for in deceiving
   Lies the dear charm of life's delightful dream;
I cannot spare the luxury of believing
   That all things beautiful are what they seem)

Who will believe that, with a smile whose blessing
   Would, like the Patriarch's, soothe a dying hour,
With voice as low, as gentle, and caressing,
   As e'er won maiden's lip in moonlit bower;

With look, like patient Job's, eschewing evil;
   With motions graceful as a bird's in air;
Thou art, in sober truth, the veriest devil
   That e'er clenched fingers in a captive's hair?

That in thy breast there springs a poison fountain,
   Deadlier than that where bathes the Upas-tree;
And, in thy wrath, a nursing cat-o'-mountain
   Is calm as her babe's sleep compared with thee!

And underneath that face, like summer ocean's,
   Its lip as moveless, and its cheek as clear,
Slumbers a whirlwind of the heart's emotions,
   Love, hatred, pride, hope, sorrow—all save fear.

Love—for thy land, as if she were thy daughter,
   Her pipe in peace, her tomahawk in wars;
Hatred—of missionaries and cold water;
   Pride—in thy rifle-trophies and thy scars;

Hope—that thy wrongs may be, by the Great Spirit,
   Remembered and revenged when thou art gone;
Sorrow—that none are left thee to inherit
   Thy name, thy fame, thy passions, and thy throne!

ALNWICK CASTLE.

HOME of the Percy's high-born race,
   Home of their beautiful and brave,
Alike their birth and burial place,
   Their cradle and their grave!
Still sternly o'er the castle gate
Their house's Lion stands in state,
   As in his proud departed hours;
And warriors frown in stone on high,
And feudal banners "flout the sky"
   Above his princely towers.

A gentle hill its side inclines,
   Lovely in England's fadeless green,
To meet the quiet stream which winds
   Through this romantic scene
As silently and sweetly still
As when, at evening, on that hill,
   While summer's wind blew soft and low,
Seated by gallant Hotspur's side,
His Katherine was a happy bride,
   A thousand years ago.

Gaze on the Abbey's ruined pile :
   Does not the succouring ivy, keeping
Her watch around it, seem to smile,
   As o'er a loved one sleeping?
One solitary turret grey
   Still tells, in melancholy glory,
The legend of the Cheviot day,
   The Percy's proudest border story.
That day its roof was triumph's arch ;
   Then rang, from aisle to pictured dome,
The light step of the soldier's march,
   The music of the trump and drum ;
And babe, and sire, the old, the young,
And the monk's hymn, and minstrel's song,
And woman's pure kiss, sweet and long,
   Welcomed her warrior home.

Wild roses by the Abbey towers
   Are gay in their young bud and bloom :
They were born of a race of funeral flowers
   That garlanded, in long-gone hours,
     A templar's knightly tomb.
He died, the sword in his mailèd hand,
On the holiest spot of the Blessed Land,
   Where the Cross was damped with his dying breath,
When blood ran free as festal wine,
And the sainted air of Palestine
   Was thick with the darts of death.

Wise with the lore of centuries,
What tales, if there be "tongues in trees,"
   Those giant oaks could tell,
Of beings born and buried here !
Tales of the peasant and the peer,
Tales of the bridal and the bier,
   The welcome and farewell,
Since on their boughs the startled bird
First, in her twilight slumbers, heard
   The Norman's curfew-bell.

I wandered through the lofty halls
    Trod by the Percys of old fame,
And traced upon the chapel walls
    Each high heroic name,
From him who once his standard set
Where now, o'er mosque and minaret,
    Glitter the Sultan's crescent moons;
To him who, when a younger son,
Fought for King George at Lexington,
    A major of dragoons.

That last half stanza—it has dashed
    From my warm lip the sparkling cup;
The light that o'er my eyebeam flashed,
    The power that bore my spirit up
Above this bank-note world—is gone;
And Alnwick's but a market town,
    And this, alas! its market day,
And beasts and borderers throng the way;
Oxen and bleating lambs in lots,
Northumbrian boors and plaided Scots,
    Men in the coal and cattle line;
From Teviot's bard and hero land,
From royal Berwick's beach of sand,
From Wooller, Morpeth, Hexham, and
    Newcastle-upon-Tyne.

These are not the romantic times
So beautiful in Spenser's rhymes,
    So dazzling to the dreaming boy:
Ours are the days of fact, not fable,
Of knights, but not of the round table,
    Of Bailie Jarvie, not Rob Roy:
'Tis what "our President," Monroe,
    Has called "the era of good feeling:"
The Highlander, the bitterest foe
To modern laws, has felt their blow,
Consented to be taxed, and vote,
And put on pantaloons and coat,
    And leave off cattle-stealing:
Lord Stafford mines for coal and salt,
The Duke of Norfolk deals in malt,
    The Douglas in red herrings;
And noble name and cultured land,
Palace, and park, and vassal band,
Are powerless to the notes of hand
    Of Rothschild or the Barings.

The age of bargaining, said Burke,
Has come: to-day the turbaned Turk

(Sleep, Richard of the lion heart!
Sleep on, nor from your cerements start)
  Is England's friend and fast ally;
The Moslem tramples on the Greek,
  And on the Cross and altar-stone,
  And Christendom looks tamely on,
And hears the Christian maiden shriek,
  And sees the Christian father die;
And not a sabre-blow is given
For Greece and fame, for faith and heaven,
  By Europe's craven chivalry.

You'll ask if yet the Percy lives
  In the armed pomp of feudal state.
The present representatives
  Of Hotspur and his "gentle Kate"
Are some half-dozen serving men
In the drab coat of William Penn;
  A chambermaid, whose lip and eye,
And cheek, and brown hair, bright and curling,
  Spoke nature's aristocracy;
And one, half groom, half seneschal,
Who bowed me through court, bower, and hall,
From donjon-keep to turret wall,
  For ten-and-sixpence sterling.

JOHN GARDNER CALKINS BRAINARD.

[Born in 1796, died in 1828. In his brief career he was first called to the bar; then undertook the editorship of a weekly gazette; and consumption closed a somewhat desultory and melancholy life].

SONNET TO THE SEA-SERPENT.

"Hugest that swims the ocean stream."

WELTER upon the waters, mighty one—
  And stretch thee in the ocean's trough of brine;
Turn thy wet scales up to the wind and sun,
  And toss the billow from thy flashing fin;
  Heave thy deep breathings to the ocean's din,
And bound upon its ridges in thy pride:
  Or dive down to its lowest depths, and in
The caverns where its unknown monsters hide
Measure thy length beneath the gulf-stream's tide—
  Or rest thee on that navel of the sea
Where, floating on the Maelstrom, abide
  The krakens sheltering under Norway's lee;
But go not to Nahant, lest men should swear
You are a great deal bigger than you are.

GEORGE P. MORRIS.

[Born in 1801, died towards 1865.[1] A general in the army, dramatist, and miscellaneous writer; especially popular for his songs, one of which is the universally known "Woodman, spare that tree"].

THE RETORT.

OLD NICK, who taught the village school,
    Wedded a maid of homespun habit;
He was stubborn as a mule,
    She was playful as a rabbit.

Poor Jane had scarce become a wife,
    Before her husband sought to make her
The pink of country polished life,
    And prim and formal as a Quaker.

One day the tutor went abroad,
    And simple Jenny sadly missed him;
When he returned, behind her lord
    She slyly stole, and fondly kissed him.

The husband's anger rose—and red
    And white his face alternate grew.
"Less freedom, ma'am!"—Jane sighed and said,
    "Oh dear! I didn't know 'twas you!"

JOHN GREENLEAF WHITTIER.

[Born in 1808 at Haverhill, Massachusetts, where his ancestors, of the Quaker denomination, had long been settled. Mr. Whittier was early engaged in farming operations; and afterwards as a political, and more especially a protectionist, journalist. In 1836 he became one of the secretaries of the Anti-Slavery Society: and some of his most vigorous and rousing poems are devoted to that noble cause. He has also written various prose works; one of the chief among which is *Supernaturalism in New England*, published in 1847. The bulk of Mr. Whittier's poetical writings is considerable. His name stands high in the United States, and ought in England to be better known than as yet it is. An upright manly energy, and the tenderness of a strong yet delicate nature, are constantly conspicuous in his writings. These fine qualities are mostly associated with a genuine poetic grace, and in many instances with art truly solid and fine].

THE DEMON OF THE STUDY.

THE Brownie sits in the Scotchman's room,
    And eats his meat and drinks his ale,
And beats the maid with her unused broom,
    And the lazy lout with his idle flail;
But he sweeps the floor and threshes the corn,
And hies him away ere the break of dawn.

---

[1] In this case and another (see Park Benjamin), where I say "towards 1865" as the date of death, I have reason to infer that the authors were alive in 1863, but have died since then, though the precise year of death is uncertain to me: 1865 is named as an approximation.

The shade of Denmark fled from the sun,
    And the Cocklane ghost from the barnloft cheer,
The fiend of Faust was a faithful one,
    Agrippa's demon wrought in fear,
And the devil of Martin Luther sat
By the stout monk's side in social chat.

The Old Man of the Sea, on the neck of him
    Who seven times crossed the deep,
Twined closely each lean and withered limb,
    Like the nightmare in one's sleep.
But he drank of the wine, and Sinbad cast
The evil weight from his back at last.

But the demon that cometh day by day
    To my quiet room and fireside nook,
Where the casement light falls dim and grey
    On faded painting and ancient book,
Is a sorrier one than any whose names
Are chronicled well by good king James.

No bearer of burdens like Caliban,
    No runner of errands like Ariel,
He comes in the shape of a fat old man,
    Without rap of knuckle or pull of bell;
And whence he comes, or whither he goes,
I know as I do of the wind which blows.

A stout old man with a greasy hat
    Slouched heavily down to his dark red nose,
And two grey eyes enveloped in fat,
    Looking through glasses with iron bows.
Read ye, and heed ye, and ye who can
Guard well your doors from that old man!

He comes with a careless "How d'ye do?"
    And seats himself in my elbow-chair;
And my morning paper and pamphlet new
    Fall forthwith under his special care;
And he wipes his glasses and clears his throat,
And, button by button, unfolds his coat.

And then he reads from paper and book,
    In a low and husky asthmatic tone,
With the stolid sameness of posture and look
    Of one who reads to himself alone:
And hour after hour on my senses come
That husky wheeze and that dolorous hum.

The price of stocks, the auction sales,
    The poet's song and the lover's glee,
The horrible murders, the seaboard gales,

The marriage list, and the *jeu d'esprit*,
All reach my ear in the selfsame tone,—
I shudder at each, but the fiend reads on !

Oh sweet as the lapse of water at noon
   O'er the mossy roots of some forest tree,
The sigh of the wind in the woods of June,
   Or sound of flutes o'er a moonlight sea,
Or the low soft music, perchance, which seems
To float through the slumbering singer's dreams,—

So sweet, so dear is the silvery tone
   Of her in whose features I sometimes look,
As I sit at eve by her side alone,
   And we read by turns from the selfsame book,—
Some tale perhaps of the olden time,
Some lover's romance or quaint old rhyme.

Then when the story is one of woe,
   Some prisoner's plaint through his dungeon-bar,
Her blue eye glistens with tears, and low
   Her voice sinks down like a moan afar ;
And I seem to hear that prisoner's wail,
And his face looks on me worn and pale.

And, when she reads some merrier song,
   Her voice is glad as an April bird's ;
And, when the tale is of war and wrong,
   A trumpet's summons is in her words,
And the rush of the hosts I seem to hear,
And see the tossing of plume and spear !—

Oh pity me then, when, day by day,
   The stout fiend darkens my parlour door ;
And reads me perchance the selfsame lay
   Which melted in music, the night before,
From lips as the lips of Hylas sweet,
   And moved like twin roses which zephyrs meet !

I cross my floor with a nervous tread,
   I whistle and laugh and sing and shout,
I flourish my cane above his head,
   And stir up the fire to roast him out ;
I topple the chairs, and drum on the pane,
And press my hands on my ears, in vain !

I've studied Glanville and James the wise,
   And wizard black-letter tomes which treat
Of demons of every name and size
   Which a Christian man is presumed to meet,
But never a hint and never a line
Can I fnd of a reading fiend like mine.

I've crossed the Psalter with Brady and Tate,
    And laid the Primer above them all,
I've nailed a horseshoe over the grate,
    And hung a wig to my parlour wall,
Once worn by a learned Judge, they say,
At Salem court in the witchcraft day.

"*Conjuro te, sceleratissime,*
    Abire ad tuum locum!"—Still
Like a visible nightmare he sits by me,—
    The exorcism has lost its skill;
And I hear again in my haunted room
The husky wheeze and the dolorous hum!

Ah!—commend me to Mary Magdalen
    With her sevenfold plagues,—to the wandering Jew,—
To the terrors which haunted Orestes when
    The furies his midnight curtains drew;
But charm him off, ye who charm him can,
That reading demon, that fat old man!

OLIVER WENDELL HOLMES.

[Born in 1809. A Physician, and Professor of Anatomy in Harvard University. Well known as author of *The Autocrat of the Breakfast-table* and other prose writings, as well as poems—humorous, critical, or occasional, for the most part].

THE TREADMILL SONG.

The stars are rolling in the sky,
    The earth rolls on below,
And we can feel the rattling wheel
    Revolving as we go.
Then tread away, my gallant boys,
    And make the axle fly;
Why should not wheels go round about,
    Like planets in the sky?

Wake up, wake up, my duck-legged man,
    And stir your solid pegs!
Arouse, arouse, my gawky friend,
    And shake your spider legs;
What though you're awkward at the trade,
    There's time enough to learn,—
So lean upon the rail, my lad,
    And take another turn.

They've built us up a noble wall,
    To keep the vulgar out;
We've nothing in the world to do
    But just to walk about;

So faster, now, you middle men,
    And try to beat the ends, —
It's pleasant work to ramble round
    Among one's honest friends.

Here, tread upon the long man's toes,
    He sha'nt be lazy here, —
And punch the little fellow's ribs,
    And tweak that lubber's ear, —
He's lost them both, — don't pull his hair,
    Because he wears a scratch,
But poke him in the further eye,
    That isn't in the patch.

Hark! fellows, there's the supper-bell,
    And so our work is done;
It's pretty sport, — suppose we take
    A round or two for fun!
If ever they should turn me out,
    When I have better grown,
Now hang me but I mean to have
    A treadmill of my own!

THE MUSIC-GRINDERS.

THERE are three ways in which men take
    One's money from his purse,
And very hard it is to tell
    Which of the three is worse;
But all of them are bad enough
    To make a body curse.

You're riding out some pleasant day,
    And counting up your gains;
A fellow jumps from out a bush,
    And takes your horse's reins,
Another hints some words about
    A bullet in your brains.

It's hard to meet such pressing friends
    In such a lonely spot;
It's very hard to lose your cash,
    But harder to be shot;
And so you take your wallet out,
    Though you would rather not.

Perhaps you're going out to dine, —
    Some filthy creature begs
You'll hear about the cannon-ball

That carried off his pegs,
  And says it is a dreadful thing
    For men to lose their legs.

He tells you of his starving wife,
  His children to be fed,
Poor little lovely innocents,
  All clamorous for bread,—
And so you kindly help to put
  A bachelor to bed.

You're sitting on your window-seat,
  Beneath a cloudless moon ;
You hear a sound that seems to wear
  The semblance of a tune,
As if a broken fife should strive
  To drown a cracked bassoon.

And nearer, nearer still, the tide
  Of music seems to come ;
There's something like a human voice,
  And something like a drum ;
You sit in speechless agony,
  Until your ear is numb.

Poor "home, sweet home," should seem to be
  A very dismal place ;
Your "auld acquaintance" all at once
  Is altered in the face ;
Their discords sting through Burns and Moore,
  Like hedgehogs dressed in lace.

You think they are crusaders, sent
  From some infernal clime,
To pluck the eyes of Sentiment,
  And dock the tail of Rhyme,
To crack the voice of Melody,
  And break the legs of Time.

But hark ! the air again is still,
  The music all is ground,
And silence, like a poultice, comes
  To heal the blows of sound ;
It cannot be,—it is,—it is,—
  A hat is going round !

No ! Pay the dentist when he leaves
  A fracture in your jaw,
And pay the owner of the bear
  That stunned you with his paw,
And buy the lobster that has had
  Your knuckles in his claw ;

But, if you are a portly man,
    Put on your fiercest frown,
And talk about a constable
    To turn them out of town;
Then close your sentence with an oath,
    And shut the window down!

And, if you are a slender man,
    Not big enough for that,
Or if you cannot make a speech
    Because you are a flat,
Go very quietly and drop
    A button in the hat!

TO AN INSECT.[1]

I LOVE to hear thine earnest voice,
    Wherever thou art hid,
Thou testy little dogmatist,
    Thou pretty Katydid!
Thou mindest me of gentlefolks,—
    Old gentlefolks are they,—
Thou say'st an undisputed thing
    In such a solemn way.

Thou art a female, Katydid!
    I know it by the trill
That quivers through thy piercing notes,
    So petulant and shrill.
I think there is a knot of you
    Beneath the hollow tree,—
A knot of spinster Katydids,—
    Do Katydids drink tea?

O tell me where did Katy live,
    And what did Katy do?
And was she very fair and young,
    And yet so wicked, too?
Did Katy love a naughty man,
    Or kiss more cheeks than one?
I warrant Katy did no more
    Than many a Kate has done.

Dear me! I'll tell you all about
    My fuss with little Jane,
And Ann, with whom I used to walk
    So often down the lane,

---

[1] Perhaps most of our readers are aware that there is an insect in America named the "Katydid," on account of its emitting a sound resembling that combination of syllables. I have been told that sometimes the insect varies its utterances into "Katydidn't."—W. M. R.

And all that tore their locks of black,
  Or wet their eyes of blue,—
Pray tell me, sweetest Katydid,
  What did poor Katy do?

Ah no! the living oak shall crash,
  That stood for ages still,
The rock shall rend its mossy base
  And thunder down the hill,
Before the little Katydid
  Shall add one word, to tell
The mystic story of the maid
  Whose name she knows so well.

Peace to the ever-murmuring race!
  And, when the latest one
Shall fold in death her feeble wings
  Beneath the autumn sun,
Then shall she raise her fainting voice,
  And lift her drooping lid,
And then the child of future years
  Shall hear what Katy did.

THE SPECTRE PIG.

A BALLAD.

It was the stalwart butcher man
  That knit his swarthy brow,
And said the gentle Pig must die,
  And sealed it with a vow.

And oh! it was the gentle Pig
  Lay stretched upon the ground,
And ah! it was the cruel knife
  His little heart that found.

They took him then, those wicked men,
  They trailed him all along;
They put a stick between his lips,
  And through his heels a thong;

And round and round an oaken beam
  A hempen cord they flung,
And, like a mighty pendulum,
  All solemnly he swung!

Now say thy prayers, thou sinful man,
  And think what thou hast done,
And read thy catechism well,
  Thou bloody-minded one;

For, if his sprite should walk by night,
   It better were for thee
That thou wert mouldering in the ground,
   Or bleaching in the sea.

It was the savage butcher then
   That made a mock of sin,
And swore a very wicked oath
   He did not care a pin.

It was the butcher's youngest son,—
   His voice was broke with sighs,
And with his pocket-handkerchief
   He wiped his little eyes;

All young and ignorant was he,
   But innocent and mild,
And, in his soft simplicity,
   Out spoke the tender child:—

"O father, father, list to me;
   The Pig is deadly sick,
And men have hung him by his heels,
   And fed him with a stick."

It was the bloody butcher then
   That laughed as he would die,
Yet did he soothe the sorrowing child,
   And bid him not to cry;—

"O Nathan, Nathan, what's a Pig,
   That thou shouldst weep and wail?
Come, bear thee like a butcher's child,
   And thou shalt have his tail!"

It was the butcher's daughter then,
   So slender and so fair,
That sobbed as if her heart would break,
   And tore her yellow hair;

And thus she spoke in thrilling tone,—
   Fast fell the tear-drops big;—
"Ah! woe is me! Alas! Alas!
   The Pig! The Pig! The Pig!"

Then did her wicked father's lips
   Make merry with her woe,
And call her many a naughty name,
   Because she whimpered so.

Ye need not weep, ye gentle ones,
  In vain your tears are shed;
Ye cannot wash his crimson hand,
  Ye cannot soothe the dead.

The bright sun folded on his breast
  His robes of rosy flame,
And softly over all the west
  The shades of evening came.

He slept, and troops of murdered Pigs
  Were busy with his dreams;
Loud rang their wild, unearthly shrieks,
  Wide yawned their mortal seams

The clock struck twelve; the Dead hath heard;
  He opened both his eyes,
And sullenly he shook his tail
  To lash the feeding flies.

One quiver of the hempen cord,—
  One struggle and one bound,—
With stiffened limb and leaden eye,
  The Pig was on the ground!

And straight towards the sleeper's house
  His fearful way he wended;
And hooting owl, and hovering bat,
  On midnight wing attended.

Back flew the bolt, up rose the latch,
  And open swung the door,
And little mincing feet were heard
  Pat pat along the floor.

Two hoofs upon the sanded floor,
  And two upon the bed;
And they are breathing side by side,
  The living and the dead!

Now wake, now wake, thou butcher man!
  What makes thy cheek so pale?
Take hold! take hold! thou dost not fear
  To clasp a spectre's tail?

Untwisted every winding coil;
  The shuddering wretch took hold;
All like an icicle it seemed,
  So tapering and so cold.

"Thou com'st with me, thou butcher man!"—
  He strives to loose his grasp,
But faster than the clinging vine
  Those twining spirals clasp.

And open, open swung the door,
  And, fleeter than the wind,
The shadowy spectre swept before,
  The butcher trailed behind.

Fast fled the darkness of the night,
  And morn rose faint and dim;
They called full loud, they knocked full long,
  They did not waken him.

Straight, straight towards that oaken beam
  A trampled pathway ran;
A ghastly shape was swinging there,—
  It was the butcher man.

PARK BENJAMIN.

[Born in 1809 at Demerara, of a New England family; died towards 1865. Practised as an attorney at Boston. Afterwards took to magazine-writing and general literature, and published a great number of compositions, in verse and prose. Two of his principal poems are satires, named *Poetry* and *Infatuation*].

INDOLENCE.

THERE is no type of indolence like this:—
  A ship in harbour, not a signal flying;
  The wave unstirred about her huge sides lying,
No breeze her drooping pennant-flag to kiss,
Or move the smallest rope that hangs aloft:
  Sailors recumbent, listless, stretched around
Upon the polished deck or canvas—soft
  To his tough limbs that scarce have ever found
A bed more tender, since his mother's knee
The stripling left to tempt the changeful sea.
  Some are asleep; some whistle, try to sing;
Some gape, and wonder when the ship will sail;
Some damn the calm, and wish it was a gale.
  But every lubber there is lazy as a king.

MATTHEW C. FIELD.

[Born in 1812, died in 1844. Irish by parentage, and a Londoner by place of birth, but living in the United States from four years of age. He published much verse, and much prose also, in journals of the Southern States, from 1834 onwards].

TO MY SHADOW.

SHADOW, just like the thin regard of men,
   Constant and close to friends while fortune's bright.
You leave me in the dark, but come again
   And stick to me as long as there is light.
Yet, Shadow, as good friends have often done,
You've never stepped between me and the sun ;
   But ready still to back me I have found you
Although, indeed, you're fond of changing sides ;
   And, while I never yet could get around you,
Where'er I walk my Shadow with me glides !
   That you should leave *me* in the dark is meet
Enough, there being one thing to remark—
   Light calls ye forth, yet, lying at my feet,
I'm keeping *you* for ever in the dark !

JOHN GODFREY SAXE.

[Born in 1816. A barrister and newspaper editor, highly popular in the States for his humorous or burlesque poems—some of them modelled very closely on Hood, and others on Barham].

THE GHOST-PLAYER.

A BALLAD.

TOM GOODWIN was an actor man,
   Old Drury's pride and boast
In all the light and sprite-ly parts,
   Especially the Ghost.

Now Tom was very fond of drink,
   Of almost every sort,
Comparative and positive,
   From porter up to port.

But grog, like grief, is fatal stuff
   For any man to sup ;
For, when it fails to pull him down,
   It's sure to blow him up.

And so it fared with ghostly Tom,
   Who day by day was seen
A-swelling, till (as lawyers say)
   He fairly lost his lean.

At length the manager observed
    He'd better leave his post,
And said, he played the very deuce
    Whene'er he played the Ghost.

'Twas only 'tother night he saw
    A fellow swing his hat,
And heard him cry, "By all the gods!
    The Ghost is getting fat!"

'Twould never do, the case was plain;
    His eyes he couldn't shut;
Ghosts shouldn't make the people laugh,
    And Tom was quite a butt.

Tom's actor friends said ne'er a word
    To cheer his drooping heart;
Though more than one was burning up
    With zeal to "take his part,"

Tom argued very plausibly;
    He said he didn't doubt
That Hamlet's father drank, and grew,
    In years, a little stout.

And so, 'twas natural, he said,
    And quite a proper plan,
To have his spirit represent
    A portly sort of man.

'Twas all in vain; the manager
    Said he was not in sport,
And, like a general, bade poor Tom
    Surrender up his *forte*.

He'd do perhaps in heavy parts;
    Might answer for a monk,
Or porter to the elephant,
    To carry round his trunk;

But in the Ghost his day was past—
    He'd never do for that;
A Ghost might just as well be dead
    As plethoric and fat!

Alas! next day poor Tom was found
    As stiff as any post—
For he had lost his character,
    And given up the Ghost!

I'M GROWING OLD.

My days pass pleasantly away;
   My nights are blest with sweetest sleep;
I feel no symptoms of decay;
   I have no cause to mourn nor weep;
My foes are impotent and shy;
   My friends are neither false nor cold;
And yet, of late, I often sigh—
        I'm growing old!

My growing talk of olden times,
   My growing thirst for early news,
My growing apathy to rhymes,
   My growing love of easy shoes,
My growing hate of crowds and noise,
   My growing fear of taking cold,
All whisper in the plainest voice,
        I'm growing old!

I'm growing fonder of my staff;
   I'm growing dimmer in the eyes;
I'm growing fainter in my laugh;
   I'm growing deeper in my sighs;
I'm growing careless of my dress;
   I'm growing frugal of my gold;
I'm growing wise; I'm growing—yes—
        I'm growing old!

I see it in my changing taste;
   I see it in my changing hair;
I see it in my growing waist;
   I see it in my growing heir;
A thousand signs proclaim the truth,
   As plain as truth was ever told,
That even in my vaunted youth
        I'm growing old.

Ah me!—my very laurels breathe
   The tale in my reluctant ears,
And every boon the Hours bequeath
   But makes me debtor to the Years!
E'en Flattery's honeyed words declare
   The secret she would fain withhold,
And tells me in "How young you are!"
        I'm growing old.

Thanks for the years—whose rapid flight
   My sombre Muse too sadly sings;
Thanks for the gleams of golden light
   That tint the darkness of their wings;

The light that beams from out the sky,
  Those heavenly mansions to unfold
Where all are blest, and none may sigh
    " I'm growing old !"

A REFLECTIVE RETROSPECT.

'TIS twenty years, and something more,
  Since, all athirst for useful knowledge,
I took some draughts of classic lore,
  Drawn, very mild, at Harvard College ;
Yet I remember all that one
  Could wish to hold in recollection, —
The boys, the joys, the noise, the fun ;
  But not a single Conic Section.

I recollect those harsh affairs,
  The morning bells that gave us panics ;
I recollect the formal prayers,
  That seemed like lessons in Mechanics ;
I recollect the drowsy way
  In which the students listened to them,
As clearly, in my wig, to-day,
  As when, a boy, I slumbered through them.

I recollect the tutors all
  As freshly now, if I may say so,
As any chapter I recall
  In Homer or Ovidius Naso.
I recollect, extremely well,
  " Old Hugh," the mildest of fanatics ;
I well remember Matthew Bell,
  But very faintly, Mathematics.

I recollect the prizes paid
  For lessons fathomed to the bottom ;
(Alas that pencil-marks should fade !)
  I recollect the chaps who got 'em—
The light equestrians who soared
  O'er every passage reckoned stony ;
And took the chalks,—but never scored
  A single honour to the pony.

Ah me !—what changes Time has wrought,
  And how predictions have miscarried !—
A few have reached the goal they sought,
  And some are dead, and some are married ;
And some in city journals war ;
  And some as politicians bicker ;
And some are pleading at the bar,
  For jury-verdicts, or for liquor.

Aud some on Trade and Commerce wait;
 And some in schools with dunces battle;
And some the gospel propagate,
 And some the choicest breeds of cattle;
And some are living at their ease;
 And some were wrecked in "the revulsion;"
Some serve the State for handsome fees,
 And one, I hear, upon compulsion.

Lamont, who in his college days
 Thought e'en a cross a moral scandal,
Has left his Puritanic ways,
 And worships now with bell and candle;
And Mann, who mourned the negro's fate,
 And held the slave as most unlucky,
Now holds him at the market-rate
 On a plantation in Kentucky.

Tom Knox, who swore in such a tone
 It fairly might be doubted whether
It really was himself alone,
 Or *Knox* and Erebus together,
Has grown a very altered man,
 And, changing oaths for mild entreaty,
Now recommends the Christian plan
 To savages in Otaheite.

Alas for young ambition's vow,
 How envious Fate may overthrow it!—
Poor Harvey is in Congress now,
 Who struggled long to be a poet;
Smith carves (quite well) memorial stones,
 Who tried in vain to make the law go;
Hall deals in hides; and "Pious Jones"
 Is dealing faro in Chicago.

And, sadder still, the brilliant Hays,
 Once honest, manly, and ambitious,
Has taken latterly to ways
 Extremely profligate and vicious;
By slow degrees—I can't tell how—
 He's reached at last the very groundsel,
And in New York he figures now,
 A member of the Common Council!

EARLY RISING.

"God bless the man who first invented sleep!"
   So Sancho Panza said, and so say I:
And bless him also that he didn't keep
   His great discovery to himself; nor try
To make it—as the lucky fellow might—
A close monopoly by patent right.

Yes—bless the man who first invented sleep
   (I really can't avoid the iteration);
But blast the man with curses loud and deep,
   Whate'er the rascal's name, or age, or station,
Who first invented, and went round advising,
That artificial cut-off—Early Rising!

"Rise with the lark, and with the lark to bed,"
   Observes some solemn sentimental owl.
Maxims like these are very cheaply said;
   But, ere you make yourself a fool or fowl,
Pray, just inquire about his rise and fall,
And whether larks have any beds at all!

"The time for honest folks to be abed"
   Is in the morning, if I reason right;
And he who cannot keep his precious head
   Upon his pillow till it's fairly light,
And so enjoy his forty morning winks,
Is up to knavery; or else—he drinks.

Thomson, who sung about the "Seasons," said
   It was a glorious thing to *rise* in season;
But then he said it—lying—in his bed,
   At ten o'clock A.M.,—the very reason
He wrote so charmingly. The simple fact is,
His preaching wasn't sanctioned by his practice.

'Tis, doubtless, well to be sometimes awake,—
   Awake to duty, and awake to truth,—
But when, alas! a nice review we take
   Of our best deeds and days, we find, in sooth,
The hours that leave the slightest cause to weep
Are those we passed in childhood or asleep!

'Tis beautiful to leave the world awhile
   For the soft visions of the gentle night;
And free, at last, from mortal care or guile,
   To live as only in the angels' sight,
In sleep's sweet realm so cosily shut in,
Where, at the worst, we only *dream* of sin.

So, let us sleep, and give the Maker praise.—
I like the lad who, when his father thought
To clip his morning nap by hackneyed phrase
Of vagrant worm by early songster caught,
Cried, "Served him right! it's not at all surprising;
The worm was punished, sir, for early rising!"

LITTLE JERRY, THE MILLER.
A BALLAD.

BENEATH the hill you may see the mill,
    Of wasting wood and crumbling stone;
The wheel is dripping and clattering still,
    But Jerry, the miller, is dead and gone.

Year after year, early and late,
    Alike in summer and winter weather,
He pecked the stones and calked the gate,
    And mill and miller grew old together.

"Little Jerry!"—'twas all the same,—
    They loved him well who called him so;
And whether he'd ever another name
    Nobody ever seemed to know.

'Twas "Little Jerry, come grind my rye;"
    And "Little Jerry, come grind my wheat;"
And "Little Jerry" was still the cry,
    From matron bold and maiden sweet.

'Twas "Little Jerry" on every tongue,
    And so the simple truth was told;
For Jerry was little when he was young,
    And Jerry was little when he was old.

But what in size he chanced to lack,
    That Jerry made up in being strong;
I've seen a sack upon his back
    As thick as the miller and quite as long.

Always busy, and always merry,
    Always doing his very best,
A notable wag was Little Jerry,
    Who uttered well his standing jest.

How Jerry lived is known to fame,
    But how he died there's none may know;
One autumn day the rumour came—
    "The brook and Jerry are very low."

And then 'twas whispered mournfully,
  The leech had come, and he was dead;
And all the neighbours flocked to see;—
  "Poor Little Jerry!' was all they said.

They laid him in his earthly bed—
  His miller's coat his only shroud—
"Dust to dust," the parson said,
  And all the people wept aloud.

For he had shunned the deadly sin,
  And not a grain of over-toll
Had ever dropped into his bin,
  To weigh upon his parting soul.

Beneath the hill there stands the mill,
  Of wasting wood and crumbling stone;
The wheel is dripping and clattering still,
  But Jerry, the miller, is dead and gone.

JAMES RUSSELL LOWELL.

[Born in Boston in 1819; Professor of Modern Languages in Harvard College. A writer of critical and other prose works, as well as of poetry. His serious poems have secured a large, and deserved a not inconsiderable, measure of admiration: but his humorous *Biglow Papers*, written in Yankee dialect, seem more likely to live with a genuine life than anything else from his pen].

FESTINA LENTE.

ONCE on a time there was a pool
Fringed all about with flag-leaves cool,
And spotted with cow-lilies garish,
Of frogs and pouts the ancient parish.
Alders the creaking redwings sink on,
Tussocks that house blithe Bob o' Lincoln,
Hedged round the unassailed seclusion,
Where muskrats piled their cells Carthusian;
And many a moss-embroidered log,
The watering-place of summer frog,
Slept and decayed with patient skill,
As watering-places sometimes will.

Now in this Abbey of Theleme,
Which realized the fairest dream
That ever dozing bull-frog had,
Sunned on a half-sunk lily-pad,
There rose a party with a mission
To mend the polliwog's condition,

Who notified the sélectmen
To call a meeting there and then.
"Some kind of steps," they said, "are needed;
They don't come on so fast as we did:
Let's dock their tails; if that don't make 'em
Frogs by brevet, the Old One take 'em!
That boy that came the other day
To dig some flag-root down this way
His jack-knife left, and 'tis a sign
That Heaven approves of our design:
'Twere wicked not to urge the step on,
When Providence has sent the weapon."

Old croakers, deacons of the mire,
That led the deep batrachian choir,
Uk! Uk! Carouk! with bass that might
Have left Lablache's out of sight,
Shook nobby heads, and said, "No go!
You'd better let 'em try to grow:
Old Doctor Time is slow, but still
He does know how to make a pill."

But vain was all their hoarsest bass,
Their old experience out of place,
And spite of croaking and entreating,
The vote was carried in marsh-meeting.

"Lord knows," protest the polliwogs,
"We're anxious to be grown-up frogs;
But do not undertake the work
Of Nature, till she prove a shirk;
'Tis not by jumps that she advances,
But wins her way by circumstances.
Pray, wait awhile, until you know
We're so contrived as not to grow.
Let Nature take her own direction,
And she'll absorb our imperfection;
You mightn't like 'em to appear with,
But we must have the things to steer with."

"No," piped the party of reform,
"All great results are ta'en by storm;
Fate holds her best gifts till we show
We've strength to make her let them go.
No more reject the Age's chrism,
Your queues are an anachronism;
No more the Future's promise mock,
But lay your tails upon the block,
Thankful that we the means have voted
To have you thus to frogs promoted."

The thing was done, the tails were cropped,
And home each philotadpole hopped,
In faith rewarded to exult,
And wait the beautiful result.
Too soon it came; our pool, so long
The theme of patriot bull-frogs' song,
Next day was reeking, fit to smother,
With heads and tails that missed each other,—
Here snoutless tails, there tailless snouts:
The only gainers were the pouts.

MORAL.

From lower to the higher next,
Not to the top, is Nature's text;
And embryo Good, to reach full stature,
Absorbs the Evil in its nature.

THE COURTIN'.[1]

God makes sech nights, all white an' still
    Fur'z you can look or listen,
Moonshine an' snow on field an' hill,
    All silence an' all glisten.

Zekle crep' up quite unbeknown,
    An' peeked in thru' the winder;
An' there sot Huldy all alone,
    'Ith no one nigh to hender.

A fireplace filled the room's one side
    With half a cord o' wood in—
There warn't no stoves (tell comfort died)
    To bake ye to a puddin'.

The wa'nut logs shot sparkles out
    Towards the pootiest, bless her,
An' leetle flames danced all about
    The chiny on the dresser.

Again the chimbley crook-necks hung,
    An' in amongst 'em rusted
The ole queen's-arm thet gran'ther Young
    Fetched back from Concord busted.

---

[1] This version of the poem appears in the *Biglow Papers*, 2nd series, being just double the length of a different version given in the 1st series. I prefer the last-named; but have thought it more befitting to abide by the author's own decision.—W. M. R.

The very room, coz she was in,
    Seemed warm from floor to ceilin',
An' she looked full ez rosy again
    Ez the apples she was peelin'.

'Twas kin' o' kingdom-come to look
    On sech a blessed cretur;
A dogrose blushin' to a brook
    Ain't modester nor sweeter.

He was six foot o' man, A 1,
    Clean grit an' human natur';
None couldn't quicker pitch a ton,
    Nor dror a furrer straighter.

He'd sparked it with full twenty gals,
    He'd squired 'em, danced 'em, druv 'em,
Fust this one, an' then thet, by spells—
    All is, he couldn't love 'em.

But long o' her his veins 'ould run
    All crinkly like curled maple;
The side she breshed felt full o' sun
    Ez a south slope in Ap'il.

She thought no v'ice hed sech a swing
    Ez hisn in the choir:
My! when he made Ole Hunderd ring,
    She *knowed* the Lord was nigher.

An' she'd blush scarlet, right in prayer,
    When her new meetin'-bunnet
Felt somehow thru' its crown a pair
    O' blue eyes sot upon it.

Thet night, I tell ye, she looked *some!*
    She seemed to've gut a new soul,
For she felt sartin-sure he'd come,
    Down to her very shoe-sole.

She heered a foot, and knowed it tu,
    A-rasping on the scraper,—
All ways to once her feelins flew,
    Like sparks in burnt-up paper.

He kin' o' l'itered on the mat
    Some doubtfle o' the sekle;
His heart kep' goin' pity-pat,
    But hern went pity Zekle.

An' yit she gin her cheer a jerk
    Ez though she wished him furder,
An' on her apples kep' to work,
    Parin' away like murder.

"You want to see my Pa, I s'pose?"
    "Wal .... no .... I come dasignin'"—
"To see my Ma? She is sprinklin' clo'es
    Agin to-morrer's i'nin'."

To say why gals acts so or so,
    Or don't, 'ould be presumin';
Mebbe to mean *yes* an' say *no*
    Comes nateral to women.

He stood a spell on one foot fust,
    Then stood a spell on t'other,
An' on which one he felt the wust
    He couldn't ha' told ye nuther.

Says he, "I'd better call agin;"
    Says she, "Think likely, Mister;"
Thet last word pricked him like a pin,
    An' .... Wal, he up an' kist her.

When Ma bimeby upon 'em slips,
    Huldy sot pale ez ashes,
All kin' o' smily roun' the lips,
    An' teary roun' the lashes.

For she was jes' the quiet kind
    Whose naturs never vary,
Like streams that keep a summer mind
    Snowhid in Jenooary.

The blood clost roun' her heart felt glued
    Too tight for all expressin',
Tell mother see how metters stood,
    And gin 'em both her blessin'.

Then her red come back like the tide
    Down to the Bay o' Fundy;
An' all I know is they was cried
    In meetin' come nex' Sunday.

BIRDOFREDOM SAWIN.[1]

I.

This kind o' sogerin' aint a mite like our October trainin';
A chap could clear right out from there ef't only looked like rainin';
An' th' Cunnles, tu, could kiver up their shappoes with bandanners,
An' send the insines skootin' to the bar-room with their banners
(Fear o' gittin' on 'em spotted), an' a feller could cry quarter
Ef he fired away his ramrod arter tu much rum an' water.
Recollect wut fun we hed, you'n' I an' Ezry Hollis,
Up there to Waltham plain last fall, along o' the Cornwallis?
This sort o' thing aint *jest* like thet,—I wish thet I wuz furder,—
Nimepunce a day fer killin' folks comes kind o' low fer murder,
(Wy I've worked out to slarterin' some fer Deacon Cephas Billins,
An' in the hardest times there wuz I ollers tetched ten shillins).
There's sutthin' gits into my throat thet makes it hard to swaller,
It comes so nateral to think about a hempen collar;
It's glory,—but, in spite o' all my tryin' to git callous,
I feel a kind o' in a cart, aridin' to the gallus.
But wen it comes to *bein'* killed,—I tell ye I felt streaked
The fust time 'tever I found out wy baggonets wuz peaked.
Here's how it wuz: I started out to go to a fandango,
The sentinul he ups an' sez, "Thet's furder 'an you can go."
"None o' your sarse," sez I; sez he, "Stan' back!" "Aint you a buster?"
Sez I; "I'm up to all thet air, I guess I've ben to muster;
I know wy sentinuls air sot; you aint agoin' to eat us;
Caleb haint no monopoly to court the seenoreetas;
My folks to hum air full ez good ez hisn be, by golly!"
An' so ez I wuz goin' by, not thinkin' wut would folly,
The everlastin' cus he stuck his one-pronged pitchfork in me,
An' made a hole right thru my close ez ef I wuz an in'my.

Wal, it beats all how big I felt hoorawin' in ole Funnel
Wen Mister Bolles he gin the sword to our Leftenant Cunnle,
(It's Mister Secondary Bolles, thet writ the prize peace essay;
Thet's why he didn't list himself along o' us, I dessay).
An' Rantoul, tu, talked pooty loud, but don't put *his* foot in it,
Coz human life's so sacred thet he's principled agin it,—
Though I myself can't rightly see it's any wus achokin' on 'em
Than puttin' bullets thru their lights, or with a bagnet pokin' on 'em.
How dreffle slick he reeled it off (like Blitz at our lyceum
Ahaulin' ribbins from his chops so quick you skeercely see 'em)
About the Anglo-Saxon race (an' saxons would be handy
To du the buryin' down here upon the Rio Grandy),

---

[1] The reader should understand B. Sawin to be a private in the United States Army, in the war against Mexico waged in 1847.

About our patriotic pas an' our star-spangled banner,
Our country's bird alookin' on an' singin' out hosanner;
An' how he (Mister B. himself) wuz happy fer Ameriky,—
I felt, ez sister Patience sez, a leetle mite histericky.
I felt, I swon, ez though it wuz a dreffle kind o' privilege
Atrampin' round thru Boston streets among the gutter's drivelage;
I act'lly thought it wuz a treat to hear a little drummin',
An' it did bonyfidy seem millanyum wuz acomin'
Wen all on us got suits (darned like them wore in the state prison),
An' every feller felt ez though all Mexico wuz hisn.

This 'ere's about the meanest place a skunk could wal diskiver
(Saltillo's Mexican, I b'lieve, fer wut we call Salt-river);
The sort o' trash a feller gits to eat doos beat all nater,—
I'd give a year's pay fer a smell o' one good blue-nosed tater;
The country here thet Mister Bolles declared to be so charmin'
Throughout is swarmin' with the most alarmin' kind o' varmin'.
He talked about delishis fruits, but then it wuz a wopper all,
The holl on't's mud an' prickly pears, with here an' there a chap-
    paral.
You see a feller peekin' out, an', fust you know, a lariat
Is round your throat an' you a copse, 'fore you can say "Wut air
    ye at?"
You never see sech darned gret bugs (it may not be irrelevant
To say I've seen a *scarabæus pilularius*[1] big ez a year-old elephant):
The rigiment come up one day in time to stop a red bug
From runnin' off with Cunnle Wright,—'t wuz jest a common
    cimex lectularius.
One night I started up on eend, an' thought I wuz to hum agin;
I heern a horn; thinks I, "It's Sol the fisherman hez come agin,
His bellowses is sound enough."—Ez I'm a livin' creeter,
I felt a thing go thru my leg,—'twuz nothin' more 'n a skeeter!
Then there's the yaller fever, tu, they call it here el vomito,—
(Come, thet wun't du, you landcrab there, I tell ye to le' *go* my
    toe!
My gracious! it's a scorpion thet's took a shine to play with't;
I darsn't skeer the tarnal thing fer fear he'd run away with't).

Afore I come away from hum I hed a strong persuasion
Thet Mexicans worn't human beans,—an ourang outang nation,
A sort o' folks a chap could kill an' never dream on't arter,
No more'n a feller'd dream o' pigs thet he hed hed to slarter.
I'd an idee thet they were built arter the darkie fashion all,
An' kickin' colored folks about, you know's, a kind o' national.
But wen I jined I wornt so wise ez thet air queen o' Sheby,
Fer, come to look at 'em, they aint much diff'rent from wut we be;

---
[1] it wuz "tumblebug" as he Writ it, but the parson put the Latten instid. i sed tother maid better meeter, but he said tha was eddykated peepl to Boston and tha wouldn't stan' it no how. idnow as tha *wood* and idnow *as* tha wood.— Hosea Biglow.

An' here we air ascrougin' 'em out o' thir own dominions,
Ashelterin' 'em, ez Caleb sez, under our eagle's pinions,—
Wich means to take a feller up jest by the slack o' 's trowsis,
An' walk him Spanish clean right out o' all his homes an' houses.
Wal, it doos seem a curus way, but then hooraw fer Jackson !
It must be right, fer Caleb sez it's reg'lar Anglo-saxon.
The Mex'cans don't fight fair, they say ; they piz'n all the water,
An' du amazin' lots o' things thet isn't wut they ough' to ;
Bein' they haint no lead, they make their bullets out o' copper,
An' shoot the darned things at us, tu, wich Caleb sez aint proper.
He sez they'd ough' to stan' right up an' let us pop 'em fairly,
(Guess wen he ketches 'em at thet he'll hev to git up airly);
Thet our nation's bigger'n theirn, an' so its rights air bigger,
An' thet it's all to make 'em free thet we air pullin' trigger ;
Thet Anglo Saxondom's idee's abreakin' 'em to pieces,
An' thet idee's thet every man doos jest wut he damn pleases.
Ef I don't make his meanin' clear, perhaps in some respex I can,—
I know thet "every man" don't mean a nigger or a Mexican.
An' there's another thing I know ; an' thet is, ef these creeturs,
Thet stick an Anglosaxon mask onto State-prison feeturs,
Should come to Jaalam Centre fer to argify an' spout on't,
The gals 'ould count the silver spoons the minnit they cleared out
    on't.

This goin' ware glory waits ye haint one agreeable feetur ;
An', ef it worn't fer wakin' snakes, I'd home agin short meter.
Oh wouldn't I be off, quick time, ef't worn't thet I wuz sartin
They'd let the daylight into me to pay me fer desartin !
I don't approve o' tellin' tales, but jest to you I may state
Our ossifers aint wut they wuz afore they left the Bay-state ;
Then it wuz "Mister Sawin, sir, you're middlin' well now, be ye ?
Step up an' take a nipper, sir ; I'm dreffle glad to see ye ;"
But now it's "Ware's my eppylet ? here, Sawin, step an' fetch it !
An' mind your eye, be thund'rin' spry, or, damn ye, you shall ketch
    it !"
Wal, ez the Doctor sez, some pork will bile so, but by mighty,
Ef I hed some on 'em to hum, I'd give 'em linkum vity ;
I'd play the rogue's march on their hides an' other music follerin'——
But I must close my letter here, fer one on 'em's ahollerin' ;
These Anglosaxon ossifers,—wal, taint no use ajawin',
I'm safe enlisted fer the war.
               Yourn,
                    BIRDOFREDOM SAWIN.

II.

I SPOSE you wonder ware I be ; I can't tell, fer the soul o' me,
Exacly ware I be myself,—meanin' by thet the holl o' me.
Wen I left hum, I hed two legs, an' they worn't bad ones neither,
(The scaliest trick they ever played wuz bringin' on me hither):

Now one on 'em's I dunno ware ;—they thought I wuz adyin',
An' sawed it off because they said 'twuz kin' o' mortifyin';
I'm willin' to believe it wuz, an' yit I don't see, nuther,
Wy one should take to feelin' cheap a minnit sooner 'n t'other,
Sence both wuz equilly to blame ; but things is ez they be ;
It took on so they took it off, an' thet's enough fer me.
There's one good thing, though, to be said about my wooden new
   one,—
The liquor can't git into it ez't used to in the true one ;
So it saves drink ; an' then, besides, a feller couldn't beg
A gretter blessin' then to hev one ollers sober peg.
It's true a chap's in want o' two fer follerin' a drum,
But all the march I'm up to now is jest to Kingdom Come.

I've lost one eye, but thet's a loss it's easy to supply
Out o' the glory that I've gut, fer thet is all my eye ;
An' one is big enough, I guess, by diligently usin' it,
To see all I shall ever git by way o' pay fer losin' it.
Off'cers, I notice, who git paid fer all our thumps an' kickins,
Du wal by keepin' single eyes arter the fattest pickins ;
So, ez the eye's put fairly out, I'll larn to go without it,
An' not allow *myself* to be no gret put out about it.
Now, le' me see, thet isn't all ; I used, 'fore leavin' Jaalam,
To count things on my finger-eends, but sutthin' seems to ail 'em :
Ware's my left hand ? Oh, darn it, yes, I recollect wut's come on't ;
I haint no left arm but my right, an' thet's gut jest a thumb on't ;
It aint so hendy ez it wuz to cal'late a sum on't.
I've hed some ribs broke,—six (I b'lieve),—I haint kep' no account
   on 'em ;
Wen pensions git to be the talk, I'll settle the amount on 'em.
An' now I'm speakin' about ribs, it kin' o' brings to mind
One thet I couldn't never break,—the one I lef' behind;
Ef you should see her, jest clear out the spout o' your invention,
An' pour the longest sweetnin' in about an annooal pension,
An' kin' o' hint (in case, you know, the critter should refuse to be
Consoled) I aint so 'xpensive now to keep ez wut I used to be ;
There's one arm less, ditto one eye, an' then the leg thet's wooden
Can be took off an' sot away whenever ther's a puddin'.

I spose you think I'm comin' back ez opperlunt ez thunder,
With shiploads o' gold images an' varus sorts o' plunder.
Wal, 'fore I vullinteered, I thought this country wuz a sort o'
Canaan, a regl'ar Promised Land flowin' with rum an' water,
Ware propaty growed up like time, without no cultivation,
An' gold wuz dug ez taters be among our Yankee nation,
Ware nateral advantages were pufficly amazin',
Ware every rock there wuz about with precious stuns wuz blazin',
Ware mill-sites filled the country up ez thick ez you could cram
   'em,
An' desput rivers run about abeggin' folks to dam 'em ;

2 F

Then there were meetinhouses, tu, chockful o' gold an' silver
Thet you could take, an' no one couldn't hand ye in no bill fer.
Thet's wut I thought afore I went, thet's wut them fellers told us
Thet stayed to hum an' speechified an' to the buzzards sold us;
I thought thet gold mines could be gut cheaper than Chiny asters,
An' see myself acomin' back like sixty Jacob Astors.
But sech idees soon melted down an' didn't leave a grease-spot;
I vow my holl sheer o' the spiles wouldn't come nigh a V spot;
Although, most anywares we've ben, you needn't break no locks,
Nor run no kin' o' risks, to fill your pocket full o' rocks.

I guess I mentioned in my last some o' the nateral feeturs
O' this all-fiered buggy hole in th' way o' awfle creeturs;
But I fergut to name (new things to speak on so abounded)
How one day you'll most die o' thust, an' 'fore the next git drownded.
The climit seems to me jest like a teapot made o' pewter
Our Prudence hed, thet wouldn't pour (all she could du) to suit her;
Fust place the leaves 'ould choke the spout, so's not a drop 'ould dreen out,
Then Prude 'ould tip an' tip an' tip, till the holl kit bust clean out;
The kiver-hinge-pin bein' lost, tea-leaves an' tea an' kiver
'ould all come down *kerswosh!* ez though the dam broke in a river.
Jest so 'tis here; holl months there aint a day o' rainy weather;
An' jest ez th' officers 'ould be alayin' heads together
Ez t' how they'd mix their drink at sech a milingtary deepot,—
'T 'ould pour ez though the lid wuz off the everlastin' teapot.
The cons'quence is thet I shall take, wen I'm allowed to leave here,
One piece o' propaty along,—an' thet's the shakin' fever;
It's reggilar employment, though, an' thet aint thought to harm one,
Nor 'taint so tiresome ez it wuz with t'other leg an' arm on;
An' it's a consolation, tu, although it doesn't pay,
To hev it said you're some gret shakes in any kin' o' way.
'Twornt very long, I tell ye wut, I thought o' fortin-makin':
One day a reg'lar shiver-de-freeze, an' next ez good ez bakin',—
One day abrilin' in the sand, then smoth'rin' in the mashes,
Git up all sound, be put to bed a mess o' hacks an' smashes.
But then, thinks I, at any rate there's glory to be had,—
Thet's an investment, arter all, thet mayn't turn out so bad.
But somehow, wen we'd fit an' licked, I ollers found the thanks
Gut kin' o' lodged afore they come ez low down ez the ranks.
The Gin'rals gut the biggest sheer, the Cunnles next, an' so on,—
We never gut a blasted mite o' glory ez I know on;
An' spose we hed, I wonder how you're goin' to contrive its
Division so's to give a piece to twenty thousand privits;

Ef you should multiply by ten the portion o' the brav'st one,
You wouldn't git more'n half enough to speak of on a grave-stun;
We git the licks,—we're jest the grist thet's put into War's hoppers;
Leftenants is the lowest grade thet helps pick up the coppers.
It may suit folks thet go agin a body with a soul in't,
An' aint contented with a hide without a bagnet hole in't;
But glory is a kin' o' thing *I* shan't pursue no furder,
Coz thet's the off'cers parquisite,—yourn's on'y jest the murder.

Wal, arter I gin glory up, thinks I, at least there's one
Thing in the bills we aint hed yet, an' thet's the glorious fun;
Ef once we git to Mexico, we fairly may presume we
All day an' night shall revel in the halls o' Montezumy.
I'll tell ye wut *my* revels wuz, an' see how you would like 'em;
We never gut inside the hall: the nighest ever *I* come
Wuz stan'in' sentry in the sun (an', fact, it *seemed* a cent'ry)
A ketchin' smells o' biled an' roast thet come out thru the entry,
An' hearin' ez I sweltered thru my passes an' repasses,
A rat-tat-too o' knives an' forks, a clinkty-clink o' glasses.
I can't tell off the bill o' fare the Gin'rals hed inside;
All I know is thet out o' doors a pair o' soles wuz fried,
An' not a hunderd miles away frum ware this child wuz posted
A Massachusetts citizen wuz baked an' biled an' roasted.
The on'y thing like revellin' thet ever come to me
Wuz bein' routed out o' sleep by thet darned revelee.

They say the quarrel's settled now; fer my part I've some doubt on't,
'T 'll take more fish-skin than folks think to take the rile clean out on't.
At any rate, I'm so used up I can't do no more fightin',
The on'y chance thet's left to me is politics or writin'.
Now, ez the people's gut to hev a milingtary man,
An' I aint nothin' else jest now, I've hit upon a plan;
The can'idatin' line, you know, 'ould suit me to a T,
An' ef I lose, 'twunt hurt my ears to lodge another flea;
So I'll set up ez can'idate fer any kin' o' office,
(I mean fer any thet includes good easy-cheers an' soffies;
Fer ez to runnin' fer a place ware work's the time o' day,
You know thet's wut I never did,—except the other way).
Ef it's the Presidential cheer fer wich I'd better run,
Wut two legs anywares about could keep up with my one?
There aint no kin' o' quality in can'idates, it's said,
So useful ez a wooden leg,—except a wooden head;
There's nothin' aint so poppylar—(wy, it's a parfect sin
To think wut Mexico hez paid fer Santy Anny's pin;)—
Then I haint gut no princerples, an', sence I was knee-high,
I never *did* hev any gret, ez you can testify;
I'm a decided peace-man, tu, an' go agin the war,—
Fer now the holl on't's gone an' past, wut is there to go *for*?

Ef, wile you're 'lectioneerin' round, some curus chaps should beg
To know my views o' state affairs, jest answer "Wooden leg!"
Ef they aint settisfied with thet, an' kin' o' pry an' doubt
An' ax fer sutthin' deffynit, jest say "One eye put out!"
Thet kin' o' talk I guess you'll find'll answer to a charm,
An' wen you're druv tu nigh the wall, hol' up my missin' arm;
Ef they should nose round fer a pledge, put on a vartoous look,
An' tell 'em thet's precisely wut I never gin nor—took!

Then you can call me "Timbertoes,"—thet's wut the people likes;
Sutthin' combinin' morril truth with phrases sech ez strikes;
Some say the people's fond o' this, or thet, or wut you please,—
I tell ye wut the people want is jest correct idees.
"Old Timbertoes," you see, 's a creed it's safe to be quite bold on,
There's nothin' in't the other side can any ways git hold on;
It's a good tangible idee, a sutthin' to embody
Thet valooable class o' men who look thru brandy-toddy;
It gives a Party Platform, tu, jest level with the mind
Of all right-thinkin', honest folks thet mean to go it blind.
Then there air other good hooraws to dror on ez you need 'em,
Sech ez the one-eyed Slarterer, the bloody Birdofredom;
Them's wut takes hold o' folks thet think, ez well ez o' the masses,
An' makes you sartin o' the aid o' good men of all classes.

There's one thing I'm in doubt about; in order to be Presidunt,
It's absolutely ne'ssary to be a Southern residunt;
The Constitution settles thet, an' also thet a feller
Must own a nigger o' some sort, jet black, or brown, or yeller.
Now I haint no objections agin particklar climes,
Nor agin ownin' anythin' (except the truth sometimes);
But, ez I haint no capital, up there among ye, may be,
You might raise funds enough fer me to buy a low-priced baby,
An' then, to suit the No'thern folks, who feel obleeged to say
They hate an' cuss the very thing they vote for every day,
Say you're assured I go full butt fer Libbaty's diffusion,
An' made the purchis on'y jest to spite the Institootion;—
But, golly! there's the currier's hoss upon the pavement pawin'!
I'll be more 'xplicit in my next.

     Yourn,
       BIRDOFREDOM SAWIN.

III.

I SPOSE you recollect thet I explained my gennle views
In the last billet thet I writ, 'way down from Veery Cruze,
Jest arter I'd a kind o' ben spontanously sot up
To run unanimously fer the Presidential cup.
O' course it worn't no wish o' mine, 'twuz ferflely distressin',
But poppiler enthusiasm gut so almighty pressin'
Thet, though like sixty all along I fumed an' fussed an' sorrered,

There didn't seem no ways to stop their bringin' on me forrerd.
Fact is, they udged the matter so I couldn't help admittin'
The Father o' his Country's shoes no feet but mine 'ould fit in,
Besides the savin' o' the soles fer ages to succeed,
Seein' thet, with one wannut foot, a pair 'd be more 'n I need ;
An', tell ye wut, them shoes 'll want a thund'rin sight o' patchin',
Ef this 'ere fashion is to last we've gut into o' hatchin'
A pair o' second Washintons fer every new election,—
Though, fur ez number one's consarned, I don't make no objection.

I wuz agoin' on to say thet wen at fust I saw
The masses would stick to't I wuz the Country's father-'n-law,
(They would ha' hed it *Father*, but I told 'em 't wouldn't du,
Coz thet wuz sutthin' of a sort they couldn't split in tu,
An' Washinton hed hed the thing laid fairly to his door,
Nor darsn't say 'tworn't hisn, much ez sixty year afore)—
But 'taint no matter ez to thet ; wen I wuz nomernated,
'Tworn't natur but wut I should feel consid'able elated,
An' wile the hooraw o' the thing wuz kind o' noo an fresh,
I thought our ticket would ha' caird the country with a resh.

Sence I've come hum, though, an' looked round, I think I seem to find
Strong argiments ez thick ez fleas to make me change my mind.
It's clear to any one whose brain ain't fur gone in a phthisis,
Thet hail Columby's happy land is goin' thru a crisis,
An' 'twouldn't noways du to hev the people's mind distracted
By bein' all to once by sev'ral pop'lar names attackted ;
'Twould save holl haycartloads o' fuss an' three four months o' jaw,
Ef some illustrous paytriot should back out an' withdraw ;
So, ez I aint a crooked stick, jest like—like ole (I swow,
I dunno ez I know his name)—I'll go back to my plough.

Whenever an Amerikin distinguished politishin
Begins to try et wut they call definin' his posishin,
Wal, I, fer one, feel sure he aint gut nothin' to define ;
It's so nine cases out o' ten, but jest that tenth is mine ;
And 'taint no more'n is proper 'n' right in sech a sitooation
To hint the course you think 'll be the savin' o' the nation.
To funk right out o' p'lit'cal strife aint thought to be the thing,
Without you deacon off the toon you want your folks should sing ;
So I 'edvise the noomrous friends thet's in one boat with me
To jest up killock, jam right down their hellum hard a lee,
Haul the sheets taut, an', laying out upon the Suthun tack,
Make fer the safest port they can, wich, *I* think, is Ole Zack.

Next thing you'll want to know, I spose, wut argiments I seem
To see thet makes me think this ere'll be the strongest team.
Fust place, I've ben consid'ble round in bar-rooms an' saloons
Agethrin' public sentiment, 'mongst Demmercrats and Coons,

An' 'taint ve'y offen thet I meet a chap but wut goes in
Fer Rough an' Ready, fair an' square, hufs, taller, horns, an' skin.
I don't deny but wut, fer one, ez fur ez I could see,
I didn't like at fust the Pheladelphy nomernee;
I could ha' pinted to a man thet wuz, I guess, a peg
Higher than him,—a soger, tu, an' with a wooden leg;
But every day with more an' more o' Taylor zeal I'm burnin',
Seein' wich way the tide thet sets to office is aturnin'.
Wy, into Bellers's we notched the votes down on three sticks,—
'Twus Birdofredum *one*, Cass *aught*, an' Taylor *twenty-six*;
An' bein' the on'y canderdate thet wuz upon the ground,
They said 'twuz no more'n right thet I should pay the drinks all round.
Ef I'd expected sech a trick, I wouldn't ha' cut my foot
By goin' an' votin' fer myself like a consumèd coot.
It didn't make no diff'rence, though; I wish I may be cust
Ef Bellers wuzn't slim enough to say he wouldn't trust!

Another pint thet influences the minds o' sober jedges
Is thet the Gin'ral hezn't gut tied hand an' foot with pledges;
He hezn't told ye wut he is, an' so there aint no knowin'
But wut he may turn out to be the best there is agoin'.
This, at the on'y spot thet pinched, the shoe directly eases,
Coz every one is free to 'xpect percisely wut he pleases.
I want free-trade; you don't; the Gin'ral isn't bound to neither;—
I vote my way; you, yourn; an' both air sooted to a T there.
Ole Rough an' Ready, tu, 's a Wig, but without bein' ultry
(He's like a holsome hayinday, thet's warm, but isn't sultry);
He's jest wut I should call myself, a kin' o' *scratch*, ez 'twere,
Thet aint exacly all a wig nor wholly your own hair.
I've ben a Wig three weeks myself, jest o' this mod'rate sort,
An' don't find them an' Demmercrats so different ez I thought.
They both act pooty much alike, an' push an' scrouge an' cus;
They're like two pickpockets in league fer Uncle Samwell's pus;
Each takes a side, an' then they squeeze the old man in between 'em,
Turn all his pockets wrong side out, an' quick ez lightnin' clean 'em;
To nary one on'em I'd trust a secon-handed rail
No furder off 'an I could sling a bullock by the tail.

Webster sot matters right in thet air Mashfiel' speech o' hisn;—
"Taylor," sez he, "aint nary ways the one thet I'd a chizzen,
Nor he aint fittin' fer the place, an' like ez not he aint
No more'n a tough ole bullethead, an' no gret of a saint;
But then," sez he, "observe my pint, he's jest ez good to vote fer
Ez though the greasin' on him worn't a thing to hire Choate fer;
Aint it ez easy done to drop a ballot in a box
Fer one ez 't is fer t'other, fer the bulldog ez the fox?"
It takes a mind like Dannel's, fact, ez big ez all ou' doors,

To find out that it looks like rain arter it fairly pours;
I 'gree with him, it aint so dreffle troublesome to vote
Fer Taylor arter all,—it's jest to go an' change your coat;
Wen he's once greased, you'll swaller him an' never know on't,
 scurce,
Unless he scratches, goin' down, with them 'ere Gin'ral's spurs.
I've ben a votin' Demmercrat, ez reg'lar ez a clock,
But don't find goin' Taylor gives my narves no gret 'f a shock.
Truth is, the cutest leadin' Wigs, ever sence fust they found
Wich side the bread gut buttered on, hev kep' a edgin' round;
They kin' o' slipt the planks frum out th' ole platform one by one,
An' made it gradooally noo, 'fore folks knowed wut wuz done;
Till, fur'z I know, there aint an inch thet I could lay my han' on,
But I, or any Demmercrat, feels comf'table to stan' on,
An' ole Wig doctrines act'lly look, their occ'pants bein' gone,
Lonesome ez staddles on a mash without no hayricks on.

I spose it's time now I should give my thoughts upon the plan,
Thet chipped the shell at Buffalo, o' settin' up ole Van.
I used to vote fer Martin, but, I swon, I'm clean disgusted,—
He aint the man thet I can say is fittin' to be trusted;
He aint half antislav'ry 'nough, nor I aint sure, ez some be,
He'd go in fer abolishin' the Deestrick o' Columby;
An', now I come to recollect, it kin' o' makes me sick'z
A horse, to think o' wut he wuz in eighteen thirty-six.
An' then, another thing;—I guess, though mebby I am wrong,
This Buff'lo plaster aint agoin' to dror almighty strong;
Some folks, I know, hev gut th' idee thet No'thun dough 'll rise,
Though, 'fore I see it riz an' baked, I wouldn't trust my eyes;
'Twill take more emptins, a long chalk, than this noo party's gut,
To give sech heavy cakes ez them a start, I tell ye wut.
But even ef they caird the day, there wouldn't be no endurin'
To stan' upon a platform with sech critters ez Van Buren;—
An' his son John, tu, I can't think how thet 'ere chap should dare
To speak ez he doos; wy, they say he used to cuss an' swear!
I spose he never read the hymn thet tells how down the stairs
A feller with long legs wuz throwed thet wouldn't say his prayers.
This brings me to another pint: the leaders o' the party
Aint jest sech men ez I can act along with free an' hearty;
They aint not quite respectable, an' wen a feller's morrils
Don't toe the straightest kin' o' mark, wy, him an' me jest quarrils.
I went to a free-soil meetin' once, an' wut d'ye think I see?
A feller was aspoutin' there that act'lly come to me,
About two year ago last spring, ez nigh ez I can jedge,
An' axed me ef I didn't want to sign the Temprunce pledge!
He's one o' them that goes about an' sez you hedn't ough' ter
Drink nothin', mornin', noon, or night, stronger 'an Taunton
 water.
There's one rule I've ben guided by, in settlin' how to vote,
 ollers,—

I take the side thet *isn't* took by them consarned teetotallers.
Ez fer the niggers, I've ben South, an' thet has changed my mind;
A lazier, more ongrateful set you couldn't nowers find.
You know I mentioned in my last thet I should buy a nigger,
Ef I could make a purchase at a pooty mod'rate figger;
So, ez there's nothin' in the world I'm fonder of an' gunnin',
I closed a bargain finally to take a feller runnin'.
I shou'dered queen's-arm an' stumped out, an' wen I come t' th' swamp,
'Twornt very long afore I gut upon the nest o' Pomp;
I come acrost a kin' o' hut, an', playin' round the door,
Some little woolly-headed cubs, ez many'z six or more.
At fust I thought o' firin', but *think twice* is safest ollers;
There aint, thinks I, not one on 'em but's wuth his twenty dollars,
Or would be, ef I hed 'em back into a Christian land,—
How temptin' all on 'em would look upon an auction-stand!
(Not but wut *I* hate Slavery in th' abstract, stem to starn,—
I leave it ware our fathers did, a privit State consarn.)
Soon'z they see me, they yelled an' run, but Pomp was out ahoein'
A leetle patch o' corn he hed, or else there aint no knowin'
He wouldn't ha' took a pop at me; but I hed gut the start,
An' wen he looked, I vow he groaned ez though he'd broke his heart;
He done it like a wite man, tu, ez nat'ral ez a pictur,
The imp'dunt, pis'nous hypocrite! wus 'an a boy constrictur.
"You can't gum *me*, I tell ye now, an' so you needn't try,
I 'xpect my eye-teeth every mail, so jest shet up," sez I.
"Don't go to actin' ugly now, or else I'll jest let strip;
You'd best draw kindly, seein' 'z how I've gut ye on the hip.
Besides, you darned ole fool, it aint no gret of a disaster
To be benev'lently druv back to a contented master,
Ware you hed Christian priv'ledges you don't seem quite aware of,
Or you'd ha' never run away from bein' well took care of.
Ez fer kin' treatment, wy, he wuz so fond on ye, he said
He'd give a fifty spot right out, to git ye, 'live or dead;
Wite folks aint sot by half ez much; 'member I run away,
Wen I wuz bound to Cap'n Jakes, to Mattysqumscot bay.
Don' know him, likely? Spose not; wal, the mean ole codger went
An' offered—wut reward, think? Wal, it wornt no *less* 'n a cent."

Wal, I jest gut 'em into line, an druv 'em on afore me;
The pis'nous brutes, I'd no idee o' the ill-will they bore me.
We walked till som'ers about noon, an' then it grew so hot
I thought it best to camp awile; so I chose out a spot
Jest under a magnoly tree, an' there right down I sot.
Then I unstrapped my wooden leg, coz it begun to chafe,
An' laid it down 'longside o' me, supposin' all wuz safe.
I made my darkies all set down around me in a ring,
An' sot an' kin' o' ciphered up how much the lot would bring.

But, wile I drinked the peaceful cup of a pure heart an' mind,
(Mixed with some wiskey, now an' then,) Pomp he snaked up
 behind,
An' creepin' grad'lly close tu, ez quiet ez a mink,
Jest grabbed my leg, and then pulled foot, quicker 'an you could
 wink.
An' come to look, they each on 'em hed gut behin' a tree ;
An' Pomp poked out the leg a piece, jest so ez I could see,
An' yelled to me to throw away my pistils an' my gun,
Or else thet they'd cair off the leg, an' fairly cut an' run.
I vow I didn't b'lieve there wuz a decent alligatur
Thet hed a heart so destitoot o' common human natur.
However, ez there worn't no help, I finally give in,
An' heft my arms away to git my leg safe back agin.
Pomp gathered all the weapins up, an' then he come an' grinned,
He showed his ivory some, I guess, an' sez, "You're fairly pinned;
Jest buckle on your leg agin, an' git right up an' come,
'Twun't du fer fammerly men like me to be so long from hum."
At fust I put my foot right down an' swore I wouldn't budge:
"Jest ez you choose," sez he, quite cool, "either be shot or
 trudge."
So this black-hearted monster took an' act'lly druv me back
Along the very feetmarks o' my happy mornin' track,
An' kep' me pris'ner 'bout six months, an' worked me, tu, like sin,
Till I hed gut his corn an' his Carliny taters in.
He made me larn him readin', tu (although the crittur saw
How much it hut my morril sense to act agin the law)
So'st he could read a Bible he'd gut; an' axed ef I could pint
The North Star out; but there I put his nose some out o' jint,—
Fer I weeled roun' about sou'west, an' lookin' up a bit,
Picked out a middlin' shiny one, an' tole him thet wuz it.
Fin'lly, he took me to the door, an', givin' me a kick,
Sez,—" Ef you know wut's best fer ye, be off, now, double-quick ;
The winter-time's a comin' on, an', though I gut ye cheap,
You're so darned lazy I don't think you're hardly wuth your keep ;
Besides, the childrin's growin' up, an' you aint jest the model
I'd like to hev 'em immertate, an' so you'd better toddle !"

Now is there anythin' on airth'll ever prove to me
Thet renegader slaves like him air fit fer bein' free ?
D'you think they'll suck me in to jine the Buff'lo chaps, an' them
Rank infidels thet go agin the Scriptur'l cus o' Shem ?
Not by a jugfull ! Sooner'n thet, I'd go thru fire an' water ;
Wen I hev once made up my mind, a meet'nhus aint sotter ;
No, not though all the crows thet flies to pick my bones wuz
 cawin',—
I guess we're in a Christian land,—
    Yourn,
        BIRDOFREDOM SAWIN.

THE PIOUS EDITOR'S CREED.

I du believe in Freedom's cause,
    Ez fur away ez Payris is ;
I love to see her stick her claws
    In them infarnal Phayrisees ;
It's wal enough agin a king
    To dror resolves an' triggers,—
But libbaty's a kind o' thing
    Thet don't agree with niggers.

I du believe the people want
    A tax on teas an' coffees,
Thet nothin' aint extravygunt,—
    Purvidin' I'm in office ;
Fer I hev loved my country sence
    My eye-teeth filled their sockets,
An' Uncle Sam I reverence,
    Partic'larly his pockets.

I du believe in *any* plan
    O' levyin' the taxes,
Ez long ez, like a lumberman,
    I git jest wut I axes :
I go free-trade thru thick an' thin,
    Because it kind o' rouses
The folks to vote,—an' keeps us in
    Our quiet custom-houses.

I du believe it's wise an' good
    To sen' out furrin missions,
Thet is, on sartin understood
    An' orthydox conditions ;—
I mean nine thousan' dolls. per ann.,
    Nine thousan' more fer outfit,
An me to recommend a man
    The place 'ould jest about fit.

I du believe in special ways
    O' prayin' an' convartin' ;
The bread comes back in many days,
    An' buttered, tu, fer sartin
I mean in preyin' till one busts
    On wut the party chooses,
An' in convartin' public trusts
    To very privit uses.

I du believe hard coin the stuff
    Fer 'lectioneers to spout on ;
The people's ollers soft enough
    To make hard money out on ;

Dear Uncle Sam pervides fer his,
  An' gives a good-sized junk to all,—
I don't care *how* hard money is
  Ez long ez mine's paid punctooal.

I du believe with all my soul
  In the gret Press's freedom,
To pint the people to the goal
  An' in the traces lead 'em.
Palsied the arm that forges yokes
  At my fat contracts squintin',
An' withered be the nose thet pokes
  Inter the gov'ment printin' !

I du believe thet I should give
  Wut's hisn unto Cæsar,
Fer it's by him I move an' live,
  Frum him my bread an' cheese air ;
I du believe that all o' me
  Doth bear his superscription,—
Will, conscience, honour, honesty,
  An' things' o' thet description.

I du believe in prayer an' praise
  To him that hez the grantin'
O' jobs,—in every thin' thet pays,
  But most of all in cantin' ;
This doth my cup with marcies fill,
  This lays all thought o' sin to rest,—
I *don't* believe in princerple,
  But oh I *du* in interest.

I du believe in bein' this
  Or thet, ez it may happen
One way or t'other hendiest is
  To ketch the people nappin'.
It aint by princerples nor men
  My preudunt course is steadied ;
I scent wich pays the best, an' then
  Go into it baldheaded.

I du believe thet holdin' slaves
  Comes nat'ral tu a Presidunt,
Let 'lone the rowdedow it saves
  To hev a wal-broke precedunt ;
Fer any office, small or gret,
  I couldn't ax with no face,
Without I'd ben, thru dry an' wet,
  Th' unrizzest kind o' doughface.

I du believe wutever trash
　'll keep the people in blindness,—
That we the Mexicuns can thrash
　Right inter brotherly kindness;
Thet bombshells, grape, an' powder'n' ball
　Air good-will's strongest magnets;
Thet peace, to make it stick at all,
　Must be druv in with bagnets.

In short, I firmly du believe
　In Humbug generally,
Fer it's a thing thet I perceive
　To hev a solid vally;
This heth my faithful shepherd been,
　In pasturs sweet heth led me,
An' this'll keep the people green
　To feed ez they hev fed me.

SUNTHIN' IN THE PASTORAL LINE.

ONCE git a smell o' musk into a draw,
An' it clings hold like precerdents in law:
Your gran'ma'am put it there,—when, goodness knows,—
To jes' this-worldify her Sunday-clo'es;
But the old chist wun't sarve her gran'son's wife,
(For, 'thout new funnitoor, wut good in life?)
An' so ole clawfoot, from the precinks dread
O' the spare chamber, slinks into the shed,
Where, dim with dust, it fust or last subsides
To holdin' seeds an' fifty things besides;
But better days stick fast in heart an' husk,
An' all you keep in't gets a scent o' musk.

Jes' so with poets: wut they've airly read
Gits kind o' worked into their heart an' head,
So's 't they can't seem to write but jest on sheers
With furrin countries or played-out ideers,
Nor hev a feelin', ef it doosn't smack
O' wut some critter chose to feel 'way back:
This makes 'em talk o' daisies, larks, an' things,
Ez though we'd nothin' here that blows an' sings,—
(Why, I'd give more for one live bobolink
Than a square mile o' larks in printer's ink)—
This makes 'em think our fust o' May is May,
Which 'tain't, for all the almanicks can say.

O little city-gals, don't never go it
Blind on the word o' noospaper or poet!
They're apt to puff, an' May-day seldom looks
Up in the country ez it doos in books;

They're no more like than hornets'-nests an' hives,
Or printed sarmons be to holy lives.
I, with my trouses perched on cow-hide boots,
Tuggin' my foundered feet out by the roots,
Hev seen ye come to fling on April's hearse
Your muslin nosegays from the milliner's,
Puzzlin' to find dry ground your queen to choose,
An' dance your throats sore in morocker shoes:
I've seen ye, an' felt proud thet, come wut would,
Our Pilgrim stock wuz pithed with hardihood.
Pleasure doos make us Yankees kind o' winch,
Ez though't wuz sunthin' paid for by the inch;
But yit we do contrive to worry thru,
Ef Dooty tells us thet the thing's to du,
An' kerry a hollerday, ef we set out,
Ez stiddily ez though 'twas a redoubt.

I, country-born an' bred, know where to find
Some blooms thet make the season suit the mind,
An' seem to metch the doubting bluebird's notes,—
Half-vent'rin' liverworts in furry coats,
Bloodroots, whose rolled-up leaves ef you oncurl,
Each on 'em's cradle to a baby-pearl,—
But these are jes' Spring's pickets; sure ez sin,
The rebel frosts'll try to drive 'em in;
For half our May's so awfully like Mayn't
'Twould rile a Shaker or an evrige saint;
Though I own up I like our back'ard springs
Thet kind o' haggle with their greens an' things,
An' when you 'most give up, without more words
Toss the field full o' blossoms, leaves, an' birds:
Thet's Northun natur', slow an' apt to doubt,
But when it doos get stirred, there's no gin-out!

Fust come the blackbirds clatt'rin' in tall trees,
An' settlin' things in windy Congresses,—
Queer politicians, though, for I'll be skinned
Ef all on 'em don't head against the wind.
'Fore long the trees begin to show belief,—
The maple crimsons to a coral-reef,
Then saffern swarms swing off from all the willers
So plump they look like yaller caterpillars,
Then grey hosschesnuts leetle hands unfold
Softer'n a baby's be at three days old.
This is the robin's almanick; he knows
Thet arter this there's only blossom-snows;
So, choosin' out a handy crotch an' spouse,
He goes to plast'rin' his adobe house.

Then seems to come a hitch,—things lag behind;
Till some fine mornin' Spring makes up her mind,

An' ez, when snow-swelled rivers cresh their dams
Heaped-up with ice thet dovetails in an' jams,
A leak comes spirtin' thru some pin-hole cleft,
Grows stronger, fercer, tears out right an' left,
Then all the waters bow themselves an' come,
Suddin, in one gret slope o' shedderin' foam,
Jes' so our Spring gits everythin' in tune,
An' gives one leap from April into June.
Then all comes crowdin' in ; afore you think,
The oak-buds mist the side-hill woods with pink,
The catbird in the laylock bush is loud,
The orchards turn to heaps o' rosy cloud,
In ellum-shrouds the flashin' hangbird clings,
An' for the summer vy'ge his hammock slings,
All down the loose-walled lanes in archin' bowers
The barb'ry droops its strings o' golden flowers,
Whose shrinking hearts the school-gals love to try
With pins,—they'll worry yourn so, boys, bimeby!
But I don't love your cat'logue style,—do you ?—
Ez ef to sell all Natur' by vendoo ;
One word with blood in't's twice ez good ez two.
'Nuff sed, June's bridesman, poet o' the year,
Gladness on wings, the bobolink, is here ;
Half-hid in tip-top apple-blooms he swings,
Or climbs aginst the breeze with quiverin' wings,
Or, givin' way to't in a mock despair,
Runs down, a brook o' laughter, thru the air.

I ollus feel the sap start in my veins
In Spring with curus heats an' prickly pains,
Thet drive me, when I git a chance, to walk
Off by myself to hev a privit talk
With a queer critter thet can't seem to 'gree
Along o' me like most folks, Mister Me.
There's times when I'm unsoshle ez a stone,
An' sort o' suffocate to be alone,—
I'm crowded jes' to think that folks are nigh,
An' can't bear nothin' closer than the sky;
Now the wind's full ez shifty in the mind
Ez wut it is ou'-doors, ef I ain't blind,
An' sometimes, in the fairest sou'west weather,
My innard vane pints east for weeks together,
My natur' gits all goose-flesh, an' my sins
Come drizzlin' on my conscience sharp ez pins.
Wal, et sech times I jes' slip out o' sight,
An' take it out in a fair stan'-up fight
With the one cuss I can't lay on the shelf,
The crook'dest stick in all the heap,—Myself.

'Twuz so las' Sabbath arter meetin'-time :
Findin' my feelins wouldn't noways rhyme

With nobody's, but off the hendle flew
An' took things from an east-wind pint o' view,
I started off to lose me in the hills
Where the pines be, up back o' 'Siah's Mills.
Pines, ef you're blue, are the best friends I know,
They mope an' sigh an' sheer your feelins so,—
They hesh the ground beneath so, tu, I swon,
You half-forgit you've gut a body on.

There's a small school'us' there where four roads meet,
The door-steps hollered out by little feet,
An' side-posts carved with names whose owners grew
To gret men, some on 'em, an' deacons tu;
'Tain't used no longer, coz the town hez gut
A high-school, where they teach the Lord knows wut.
Three-story larnin' 's pop'lar now; I guess
We thriv ez wal on jes' two stories less,
For it strikes me there's sech a thing ez sinnin'
By overloadin' children's underpinnin':
Wal, here it wuz I larned my A B C,
An' it's a kind o' favorite spot with me.

We're curus critters: Now ain't jes' the minute
Thet ever fits us easy while we're in it;
Long ez 'twuz futur', 'twould be perfect bliss,—
Soon ez it's past, *thet* time's wuth ten o' this;
An' yit there ain't a man thet need be told
Thet Now's the only bird lays eggs o' gold.
A knee-high lad, I used to plot an' plan,
An' think 'twuz life's cap-sheaf to be a man;
Now, gittin grey, there's nothin' I enjoy
Like dreamin' back along into a boy:
So the ole school'us' is a place I choose
Afore all others, ef I want to muse.
I set down where I used to set, an' git
My boyhood back, an' better things with it,—
Faith, Hope, an' sunthin', ef it isn't Cherrity,
It's want o' guile, an' thet's ez gret a rerrity.

Now, 'fore I knowed, thet Sabbath arternoon
Thet I sot out to tramp myself in tune,
I found me in the school'us' on my seat,
Drummin' the march to no-wheres with my feet.
Thinkin' o' nothin', I've heerd ole folks say,
Is a hard kind o' dooty in its way:
It's thinkin' everythin' you ever knew,
Or ever hearn, to make your feelins blue.
I sot there tryin' thet on for a spell:
I thought o' the Rebellion, then o' Hell,
Which some folks tell ye now is jest a metterfor
(A the'ry, p'raps, it wun't *feel* none the better for);

I thought o' Reconstruction, wut we'd win
Patchin' our patent self-blow-up agin:
I thought ef this 'ere milkin' o' the wits,
So much a month, warn't givin' Natur' fits,—
Ef folks warn't druv, findin' their own milk fail,
To work the cow thet hez an iron tail,
An' ef idees 'thout ripenin' in the pan
Would send up cream to humour ary man:
From this to thet I let my worryin' creep,
Till finally I must ha' fell asleep.

Our lives in sleep are some like streams thet glide
'Twixt flesh an' sperrit boundin' on each side,
Where both shores' shadders kind o' mix an' mingle
In sunthin' thet ain't jes' like either single;
An' when you cast off moorins from To-day,
An' down towards To-morrer drift away,
The imiges thet tengle on the stream
Make a new upside-down'ard world o' dream:
Sometimes they seem like sunrise-streaks an' warnins
O' wut'll be in heaven on Sabbath-mornins,
An', mixed right in ez ef jest out o' spite,
Sunthin' thet says your supper ain't gone right.
I'm gret on dreams, an' often, when I wake,
I've lived so much it makes my mem'ry ache,
An' can't skurce take a cat-nap in my cheer
'Thout hevin' em, some good, some bad, all queer.

Now I wuz settin' where I'd ben, it seemed,
An' ain't sure yit whether I r'ally dreamed,
Nor, ef I did, how long I might ha' slep',
When I hearn some un stompin' up the step;
An' lookin' round, ef two an' two make four,
I see a Pilgrim Father in the door.
He wore a steeple-hat, tall boots, an' spurs,
With rowels to 'em big ez chesnut-burrs,
An' his gret sword behind him sloped away
Long'z a man's speech thet dunno wut to say.—
"Ef your name's Biglow, an' your given-name
Hosee," sez he, "it's arter you I came;
I'm your gret-gran'ther multiplied by three."—
"My *wut?*" sez I—"Your gret-gret-gret," sez he:
"You wouldn't ha' never ben here but for me.
Two hunderd an' three year ago this May
The ship I come in sailed up Boston Bay;
I'd ben a cunnle in our Civil War,—
But wut on airth hev *you* gut up one for?
I'm told you write in public prints: ef true,
It's nateral you should know a thing or two."—
"Thet air's an argymunt I can't endorse,—

'Twould prove, coz you wear spurs, you kep' a horse :
For brains," sez I, "wutever you may think,
Ain't boun' to cash the drafs o' pen-an'-ink,—
Though mos' folks write ez ef they hoped jes' quickenin'
The churn would argoo skim-milk into thickenin';
But skim-milk ain't a thing to change its view
O' usefleness, no more'n a smoky flue.
But du pray tell me, 'fore we furder go,
How in all Natur' did you come to know
'Bout our affairs," sez I, "in Kingdom-Come?"—
"Wal, I worked round at sperrit-rappin' some,
In hopes o' larnin' wut wuz goin' on,"
Sez he, "but mejums lie so like all-split
Thet I concluded it wuz best to quit.
But, come now, ef you wun't confess to knowin',
You've some conjecturs how the thing's a-goin'."—
"Gran'ther," sez I, "a vane warn't never known
Nor asked to hev a jedgment of its own;
An' yit, ef't ain't gut rusty in the jints,
It's safe to trust its say on certain pints:
It knows the wind's opinions to a T,
An' the wind settles wut the weather'll be."—
"I never thought a scion of our stock
Could grow the wood to make a weathercock;
When I wuz younger'n you, skurce more'n a shaver,
No airthly wind," sez he, "could make me waver!"
(Ez he said this, he clinched his jaw an' forehead,
Hitchin' his belt to bring his sword-hilt forrard.)—
"Jes' so it wuz with me," sez I, "I swow,
When *I* wuz younger'n wut you see me now,—
Nothin', from Adam's fall to Huldy's bonnet,
Thet I warn't full-cocked with my jedgment on it;
But, now I'm gettin' on in life, I find
It's a sight harder to make up my mind,—
Nor I don't often try tu, when events
Will du it for me free of all expense.
The moral question's ollus plain enough,—
It's jes' the human-natur' side thet's tough;
Wut's best to think mayn't puzzle me nor you,—
The pinch comes in decidin' wut to *du*.
Ef you *read* History, all runs smooth ez grease,
Coz there the men ain't nothin' more'n idees,—
But come to *make* it, ez we must to-day,
Th' idees hev arms an' legs an' stop the way:
It's easy fixin' things in facts an' figgers,—
They can't resist, nor warn't brought up with niggers;
But come to try your the'ry on,—why, then
Your facts an' figgers change to ign'ant men
Actin' ez ugly"——" Smite 'em hip an' thigh!"
Sez gran'ther, "and let every man-child die!

Oh for three weeks o' Crommle an' the Lord!
O Israel, to your tents an' grind the sword!"—
"Thet kind o' thing worked wal in ole Judee,
But you forgit how long it's ben A.D. ;
You think thet's ellerkence,—I call it shoddy,
A thing," sez I, "wun't cover soul nor body;
I like the plain all-wool o' common-sense,
Thet warms ye now, an' will a twelvemonth hence.
You took to follerin' where the Prophets beckoned,
An', fust you knowed on, back come Charles the Second;
Now wut I want's to hev all *we* gain stick,
An' not to start Millennium too quick ;
We hain't to punish only, but to keep,
An' the cure's got to go a cent'ry deep."—
"Wal, milk-an'-water ain't a good cement,"
Sez he, "an' so you'll find it in th'event ;
Ef reshness venters sunthin', shilly-shally
Loses ez often wut's ten times the vally.
Thet exe of ourn, when Charles's neck gut split,
Opened a gap thet ain't bridged over yit ;
Slav'ry's your Charles, the Lord hez gin the exe."—
"Our Charles," sez I, "hez gut eight million necks.
The hardest question ain't the black man's right,—
The trouble is to 'mancipate the white ;
One's chained in body, an' can be sot free,—
The other's chained in soul to an idee:
It's a long job, but we shall worry thru it;
Ef bag'nets fail, the spellin'-book must do it."
"Hosee," sez he, "I think you're goin' to fail :
The rettlesnake ain't dangerous in the tail ;
This 'ere rebellion's nothin' but the rettle,—
You'll stomp on thet an' think you've won the bettle.
It's Slavery thet's the fangs and thinkin' head,
An' ef you want salvation, cresh it dead,—
An' cresh it suddin, or you'll larn by waitin'
Thet Chance wun't stop to listen to debatin'!"—
"God's truth!" sez I,—"an' ef *I* held the club,
An' knowed jes' where to strike,—but there's the rub!"—
"Strike soon," sez he, "or you'll be deadly ailin',—
Folks thet's afeared to fail are sure o' failin';
God hates your sneakin' creturs thet believe
He'll settle things they run away an' leave!"

He brought his foot down fercely, ez he spoke,
An' give me sech a startle thet I woke.

MR. HOSEA BIGLOW TO THE EDITOR OF THE ATLANTIC
    MONTHLY.

DEAR SIR,—Your letter come to han',
  Requestin' me to please be funny;
But I a'n't made upon a plan
  Thet knows wut's comin', gall or honey:
There's times the world doos look so queer,
  Odd fancies come afore I call 'em;
An' then agin, for half a year,
  No preacher 'thout a call's more solemn.

You're'n want o' sunthin' light an' cute,
  Rattlin' an' shrewd an' kin' o' jingleish,
An' wish, pervidin' it 'ould suit,
  I'd take an' citify my English.
I *ken* write long-tailed, ef I please,—
  But when I'm jokin', no, I thankee;
Then, 'fore I know it, my idees
  Run helter-skelter into Yankee.

Sence I begun to scribble rhyme,
  I tell ye wut, I ha'n't ben foolin';
The parson's books, life, death, an' time,
  Hev took some trouble with my schoolin';
Nor th' airth don't git put out with me,
  Thet love her'z though she wuz a woman;
Why, th' a'n't a bird upon the tree
  But half forgives my bein' human.

An' yit I love th' unhighschooled way
  Ol' farmers hed when I wuz younger;
Their talk wuz meatier, an' 'ould stay,
  While book-froth seems to whet your hunger.
For puttin' in a downright lick
  'Twixt Humbug's eyes, there's few can match it,
An' then it helves my thoughts ez slick
  Ez stret-grained hickory doos a hatchet.

But when I can't, I can't, thet's all,
  For Natur' won't put up with gullin';
Idees you hev to shove an' haul
  Like a druv pig a'n't wuth a mullein;
Live thoughts a'n't sent for; thru all rifts
  O' sense they pour an' resh ye onwards,
Like rivers when south-lyin' drifts
  Feel thet the airth is wheelin' sunwards.

Time wuz, the rhymes come crowdin' thick
  Ez office-seekers arter 'lection,
An' into ary place 'ould stick
  Without no bother nor objection;

But sence the war my thoughts hang back
  Ez though I wanted to enlist 'em,
An' substitutes,—wal, *they* don't lack,
  But then they'll slope afore you've mist 'em.

Nothin' don't seem like wut it wuz;
  I can't see wut there is to hinder,
An' yit my brains jes' go buzz, buzz,
  Like bumblebees agin a winder.
'Fore these times come, in all airth's row,
  There wuz one quiet place, my head in,
Where I could hide an' think,—but now
  It's all one teeter, hopin', dreadin'.

Where's Peace? I start, some clear-blown night,
  When gaunt stone walls grow numb an' number,
An', creakin' 'cross the snow-crust white,
  Walk the col' starlight into summer;
Up grows the moon, an' swell by swell
  Thru the pale pasturs silvers dimmer
Than the last smile thet strives to tell
  O' love gone heavenward in its shimmer.

I hev been gladder o' sech things
  Than cocks o' spring or bees o' clover;
They filled my heart with livin' springs,—
  But now they seem to freeze 'em over;
Sights innercent ez babes on knee,
  Peaceful ez eyes o' pastured cattle,
Jes' coz they be so, seem to me
  To rile me more with thoughts o' battle.

In-doors an' out by spells I try;
  Ma'am Natur' keeps her spin-wheel goin',
But leaves my natur' stiff an' dry
  Ez fiel's q' clover arter mowin';
An' her jes' keepin' on the same,
  Calmer than clock-work, an' not carin',
An' findin' nary thing to blame,
  Is wus than ef she took to swearin'.

Snow-flakes come whisperin' on the pane
  The charm makes blazin' logs so pleasant,
But I can't hark to what they're say'n',
  With Grant or Sherman ollers present;
The chimbleys shudder in the gale,
  Thet lulls, then suddin takes to flappin'
Like a shot hawk, but all's ez stale
  To me ez so much sperit-rappin'.

Under the yaller-pines I house,
  When sunshine makes 'em all sweet-scented,
An' hear among their furry boughs
  The baskin' west-wind purr contented,—
While 'way o'erhead, ez sweet an' low
Ez distant bells thet ring for meetin',
The wedged wil' geese their bugles blow,
Further an' further south retreatin'.

Or up the slippery knob I strain,
  An' see a hunderd hills like islan's
Lift their blue woods in broken chain
  Out o' the sea o' snowy silence;
The farm-smokes, sweetes' sight on airth,
  Slow thru the winter air a-shrinkin',
Seem kin' o' sad, an' roun' the hearth
  Of empty places set me thinkin'.

Beaver roars hoarse with meltin' snows,
  An' rattles di'mon's from his granite;
Time wuz, he snatched away my prose,
  An' into psalms or satires ran it;
But he, nor all the rest thet once
  Started my blood to country-dances,
Can't set me goin' more'n a dunce
  Thet ha'n't no use for dreams an' fancies.

Rat-tat-tat-tattle thru the street
  I hear the drummers makin' riot,
An' I set thinkin' o' the feet
  Thet follered once an' now are quiet,—
White feet ez snowdrops innercent,
  Thet never knowed the paths o' Satan,
Whose comin' step there's ears thet won't,
  No, not lifelong, leave off awaitin'.

Why, ha'n't I held 'em on my knee?
  Didn't I love to see 'em growin',
Three likely lads ez wal could be,
  Handsome an' brave an' not tu knowin'?
I set an' look into the blaze
  Whose natur', jes' like their'n, keeps climbin',
Ez long'z it lives, in shinin' ways,
  An' half despise myself for rhymin'.

Wut's words to them whose faith an' truth
  On War's red techstone rang true metal,
Who ventered life an' love an' youth
  For the gret prize o' death in battle?

To him who, deadly hurt, agen
    Flashed on afore the charge's thunder,
Tippin' with fire the bolt of men
    Thet rived the Rebel line asunder?

'Ta'n't right to hev the young go fust,
    All throbbin' full o' gifts an' graces,
Leavin' life's paupers dry ez dust
    To try an' make b'lieve fill their places:
Nothin' but tells us wut we miss,
    There's gaps our lives can't never fay in,
An' thet world seems so fur from this
    Lef' for us loafers to grow grey in!

My eyes cloud up for rain; my mouth
    Will take to twitchin' roun' the corners;
I pity mothers, tu, down South,
    For all they sot among the scorners:
I'd sooner take my chance to stan'
    At Jedgment where your meanest slave is
Than at God's bar hol' up a han'
    Ez drippin' red ez your'n, Jeff Davis!

Come, Peace! not like a mourner bowed
    For honour lost an' dear ones wasted,
But proud, to meet a people proud,
    With eyes that tell o' triumph tasted!
Come, with han' grippin' on the hilt,
    An' step that proves ye Victory's daughter!
Longin' for you, our sperits wilt
    Like shipwrecked men's on raf's for water!

Come, while our country feels the lift
    Of a gret instinct shoutin' forwards,
An' knows thet freedom a'n't a gift
    Thet tarries long in han's o' cowards!
Come, sech ez mothers prayed for when
    They kissed their cross with lips thet quivered,
An' bring fair wages for brave men,
    A nation saved, a race delivered!

WALT WHITMAN.

[Born on 31st May 1819, at West Hills, Long Island, in the State of New York. Mr. Whitman appears to me to be by far the greatest poet that America has produced, and great among the poets of any age or country. This, however, would not be an apposite place in which to enlarge upon his powers or his career, and I shall therefore confine myself to a few words regarding his relation to the Humorous in poetry. In this respect there is little to be said, save in a negative sense: the only piece of his that can in any way be termed humorous is the one here extracted, and even this has more of a grim grotesque suggestiveness than of humour properly so called. In fact, the absence of humour from the writings of Whitman—treating as he does of every possible aspect of life, work, scene, and association, in America—is a noticeable point, and may even be said to argue one limitation in his enormously capacious and sympathetic mind, and in his faculty for expressing the actualities (to which in other regards he is so intensely responsive) of modern life. And it may be added that the Americans generally—whether writers or others—have a peculiar readiness in seizing, and in realizing in words, anything amenable to the faculties of humour, wit, or (perhaps more especially) whim and ridicule. The reason for Whitman's deficiency may be that to him nothing is "common or unclean." Accepting as he does every fact of life and of circumstance, oddity is not to him so odd as to be worth "showing up" from that point of view, nor absurdity deserving of castigation or introspection, but simply of notice and appraisement: he observes these among a myriad of other phenomena, understands them for what they are worth to him, and passes. He does not turn-on (if I may use such an expression) any special part of his mind to take cognizance of these special qualities and appearances in man: but he rates them, along with all other *matériel*, by his perceptive power as a whole. They have their place in the show, and he has his place as spectator of it, and does not care to change that place for the sake of observing these particulars more closely, or with a greater amount of either fellow-feeling or distaste. Whatever may be the true explanation of the want of humorous turn in Whitman, this deficiency is, I think, one of the reasons why his writings raise so much dislike and opposition. He says a number of things that people consider out-of-the-way; and, finding that he either does not consider them out-of-the-way at all, or has not a humorous relish for them as such, readers detect a certain lack of *rapprochement* between the author and themselves, and resent it accordingly].

A BOSTON BALLAD.

(1854).

To get betimes in Boston town, I rose this morning early;
Here's a good place at the corner—I must stand and see the show.

Clear the way there, Jonathan!
Way for the President's marshal! Way for the government cannon!
Way for the Federal foot and dragoons—and the apparitions
    copiously tumbling.

I love to look on the stars and stripes—I hope the fifes will play
    Yankee Doodle.

How bright shine the cutlasses of the foremost troops!
Every man holds his revolver, marching stiff through Boston town.

A fog follows—antiques of the same come limping,
Some appear wooden-legged, and some appear bandaged and
    bloodless.

Why this is indeed a show ! It has called the dead out of the
    earth !
The old grave-yards of the hills have hurried to see !
Phantoms ! phantoms countless by flank and rear !
Cocked hats of mothy mould ! crutches made of mist !
Arms in slings ! old men leaning on young men's shoulders !

What troubles you, Yankee phantoms ? What is all this chattering
    of bare gums ?
Does the ague convulse your limbs ? Do you mistake your crutches
    for fire-locks, and level them ?

If you blind your eyes with tears, you will not see the President's
    marshal ;
If you groan such groans, you might balk the government cannon.

For shame, old maniacs ! Bring down those tossed arms, and let
    your white hair be ;
Here gape your great grand-sons—their wives gaze at them from
    the windows,
See how well dressed—see how orderly they conduct themselves.

Worse and worse ! Can't you stand it ? Are you retreating ?
Is this hour with the living too dead for you ?

Retreat then ! Pell-mell !
To your graves ! Back ! back to the hills, old limpers !
I do not think you belong here, anyhow.

But there is one thing that belongs here—shall I tell you what
    it is, gentlemen of Boston ?

I will whisper it to the Mayor—he shall send a committee to England ;
They shall get a grant from the Parliament, go with a cart to the
    royal vault—haste !
Dig out King George's coffin, unwrap him quick from the grave-
    clothes, box up his bones for a journey ;
Find a swift Yankee clipper—here is freight for you, black-bellied
    clipper,
Up with your anchor ! shake out your sails ! steer straight toward
    Boston bay.

Now call for the President's marshal again, bring out the government cannon,
Fetch home the roarers from Congress, make another procession,
    guard it with foot and dragoons.

This centre-piece for them :
Look ! all orderly citizens—look from the windows, women !

The committee open the box, set up the regal ribs, glue those that
  will not stay,
Clap the skull on top of the ribs, and clap a crown on top of the
  skull.

You have got your revenge, old buster ! The crown is come to its
  own, and more than its own.

Stick your hands in your pockets, Jonathan—you are a made man
  from this day ;
You are mighty cute—and here is one of your bargains.

CHARLES G. LELAND.

[Born in 1824, of a family which has been settled in America since about 1570, and to which the antiquary John Leland belonged. Our author studied chiefly in Europe, and was a writer of position long before his *Breitmann Ballads* (the semi-German *patois* of which is well known in his native Philadelphia) set all sorts of people laughing. *Meister Karl's Sketch-book*, and *The Poetry and Mystery of Dreams*, are two of his principal works.]

MANES.

There's a time to be jolly, a time to repent,
A season for folly, a season for Lent.
The first as the worst we too often regard ;
The rest as the best, but our judgment is hard.

There are snows in December and roses in June,
There's darkness at midnight and sunshine at noon :
But, were there no sorrow, no storm-cloud or rain,
Who'd care for the morrow with beauty again?

The world is a picture both gloomy and bright,
And grief is the shadow, and pleasure the light,
And neither should smother the general tone :
For where were the other if either were gone?

The valley is lovely ; the mountain is drear,
Its summit is hidden in mist all the year ;
But gaze from the heaven, 'high over all weather,
And mountain and valley are lovely together.

I have learned to love Lucy, though faded she be ;
If my next love be lovely, the better for me.
By the end of next summer, I'll give you my oath,
It was best, after all, to have flirted with both.

In London or Munich, Vienna, or Rome,
The sage is contented, and finds him a home ;
He learns all that is bad, and does all that is good,
And will bite at the apple, by field or by flood.

JOHN HAY.

[Colonel Hay, born towards 1830, is author of *Little Breeches, and other Pieces, Humorous, Descriptive, and Pathetic*, published a year or two ago. They comprise some noteable specimens of that peculiar American knack of saying things with a twinge (as it were)—vigorously, unexpectedly, and with a pungency not exactly unpleasant, yet not quite pleasant assuredly].

JIM BLUDSO.

Wal, no! I can't tell whar he lives,
  Because he don't live, you see:
Leastways, he's got out of the habit
  Of livin' like you and me.
Whar have you been for the last three years,
  That you haven't heard folks tell
How Jemmy Bludso passed-in his checks,
  The night of the Prairie Belle?

He weren't no saint—them engineers
  Is all pretty much alike—
One wife in Natchez-under-the-Hill,
  And another one here in Pike.
A keerless man in his talk was Jim,
  And an awkward man in a row—
But he never flunked, and he never lied;
  I reckon he never knowed how.

And this was all the religion he had—
  To treat his engine well;
Never be passed on the river;
  To mind the pilot's bell;
And if ever the Prairie Belle took fire—
  A thousand times he swore,
He'd hold her nozzle agin the bank
  Till the last soul got ashore.

All boats has their day on the Mississip,
  And her day come at last.
The Movastar was a better boat,
  But the Belle she wouldn't be passed;
And so come tearin' along that night—
  The oldest craft on the line,
With a nigger squat on her safety valve,
  And her furnace crammed, rosin and pine.

The fire bust out as she clared the bar,
  And burnt a hole in the night,
And quick as a flash she turned, and made
  For that willer-bank on the right.

There was runnin' and cursin', but Jim yelled out
  Over all the infernal roar,
"I'll hold her nozzle agin the bank
  Till the last galoot's ashore."

Through the hot black breath of the burnin' boat
  Jim Bludso's voice was heard,
And they all had trust in his cussedness,
  And knowed he would keep his word.
And, sure's you're born, they all got off
  Afore the smokestacks fell,—
And Bludso's ghost went up alone
  In the smoke of the Prairie Belle.

He weren't no saint—but at jedgment
  I'd run my chance with Jim,
'Longside of some pious gentlemen
  That wouldn't shook hands with him.
He'd seen his duty, a dead sure thing—
  And went for it thar and then;
And Christ aint a going to be too hard
  On a man that died for men.

THE MYSTERY OF GILGAL.

The darkest, strangest mystery
  I ever read, or heern, or see,
Is 'long of a drink at Taggart's Hall—
  Tom Taggart's, of Gilgal.

I've heern the tale a thousand ways,
  But never *could* git through the maze
That hangs around that queer day's doin's:
  But I'll tell the yarn to youuns.

Tom Taggart stood behind his bar;
The time was fall, the skies was far;
The neighbours round the counter drawed,
  And ca'mly drinked and jawed.

At last come Colonel Blood, of Pike,
And old Jedge Phinn, permiscus-like;
And each, as he meandered in,
  Remarked "A whisky-skin."

Tom mixed the beverage full and far,
And slammed it, smoking, on the bar.
Some says three fingers, some says two,—
  I'll leave the choice to you.

Phinn to the drink put forth his hand ;
Blood drawed his knife, with accent bland,
"I ax yer parding, Mister Phinn—
    Jest drap that whisky-skin."

No man high-toneder could be found
Than old Jedge Phinn the country round.
Says he, " Young man, the tribe of Phinns
    Knows their own whisky-skins !"

He went for his 'leven-inch bowie knife :—
" I tries to foller a Christian life ;
But I'll drap a slice of liver or two,
    My bloomin' shrub, with you."

They carved in a way that all admired,—
Tell Blood drawed iron at last, and fired.
It took Seth Bludso 'twixt the eyes,
    Which caused him great surprise.

Then coats went off, and all went in ;
Shots and bad language swelled the din ;
The short sharp bark of Derringers,
    Like bull-pups, cheered the furse.

They piled the stiffs outside the door ;
They made, I reckon, a cord or more.
Girls went that winter, as a rule,
    Alone to spellin'-school.

I've sarched in vain, from Dan to Beer-
Sheba, to make this mystery clear ;
But I end with *hit* as I did begin,—
    WHO GOT THE WHISKY-SKIN?

EDMUND CLARENCE STEDMAN.

[Born about 1835. Author of *The Blameless Prince, and other Poems*, published in 1869, and of at least two other volumes of poetry, previously issued].

PAN IN WALL STREET.
A.D. 1867.

JUST where the Treasury's marble front
    Looks over Wall Street's mingled nations,—
Where Jews and Gentiles most are wont
    To throng for trade and last quotations,—
Where, hour by hour, the rates of gold
    Outrival, in the ears of people,
The quarter-chimes, serenely tolled
    From Trinity's undaunted steeple ;—

Even there I heard a strange wild strain
   Sound high above the modern clamour,
Above the cries of greed and gain,
   The kerbstone war, the auction's hammer,—
And swift, on Music's misty ways,
   It led, from all this strife for millions,
To ancient, sweet-do-nothing days
   Among the kirtle-robed Sicilians.

And as it stilled the multitude,
   And yet more joyous rose and shriller,
I saw the minstrel, where he stood
   At ease against a Doric pillar :
One hand a droning organ played ;
   The other held a Pan's-pipe (fashioned
Like those of old) to lips that made
   The reeds give out that strain impassioned.

'Twas Pan himself had wandered here
   A-strolling through this sordid city,
And piping to the civic ear
   The prelude of some pastoral ditty !
The demigod had crossed the seas,—
   From haunts of shepherd, nymph, and satyr,
And Syracusan times,—to these
   Far shores and twenty centuries later.

A ragged cap was on his head :
   But—hidden thus—there was no doubting
That, all with crispy locks o'erspread,
   His gnarlèd horns were somewhere sprouting ;
His club-feet, cased in rusty shoes,
   Were crossed, as on some frieze you see them,
And trousers, patched of divers hues,
   Concealed his crooked shanks beneath them.

He filled the quivering reeds with sound,
   And o'er his mouth their changes shifted,
And with his goat's-eyes looked around
   Where'er the passing current drifted ;
And soon, as on Trinacrian hills
   The nymphs and herdsmen ran to hear him,
Even now the tradesmen from their tills,
   With clerks and porters, crowded near him.

The bulls and bears together drew
   From Jauncey Court and New Street Alley,
As erst, if pastorals be true,
   Came beasts from every wooded valley ;
The random passers stayed to list,—
   A boxer Ægon, rough and merry,—
A Broadway Daphnis, on his tryst
   With Naïs at the Brooklyn Ferry.

A one-eyed Cyclops halted long
　In tattered cloak of army pattern,
And Galatea joined the throng,—
　A blowsy, apple-vending slattern ;
While old Silenus staggered out
　From some new-fangled lunch-house handy,
And bade the piper, with a shout,
　To strike up Yankee Doodle Dandy !

A newsboy and a peanut-girl
　Like little Fauns began to caper :
His hair was all in tangled curl,
　Her tawny legs were bare and taper ;
And still the gathering larger grew,
　And gave its pence and crowded nigher,
While aye the shepherd-minstrel blew
　His pipe, and struck the gamut higher.

O heart of Nature, beating still
　With throbs her vernal passion taught her ;—
Even here, as on the vine-clad hill,
　Or by the Arethusan water !
New forms may fold the speech, new lands
　Arise within these ocean-portals,
But Music waves eternal wands,—
　Enchantress of the souls of mortals !

So thought I,—but among us trod
　A man in blue, with legal baton,
And scoffed the vagrant demigod,
　And pushed him from the step I sat on.
Doubting I mused upon the cry
　" Great Pan is dead !"—and all the people
Went on their ways :—and clear and high
　The quarter sounded from the steeple.

F. BRET HARTE.

[Born about 1835. A name now universally known, by the authorship of *The Luck of Roaring Camp*, and especially of the verses on *That Heathen Chinee*].

THE SOCIETY UPON THE STANISLAUS.

I RESIDE at Table Mountain, and my name is Truthful James ;
I am not up to small deceit, or any sinful games ;
And I'll tell in simple language what I know about the row
That broke up our society upon the Stanislow.

But first I would remark that it is not a proper plan
For any scientific gent to whale his fellow-man,
And, if a member don't agree with his peculiar whim,
To lay for that same member for to " put a head " on him.

Now nothing could be finer or more beautiful to see
Than the first six months' proceedings of that same society,
Till Brown of Calaveras brought a lot of fossil bones
That he found within a tunnel near the tenement of Jones.

Then Brown he read a paper, and he reconstructed there,
From those same bones, an animal that was extremely rare;
And Jones then asked the Chair for a suspension of the rules,
Till he could prove that those same bones was one of his lost
     mules.

Then Brown he smiled a bitter smile, and said he was at fault:
It seemed he had been trespassing on Jones's family vault.
He was a most sarcastic man, this quiet Mr. Brown,
And on several occasions he had cleaned out the town.

Now I hold it is not decent for a scientific gent
To say another is an ass,—at least, to all intent;
Nor should the individual who happens to be meant
Reply by heaving rocks at him to any great extent.

Then Abner Dean of Angel's raised a point of order—when
A chunk of old red sandstone took him in the abdomen,
And he smiled a kind of sickly smile, and curled up on the floor,
And the subsequent proceedings interested him no more.

For, in less time than I write it, every member did engage
In a warfare with the remnants of a palæozoic age;
And the way they heaved those fossils in their anger was a sin,
Till the skull of an old mammoth caved the head of Thompson in.

And this is all I have to say of these improper games,
For I live at Table Mountain, and my name is Truthful James;
And I've told in simple language what I know about the row
That broke up our society upon the Stanislow.

PENELOPE.

SIMPSON'S BAR, 1858.

So you've kem 'yer agen,
  And one answer won't do?
Well, of all the derned men
  That I've struck, it is you.
O Sal! 'yer's that derned fool from Simpson's,
  cavortin' round 'yer in the dew.

Kem in, ef you *will*.
  Thar,—quit! Take a cheer.
Not that; you can't fill
  Them theer cushings this year,—
For that cheer was my old man's, Joe Simpson, and
  they don't make such men about 'yer.

He was tall, was my Jack,
    And as strong as a tree.
Thar's his gun on the rack,—
    Jest you heft it, and see.
And *you* come a courtin' his widder. Lord! where
    can that critter, Sal, be?

You'd fill my Jack's place?
    And a man of your size,—
With no baird to his face,
    Nor a snap to his eyes,
And nary—Sho! thar! I was foolin',—I was,
    Joe, for sartain,—don't rise.

Sit down. Law! why, sho!
    I'm as weak as a gal.
Sal! Don't you go, Joe,
    Or I'll faint,—sure I shall.
Sit down,—*anywheer* where you like, Joe,—in that
    cheer, if you choose,—Lord, where's Sal?

TO THE PLIOCENE SKULL.

A GEOLOGICAL ADDRESS.

"SPEAK, O man less recent! Fragmentary fossil!
Primal pioneer of pliocene formation,
Hid in lowest drifts below the earliest stratum
    Of volcanic tufa!

"Older than the beasts, the oldest Palæotherium;
Older than the trees, the oldest Cryptogami;
Older than the hills, those infantile eruptions
    Of earth's epidermis!

"Eo—Mio—Plio—whatsoe'er the '-cene' was
That those vacant sockets filled with awe and wonder,—
Whether shores Devonian or Silurian beaches,—
    Tell us thy strange story!

"Or has the professor slightly antedated
By some thousand years thy advent on this planet,
Giving thee an air that's somewhat better fitted
    For cold-blooded creatures?

"Wert thou true spectator of that mighty forest
When above thy head the stately Sigillaria
Reared its columned trunks in that remote and distant
    Carboniferous epoch?

"Tell us of that scene,—the dim and watery woodland
Songless, silent, hushed, with never bird or insect
Veiled with spreading fronds and screened with tall club-mosses,
    Lycopodiacea,—

"When beside thee walked the solemn Plesiosaurus,
And around thee crept the festive Ichthyosaurus,
While from time to time above thee flew and circled
    Cheerful Pterodactyls.

"Tell us of thy food,—those half-marine refections,
Crinoids on the shell and Brachipods *au naturel*,—
Cuttle-fish to which the *pieuvre* of Victor Hugo
    Seems a periwinkle.

"Speak, thou awful vestige of the Earth's creation,—
Solitary fragment of remains organic !
Tell the wondrous secret of thy past existence,—
    Speak ! thou oldest Primate !"

Even as I gazed, a thrill of the maxilla,
And a lateral movement of the condyloid process,
With post-pliocene sounds of healthy mastication,
    Ground the teeth together.

And, from that imperfect dental exhibition,
Stained with expressed juices of the weed Nicotian,
Came these hollow accents, blent with softer murmurs
    Of expectoration ;

" Which my name is Bowers, and my crust was busted
Falling down a shaft in Calaveras County ;
But I'd take it kindly if you'd send the pieces
    Home to old Missouri !"

ROBERT H. NEWELL.

[This popular writer is author of the *Orpheus C. Kerr* (*i.e.* Office-seeker) *Papers;* from which book the following piece is taken].

THE AMERICAN TRAVELLER.

To Lake Aghmoogenegamook,
  All in the State of Maine,
A man from Wittequergaugaum came
  One evening in the rain.

" I am a traveller," said he,
  " Just started on a tour,
And go to Nomjamskillicook
  To-morrow morn at four."

He took a tavern-bed that night;
  And, with the morrow's sun,
By way of Sekledobskus went,
  With carpet-bag and gun.

A week passed on; and next we find
  Our native tourist come
To that sequestered village called
  Genasagarnagum.

From thence he went to Absequoit,
  And there—quite tired of Maine—
He sought the mountains of Vermont,
  Upon a railroad train.

Dog Hollow, in the Green Mount State,
  Was his first stopping-place;
And then Skunk's Misery displayed
  Its sweetness and its grace.

By easy stages then he went
  To visit Devil's Den;
And Scrabble Hollow, by the way,
  Did come within his ken.

Then *via* Nine Holes and Goose Green
  He travelled through the State;
And to Virginia, finally,
  Was guided by his fate.

Within the Old Dominion's bounds
  He wandered up and down;
To-day, at Buzzard Roost ensconced,
  To-morrow, at Hell Town.

At Pole Cat, too, he spent a week,
  Till friends from Bull Ring came,
And made him spend a day with them
  In hunting forest-game.

Then, with his carpet-bag in hand,
  To Dog Town next he went;
Though stopping at Free Negro Town,
  Where half a day he spent.

From thence, into Negationburg
  His route of travel lay;
Which having gained, he left the State,
  And took a southward way.

North Carolina's friendly soil
 He trod at fall of night,
And, on a bed of softest down,
 He slept at Hell's Delight.

Morn found him on the road again,
 To Lousy Level bound;
At Bull's Tail, and Lick Lizard too,
 Good provender he found.

The country all about Pinch Gut
 So beautiful did seem
That the beholder thought it like
 A picture in a dream.

But the plantations near Burnt Coat
 Were even finer still,
And made the wondering tourist feel
 A soft delicious thrill.

At Tear Shirt, too, the scenery
 Most charming did appear,
With Snatch It in the distance far,
 And Purgatory near.

But, spite of all these pleasant scenes,
 The tourist stoutly swore
That home is brightest, after all,
 And travel is a bore.

So back he went to Maine, straightway;
 A little wife he took;
And now is making nutmegs at
 Moosehicmagunticook.

INDEX TO FIRST LINES.

	PAGE
A Band, a Bob-wig, and a Feather	156
A brace of sinners, for no good	231
A country that draws fifty foot of water	123
A Fox, in life's extreme decay	190
A gentle maid, of rural breeding	212
A gentle squire would gladly entertain	85
A great Law Chief whom God nor demon scares	232
A Jubilee is but a spiritual fair	124
A learn'd society of late	103
A Lion, tired with state affairs	185
A man, in many a country town, we know	299
A modest love of praise I do not blame	255
A poore widow, somedeal stope in age	12
A shifting knave about the town	97
A spending hand that alway poureth out	44
A Tailor, a man of an upright dealing	77
Alas! how dismal is my tale	350
All the Bard's rhymes, and all his inks	352
All upstarts, insolent in place	189
Almighty God, Maker of all	26
An oaken broken elbow-chair	157
As Bathian Venus t'other day	206
As he that makes his mark is understood	124
As I went to the wake that is held on the green	409
As it befell one Saturday at noon	365
As some raw youth in country bred	166
At Wapping I landed, and called to hail Mog	269
Away, fond dupes! who, smit with sacred lore	344
Back and side, go bare, go bare	362
Balmy Zephyrs lightly flitting	343
Before I sigh my last gasp, let me breathe	81
Begin, my Muse, the imitative lay	275
Behold the hero, who has done all this	402
Beneath the hill you may see the mill	440
Blow, Boreas, foe to human kind	210

INDEX TO FIRST LINES. 485

	PAGE
Chloe brisk and gay appears	406
Chloe's the wonder of her sex	172
Clarendon had law and sense	148
Come, a brimmer, my bullies, drink whole ones or nothing	146
Come, lasses and lads, take leave of your dads	384
Confound the Cats! all Cats—alway	354
Cooper, whose name is with his country's woven	417
Cosmelia's charms inspire my lays	402
Dear friend, since I am now at leisure	203
Dear mother, dear mother, the Church is cold	298
Dear Sir, your letter come to han'	467
Death went upon a solemn day	170
Distracted with care	151
Do what you come for, captain, with your news	82
Fair Doris, break thy glass; it hath perplexed	92
Farewell, rewards and fairies	90
Fathers of wisdom, a poor wight befriend	248
Fight on, brave soldiers, for the cause	388
For a man that is almost blind	358
Freeborn Pindaric never does refuse	154
Friar Bacon walks again	398
From an extempore prayer and a godly ditty	386
From Oberon, in fairy-land	379
Geron his mouldy memory corrects	78
Gil's history appears to me	201
Go and catch a falling star	79
God bless the man who first invented sleep	439
God makes sech nights, all white an' still	443
Hail, glorious edifice, stupendous work	337
Happy the man who, void of cares and strife	175
Harriet at school was very much the same	288
He that spendeth much	48
Here, for the nonce	91
Holland, that scarce deserves the name of land	141
Home of the Percy's high-born race	419
How fond are men of rule and place	186
I am a rogue and a stout one	381
I am a young fellow	410
I am an Irishman, in Ireland I was born	41
I am as I am, and so will I be	42
I asked of my dear friend orator Prig	299
I breathe, sweet Ghib, the temperate air of Wrest	93
I can love both fair and brown	80
I du believe in Freedom's cause	458
I know your heart cannot so guilty be	126
I lately saw what now I sing	202
I lately thought no man alive	221
I love to hear thine earnest voice	429
I marched three miles through scorching sand	157
I reside at Table Mountain, and my name is Truthful James	478
I went from England into France	87
I will you tell a full good sport	360
If e'er to writing you pretend	198
If I address the Echo yonder	405
If thou didst feed on western plains of yore	313
Ill husbandry braggeth	46
In ancient times, as story tells	159

INDEX TO FIRST LINES.

	PAGE
In foreign universities	123
In London I never know what I'd be at	257
In London was a priest, an annueler	1
In Love's name you are charged hereby	96
In other men we faults can spy	192
In this little vault she lies	98
Is that dace or perch	412
It fell upon a Martinmas time	406
It is your pardon, sir, for which my Muse	121
It was a poor man, he dwelled in Kent	371
It was the month in which the righteous maid	49
It was the stalwart butcher man	430
Just where the Treasury's marble front	476
Know this, my brethren, heaven is clear	100
Ladies turn conjurers, and can impart	130
Last Sunday at St. James's prayers	408
Let's not rhyme the hours away	138
Libertas et natale solum	169
Lords, knights, and squires, the numerous band	152
Love drunk, the other day, knocked at my breast	136
Margarita first possessed	132
May the Babylonish curse	329
Most gracious and omnipotent	126
Must then my crimes become thy scandal too	149
My brother Jack was nine in May	332
My days pass pleasantly away	436
My passion is as mustard strong	195
Nature and Fortune, blithe and gay	407
Now hardly here and there an hackney-coach	163
Now that, thanks to the powers below	390
Now thou hast loved me one whole day	80
O fair maid of Passage	307
O thou whose all-consoling power	271
O thou! whose daring works sublime	252
Oh! be the day accurst that gave me birth	314
Oh how my lungs do tickle! ha ha ha!	86
Oh what a pain is love	403
Old Nick, who taught the village school	423
On Thames's bank, a gentle youth	209
One day, it matters not to know	327
One of the kings of Scanderoon	349
Once git a smell o' musk into a draw	460
Once on a time there was a pool	441
Out upon it, I have loved	125
Pagget, a schoolboy, got a sword, and then	99
Peter, like famed Christina, queen of Sweden	253
Pope has the talent well to speak	165
Rebellion hath broken up house	396
Rhyme, the rack of finest wits	83
See who ne'er was nor will be half read	195
Shadow, just like the thin regard of men	434

INDEX TO FIRST LINES. 487

	PAGE
She sat and sewed that hath done me the wrong	43
Since last we met, thou and thy horse, my dear	144
Sly Merry Andrew, the last Southwark Fair	153
So you've kem 'yer again	479
Some of my friends (for friends I must suppose	226
Songs of shepherds, rustical roundelays	377
Speak, O man less recent! Fragmentary fossil	480
Stella this day is thirty-four	163
Survey this shield all bossy bright	338
Tell me not of Lords and laws	393
That all men would be cowards if they dare	277
The Brownie sits in the Scotchman's room	423
The darkest, strangest mystery	475
The fox and the cat, as they travelled one day	226
The learned, full of inward pride	192
The little boy to show his might and power	126
The mean, the rancorous jealousies, that swell	251
The rats by night such mischief did	186
The shepherd heretofore did keep	102
The stars are rolling in the sky	426
The town of Passage is neat and spacious	308
The world's a printing-house. Our words, our thoughts	384
There are three ways in which men take	427
There is no type of indolence like this	433
There needs no other charm nor conjurer	124
There once was a painter in Catholic days	324
There's a time to be jolly, a time to repent	473
There was a Cameronian cat	401
There was a man bespake a thing	78
There was an old man came over the Lea	385
There was an old woman, as I've heard tell	409
There were six jovial tradesmen	392
This is the prettiest motion	134
'This kind o' sogerin' aint a mite like our October trainin'	446
This one request I make to him that sits the clouds above	125
Those who in quarrels interpose	191
Thy charms, O sacred Indolence, I sing	181
Time was when round the lion's den	414
'Tis sweet to view, from half-past five to six	334
'Tis twenty years, and something more	437
'Tis well that equal Heaven has placed	118
To all you ladies now at land	150
To get betimes in Boston town, I rose this morning early	471
To Lake Aghmoogenegamook	481
To pass the time thereas I went	367
To sup with thee thou didst me home invite	99
Toll, toll	130
Tom Goodwin was an actor man	434
'Twas on a lofty vase's side	220
Up the Mediterranin	270
Vesey! of Verse the judge and friend	259
Wal, no! I can't tell whar he lives	474
Well, Heaven be thanked! friend Allan, here I am	315
Well, if ever I saw such another man since my mother bound my head	164
Welter upon the waters, mighty one	422
Were men so dull they could not see	101
What gossips prattled in the sun	302
What! put off with one denial	405

	PAGE
When first I sought fair Cœlia's love	206
When Johnson sought (as Shakspeare says) that bourn	233
When, now mature in classic knowledge	222
When Orpheus went down to the regions below	197
When owls are stripped of their disguise	400
When these things following be done to our intent	358
Where gentle Thames through stately channels glides	173
Where others love and praise my verses, still	99
Where the Red Lion, staring o'er the way	225
Whether on earth, in air, or main	194
While at the helm of State you ride	208
While Butler, needy wretch, was yet alive	198
Who friendship with a knave hath made	188
Who marrieth a wife upon a Monday	383
Who says that Giles and Joan at discord be	82
Whoever pleaseth to enquire	158
Why flyest thou away with fear	230
Why, how now, old sexton? why shake you with dread	309
Why should the world be so averse	114
Wise emblem of our politic world	137
With face and fashion to be known	128
Women, women, love of women	357
Would you that Delville I describe	180
You ask a story, not more strange than true	178
You that decipher out the fate	140
You won not verses, madam, you won me	84